Understanding Vision
An Interdisciplinary Perspective

Edited by

Glyn W. Humphreys

BLACKWELL
Oxford UK & Cambridge USA

Copyright © Basil Blackwell Ltd. 1992

First published 1992

First published in USA 1992

Blackwell Publishers
238 Main Street, Suite 501
Cambridge, Massachusetts 02142
USA

108 Cowley Road
Oxford OX4 1JF
UK

Library of Congress Cataloging-in-Publication Data

Understanding vision: an interdisciplinary perspective/edited by Glyn W. Humphreys.
    p.   cm. — (Readings in mind and language)
    Includes bibliographical references and index.
    ISBN 0–631–17908–9 (hard). — ISBN 0–631–17909–7 (pbk.)
    1. Visual perception. I. Humphreys, Glyn W. II. Series.
BF241.U5   1992   92–2627
152.14—dc20   CIP

British Library Cataloguing in Publication Data

A CIP catalogue record for this book is available from the British Library.

Typeset in 9.5 on 11 pt Palatino
by Graphicraft Typesetters, Hong Kong
Printed in Great Britain by T.J. Press Ltd, Padstow, Cornwall

This book is printed on acid-free paper

Contents

List of Contributors

Muriel Boucart   Laboratorie de Psychologie Experimentale, Université Paris V

Vicki Bruce   Department of Psychology, University of Nottingham

Chris Christou   University Laboratory of Physiology, Oxford

Bruce G. Cumming   University Laboratory of Physiology, Oxford

Tom Freeman   Cognitive Science Research Centre, School of Psychology, University of Birmingham

Stephen Grossberg   Center for Adaptive Systems, Boston University

Mike Harris   Cognitive Science Research Centre, School of Psychology, University of Birmingham

Michael J. Hawken   Center for Neural Sciences, New York University

Glyn W. Humphreys   Cognitive Science Research Centre, School of Psychology, University of Birmingham

Elizabeth B. Johnston   Center for Neural Sciences, New York University

Pierre Jolicoeur   Department of Psychology, University of Waterloo

Kris N. Kirby   Department of Psychology, Harvard University

Stephen M. Kosslyn   Department of Psychology, Harvard University

Stephen E. Palmer   Department of Psychology, University of California, Berkeley

Andrew J. Parker   University Laboratory of Physiology, Oxford

M. Jane Riddoch Cognitive Science Research Centre, School of Psychology, University of Birmingham

Keith H. Ruddock Department of Physics and Biology, Imperial College

Kent A. Stevens Department of Computer Science, University of Oregon

Roger J. Watt Department of Psychology, Stirling University

Glen Williams Cognitive Science Research Centre, School of Psychology, University of Birmingham

Andrew Zisserman Center for Neural Sciences, New York University

Acknowledgments

This book arose from a special issue of *Mind and Language*, which appeared in December 1990. The special issue itself arose through the encouragement of Martin Davies, who agreed to this attempt to bring recent work in artificial intelligence and experimental psychology to the broader sphere of journal readers. I thank Martin for giving me the opportunity to bring the research reported in the special issue to a wider stage. My family bore with the tendency for editorial work to encroach upon weekends (mostly with good humour). To them, many thanks.

Glyn W. Humphreys

Introduction

GLYN W. HUMPHREYS

In the past ten years or so, vision research has made undoubted progress. So much so that, within the confines of their laboratories (and sometimes beyond), researchers may be heard proclaiming that certain problems in vision are now "solved." For instance, algorithms have been developed that allow depth to be coded from stereo images, edges to be detected at the boundaries of objects, and shape to be coded from patterns of movement. In developing such algorithms, surely the answers to some of the most mysterious visual capacities – those that arise so rapidly that we have little introspective knowledge of how the processes operate – are known.

It can be argued that this apparent success is a by-product of a convergence of research from different parent disciplines: of experimental work (on the processing algorithms that characterize human vision), computational studies (on the computational problems of vision and how they might be solved by any intelligent processing system), and neurophysiological research (on how visual processes are implemented in the brain). That is, vision research provides one of the success stories for an interdisciplinary approach to cognitive science.

However, despite the sometimes expressed confidence, the convergence on a solution may be more apparent than real. Many of the best implementations of visual processes in computers fail catastrophically when wheeled out into the real world of noisy images (where the lighting is imperfect, shadows fall and cameras have limited resolution). Experimental work can disagree with the "optimal" algorithms that may best suit practical application. The boundaries found useful for dividing problems in computer vision (e.g. between so-called low- and high-level vision, according to whether stored knowledge of objects and particular environments needs to be drawn upon) may not correspond to those forced upon human vision by evolution. The list of possible areas of divergence is immense; indeed, it comes to be writ large as research in each component discipline progresses. It is thus timely to raise the issue of the relations among the different approaches that are currently at the forefront of vision research. Is there convergence or divergence? If there is divergence, can any lessons be profitably drawn?

This book is concerned with the different approaches taken towards understanding vision. There are eleven chapters, each written by leading researchers in their own field. In each chapter, the authors attempt to introduce their work in a comprehensible way, and to try to discuss this work in the wider context of developing complete models of visual processing. Each chapter stands as a state of the art summary of work in a particular area of "vision research." However, in juxtaposing the chapters, the intention is to contrast the different approaches taken. It is my own belief that no one approach will lead to a full understanding of vision. Hence each chapter may contribute but one part of a broader-reaching mosaic in which, to coin a *Gestalt* phrase, the whole is greater than the sum of the parts.

The chapters range from computational analyses of visual processing, to computational implementation of visual processes in neuronal networks, by way of psychophysical analyses of 2D pattern processing and 3D surface processing, cognitive studies of face and object recognition, analyses of visual aspects of thought, and studies of selective visual disorders after brain damage.

Chapters 1 and 2 by Stevens and by Watt take a computational approach to vision. Stevens addresses the issue of how the visual system constructs the perception of surfaces from multiple cues, a theme returned to at a number of stages in the book (e.g. Parker et al. in chapter 8). Stevens's work is informed both by a knowledge of existing computational algorithms used to derive surface representations, and by experimental studies of surface perception in human observers. This chapter provides a good introduction to the interdisciplinary approach to vision.

Watt is concerned with a somewhat different problem; namely, how spatial information is represented. In discussing this topic, Watt points to a distinction between subjective and objective vision, and notes that functional processes in vision (objective vision) may operate in ways quite unlike our subjective impressions. Having given this issue a little thought, most people would probably agree that vision can function independently of conscious introspection. This is illustrated by visual illusions where even when the observer is told that their response is incorrect, the conscious knowledge fails to overrule the functional response of the system (a theme taken up in chapter 6 by Humphreys et al.). Similarly, one of the lessons that can be gleaned from neurophysiological studies of visual processing is that basic dimensions of visual stimuli – motion, color, spatial patterns – are to some degree processed independently in the brain (e.g. Desimone and Ungerleider, 1989); this functional decomposition of the image takes place underneath our subjective impressions of a coherent world of moving, colored objects. However, Watt's case is perhaps even more radical than this. Watt argues that the functional representation of space itself is different from our subjective impression. Functionally, space is not represented metrically, with the distance and direction of objects being coded on the basis of metric position; rather, distance and direction are encoded directly, and position is derived from these. The notion of a metric spatial representation underlying human cognition lies at the heart of our subjective perception of the world; Watt's proposal that the visual system encodes space in a quite different way cuts this idea to the quick. It remains to be seen how this proposal stands up to vigorous empirical investigation; however, if it does then future work must address the question of how the objective coding of space by the visual system can mesh with studies stressing the analog nature of visual thought (see Kirby and Kosslyn in chapter 4).

The chapters dealing with computational approaches to vision are followed by chapters on aspects of visual cognition: how descriptions of objects and faces are encoded, and how visual memories are best characterized. Palmer (in chapter 3) looks at the problem of perceptual organization and grouping – how the parts of objects are related to the perceptual whole. Palmer reviews current work which provides empirical measures of many of the original *Gestalt* demonstrations. He also goes beyond this to relate the *Gestalt* idea of "perceptual wholes," created by patterns of interaction between electrical fields in the brain, to recent developments in artificial neural networks in which perceptual wholes may be represented in terms of "minimal energy states" within a network. This chapter illustrates how old ideas have been put to recent empirical test, and how they can be given a new suit of clothes by developments in computational modelling.

Kirby and Kosslyn (chapter 4) review empirical work on visual thought, and in particular on whether visual images are depictive: that is, whether images are combined solely on the basis of spatial juxtaposition (and not on the basis of semantic or syntactic relations), and whether they convey meaning solely from visual resemblance. Kirby and Kosslyn argue strongly that images are indeed depictive. It is because of this that images are useful for solving certain types of problems, and that imagery can be conceptualized as part of the visual system. Note, though, that as our view evolves of how the visual system encodes space for particular tasks (Watt, chapter 2), so may our view of imagery.

Bruce (chapter 5) is concerned with the encoding and recognition of a particular class of visual objects, namely faces. As a visual-processing problem, face recognition is of some interest. For instance, faces are visually very similar, yet face recognition proceeds in an impressively efficient fashion for the majority of normal individuals. What kinds of perceptual structures are useful for face recognition, and how might algorithms be developed to encode such structures? Bruce highlights how different approaches to face recognition can complement each other, taking as her starting point Marr's (1982) distinctions among computational, algorithmic and implementational levels of analysis.

Following brain damage, selective disorders of visual processing can occur: problems in face recognition being a striking case. In chapter 6, Humphreys et al. discuss the utility of neuropsychological analyses of object recognition for understanding basic components of the normal object recognition system.

They draw an analogy between neuropsychological studies and other attempts to understand vision by means of the breakdown of visual processing; for instance, in the study of visual illusions. They point out that neuropsychological studies have their limitations; for example, they depend often on single patients, and on the assumption that brain damage selectively reduces the normal processing system rather than making it function in some new way. One way around the problems caused by such assumptions is to show that the pattern of performance found in the neuropsychology literature meshes with that produced when simulated "lesions" are performed on computational models of behavior. That is, some of the problems related to a particular approach to understanding vision can be overcome by looking for convergent evidence from a different discipline. Humphreys et al. illustrate this by means of studies of simulated lesions on the operation of connectionist models.

Chapters 7 and 8 by Ruddock and by Parker et al. discuss psychophysical studies of human perception of 2D patterns and 3D surfaces. Psychophysical studies may be characterized by the attempt to understand the operation of underlying processing mechanisms by studying their performance at threshold. These studies can also be closely related to physiological studies of vision, based on the assumption that separate physiological mechanisms can be identified by characteristically different threshold functions. Ruddock's chapter is concerned with the way in which the visual system analyzes simple 2D patterns containing many elements ("distributed images.") Such patterns are characteristic of many everyday environments, where images contain multiple disparate elements (e.g. the leaves of a tree, the surface of a desk). Ruddock argues that such patterns are analyzed in a hierarchical fashion, in which images are first analyzed for color, then contrast polarity, then magnification, and then orientation. Hence a target differing in color from its background can be detected at the first processing stage, whilst a target differing in orientation from its background can only be detected after the prior encoding of color, contrast polarity, and magnification. One question for future neurophysiological research is whether a functional hierarchy of this sort is physically implemented within the brain. Ruddock also examines the case of a patient, HJA, with a selective impairment in particular processes in 2D pattern perception. This patient is also discussed in chapter 6 by Humphreys et al., so providing a link across two chapters.

Parker et al. are concerned with the analysis of 3D surfaces, and describe a number of ingenious experiments that attempt to decompose the mechanisms underlying surface perception. They also discuss in some detail how the mechanisms revealed by psychophysical study can be linked to neurophysiological evidence. In the future, we can look to computational work which implements these functional mechanisms in a way that relates directly to their implementation in biological visual systems.

Jolicoeur (chapter 9) moves beyond the treatment of objects in terms of their surfaces to discuss the processes involved in object recognition: how stored knowledge about objects is contacted. Jolicoeur is particularly concerned with how we recognize disoriented objects – objects rotated within-the-plane into a novel orientation. It turns out that the time taken to identify such objects can be a linear function of the angle of disorientation (at least up until the objects are inverted). Such linear effects are reminiscent of the functions found when subjects have to imagine whether two objects at different orientations are the same or mirror reflections of one another (see Kirby and Kosslyn, chapter 4), suggesting that some form of mental rotation process can be involved in on-line object recognition. Jolicoeur goes on to discuss some of the possible mechanisms mediating the recognition of disoriented objects, and how these mechanisms relate to some current models of object recognition in the computer vision literature.

We have already noted how chapters 1 and 2 by Stevens and Watt attempt to present a computational analysis of certain processes in vision, and this computational perspective is also emphasized by Bruce (chapter 5). In his influential analysis of vision, David Marr (1982) pointed out that J. J. Gibson's work provides a good example of a computational approach to vision. Gibson (e.g. Gibson, 1979), it may be remembered, placed great emphasis on the properties of the visual world and the way in which these properties constrain visual processing. The influence of Gibson's work on recent psychophysical and mathematical treatments of one aspect of vision – motion perception – is illustrated in chapter 10 by Harris et al. They discuss aspects of the image that change in direct correlation with patterns of movement by the observer, and how these patterns of movement can be used to encode information about 3D surfaces. They go on to present evidence that distinct functional mechanisms exist for encoding different types of motion (for rotation, expansion, translation, and so forth); thus these mechanisms can provide direct inputs to control particular behaviors. Again, one is reminded here of Watt's argument that vision is functionally specialized for delivering the appropriate information for particular actions, rather than for "depicting" scenes. We may also again look to future neurophysiological and computational studies to provide convergent support for Harris et al.'s proposals.

In the final chapter, Grossberg presents an account of the way in which processes concerned with form, color, motion, and depth may interact: the FACADE model. As discussed by Stevens (chapter 1) and Parker et al. (chapter 8), it can be argued that processes concerned with form, color, motion, and depth perception operate in a modular fashion; for instance, this is suggested by neurophysiological evidence indicating the separate neural representation of these properties of visual stimuli in the brain (Desimone and Ungerleider, 1989). Grossberg, however, proposes that these different types of information interact cooperatively, so that (for example) changes in perceived color produce changes in perceived form and depth. Grossberg goes on to propose specific mechanisms for these cooperative interactions, based on patterns of interaction between simple processing units sensitive to the different image properties. In the spirit of interdisciplinary work, we can now hope that explicit computational theories, such as the FACADE model, serve as a framework for future experimentation aimed at testing how different visual properties interact in human vision.

These eleven chapters provide a wide-ranging tour of vision research, and current approaches to the topic are well illustrated. The chapters move from the representation of basic visual dimensions (e.g. space), to the treatment of objects in terms of their surfaces, to the recognition of particular types of objects, and to the modelling of interactions among different image properties. Eight of the chapters appeared in a special issue of *Mind and Language* in 1990; three have been added to fill in some of the gaps in the special issue. It is hoped that this volume will encourage future work that attempts to step across the parent disciplines of vision research to provide us with a better understanding of human visual processing.

One technical point needs to be mentioned. In chapter 1, Stevens presents a number of stereograms, consisting of pairs of images which are otherwise identical but they have a slight disparity in the locations of some of the components in each image (e.g. some of the components in one image are shifted to a slightly different location relative to the components in the other image). When viewed stereoscopically (i.e. separately by each eye), the disparate components stand out in depth from the background. One way to view the images stereoscopically (without the use of a special instrument for stereo viewing, such as a stereoscope) is to hold a pen about halfway between you and the central point between the images. Look first at the pen and then try to shift attention from the pen to the images. With some effort and concentration, the two images should fuse into one.

1
Constructing the Perception of Surfaces from Multiple Cues

KENT A. STEVENS

When we attend to the surfaces about us, we readily appreciate their overall three-dimensional (3D) shape, as well as the curvature, orientation, and distance of small patches across their extent. Beyond allowing us to appreciate these quantities in and of themselves, surface perception contributes to the recognition of objects on the basis of 3D shape, as well as many visually guided motor skills, from determining where to grasp an object to deciding which path to ski down a slope. How is 3D surface information encoded or, in other words, how do we construct the perception of surfaces?

It is virtually a given that 3D perception amounts to the recovery of the third dimension (measured along the line of sight and perpendicular to the image plane). Intuition has suggested to many investigators that *depth* (the variation in the distance from the observer to points across a surface and between surfaces) constitutes the fundamental basis for the encoding of surfaces. It is recognized that depth information might be recovered only up to a scale factor: one might construct an accurate impression of the shape of a surface without appreciation for the overall size or scale of those relief features. Is depth, specified up to a scale factor, the means by which surface shape is described? And, specifically, is depth the means by which one reconciles or combines surface information from different depth cues (such as stereopsis, motion parallax, linear perspective)?

Apparent depth does seem intimately related to the appreciation of 3D shape. It varies in magnitude according to the vividness of the 3D impression one experiences. Moreover, overall distance, ratios of distances, and distance intervals can be perceived with reasonable precision when viewed binocularly and with free head movements, provided the 3D points concerned lie within a few meters of the observer (Johansson, 1973; Ritter, 1979; Foley, 1980). But our ability to perform specific distance measurements does not necessarily extend to the perception of continuous surfaces. That is to say, the visual system might well have the ability to determine, with admirable skill, the distance to specific 3D locations, and yet not use that information across extended surfaces as the means for describing their layout in space. As this chapter will review, it is doubtful that distance or depth information is the basis on which we construct our impressions of surface shape from different "depth cues" (such as monocular perspective, motion, and binocular disparities). Instead, apparent depth might be largely a derivative property that emerges after first describing the surface primarily in terms of curvature and discontinuity information.

In addition to directly encoding the distance across a surface, surface layout might be described locally in terms of the orientation of the tangent plane and surface curvature across smooth regions, and by marking a variety of distinguished loci across the surface, such as discontinuities in depth (edges) or orientation (creases). These quantities are immediately and vividly experienced, and can be reported with some confidence and precision under experimental circumstances, which suggests that they might be involved in the internal description of surface shape, or at least closely related to those primitives. But many other shape descriptors are also conceivable. We are in a rather difficult situation, both theoretically and empirically, when it comes to understanding the visual description of surface shape, because of the mathematical interconvertability of many of these quantities. For example, depth, slant, and curvature are related by differentiation and integration across smooth regions. An internal representation that provides an interpolated, effectively continuous distribution of these quantities would allow conversion from one form to another, within limits.[1] As will be reviewed, there is evidence that we can convert among these forms of information. This complicates our understanding of the internal representation, for an ability to make a given judgment does not necessarily imply that quantity is explicitly stored in some map-like representation; it might be computed "on demand," i.e. only where necessary (see Ullman, 1984). On the other hand, marked difficulty in performing a given task might suggest that the corresponding information is either not explicitly represented or not readily derived. But, as discussed below, that conclusion also requires some care.

Under natural circumstances, the 3D information we extract and represent within the visual system supports a remarkable range of judgments – many more than could conceivably be derived directly from some explicit representation of that information. For instance, consider the simple task of determining which of two specified 3D points, lying in different visual directions, is the nearer. We can safely conclude that this judgment is not directly mediated by accessing a representation of relative distance: it is not feasible to explicitly represent that information for all possible pairs of 3D points in a scene. To the extent that this perceptual task is possible, it would appear to be based on comparing the apparent distances to the specific points. Even then, the two distances might be determined only as a consequence of needing the information for that task. The robustness and generality of our visual system might lead us to believe we perceive, at any moment, far more than we in fact do.

What 3D representation supports our ability to report the apparent orientation of a patch of a depicted surface? Surface orientation has two degrees of freedom, which are naturally characterized as *slant*, the angle between the line of regard and the surface normal, and *tilt*, the direction of slant, which corresponds to the direction to which the surface normal projects, as well as the direction of the gradient of depth relative to the observer (Stevens, 1983a).[2] The two components, being orthogonal, might be known to differing precision; tilt is often more reliably determined from the image than slant (Stevens, 1981b, 1983a). Slant is in fact a difficult and unnatural judgment to make on the basis of some cues, such as simple shading (Todd and Reichel, 1989). But other stimuli, even simple line drawings, allow observers an immediate and reliable impression of both slant and tilt (Stevens, 1983a,b; Stevens and Brookes, 1987).[3] This situation is not unique to slant: the quality of many 3D judgments depends on the quality of the stimulus information. Thus it may be difficult to shed light on the underlying *representation* by impoverishing the stimulus.

Another way to explore representational issues is to contrive stimuli which place in conflict cues that usually covary. But when cues are placed in direct conflict, the results are often unpredictable and idiosyncratic; for example, when one reverses binocular disparity (and the depth that disparity implies) in a stereo photograph by swapping left and right images, suggesting a depth ordering opposite to that provided by the monocular cues. In that case the monocular interpretation usually dominates, but the story is complicated. The validity of cue conflict as a research paradigm can well be challenged when one presents situations for which the visual system might never have evolved a strategy. But, as will be discussed, more subtle conflicts can be posed that are ecologically plausible. In these cases, if the observer is "blind" to a given type of conflict, that observation might suggest something about either the strategy by which such conflicts are resolved or, perhaps, something about what constitutes a feature. This chapter summarizes a recent line of work that follows this approach. The next section describes an experiment that demonstrates the robustness with which binocular depth and monocular depth can be compared, which underscores the above observation regarding the conversion of 3D information from one form to another. Subsequent sections describe limitations in the ability of binocular disparity to combine with monocular interpretations. The final discussion presents recent conjectures regarding the construction of continuous surfaces from surface features derived from those findings.

Recent Observations

Depth from Monocular Contours is Commensurate with Depth from Stereopsis

A prerequisite of combining sources of 3D information is that they be commensurate. Stevens and Brookes (1987) describe experiments in which subjects viewed a curved surface rendered by a family of parallel surface contours.[4] The surface was presented monocularly (to the dominant eye) and a binocular probe was then briefly presented at one of several locations across the image. The task was to compare the depth of the probe with that of the surface at that point. Subjects adjusted the disparity of the probe in a manner roughly consistent with the depth suggested by the monocular surface, and could do so for stimuli presented for only 150 ms, which precludes eye movements. In order to compare the depth of a binocular probe with that seen monocularly, the two forms must be made commensurate. It is particularly interesting that depth comparisons were possible when the monocular image was in orthographic (parallel) projection, since in this case there is objectively only information about the curvature and orientation of the surface, no depth or distance information *per se*. This demonstrates some ability to convert slant information to distance information. The data also suggest that the distance to the (monocular) surface at the point of fixation is assumed to coincide with the 3D point of convergence of the two eyes. This would be a natural extension of the fact that binocular vision generally brings the 3D point of fixation into sharp focus and (approximately) zero disparity. Most relevant to the current topic is our ability to relate depth from binocular disparity with purely monocular 3D information. What might that say about the internal representation of 3D information? Does the rapidity with which the judgment can be made argue for monocular and binocular depth being combined effortlessly and preattentively, or does the task, while performed naturally and rapidly, nonetheless require scrutiny? This question remains open.

Depth is Reconstructed from Disparity Contrast, not Directly Computed from Absolute Disparity

As mentioned earlier, it has been demonstrated that observers can derive from binocular disparity rather precise information about the distance to specific points in nearby space. The theoretical basis for this ability has been shown by various authors: depth, surface orientation, and even absolute distance can be derived directly from disparity, provided one has knowledge of the angle of convergence of the two eyes and other geometrical parameters (Mayhew, 1982; Mayhew and Longuet-Higgins, 1982; Prazdny, 1983b). It would be reasonable to expect the visual system to use distance information from stereopsis to constrain or disambiguate the interpretation of a monocular image. For example, can stereopsis effectively contradict the apparent surface orientation of a planar surface suggested by a simple line drawing? Stevens and Brookes (1988) report experiments in which wire-frame renditions of slanted planes were presented as stereograms. The stereo information consisted of a constant disparity gradient, corresponding to a slanted plane; the monocular information (e.g. provided by the perspective projection of grid lines) also suggested a slanted plane. To make things interesting, the directions of the monocular and stereo depth gradients were varied

Figure 1.1   *A stereogram presenting a constant disparity gradient which corresponds to a slanted plane. The monocular 3D interpretation is of a corridor in perspective receding from the viewer. It is difficult to see these lines as lying on a common slanted plane; rather, they appear in perspective according to the monocular interpretation. Practiced observers can usually determine which of the two sides is the nearer, nonetheless.*

independently. For example, one can derive a substantial impression of a slanted plane by simply displaying two lines that intersect at an oblique angle; the observer tends to interpret this as a foreshortened view of a right angle (Stevens, 1983b). The stereo version, however, was constructed to accurately depict two lines intersecting at a 45 degree angle. The stereo and the monocular information specified very different orientations for the plane containing the two lines. When the two lines were viewed binocularly, with no other features visible, the stereo information was quite ineffective in dispelling the assumption that the two lines were perpendicular. In a variety of manipulations along these lines, subjects viewed renditions of planar surfaces and were asked to judge quantities such as the direction of the depth gradient (by indicating whether a line segment appeared normal to the surface, or by comparing the relative depth of pairs of distinguished points on the surface). The monocular interpretation dominated the appearance of three-dimensionality; constant disparity gradients (corresponding to slanted planes) are quite ineffectual. That is not to say that we have no sensitivity to stereo slant: Gillam (1968) reported that observers compromise between the slant suggested monocularly and stereoscopically when the two are brought into opposition (figure 1.1).

When the monocular impression is compelling, constant stereo disparity gradients have a weak contribution, particularly in comparison with non-linear gradients (as discussed below). Figure 1.2 shows a rendition of a slanted plane (the monocular interpretation) with a superposed disparity distribution that corresponds to a Gaussian centered in the figure. Most observers have little difficulty, after a moment, in seeing the figure as a slanted plane with a central protrusion in depth. Spatial distributions of disparity, which correspond to curvature features, are usually quite salient, and much more effective than constant disparity gradients in influencing the monocular interpretation.

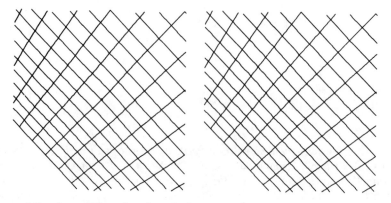

Figure 1.2   *A rendition of a slanted plane in perspective. The stereo information corresponds to a Gaussian in depth. Most, but not all, observers that have good stereo vision see the Gaussian feature, usually smoothly integrated with the interpretation of a slanted plane. Use free (uncrossed) fusion or a stereo viewer in this and the following figures.*

We hypothesized that stereopsis contributes 3D surface information primarily where the second spatial derivatives[5] of disparity are non-zero, which correspond to regions where the surface is curved, creased, or discontinuous. Binocular depth, by this view, is reconstructed from disparity contrast, rather than computed directly from absolute disparity. Gillam et al. (1984) also found that disparity discontinuities are much more effective in inducing depth than constant gradients. Rogers (1986) and Rogers and Cagenello (1989) similarly propose that disparity curvature is the basis of binocular depth constancy (see also Mitchison and Westheimer, 1984; Gillam et al., 1988; Brookes and Stevens, 1989a).

This research suggests that binocular depth perception is a reconstruction indirectly determined from higher spatial derivatives of disparity, very different from the direct computation of depth from disparity suggested by the mathematical analyses in the literature. The explanation likely rests on the fact that the visual system cannot, in fact, derive reliable measurements of absolute disparity due to uncontrolled misregistration between the two eyes. Anderson and Van Essen (1987) propose that the two retinal images are shifted dynamically in order to maintain spatial registration; that operation preserves disparity contrast but not absolute disparity.

Depth is Analogous to Brightness in Effects due to Reconstruction but not in Effects due to Spatial Lateral Inhibition

The salience of disparity contrast in the perception of binocular depth suggests an analogy with luminance contrast and the perception of brightness.

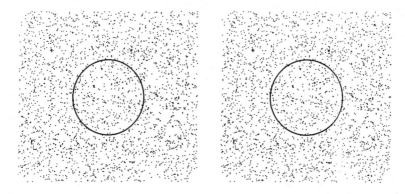

Figure 1.3 *A constant disparity ring (which should be seen as parallel to the image plane) embedded in a constant disparity background. The background gradient induces anomalous slant in the ring analogous to the Koffka ring illusion in the luminance domain.*

In the luminance domain, it is generally accepted that the retinal luminance distribution is bandpass filtered by a family of center-surround operators of differing size that roughly approximate a Laplacian. If the luminance signal is modeled as being conveyed to the cortex in terms of second spatial derivatives, the perception of brightness can be described mathematically as a 2D reconstruction or integration (Arend, 1973; Arend and Goldstein, 1987). Similarly, depth appears to be a reconstruction. Various illusions in the luminance domain have counterparts in the disparity domain, such as demonstrated in figure 1.3.

The analogy between depth and brightness was first explicitly proposed in the discussion of a stereoscopic counterpart of the Craik–O'Brien–Cornsweet illusion (Anstis et al., 1978; Rogers and Graham, 1983). In the luminance version of this illusion, two fields of equal luminance meet at a border whose profile is shaped like a double spur. The impression is of two homogeneous regions differing in brightness separated by a sharp step edge. In the depth version, one of the fields is seen as closer. The illusion demonstrates that depth information is extrapolated over extended regions bounded by sharp disparity edges, much like the extrapolation of brightness information away from intensity edges.

Brookes and Stevens (1989b) explored this analogy by comparing known brightness illusions with their depth counterparts. Various types of illusions were compared to examine the analogy. Stereograms were constructed in which disparity varied spatially in close correspondence to the luminance distributions in well-known brightness illusions (such as the Koffka ring analogue in figure 1.3). It was found that illusions due to reconstruction of brightness values have counterparts in binocular depth perception but that those due to lateral inhibition do not. The center-surround mechanisms involved in the detection of luminance differences produce lateral inhibition effects which take the form of illusory bands or spots at areas of changing contrast (e.g. Mach bands, Hermann grid). Analogous effects in the stereo versions of these patterns have not been observed. Brookes and Stevens (1989b) offer several reasons against expecting second derivatives of disparity to be computed by center-surround operators, including the observation that the first derivative might be effectively performed by the process of achieving image registration (as mentioned earlier).

Neither Additivity Models nor Winner-take-all Schemes Account for Cue Integration Phenomena

Cue integration is usually characterized in terms of how information from different sources is reconciled in order to produce the 3D interpretation which is most consistent with the evidence provided by these cues. When the 3D information provided by different cues is not consistent, observers tend to see a compromise surface which reflects a linear weighted combination of the information from different cues (Gillam, 1968; Attneave, 1972; Bruno and Cutting, 1988). Cue integration must also deal with the presence and absence of information from independent cues, and not merely their consistency, for information is not always available from any given cue. Also, 3D information might be provided in a patchwork manner, with stereo information available in one region, perhaps in conjunction with other monocular cues, and not in another (e.g. the surface projecting into a monocular portion of the field of view). The global coherence of the surface across the 2D field of view then becomes an issue. We believe that some measure of coherence governs whether the visual system will seek a compromise percept or a winner-take-all solution (in which one cue is favored to the exclusion of others, see Dosher et al., 1986; Bülthoff and Mallot, 1988).

The work discussed thus far suggests a framework for describing spatial coherence in cue integration. Recall the earlier observations that constant gradients of stereo information (corresponding to planar surfaces) were found to be relatively ineffective in influencing the perception of surface layout, compared to disparity gradients that vary spatially either continuously or discontinuously (corresponding to curbed, creased, or discontinuous surfaces). The reconstructive nature of binocular depth, which was demonstrated by a variety of disparity contrast illusions, might reflect a general strategy in which the reconstruction of depth is constrained by curvature, discontinuity, and orientation information contributed by several cues, and not merely disparity contrast. Stevens and Brookes (1988) propose that the role of stereopsis in the determination of overall surface shape is limited, in that linear gradients place only weak constraints on the perception of the depth gradient compared to monocular perspective (and other slant cues). Binocular disparities are much more effective in indicating surface curvature and discontinuities. This hypothesis offers a basis for describing coherence (and conflict) in the integration of 3D cues.

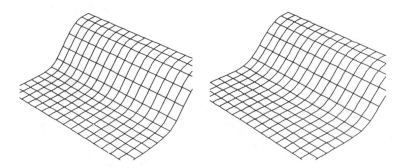

Figure 1.4   *A combination of stereo and mono edges results in an apparent trough.*

Stevens et al. (in press) examined the perception of surfaces defined by a spatial combination of mono and stereo curvature information. The curvature features were independently defined by surface contours and by binocular disparity. A simple illustration of combining binocular and monocular curvature information is provided in figure 1.4, where a smooth stereo edge (having a sigmoid depth profile) is placed adjacent to a smooth monocular edge of similar profile. Where the stereo information suggests surface curvature, the monocular information suggests a plane, and vice versa. The overall perceived surface has the shape of a smooth trough, with one side defined solely by monocular information and the other defined solely by the pattern of binocular disparities. The trough constitutes an emergent surface feature defined by the combination of mono and stereo cues.

In figure 1.4 the stereo and mono curvature features are spatially separated. More interesting cases are presented when the features are spatially superposed, and either orthogonal or spatially coincident and aligned in orientation, wherein one can examine the effect of consistency in the sign of curvature implied by the two cues. Figure 1.5 presents a ridge defined by surface contours that is intersected by a similarly shaped ridge defined by binocular disparities. The central question concerns how the two curvature descriptions are combined where the ridges intersect. Observers vary in the extent to which they report additivity (a bump or protrusion at the intersection); many observers fail to report it at all.

The perceptual effects which we found resulting from the combination of these conflicting cues are summarized as follows. The monocular interpretation of a set of surface contours, whether planar or curved, tends to dominate the combined percept at locations in the display where the disparity pattern indicates planarity. The binocular interpretation tends to dominate where the disparity pattern indicates curvature and where the monocular pattern indicates planarity. Where both stereo and monocular interpretations indicate inconsistent surface curvature features, more complex resolution strategies are suggested, sometimes involving conscious attention to either the

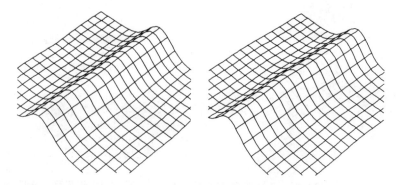

Figure 1.5   *A combination of crossed stereo and mono ridges.*

stereo or the mono interpretation, sometimes involving a compromise between both, but varying among observers and among presentations for the same observer. Combinations in which the curvature signs are opposed generally produce stimuli which are unstable and difficult to interpret, with wide variability in effect among different observers. Observers show a variety of strategies, when faced with such conflicts. In some cases, a perspective reversal of the monocular feature provides a resolution of conflict with the stereo feature. In other cases, an unstable shifting between stereo and monocular interpretations is reported. In general, subjects experience considerable difficulty in composing an adequate description of the appearance of such stimuli, which seem particularly liable to change as the focus of attention changes.

Discussion

We are seldom aware of the fact that our perception of surfaces is constructed from the information provided by multiple 3D sources. The fabric of the internal representation is still unknown, even in the case where the percept is derived from a single cue, such as stereopsis. Intuition suggests the fundamental data correspond to distance or depth information. That may be only one of the forms in which 3D shape is made explicit; the individual cues differ in the quality of information they provide. Common to many of these cues is availability of information about curvature and discontinuities. Even shading, one of the weakest 3D cues, provides some constraint on surface curvature, but little if any constraint on slant or depth (see Todd and Mingolla, 1983). Curvature can be quantified with more or less specificity, either as a simple viewer-centered measure of image properties (gradients of disparity, for example), or projected in 3D in order to correspond to intrinsic surface curvature (independent of viewpoint). The extent to which the curvature information from a given cue is interpreted in 3D is an open question.

Koenderink and van Doorn (1982) show how one can interpret monocular configurations in an image, such as contour terminations, as qualitative evidence for the intrinsic geometry of corresponding surface regions in 3D. It is worth considering to what extent other cues can be interpreted in terms of intrinsic geometry (such as the inferences afforded by surface contours interior to the silhouette boundary, Stevens, 1981a). In this chapter we further suggest that curvature is used as a measure on which consistency across cues is decided as part of the integration process. The use of curvature is attractive as a means for describing cue compatibility both because of its general availability, and for its ability to summarize local surface shape in a way that is more robust than a pointwise estimate of depth (assuming that it were available from each cue).

Usually, all 3D cues available in a scene will be in approximate agreement. There are, however, natural cases in which independent cues suggest that surfaces will be more than merely quantitatively inconsistent. Perhaps the simplest strategy for resolving this conflict is a winner-take-all scheme, in which a decision is made on which cue is providing the best evidence and the information is then accepted from that cue and rejected from the other. What occurs in that case, in terms of the representations? Are the individual representations available for scrutiny or are they lost after constructing the final percept? When the 3D curvature information provided by surface contours is inconsistent with curvature information provided by binocular disparities, experienced subjects are generally able to consciously attend to the stereo or the mono information, to the virtual exclusion of the other. It might therefore not be necessary to postulate a single, combined representation mediating the perception of 3D form. An alternative hypothesis would hold that (approximately) independent representations of the various 3D cues are generated automatically, with integration of information between different cues occurring only when it is required for some particular task, and then only according to some task-specific strategy.

On the above theory, one might predict that judgment tasks will tend to be based on the cue providing information which is most directly applicable to the particular task at hand: for example, if linear perspective provides information which is represented in the form of surface orientation, while binocular disparity provides information which is represented in the form of depth contrast, a task requiring judgment of surface orientation might tend to be performed using the perspective information, while a depth comparison task might be performed on the basis of the disparity information. Where the two cues are in agreement, as they would be in most natural viewing situations, the two tasks would be expected to yield compatible results. Where the two cues conflict, however, one might expect the performance on the two tasks to conflict also, in contrast to the result predicted by the theory that both tasks are performed on the basis of a single, combined representation.

Acknowledgments

This research was supported by ONR contract N00014–87–K–0321. Work summarized in this chapter was performed in close collaboration with Allen Brookes and Marek Lees.

Notes

1   The internal representation is often expected to be organized as 2D arrays, or maps, containing pointwise depth or surface orientation information as well as spatially extended surface features such as ridges, depth discontinuities, and creases (Attneave, 1972; Barrow and Tenenbaum, 1978; Marr, 1978, 1982). These maps are expected to be indexed by visual direction.

2   One can indicate apparent surface orientation, for example, by adjusting the direction of a line segment until it appears to extend in space perpendicularly to the tangent plane of the surface, or by setting the shape and orientation of an ellipse so that it corresponds to the foreshortened image of a circle lying on the surface (see methods in Stevens, 1983a,b; Stevens and Brookes, 1987, 1988).

3   Just as line drawings are readily capable of conveying a familiar face or scene, they are equally capable of depicting the 3D shape and orientation of an abstract surface. Surface shading, on the other hand, does not provide a viewer as unambiguous a 3D impression. While shading tends to enhance a simple line drawing, its interpretation requires strong boundary constraints, and thus attempts to remove all cues but shading result in weak 3D impressions.

4   Parallel contours provide a highly effective means for depicting smooth surfaces. The visual system seemingly infers, from their parallelism and image curvature, geometric properties of the underlying surface and its orientation relative to the observer. See Stevens (1981a) for a theory of constraints that permit these inferences.

5   A slanted plane produces a constant gradient (first derivative) of disparity; a curved surface results in a spatially varying gradient, i.e. a nonzero second derivative. See below for how these derivatives might be computed.

2
Visual Analysis and Representation of Spatial Relations

ROGER J. WATT

Subjective and Objective Vision

Vision is a subjective experience, not to be questioned, and very much a personal business that depends on who we are. However, there is also a more prosaic, objective side to vision: without it we would not be able to see what to do; see how to do it; and then see to do it. This side of vision is concerned with interactions with a physical world, a world that is very much the same for all of us, at least in current scientific philosophy. This side is objective because a person either succeeds in catching the ball, or does not. Our effector organs have to act in a world that is outside their own individual psychology, and our eyes provide the source of information for many of these actions. If our actions do not succeed then we have to question the source of information. Vision as subjective experience and vision as physical source of information are two logically distinct systems, and must be studied in different ways (figure 2.1).

Confusion between the subjective and objective aspects of vision is responsible for the fact that a number of serious difficulties in our understanding of vision have been overlooked. There are as yet no satisfactory methods for treating the properties of dimensions of space and of time; in each case the scientific theory of spatial perception is based four-square on subjective experience. The confusion between the subjective and objective aspects of vision is particularly rife in some areas where work in understanding machine vision and in understanding human vision are examining similar topics. This is bizarre because machine vision systems are embodiments of the physical process, not the subjective experience. To use subjective experience as a source of inspiration, encouragement, and information in machine vision is a nonsense.

Figure 2.1   *Image of the view from my office. The view can be taken as an experience which is vivid, dramatic, inspiring, or whatever. However, the image can also be used as a source of information about the weather and used to determine whether to go for an outdoor walk at lunchtime.*

A simple instance of the confusion is given by work on the processes of edge analysis in human vision. There are several models of this process, and they can be split into two categories. There are those that are concerned with the phenomenal appearance of edges, with the locations where subjects report edges, and with the edge-like appearance of certain luminance configurations, such as Mach bands (figure 2.2). There are those that are concerned with the information content of the edge stimulus, and the precision with which the edge information can be used, irrespective of how or where it appears to the observer's consciousness. For example, MIRAGE (Watt and Morgan, 1985) is a model of the manner in which information is made available for psychophysical judgments, rather than a model of the psychological appearance of edges. Watt and Morgan were concerned to find an algorithm that showed the same variations in the precision with which edge information could be used as did their subject. In contrast, the local energy model (Morrone and Burr, 1988), for example, was concerned to find an algorithm that found edges at the same locations as their subjects' experiences. The latter model can be implemented as an image processing algorithm that produces a picture output which contains lines where edges and lines should be seen in the original. It is not clear whether this pictorial property is necessary, unless one supposes that the visual system likewise produces a pictorial output. The point is that, whether or not a particular algorithm for edge detection produces something that looks nice, or looks as if it could be what

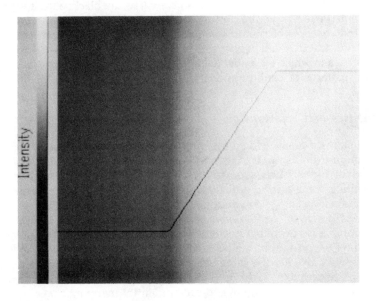

Figure 2.2   *Mach bands: an image of a simple pattern of luminance. The image has an appearance that has rather little to do with the exact luminance profile. The image can also be processed to allow subjects to judge whether the contrast of the figure is greater or less than that of some other and so on. These two aspects are quite distinct, and different explanations are to be required.*

we see, is quite irrelevant. The appearance does not indicate the information value of the edges that are found. The information value of the edges that are found has two components: one is how reliable they are, given some noise and other forms of uncertainty in the image-formation process; the other component is how useful they are. To evaluate these is to determine the potential role of a particular algorithm in a vision process.

At its most blatant, the "picture-in-the-head" idea is that the outcome of vision is a picture inside the system somewhere, and the problem with this approach is that pictures are for looking at. Replacing the picture by an image of its edges is no different. It is generally accepted that some form of description of the things in the scene has to be invoked to avoid the "picture-in-the-head" problem. Each thing in the scene is then represented by an item of information. It is then usual to suppose that there is a spatial structure inside the system, rather like a blackboard, on which items of information are recorded at the appropriate positions. This blackboard implicitly represents the spatial relations between different parts of the image or scene and these relations can be measured off it if needed. The appropriate positions for items of information are taken to be where they are in the image or the things are in the scene. However, this just makes the blackboard a screen to be examined like the picture. It has the same, or a similar, geometry built up out of the concepts of points and lines, of positions and distances, and of geometrical transformation and congruence. In this chapter, I offer a different approach in which all spatial relations are taken to be represented explicitly by local patterns or configurations with the image.

Quantities and Information

We can start by considering a physical system that has the task of mapping information from its input to its output (figure 2.3). The information may be in different forms, such as an optical image for the input and a number representing some attribute of that image for the output. For example, we might show it an image containing a line of a particular length, and get the response "31.415926" as its response. How can we interpret this number?

The number is part of a number system and conforms to certain standards and behaviors. A number can be used to represent a *quantity* such as length, if the quantity also has the same behaviors. We can treat the number system as a set of devices that do things to numbers. To start with, consider a device that appears to do nothing, the so-called identity mapping:

$$A \leftarrow A$$

The symbol "$\leftarrow$" means "is obtained from." We can now define an *origin*, 0, for the number system as a constant that is equivalent to the identity mapping under addition:

$$A \leftarrow A + 0$$

We can then define a *scale*, 1, for the number system as the constant which gives the identity mapping under multiplication:

$$A \leftarrow A \times 1$$

A number can be used to represent a physical property, such as the length of a line. We can define a system that measures length as a device that effects a mapping from a stimulus line, A', to a number, A:

$$A \leftarrow A'$$

which says that the system produces an output A in response to an input A'. We have to decide on a value of length which will be represented by the number 0 and a value which will be represented by the number 1. These two values then determine the mapping from physical lengths to numbers. The choice of origin and scale have an impact on the manner in which the device responds to differences in its input. If we think of line length as the amount of distance between two points on a line, then there is one line length, the

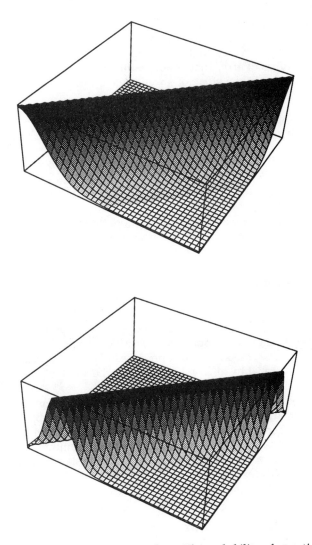

Figure 2.3 *Two different system mappings. The probability of a particular output value, for a given input value, is shown as a grey level: the darkest points are the most probable. Two different variable errors and two different constant errors are shown.*

addition of which is physically equivalent to the identity mapping. If we call this degree of length the origin, and assign it to the number 0, then the numbers used to represent length will have similar properties to the physical domain itself, such as being additive.

Any physical system is prone to errors that place a limit on its *information capacity* and its performance. In the context of information-processing systems, there are two types of error that are quite different. The system has no error if we can characterize the effect of an information processing system by the mapping:

$$A \leftarrow A'$$
where $A \equiv A'$

The symbol $\equiv$ means "is equivalent to." However, the output may be subject to a constant error, β:

$$A + \beta \equiv A' \tag{1}$$

in which case the system is biased. In addition, the system may be subject to a random, variable error, ε:

$$A + \varepsilon \leftarrow A' \tag{2}$$

The two expressions, (1) and (2) then define the system mapping.

We can treat the amount of information available in the output of a system as being related, in some unspecified way, to the number of reliably different outputs that the system can produce. A system may produce an output that had three significant figures, but was so built that the final figure was simply random. In this case, the system can produce 10^3 different outputs, but only 10^2 of them are reliably different. What sets the limit of the information output from a system?

The two types of error, constant and variable, that a system can make have different information consequences. If a system is always subject to the same constant error, there is no actual information loss, according to our definition of information. It is only variable error that limits the amount of information in the output of a system. If the variable error has a standard deviation of 1 then the smallest difference that can be distinguished reliably in the output of the system is of the same order.

Psychophysical Measurements

The usual way to study vision in humans is to use psychophysics. Why does psychophysics have its name? What justifies the implication that it is partly a physical and partly a psychological science? The term has become synonymous in many circles with all types of investigations into the nature of sensory processes, especially vision. It is not uncommon to hear the term used to describe the look-and-see type of demonstration that is thought by many to offer proof of some point of view. These demonstrations rely on the spectator having a particular experience with a particular stimulus, which in turns relies upon the spectator having the same interpretation of the context. It is assumed that there is only one way to see an image. The term "psychophysics" should obviously be applied to the vision process that is concerned with the transfer of information from the eyes to the effectors, either directly or through the medium of memory. As I sit here, I can pick up the mug of coffee beside me without looking, because the visual information that is necessary has been temporarily stored into a suitable memory. I can see the mug, experience its roundness, but have I actually accessed the physical information, or do I just think that I have? The proof requires that I successfully pick it up.

Psychophysical measurements are made to gain insight into the nature and mechanisms of vision processes. If you want to find out how some device does something, you can either take it apart and hope to recognize the function of the bits that you find, or you can watch, from the outside, and hope to spot a pattern in the limitations on what it can do. The gears inside a car engine have an appearance that is visually suggestive of their function; neurones inside the head do not. From a functional point of view the pattern of limitations in the performance seems a more likely source of insight into how vision works. Psychophysics provides a systematic theory of how these limitations can be observed, measured, and organized.

Psychophysics is a technique for examining an information-processing system. Psychophysics is concerned with the measurement of the fundamental parameters of the system, its variable error, and its constant error. These two are somewhat analogous to the older terms, threshold and point of subjective equality. We treat stimuli as having values which are points on a continuous dimension of interest. A standard stimulus is defined and takes one place on the continuum; a set of test stimuli are then taken about this standard. The threshold difference is the smallest difference on that continuum about the standard stimulus that can be reliably reported by a subject. The point of subjective equality is the value of the test stimulus at which it appears equal to the standard. Neither term is particularly useful, and both are somewhat misleading. The threshold is not a fixed step, above which stimuli are discriminable and below which they are not. The point of subjective equality is actually the point at which some specific aspect of the two stimuli appears equal. The terms variable and constant error are more appropriate.

The standard technique to measure the distribution of $(A + \varepsilon)$ is as follows. The subject is shown two stimuli, one with a value of A and one with a value of $(A + \delta A)$, and asked to discriminate which of them is the greater. The proportion of trials on which that with the value of $(A + \delta A)$ is chosen is then measured. For large positive δA, the proportion of trials will approach 1.0; for large negative δA, the proportion of trials will approach 0.0. Between these two there is a continuous function, and this is sampled by measuring the proportion for a range of values δA (figure 2.4).

The two stimuli give rise to two probability density functions through the system mapping. They give rise to two actual values that are drawn from

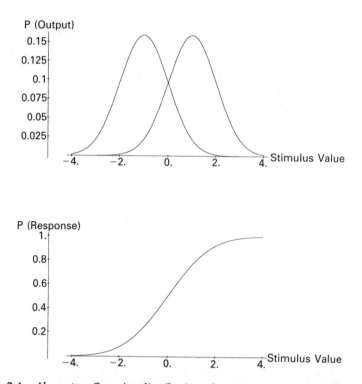

Figure 2.4   *Above, two Gaussian distributions that represent the probability density functions arising from two stimuli, S and ∂S. The distance between the two distributions, measured in units of their standard deviations, determines how discriminable the two stimuli are. Below a typical psychometric function.*

their respective distributions. Whether the subject correctly reports $(A + \delta A)$ to be greater than A is then determined by these two values. The larger the value of δA, the smaller the degree of overlap between their two probability density functions and the more likely is the subject to report the difference correctly. A function giving the probability of correct response for values of δA then encapsulates all the information about the constant and the variable errors. An estimate of this function can be obtained by observing the proportion of trials on which a correct response is made for various values of δA. A graph of this is called a *psychometric function*.

If the random error is assumed to have a Gaussian density function, the psychometric function will have the form of a cumulative Gaussian function with a variance that is given by the variance of the random error and a mean that is given by the constant error. From the psychometric function it is possible to estimate these two parameters, the mean and variance, and hence to characterize the system mapping with the vicinity of A.

How should we interpret the two types of error, constant and variable? The constant error is always difficult to interpret, because it is affected by the way in which the subject responds when uncertain. In order to assess the psychometric function with accuracy, it is necessary to include many trials where the subject's responses are variable, which is where the subject will be forced on occasions to guess. If the subject has an innocent bias in guessing, showing a preference for one of the two responses, then this will shift the constant error. Whether such a bias is a proper part of vision or not is a question that belongs to the subjective approach. Variations in constant error as the stimulus changes can be interpreted more readily, particularly if they are not associated with any change in the variable error. In these circumstances, it is reasonable to suppose that the subject's guessing strategy is not changing, and that the changes in constant error must be due to an effect of the vision process. The variable error is easier to interpret. The higher the variable error, the less information that the vision process is transferring between stimulus input and response output. The variable error indicates how reliable the information is. The constant error indicates how the information has been distorted.

Relations and Metrics

When we use numbers to represent quantities in the way that I have described, the *relations* between different numbers reflect some of the relations between the different values of the physical property. These relations can be of several different varieties. *Ordinal* relations are those where the qualitative <greater than> <equal to> <less than> and their negations are defined. *Cardinal* relations are those where these relations are enhanced through the use of arithmetic operators providing a system of interpreting the numerical values that are assigned to a physical property so that the arithmetic operations of addition and multiplication are understood:

$$
\begin{aligned}
& A && \leftarrow A' \\
\text{and} \quad & B && \leftarrow B' \\
\text{then} \quad & (A + B) && \leftarrow (A' \oplus B') \\
\text{then} \quad & (A - B) && \leftarrow (A' \oplus - B')
\end{aligned}
$$

where the symbol, $\oplus$, represents the physical addition of two lengths. We also have:

$$(A \times 2) \equiv (A + A) \leftarrow (A' \oplus A') \equiv (A' \bigcirc 2)$$

where the symbol, $\bigcirc$, represents the repetition of physical lengths.

All relations have certain properties which may be:

transitive: $(A = B)$ & $(B = C) \Rightarrow (A = C)$
symmetric: $(A = B)$ $\qquad\qquad \Rightarrow (B = A)$
and reflexive: $(A = A)$

The symbol $\Rightarrow$ means "implies that." These properties will vary from relation to relation.

Some quantities are not described by one number, but need instead a list of numbers. Position is an example, where a list of two numbers is required to specify any value of the quantity in the plane of a 2D image. If we have:

$$P(x_1, y_1) \leftarrow P(x_1', y_1')$$
$$\text{and}\quad P(x_2, y_2) \leftarrow P(x_2', y_2')$$

we can define several types of relation on these. For example, using the familiar orientation of coordinates, we have:

$$P_1 \text{ <left of> } P_2 \Leftarrow x_1 \text{ <less than> } x_2$$
$$P_1 \text{ <above> } P_2 \Leftarrow y_1 \text{ <greater than> } y_2$$

The symbol $\Leftarrow$ means "is implied by." We can define:

$$P_1 \oplus P_2 \equiv P(x_1 + x_2, y_1 + y_2)$$

All of these relations treat the two numbers, or coordinates, as separate entities that are not to be combined.

When we come to consider the distance between two points and the direction of one point from another, we need to define a *metric* that specifies how distance is to be calculated. Metrics specify how the various numbers in a multidimensional relation should be combined. We write ∂s for the distance that is passed as we move through a change in position of $(\partial x, \partial y)$. Distance in the standard Euclidean metric is given by:

$$\partial s \leftarrow (\partial x^2 + \partial y^2)^{1/2}$$

and direction is given by:

$$\theta \leftarrow \tan^{-1}(\partial y / \partial x)$$

Things, Edges, and Edge Maps

Edge detection is a common starting point in many machine vision systems. The logic is simple. The scene is made up of a number of compact (i.e. not diffuse) things, and viewed from a particular place in the scene; each of these things has a characteristic occluding edge, or silhouette. Different things in the scene have different surface reflectances and different illuminances.

Therefore, occluding edges between different objects project a sudden change in image intensity. Image intensity changes of this variety can be detected by a suitable algorithm, and the presence of an occluding edge inferred. A number of algorithms have been devised to select those intensity edges that have the highest probability of deriving from occluding edges in the scene and correspondingly low probabilities of finding intensity changes that are not due to occluding edges. The output of edge-finder algorithms of this type is a new image, the edge map, containing non-zero values at all locations where the evidence suggests that there lies the effect of an occluding edge.

Edge maps may have a certain utility in many machine vision systems, providing a useful reduction in the information content of the image. They also have an intuitive appeal, in that they look like a sort of summary of an image. It has been supposed that an important function of the earlier parts of the human visual process would also be to construct an edge map. The reasons for such a supposition are also largely intuitive, although it has proved easy enough to make models that can be tested by psychophysical procedures. The success of such models, as predictors of data, can easily lead to the unjustified confirmation of the theory of the model, i.e. that edge maps exist in human vision. This is unjustified because a different type of model, for the same set of data but interpreted in a different theory, might be equally successful.

A model for an edge map would be a specification of the algorithm whereby the edge map is created. Normally this will have several parts. First, the model will specify the conditions under which an edge is detected; then the model will specify how the edge will be characterized. How should models of edge maps be evaluated? Whether in machine vision or in human vision, this is a serious question. In the case of human vision, what type of data can be used to test a model? There are many approaches, that could be used. The least satisfactory is the approach of creating an image edge map, inspecting it, and noting that it looks like the original image. This is unsatisfactory because there are no objective criteria for the evaluation. Hardly more satisfactory is a second approach, where an algorithm is used to locate edges in some simple synthetic image, such as a square, and then the locations are compared with those reported by subjects. This is also unsatisfactory, because it is based on a subjective model of vision. There would need to be a theory of the conscious appearance of images before the model and the observation could be properly compared. A third technique is more satisfactory. The nature and reliability of the information available for different attributes of edges can be measured psychophysically, and can be compared directly with the model.

The edge map has a metric, normally 2D Euclidean, and this determines how the spatial relations between different edges are to be treated. In a map, items have coordinate location, and this is used to calculate the spatial relations. I believe that this is the fundamental problem with the concept of maps in vision, and in the next section I describe an alternative approach to spatial relations.

Spatial Ordering

It is often very convenient to say that something has a particular location in a display and in an image. There are certain implications of doing this that deserve consideration. For example, it is quite reasonable to say that a point has a particular position in an image: it is not reasonable to say that a color has a particular position in an image. We can define qualitative relations between positions in an image, such as <left of> <above> <near to> <far from> and we can go on to define quantitative relations between positions in an image, such as <10 cm away from> and <bearing 45° from>.

Let us return to the ordinary number system, to consider how the position of points on the continuum of natural numbers can be represented. The value of a particular number records its distance from the origin in scale units. This is a *direct code* for position, that does not depend on any other points on the continuum. We can also define the position of each point by giving its two neighbors, and identifying which is which. This would give a *relational code* for position, where the position of any one point can be computed by counting the number of increments in position from the origin as are necessary to reach the point in question (figure 2.5).

For each of these two types of code, we could have a hierarchical version (figure 2.6). In the case of a *hierarchical direct code*, some of the points, the P^1 points, would have direct position codes with respect to the origin; others, the P^2 points, would have direct codes with respect to the P^1 points; more still, the P^3 points, would have direct codes with respect to the P^2 points; and so on. The position of any point would then be given by the sum of the direct codes of all of its ancestors up to the P^1 generation. In the case of a *hierarchical relational code*, some of the points, the P^1 points, would have incremental position codes amongst themselves; about each one of these P^1 points, a set of P^2 points would have a local relational code; about each one of these P^2 points, a set of P^3 points would have a local relational code; and so on. The position of any point would then be given by the sum of the relations to the parent of the current level, multiplied by the relation size at this level, plus the same sum at the next level, multiplied by its relation size, and so on up to and including the P^1 generation. This is how the decimal notation for numbers works.

It might be thought that the spatial ordering of items in a display was always available to subjects, but it is possible that this is not the case (Watt, 1985).

Distance

With the use of a metric, we can define the meaning of the distance between the positions of two points. The numerical value of the distance can then be calculated from the coordinate values of the two positions. This is the

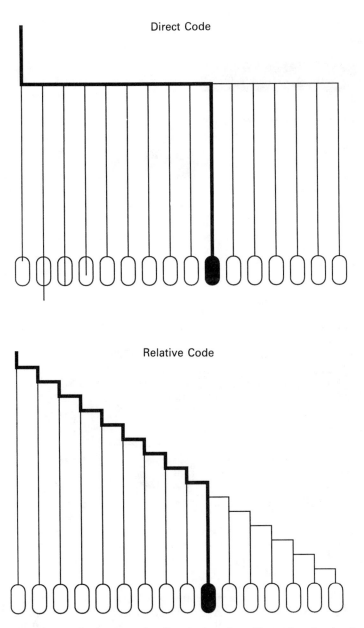

Figure 2.5 *The two basic types of coding for location. Above, location is given by the identity of the entry and its difference from the origin. Below, it is given by the sum of the neighborhood differences from the entry to the origin.*

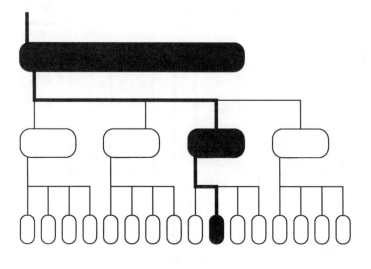

Hierarchical Relative Code

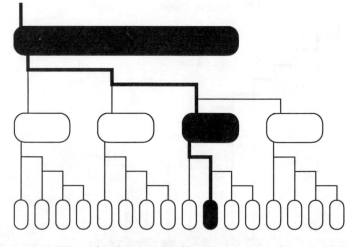

Figure 2.6 *Hierarchical types of coding for location. Above, location is given by the entries at each level and the sum of the differences from the origin. Below, it is given by the sum of the relational differences from the entry to the origin.*

standard physical model of distance, and in this sec
appropriate as a model for the role of distances in

It is possible to achieve very high precision in t]
location under some circumstances. One arc secon
and a typical foveal receptor has a diameter of ar
Vernier target of two abutting lines with an offset
of visual angle can be reliably discriminated from
et al., 1973). This is misleading, however, and it ha₋ ₋₋
better described as a shape judgment task, rather than one of direc₋ ₋₋₋
relation judgment (Watt et al., 1987). Such high precisions rely on the two
lines being treated as one item (Watt and Campbell, 1985).

It is known that visual judgments of distance can also, under some circumstances, be very accurate, having a very low variable error. For comparisons of distances, as defined by the separation between two dots, that are not more than around 5 arc minutes, the typical variable error has a magnitude of less than 10 arc seconds (Westheimer and McKee, 1977; Watt, 1984). For greater distances, the variable error can be expressed by a Weber law, so that the variable error is a simple fraction of the distance that is being judged. There is a rise in Weber fraction for dot separations that is less than about 5 arc minutes. A similar pattern of results holds for judgments of line length, although the finest precision is found for lengths of around 10 arc minutes. Judgments of line length are always of higher precision than judgments of dot separation, even though the information in the two cases is identical (Andrews et al., 1974).

What does the Weber law signify? If distance is just determined by the separation of two points, then the variable error in distance comparison should arise only from the variable error with which the two points can be individually located. There is no reason to suppose that two points that are separated by 1 arc degree will be located with any less accuracy than when they are separated by 10 arc minutes. The effects of eccentricity are not great enough over this range, and have been ruled out (Morgan and Watt, 1989). It therefore follows that the process of combining the positions of two points to form an estimate of distance is not simple.

For short separations, Weber's law breaks down, and the variable errors are much higher than they should be. Watt (1984) has shown that this is what would be expected, if the stimulus that is being judged were to have been filtered by a blurring function with an appreciable width, and that it was the resulting blurred length that was being judged. Suppose that the stimulus was a line of length L, and that it is "seen" through a filter of standard deviation f. The line has a standard deviation of $L/\sqrt{12}$, the square of which adds to the square of the filter standard deviation:

$$L' = \sqrt{(L^2/12 + f^2)}$$

The rate of change of this as L changes will then be one determinant of the threshold function:

$$\frac{L}{12L'} = \frac{L}{\sqrt{(L^2/12 + f^2)}} = \frac{1}{\sqrt{(1/12 + f^2/L^2)}}$$

The reciprocal of this is a measure of the change in L that is required to produce a fixed change in L', as a function of L. When L is large (larger than f), then this tends to a constant value. This function is a good model for the experimental data, for a value of f of around 3 minutes of arc.

There is a paradox here, in that the blurring of the degree necessary to generate the right sort of function is very much larger than that introduced by the optics of the eye. In these experiments, the stimuli look sharp and well focussed, but behave as if they were significantly blurred. This is even more marked when exposure duration is restricted (Watt, 1987a). For brief presentations, the stimulus still looks sharp and well focussed, but the size of filter that is needed to explain the results is increased: filter size is reciprocally related to the exposure duration.

Distance is also often judged with constant errors. The Müller–Lyer illusion is probably an illusion of apparent length, but there is another, less familiar illusion of distance that is better for our purposes here. The Oppel–Kundt illusion of filled space is shown in figure 2.7. It is generally agreed that the distance between the outer lines of a filled spatial interval is seen as wider than the distance between the two lines of an equivalent empty interval. The figure shows a standard empty interval and a collection of filled intervals: the empty interval actually physically matches the central filled interval, but it does not appear to do so (see also figure 2.8).

The magnitude of the Oppel–Kundt illusion depends on the number of lines between the two outer ones, being greatest for about ten lines, and smaller for either fewer or more lines. Craven and Watt (1989) have measured the constant errors in the illusion and have shown that the illusion, and its dependence on the number of lines can be modeled by a system that measures distance by counting contours across a range of spatial scales. The principle that this would indicate is that for a field that has a reliable density of contours, on average and across scales, there is no need to use an internal scale, the field itself provides one. Fractal images are just such fields, with statistically reliable contour densities. Since many natural images have the characteristics of Brownian fractals, this would also apply, usually, to retinal images. Craven and Watt were able to show that the judged sizes of the various Oppel–Kundt figures, when compared with a patch of fractal image, were exactly as predicted by the contour densities.

In this section, I have described three oddities in the way in which distances are judged and "seen." First, the Weber law indicates that the simple Pythagorean approach is not employed. Secondly, the distances that are judged are not those that we would define on the stimuli, but are instead defined by the visual system on some type of blurred version of the stimulus. Thirdly, constant errors in optical illusions can be attributed to statistical

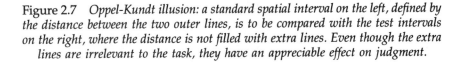

Figure 2.7   *Oppel-Kundt illusion: a standard spatial interval on the left, defined by the distance between the two outer lines, is to be compared with the test intervals on the right, where the distance is not filled with extra lines. Even though the extra lines are irrelevant to the task, they have an appreciable effect on judgment.*

differences between those figures and natural images. The idea is introduced that counting contours is used to measure distance.

Direction

A metric also allows the specification of direction. Direction, or as it is more usually regarded, orientation, shows many of the same psychophysical properties as does distance.

The direction of a line can be judged very accurately (Andrews, 1967). This precision is subject to an equivalent restriction to the Weber law, so that for line lengths greater than about 10 arc minutes, variable errors are a fixed proportion of the length of the line, i.e. a fixed orientation difference (Watt, 1984). Just as with distance, line stimuli are judged more accurately than dot stimuli (Watt, 1984). Moreover, variable errors for smaller line lengths, when expressed as orientation differences, rise in a manner that can be modeled by the effects of blurring the stimulus, and the degree of blurring necessary is of the order of 3 arc minutes, as for line length judgments. For brief exposure durations, a much larger degree of blurring is required.

There is even an orientation equivalent to the Oppel–Kundt illusion, which

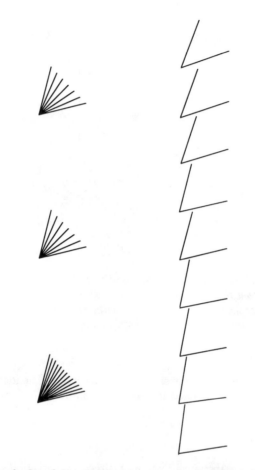

Figure 2.8   *Angle Oppel–Kundt illusion: a standard angle on the left, defined by the two outer lines, is to be compared with the test angles on the right, that are not filled with extra lines. Even though the extra lines are irrelevant to the task, they have an appreciable effect on judgment.*

shows a similar variation in constant error with number of lines as does the distance version (Rentschler et al., 1981).

Spatial Configurations

Finally, I consider briefly how spatial configurations can be represented. Consider this problem: a subject is shown three patterns of randomly placed dots, and is asked to discriminate which is the odd one out, that is, which

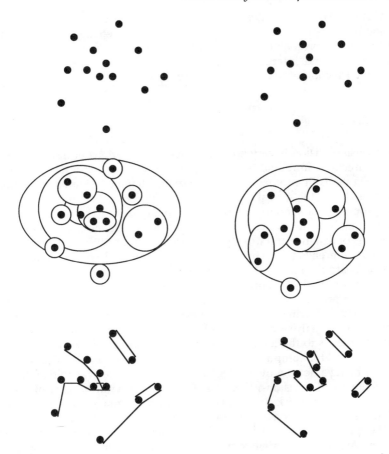

Figure 2.9 *Two patterns of dots plus relation codes: the slight difference in the two random dot patterns could give rise to different patterns of spatial relation representation. The middle panels show a notional neighborhood code, and the bottom panels show a notional nearest neighbor code.*

is different from the other two. How can the necessary information be made explicit, so that the task can be performed?

This task could be done with direct codes for position by creating a set of the coordinates of all the dots in each pattern, normalizing by subtracting the mean coordinate in each case, and then comparing the three sets. I suggest that it is not done in this way but is done instead by using relational codes. All that is required is that different spatial configurations in the random dot patterns should give rise to different representations so that the patterns can be told apart (figure 2.9).

This task shows considerable improvements in precision as exposure duration is increased (Watt, 1987b), and this is interpreted as indicating that a hierarchical representation is used. I have speculated elsewhere that it is the construction and internal maintenance of such a representation that is a primary function of visual attention (Watt, 1988).

Conclusion

Our sense of vision is very spatial. Items have locations in three-space, and have directions in retinal two-space. Spatial relations exist and can be used between items in an image. In this chapter, I have considered the rationale for considering the spatial aspects of human vision and what is known about the properties of spatial perception in human vision. The tentative conclusion is that human vision does not use position in the metrical sense, and the relations of distance and direction as derived from positions. Instead, spatial relations are encoded explicitly as the fundamental spatial quantity, and positions are then derived from these.

An important distinction in the argument has been the notion of an objective vision process or processes that deliver information for subsequent use, rather than delivering a "view" or reconstruction of the scene. Our subjective impression is that we can relate all possible pairs of visual inputs and this naturally leads to the idea of a space with coordinate systems for indexing locations and for computing relations. If we mistrust our subjective impression as being a heavily over-interpreted version of the available information for actions and decisions, then we can dispense with the idea of a spatial coordinate framework and replace it with a system within which useful relations are computed and made explicit.

The question that such a point raises concerns the competence of such a system. Are there immediate visually initiated and controlled tasks that require the spatial coordinate framework or, as I would tend to suspect, is it the case that relational descriptions are sufficient for all practical purposes? The answer to this question does not yet exist.

Acknowledgments

This chapter was written with the support of a BP Royal Society of Edinburgh Research Fellowship and ESPRIT Basic Research Action 3001.

3
Modern Theories of Gestalt *Perception*

STEPHEN E. PALMER

Some of the most interesting phenomena of visual perception were discovered by *Gestalt* psychologists early in this century. Most of them concern *holistic* aspects of perception, such as the familiar laws of grouping and figure/ground relationships. Given the considerable advances that have been made recently in computational, psychophysical, and physiological studies of vision, one would think that such basic problems would now be well understood. In fact, most *Gestalt* phenomena are as enigmatic as ever.

In this chapter I will discuss four modern theories that address the problem of how holistic contextual effects might occur in the perception of simple geometric figures. The first three theories attempt to specify the stimulus factors that produce the (emergent) structure characteristic of *Gestalt* phenomena. These three stimulus theories contend that the dominant factor is (a) the axis of elongation (Palmer, 1975; Marr and Nishihara, 1978), (b) axes of reflectional symmetry (Brady, 1983; Palmer, 1983, 1985), or (c) the orientation at which there is maximal power in low spatial frequencies (Ginsburg, 1971; Janez, 1983). Each theory will be described in detail later in the chapter, and experiments will be presented that test important predictions of each. The fourth theoretical approach is a much more speculative attempt to specify a mechanism for *Gestalt* effects in the form of dynamic "connectionist" networks (e.g. Hopfield, 1982, 1984). After explaining how such networks work, I will argue that these modern theories are closely related to the original ideas of *Gestalt* theorists and that they offer a promising approach for constructing new theories to account for *Gestalt* phenomena. Before considering these modern approaches to *Gestalt* perception in detail, however, it will be useful to give a quick sketch of *Gestalt* ideas to place the present theories in proper historical context.

A Brief History of Gestalt Theory

The founding of the *Gestalt* movement early in this century was one of the most important events in the history of perception. Led by Max Wertheimer, ·
Kurt Koffka, and Wolfgang Kohler, this group of psychologists challenged the prevailing theoretical position of "structuralism" and largely succeeded in overturning it. Structuralism was built on two major theoretical assumptions. The first, *atomism* or *elementarism*, was that complex percepts could be analyzed into indivisible, local sensory experiences. The second, *empiricism* or *associationism*, was that these sensory atoms were held together by mental associations due to their having occurred contiguously in space and time. The structuralist approach is sometimes referred to as "mental chemistry" because of the fairly obvious similarities between their ideas and those underlying the atomic theory of chemistry.

The *Gestalt* theorists rejected both of these assumptions and replaced them with ones of their own design. In place of atomism, they advocated *holism*:·
· the idea that a perceptual whole is different from – and not reducible to – the sum of its parts. In place of associationism, they offered the concept of *or*-
· *ganization*: the notion that visual experience is inherently structured by the nature of the stimulus as it interacts with the visual nervous system. These ideas promoted a new way of thinking about visual perception, one that led to a remarkable series of discoveries about perception. The examples most
· familiar to modern psychologists are the laws of grouping and figure/ground organization, now discussed in virtually every introductory textbook. There are many other perceptual phenomena that can be traced to the *Gestalt* movement, however, including the various perceptual constancies, apparent motion, induced motion, and a host of other contextual effects. Such demonstrations convinced most psychologists that the underlying assumptions of structuralism were untenable and needed to be supplanted by a more adequate theoretical conception.

Despite their facility for finding fatal flaws in opposing viewpoints, *Gestalt* theorists were notably less successful in formulating a viable replacement theory. The abstract principles of holism and organization that guided their search for phenomena did not, in and of themselves, constitute a coherent theory that could explain perception in any specific sense. Wolfgang Kohler attempted to bridge this gap in 1920 by his proposal that the brain constitu-
· tuted what he called a "physical *Gestalt*": a holistic physical system whose behavior is governed by complex dynamic interaction. A favorite example of such a *Gestalt* system was a soap bubble. Soap bubbles have the intriguing property that, no matter what shape they start out, they always evolve over time into a perfect sphere. The distribution of local stresses and strains in the surface of the bubble are propagated to neighboring regions so that, eventually, they are spread uniformly over the entire surface. In the end, the entire soap bubble achieves a state of global stability when the forces on its surface achieve a minimum of physical energy. Kohler argued that there were many

other "physical *Gestalts*" that have this general character – systems that · evolve dynamically toward a stable state of minimum energy – and that the brain was among them. He conceived that it worked by coming to an optimal compromise between the constraints imposed by incoming sensory data and its own internal constraints toward achieving holistically "good" organizations.

The specific mechanism Kohler proposed to account for perception (and all other mental events) was electrical fields within the brain. They had all of the important properties of physical *Gestalts* and were deemed to be physiologically plausible in Kohler's day. For many years there were no direct physiological tests of his idea, but in 1949 Kohler and Held obtained scalp recordings of direct electrical currents that correlated with a percept of a point moving along a straight path. What was unclear, however, was · whether these fields played a *causal* role in determining perception, as Kohler maintained, or whether they were ineffectual side-effects of the *real* causal events that took place in the brain: the firing of neurons.

Several important physiological experiments were performed to test Kohler's field theory. In one study, Lashley et al. (1951) spread strips of gold foil over the visual cortex of monkeys and inserted gold pins into the macular area. Because gold is an excellent conductor of electrical current, they reasoned that the strips would play havoc with the flow of current allegedly producing perception. In another experiment, Sperry and Milner (1955) inserted mica strips into the visual cortex of monkeys. Because mica is an electrical insulator, these strips were expected to interrupt and distort the flow of current. In both experiments the implantation was done after the animals had already learned a visual shape discrimination problem. After recovering from surgery, the monkeys were tested on the same shape problem to find out whether the disrupted electrical fields had correspondingly disrupted their perception. Contrary to the prediction of field theory, the results showed no significant decrease in performance. Although Kohler subsequently argued that serious objections could be raised against these experiments, they were generally accepted as decisive by the psychological community, thus sounding the death knell for his theory of brain interaction through electrical fields.

Although *Gestalt* field theory has not survived intact over the years, most *Gestalt* phenomena have. Moreover, many further demonstrations of holistic and organizational effects have been added to the perceptual literature that support the *Gestalt* theorists' view that a non-atomic, non-associationistic approach to perceptual theory is required. Despite their theoretical importance, these *Gestalt* phenomena continue to be poorly understood. In the past several years, however, some new proposals have been made. I will describe four that have been recently applied to a particular *Gestalt* phenomenon that I have been studying for several years: contextual effects on the perceived pointing of ambiguous triangles. After describing the basic phenomena of interest, I will describe the theories and some experimental tests my colleagues and I have made of their predictions.

Contextual Effects on Perceived Pointing of Ambiguous Triangles

The *Gestalt* effects that we have been using as a crucible for theory testing occur in the phenomenon of perceived pointing of ambiguous triangles (Palmer, 1980, 1985; Palmer and Bucher, 1981, 1982; Bucher and Palmer, 1985; Palmer et al., 1988). It concerns the fact that equilateral triangles are perceptually ambiguous in the sense that they can be perceived to point in any of three directions, but only one of them at once (Attneave, 1968). Thus, the triangle in figure 3.1A can be seen to point toward 3, 7 or 11 o'clock and can sometimes be perceived to flip back and forth among these numbers. Figure 3.1B shows that a random arrangement of such triangles all point in the same direction at once and that they all change direction at the same time. The phenomenon that most intrigues me, however, is a *Gestalt*-like configural effect that results when several triangles are placed in well-structured configurations. As shown in figure 3.1C, when several triangles are aligned along one of their axes of symmetry, perception is strongly biased toward seeing them point in a direction that coincides with the configural line. When they are aligned along one of their sides (figure 3.1D), they are seen to point in a direction perpendicular to the configural line. Both of these effects have been verified experimentally using self-report measures (Palmer, 1980) and perceptual performance techniques (Palmer and Bucher, 1981).

In a series of further experiments we have shown that qualitatively similar bias effects can be produced by placing textural stripes inside a single triangle (figure 3.1E and F). Stripes parallel to an axis of symmetry bias perceived pointing in that direction, and stripes parallel to a side bias it in a direction perpendicular to the stripes (Palmer and Bucher, 1982). It turns out that stripes on the perceptual ground produce similar, but weaker, effects. Another contextual factor that produces this type of effect is the presence of a rectangular frame that surrounds a triangle (figure 3.1G and H). Again, perception of the triangle is biased toward pointing along the long axis of the rectangle when it is aligned with one of the triangle's axes and perpendicular to the long axis when it is parallel to one of the triangle's sides (Palmer, in preparation).

Although these contextual effects were discovered long after *Gestalt* psychologists did their ground-breaking work, they are nevertheless good examples of *Gestalt* phenomena. They are holistic in the sense that the perception of each individual triangle is strongly influenced by the spatial structure around it. The fact that all triangles are seen to point in the same direction in figure 3.1B demonstrates this fact quite directly. These contextual effects also exhibit intrinsic organization because the way the triangles affect each other seems to depend importantly on the structure of the perceived whole. This is demonstrated in figure 3.1C and D by the fact that the direction of perceived pointing is clearly influenced by the overall orientation of the configurations.

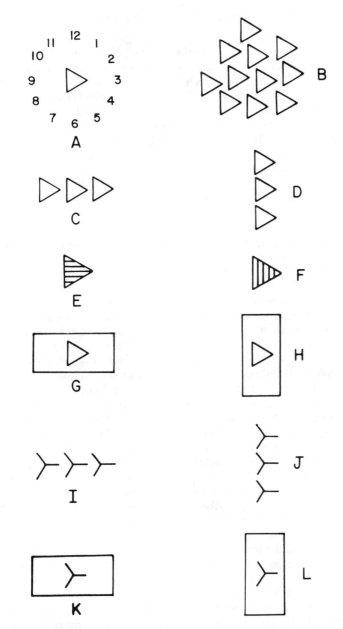

Figure 3.1 *Ambiguous triangles (and Ys) in orientationally neutral conditions (A and B) and in contextual conditions that systematically bias perceived direction of pointing toward 3 o'clock (C–L).*

Reference Frame Accounts of Contextual Effects

Before discussing any specific theories of these contextual effects, it will be useful to consider briefly the general theoretical approach that seems best suited to account for them: namely, perceptual frames of reference. This concept was also introduced by *Gestalt* psychologists. For example, Karl Duncker (1929) used it to explain a phenomenon called "induced motion." Induced motion occurs when a single stationary point of light is surrounded by a luminous rectangle that moves slowly back and forth in an otherwise dark room. Under these conditions observers perceive the moving rectangle as stationary and the stationary point as moving, quite the opposite of what is actually taking place. An everyday example of induced motion occurs when we perceive the moon as moving through a motionless cloud, when actually it is the cloud that is moving in front of a stationary moon. Duncker argued that the perceptual system selects the large surrounding figure as the stationary *frame of reference* for perceiving the smaller surrounded figure, as if the surrounding object were taken to stand for the stationary environment.

The concept of reference frame has also been applied to orientation perception, perhaps most notably by Asch and Witkin (1948). For example, when an observer stands inside a slightly tilted room, he or she will typically perceive the room as upright and himself as tilted! Here the reference frame of the room seems to define what is vertical and what is horizontal. Thus the room becomes the frame of reference with respect to which the orientation of other objects, including the body of the observer, is gauged.

Although the present stimuli do not look much like tilted rooms around observers, the application of reference frames to pointing triangles is relatively straightforward. One sees the triangles point as they do because the surrounding context of the whole display induces a reference frame relative to which the orientations of the triangles are perceived. Thus, a whole row of triangles might define the orientation of the reference frame, and each individual triangle would then be perceived to point along one of the axes of this perceptual frame, if they were so aligned.

The motivation for invoking the concept of perceptual reference frames in modern theories of vision is that they offer an important computational advantage in understanding the perception of shape and orientation (Palmer, 1975; Marr and Nishihara, 1978). The problem they solve is how to encode the shape of an object in a way that is independent of its orientation. This would allow the same object to be perceived as having the same shape when seen in different orientations. This is an important aspect of perceptual constancy, even though not all shapes are constant over changes in orientation, as Rock (1973) has demonstrated. The fundamental insight provided by reference frame theory is that if one encodes the object's shape relative to a reference orientation that coincides with an orientation-invariant property of the object itself – such as its axis of elongation or axis of symmetry – then its shape can be described in an orientation-invariant way (Palmer, 1975). Figure 3.2 shows how this might happen for a schematic human face. The overall face is represented as approximately oval, with its center and axis of elongation defining the position and orientation (respectively) of its intrinsic frame of reference. Each of the facial parts is similarly represented within its own intrinsic reference frame, and these part-frames are related to the larger face-frame by similarity transformations (i.e. translations, rotations, and dilations). These are symbolized in the hierarchical network by the ovals within which vectors indicate translations, angle sizes indicate rotations, and size ratios indicate dilations. Note that these frame relations remain invariant when the orientation of the face as a whole changes. (For a more complete discussion of the role of reference frames in shape and orientation perception, see Palmer, 1989; Rock, 1990.)

Marr and Nishihara (1978) have made similar proposals about using reference frames to achieve constancy. They extended the idea to encompass 3D shapes and couched it within an explicit theory of object representation based on a particular set of shape primitives. Specifically, they proposed that 3D objects can be represented in "object-centered coordinates" by a hierarchical description in terms of primitive shapes (called "generalized cylinders") at various levels of resolution, as illustrated in figure 3.3. "Object-centered coordinates" means that the shape of the object is described relative to the intrinsic properties of the object itself – such as its axis of elongation – rather than to the viewer or to the surrounding environment. "Generalized cylinders" are just extensions of the usual idea of cylinders to include cases in which the axis is curved (such as a C-shaped or S-shaped tube) and the diameter of the cylinder can vary along its axis (such as an hourglass- or bell-shaped object). Because each generalized cylinder has its own intrinsic axis, this axis can be used to define the reference orientation relative to which the object's shape can be represented, thus providing an orientation-invariant description that can be used to identify the object. Figure 3.3 shows how Marr and Nishihara proposed to represent the 3D shape of a human body in terms of generalized cylinders at different levels of resolution (see Marr and Nishihara, 1978; Marr, 1982, for more detailed descriptions).

Thus, modern computational theorists would argue that reference frame effects occur in visual perception because they help to solve the problem of perceiving shape invariance over changes in orientation, and perhaps other variables as well (Palmer, 1989). The present case of contextual effects on perceived pointing of triangles would be understood as resulting from the operation of this important mechanism. If so, we can gain insight into its nature by studying this effect in detail.

Although our initial experiments on this topic were largely empirically driven, our more recent work has been directed at testing several explicit theories of such reference frame effects. I will now describe three theories that attempt to specify what stimulus variables control these effects – axis of elongation, axes of symmetry, and low spatial frequency power – and some experiments that test their predictions.

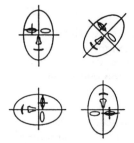

A

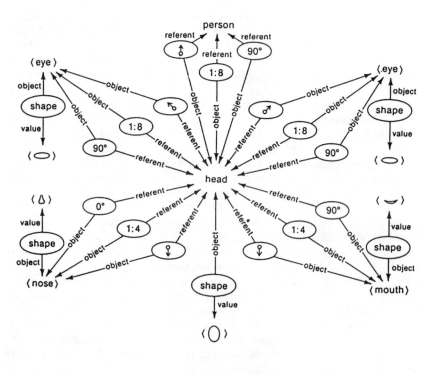

B

Figure 3.2 *Using reference frames to maintain constancy over orientations in a schematic face. a, the invariance of the relation between the frame of the head and that of the eye in different orientations. b, a propositional network representation of a "face schema" that specifies the transformational relations between the face frame and the various facial feature frames. (From S. E. Palmer, 1975. Visual perception and world knowledge, in D. A. Norman and D. E. Rumelhart (eds),* Explorations in Cognition, *San Francisco: Freeman, figure 11.4, p. 290.)*

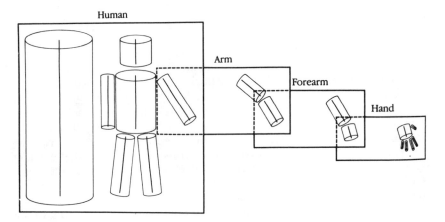

Figure 3.3 *Marr and Nishihara's hierarchical cylinder model of a human body. The person is coarsely modeled as a single cylinder of the appropriate orientation, size, and shape. At the next lower level, this is decomposed into six component cylinders representing the head, torso, arms, and legs. Insets show the arm and hand at finer levels of resolution. (From D. Marr 1982: Vision, San Francisco: Freeman, figure 5.3, p. 306. Reproduced with permission.)*

Axis of Elongation Theory

In trying to account for the contextual effects described above, I was initially drawn to the global elongation of the stimuli as the spatial structure that might have produced these biases. That is, it seemed possible that the visual system was strongly biased toward establishing the perceptual reference frame along the longest axis of the figure, such as the major axis of an ellipse or a rectangle. This notion had its genesis in some of my own previous theoretical work on perceptual representation of objects (Palmer, 1975), but gained much wider currency when Marr and Nishihara (1978) advanced it as part of their computational theory of object recognition. There is also some psychological support for it as an important factor in recovering intrinsic descriptions of shape (e.g. Wiser, 1981; Humphreys, 1983).

In applying this idea to the present phenomena, however, it is not entirely clear why an elongated stimulus should produce a bias along a direction *perpendicular* to its axis of elongation, especially given that the perpendicular effect is every bit as strong as the one *along* its axis of elongation. This problem can be overcome simply by postulating an internal reference frame that contains two perpendicular axes, such as in a standard Cartesian coordinate system (e.g. Palmer, 1980; Palmer and Bucher, 1981; Janez, 1983). If one then assumes that elongation along a given orientation drives the frame selection process toward frames that have either axis along that line of elongation, both the parallel and perpendicular effects can be easily explained.

Testing the Elongation Theory

We set out to test the elongation theory using the same methods we had developed previously to study other contextual effects on perception of ambiguous triangles (e.g. Palmer and Bucher, 1981). In our paradigm, subjects are required to discriminate in which of two or more directions an equilateral triangle can be seen to point. These directions usually coincide with salient extrinsic orientations such as gravitational horizontal or vertical. For instance, subjects would be asked to determine whether the triangles point directly right (toward 3 o'clock) or directly left (toward 9 o'clock), ignoring all other possible directions in which they might be seen to point. For instance, they would have to see the triangle in figure 1A point directly to the right (toward 3 o'clock) rather than obliquely (toward 7 or 11 o'clock) in order to perform the task. The amount of time subjects take to achieve this percept is measured by requiring them to make a simple directional response as soon as they can determine in which of the designated directions the presented triangle points. Reaction time (RT) is taken as the primary measure of the difficulty in achieving the required percept for different stimulus conditions. Error rate is also measured, but its correlation with RT is so strongly positive that it provides little additional information.

All of the studies I will describe are based on the following rationale. If the target triangle is presented within a context whose orientation biases perception of pointing in a direction *consistent* with the required directional response – toward 3 o'clock in figure 3.4A and D – then RTs will be faster than if the same triangle is presented within a context whose orientation biases a direction *inconsistent* with the required response – toward 11 o'clock in figure 3.4B and E or 7 o'clock in figure 3.4C and F. The magnitude of the perceptual bias introduced by a given type of contextual structure can then be computed as the signed difference between the response times in corresponding inconsistent and consistent conditions. Reliable differences of this sort have been obtained in many previous experiments using a variety of stimuli (Palmer and Bucher 1981, 1982; Palmer, 1985; Palmer et al., 1988). The present "interference paradigm" was chosen over a more direct methodology in which subjects merely indicate the direction in which they first see the triangle point (Palmer, 1980) because it is less subject to alternative interpretations in terms of "demand characteristics" or other "optional perceptual processes" that might contaminate the results.

There is an obvious way to test the elongation theory using rectangular frames as the oriented context: simply measure the effect of changing their aspect (length-to-width) ratios. If the elongation hypothesis is correct, there should be no bias effects for square frames because they are not globally elongated. Moreover, the magnitude of the bias effect should increase monotonically as the aspect ratio increases from unity. The perpendicular structure of the hypothesized Cartesian frame further predicts that the effects of elongation will be equal for axis- and base-aligned frames.

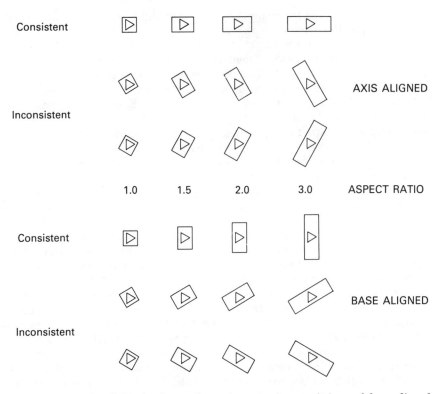

Figure 3.4 *Stimuli in the frame elongation experiment. Axis- and base-aligned rectangular frames with aspect ratios of 1.0, 1.5, 2.0, and 3.0 were presented at orientations either consistent or inconsistent with the required response. All right-pointing conditions are shown; mirror-image left-pointing conditions were also included.*

The stimuli for this experiment consisted of single equilateral triangles surrounded by frames of constant width and varying aspect ratios: 1 : 1 (squares), 1.5 : 1, 2 : 1, and 3 : 1 (see figure 3.4). The triangles were oriented so that each could be seen as pointing either directly leftward (toward 9 o'clock) or directly rightward (toward 3 o'clock). Subjects were instructed to discriminate between these two cases as quickly and accurately as possible by pressing the rightmost response key with their right hand for the right-pointing triangles and the leftmost response key with their left hand for the left-pointing triangles. On one-third of the trials, the frame orientation was *consistent* with the required percept. In the axis-aligned consistent conditions (figure 3.4A) the long axis of the frame coincided with the axis of symmetry that bisected the right- or left-pointing angle of the triangle. In the base-aligned consistent condition (figure 3.4D) the long axis of the frame was parallel to the side of the triangle opposite the right- or left-pointing angle of the triangle. Responses on these consistent trials should be fast and accurate, to the extent that the frame has a large aspect ratio. On the other two-thirds of the trials, the frame orientation was *inconsistent* with the required percept. For each of the other two possible directions of pointing there were both axis- and base-aligned inconsistent frames defined in analogous ways for the other two angles as shown in figures 4B, C, E, and F. Responses on these trials should be slower and/or less accurate to a degree that depends on the size of the aspect ratio. In square frames (whose aspect ratio is 1.0) the axis- and base-aligned conditions are identical, and the elongation theory predicts no difference between consistent and inconsistent frame orientations.

Mean RTs are shown in figure 3.5 for consistent and inconsistent conditions as a function of frame elongation (aspect ratio). They show that neither of the two critical predictions of elongation theory is confirmed. Contrary to the prediction that square frames would have no bias effect, they produced a highly reliable bias effect: responses in the presence of inconsistent square frames took nearly 150 ms longer than those in the presence of consistent ones. Concerning the prediction of a monotonic increase in bias effects for increasingly elongated frames, there does seem to be a slight trend towards higher RTs for the longer frames especially for the base-aligned ones, but even the difference between the most extreme aspect ratios fails to reach statistical significance. It seems safe to say that the measured variation in the amount of interference (inconsistent RT minus consistent RT) due to differences in frame elongation are quite unimpressive relative to the amount of interference for the unelongated square frame. We conclude, therefore, that global elongation is not a major factor, at least for this particular contextual effect.

Symmetry Theory

A second theory that has been advanced to account for contextual effects on perceived pointing of ambiguous triangles is formulated in terms of symmetry conditions (Palmer and Bucher, 1982; Palmer, 1983, 1985). The proposal is that, roughly speaking, the visual system uses symmetry rather than elongation as the principal type of spatial structure used to select the orientation of its reference frame.[1] In this case, however, the theory is a bit more elaborate, and it makes a number of interesting predictions that have turned out to be true. The following is a brief description of a qualitative theory that attempts to account for how several contextual phenomena might arise from symmetry structure and how they are related to each other.

As with all reference frame accounts, we begin by assuming that people perceive a triangle's *shape* relative to an intrinsic, oriented reference frame and its *orientation* by the relation of this frame to a larger environmental reference frame. We further assume that the visual system has a powerful tendency to establish the orientation of a reference frame along an axis of reflectional symmetry, if one exists. Equilateral triangles have three such

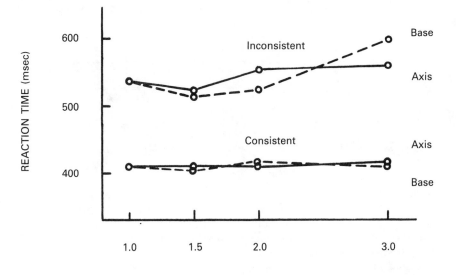

Figure 3.5 *Results of the frame elongation experiment. Mean RTs are plotted for axis- and base-aligned frames in consistent and inconsistent orientations as a function of aspect ratio.*

axes in their symmetry subgroup, the dihedral group D3 (Weyl, 1952).[2] In this way, the theory accounts for the fact that equilateral triangles are three-ways ambiguous in perceived orientation and direction of pointing: the percept depends on which axis of symmetry is selected for the orientation of the frame (see figure 3.6). The triangle's *shape* is not correspondingly ambiguous because all of its geometrical properties are invariant over the transformations that relate alternative frames (i.e. rotations through an angle of 120 degrees and its integer multiples).

When additional elements are added to the display, their symmetries may or may not align with those of the original triangle. In the present cases – configural lines, textural stripes, and rectangular frames – the biasing factors all have a two-fold symmetry subgroup (the dihedral group D2) as illustrated in figure 3.6B for a rectangular frame. The intersection of these two sets of transformations is the symmetry subgroup of the resulting composite display. Because of the structure of the two component groups, D2 and D3, their intersection can contain, at most, one transformation, and this is a reflection about a global axis of symmetry. The theory assumes that the reference orientation is established along an axis of symmetry, if one exists. The reference orientation established for the whole display, then, will coincide with its global axis of symmetry, if one exists (figure 3.6C). The two merely local axes of symmetry of the triangle will therefore be less likely to be

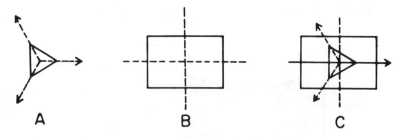

Figure 3.6   *A symmetry analysis of bias effects in perceived pointing of an ambiguous triangle.*

selected, and the triangle will tend to be seen pointing along the line of global reflectional symmetry. Note that this analysis holds equally for all three types of bias – due to configurations, textural stripes, and rectangular frames – and for both the axis-aligned and base-aligned versions of each. No further assumptions about interactions among perpendicular orientations are required for the cases we have considered. Moreover, it clearly predicts bias effects for square frames as well as rectangular ones, as was found in the experiment on aspect ratios of rectangles.

This theory has the virtue of being easily extended to other cases because it appeals only to the symmetry structure of the component stimuli. Therefore, it should apply equally to any other composite display whose components have the same symmetry subgroups, D3 and D2. Figure 3.1I through L show one such extension to Y-shaped figures (symmetry group D3) positioned in configural lines or inside rectangular frames (symmetry group D2). These Ys, like equilateral triangles, are ambiguous in that they are seen to "point" in one of three directions. They also can be biased toward pointing along axes of global symmetry within linear configurations and rectangular frames.

A second advantage of the present account is that it can be extended to other, analogous symmetry structures. One important example is the ambiguous square/diamond figure discussed by Mach (1886/1959). The perceived shape of a square tilted 45 degrees can be that of either an upright diamond or a tilted square, depending on what one takes to be the reference axis (see figure 3.7). This ambiguity in shape of the square/diamond is analyzed in terms of symmetry structure as follows. This figure has four-fold symmetry (the dihedral group D4), and so its reference axes can be chosen in any of four ways. However, there are only two possible shape descriptions of the figure within these four possible reference frames. The geometrical properties of this figure are the same for frames that share the same axes – because squares are rotationally symmetrical about a 90 degree angle and its integer multiples – so there are really only two sets of frames that matter: the side-bisector frames and the angle-bisector frames. The properties of the figure *do* differ between these two sets of frames, however, and so the shape of the figure is two-ways ambiguous. The side-bisector frames produce a

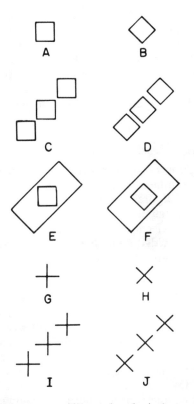

Figure 3.7   *The ambiguous square/diamond and +/× in contextual conditions that bias their perceived shape.*

shape description in which the sides are parallel and perpendicular to the frame axes, and so selecting one of them results in the perception of a "square" shape. The angle-bisector frames produce a shape description in which the sides are oblique relative to the frame axes, and so selecting one of them results in the perception of a "diamond" shape.

The symmetry theory further predicts that adding contextual figures with symmetry axes that align selectively with one set of frames and not the other should selectively bias the corresponding shape percepts. Indeed, this is the case, as illustrated in figure 3.7A through F. Squares aligned along a 45-degree diagonal (figure 3.7C) are generally seen as a tilted column of diamonds, and diamonds aligned along a 45-degree diagonal (figure 3.7D) are generally seen as a tilted column of squares (Attneave, 1968; Palmer, 1985). Similar effects due to rectangular frames (figure 3.7E and F) were demonstrated many years ago by the *Gestalt* psychologist Kopfermann (1930). The present explanation in terms of symmetry further predicts that analogous effects should result for other figures whose symmetry structure is the same as for the ambiguous square/diamond. It can be readily observed in figure 3.7G and H that a + and a × are correspondingly ambiguous shape percepts for the same figure. They too can be biased by configural alignment along the 45-degree diagonal or by rectangular frames tilted by 45 degrees (Palmer, 1985). Thus, the symmetry theory seems to be supported by several confirmed predictions. In the next section I will describe some as yet unpublished research we have recently completed to test the symmetry theory more rigorously.

Testing the Symmetry Theory

The obvious strategy for testing a theory based on symmetry is to examine conditions in which symmetries are systematically broken. If symmetry is the key factor, then configural bias effects should disappear, or at least be significantly reduced, when one destroys a symmetry axis to which the process of reference frame selection is supposedly drawn. Several experiments were conducted that provided a number of different tests of this prediction, only two of which are described here.

Curved Frames.   In one experiment the symmetry of a rectangular frame was broken by bending it along its long axis. This has the effect of breaking the axis-aligned symmetry (the one along the long axis) while preserving the base-aligned symmetry (the one along the short axis). This makes a very interesting prediction: namely, that "straight" frames should have approximately equal bias effects on an interior triangle in their axis-aligned and base-aligned orientations, but curved base-aligned frames should have a much bigger biasing effect than curved axis-aligned frames. The reason is simply that the base-aligned symmetry axis is intact after bending the frame, whereas the axis aligned symmetry axis is broken. This prediction was strongly confirmed (see figures 3.8 and 3.9).

Other experiments have broken the symmetry of displays containing an ambiguous triangle in other ways, and most have produced substantial evidence for the prediction of the symmetry hypothesis (see Palmer, 1989). In testing the symmetry theory, however, the most informative experiments are those that do *not* support the hypothesis, and so I will now describe one such experiment.

Parts of a Frame.   This experiment was actually undertaken for a slightly different purpose, but it turns out to provide an interesting test of the symmetry hypothesis. The idea was to study the compositionality of the frame effect by measuring the bias effects produced by its individual sides and all possible combinations of them: pairs, triples, and the complete square frame (see figure 3.10). The set of stimuli thus defined has the property of systematically breaking symmetries of the frame in certain cases while preserving them in other cases. The unadorned symmetry hypothesis predicts that the symmetrical cases will produce reliable bias effects whereas the asymmetrical cases will not.

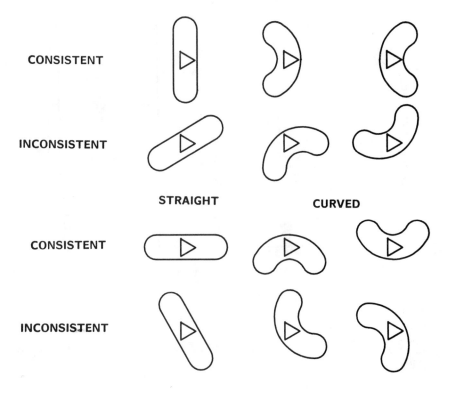

BASE ALIGNED

CONSISTENT

INCONSISTENT

STRAIGHT   **CURVED**

CONSISTENT

INCONSISTENT

AXIS ALIGNED

Figure 3.8   *Example of stimuli from the curved frames experiment. Bending the frame along its long axis preserves the symmetry of base-aligned conditions but breaks the symmetry of axis-aligned conditions.*

The experimental design consisted of the 15 configural conditions shown in figure 3.10 in consistent and inconsistent orientations for both left- and right-pointing triangles. Each subject was shown each condition three times and RTs to discriminate left- from right-pointing triangles were measured.

The results are shown below each stimulus in terms of interference RT (inconsistent RT minus consistent RT). There is some good news and some bad news for the symmetry theory. The good news is that the conditions with the largest bias effects were systematically associated with symmetrical configurations: in fact, the six highest bias scores all came from symmetrical figures. The bad news comes in two parts. First, all but one of the asymmetrical configurations produced statistically reliable amounts of bias.

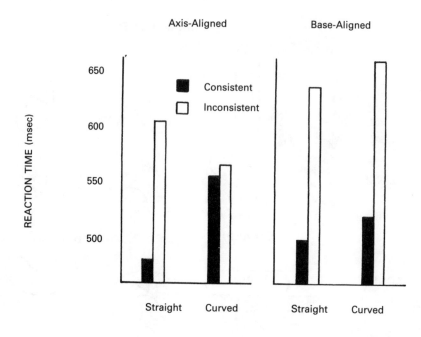

Figure 3.9   *Results of the curved frames experiment. Bending the axis-aligned frames eliminates the bias effect, whereas bending the base-aligned frames does not, as predicted by symmetry theory.*

Secondly, the configuration that produced the *least* bias of all was, in fact, a symmetrical one.

There are various ways in which one could try to accommodate this pattern of results by modifying the symmetry hypothesis. For example, the one case in which a symmetrical configuration produces a minuscule effect might well be due to the fact that it looks, at first glance, pretty much like a bigger triangle. Unfortunately, this observation sheds no light on the often-substantial effects of the asymmetrical configurations. It might be premature to reject the symmetry theory based on the results of this one experiment, but they do tend to reduce one's confidence in it as a sole explanation.

Low Spatial Frequency Theory

A third theory to account for reference frame selection has been proposed by Luis Janez (1983), based on a proposal originally made by Arthur Ginsburg (1971, 1986). Ginsburg claimed that *Gestalt* phenomena, such as the

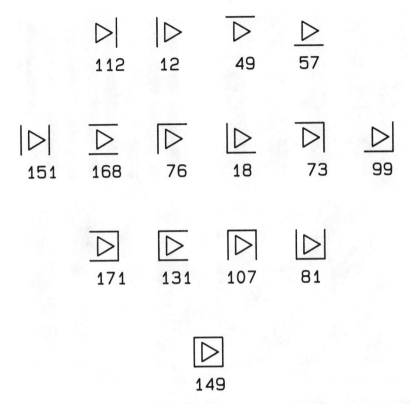

Figure 3.10 *Example stimuli and results of the parts-of-a-frame experiment. All possible combinations of sides of a square frame were measured for the amount of interference they produced. Numbers below each stimulus show the results: inconsistent RT – consistent RT = interference (in ms).*

contextual effects we have been studying, can be explained in terms of the content of images at *low spatial frequencies*. Ginsburg's theory rests on an idea originally formulated and tested by Campbell and Robson (1968): namely, that early stages in the human visual system contain separate channels for processing information at different spatial frequencies and orientations. The idea is that, despite the apparent unity of complex spatial percepts, the visual system actually decomposes them into a particular set of primitive spatial patterns (called "sinusoidal gratings") in which the amount of light varies as a sine wave along one orientation. Some examples of sinusoidal gratings are shown in figure 3.11. It is a mathematical fact, proved in a well-known theorem by Fourier, that any two-dimensional pattern can be analyzed into the sum of many such gratings at different spatial frequencies, orientations, and amplitudes. For example, figure 3.12 shows how a square-wave grating

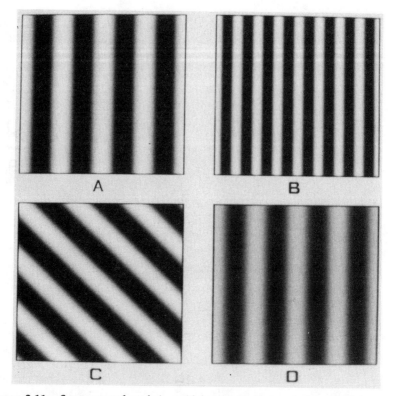

Figure 3.11 *Some examples of sinusoidal gratings that vary in spatial frequency (A versus B), orientation (A versus C), and amplitude (A versus D). "Spatial frequency" refers to the inverse of the width of the light/dark cycle of luminance variation, with low frequencies corresponding to wide gratings, and "amplitude" refers to the degree of contrast between the lightest and darkest parts of the grating, with low amplitude corresponding to low contrast.*

pattern can be constructed by adding together several sinusoidal gratings. There is now massive evidence, from both psychophysics and physiology, supporting the hypothesis that the visual system analyzes retinal images into responses within visual channels defined by spatial frequency and orientation (cf. DeValois and DeValois, 1980).

Ginsburg proposed that *Gestalt* configural effects correspond to the pattern of output in visual channels selectively tuned to *low spatial frequencies*. As evidence, he showed that when images are low-pass filtered, so that only the component gratings at low spatial frequencies remain, the "emergent" properties to which the *Gestalt* theorists referred are often explicitly present in the filtered images. Some examples consisting of circular and linear

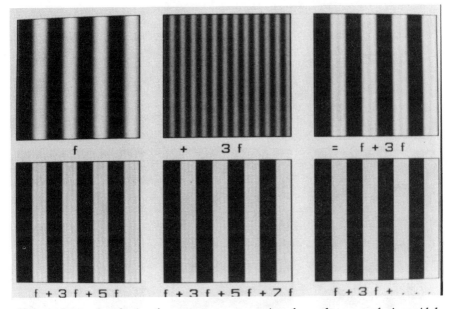

Figure 3.12 *Synthesis of a square-wave grating from the sum of sinusoidal components. The upper left image shows the sinusoidal grating at the fundamental spatial frequency (f) of the square-wave at full amplitude. The upper middle image shows the third harmonic at three times the fundamental spatial frequency (3f) with one-third the amplitude. The upper right image shows the sum of these two gratings (f+3f). The lower row of images shows the result of adding further odd harmonies – the fifth harmonic (f+3f+5f) at one-fifth amplitude, the seventh harmonic (f+3f+5f+7f) at one-seventh amplitude, and so on (f+3f+. . .) – to construct a square-wave grating with sharp rather than fuzzy edges.*

configurations of triangles are presented in figure 3.13. The top row shows the initial spatial patterns, the middle row shows their two-dimensional power spectra,[3] and the bottom row shows the result of "low-pass filtering": taking out all of the power at high spatial frequencies in the corresponding patterns in the top row so that only the low spatial frequencies remain. Notice that the overall shape of the configuration is preserved whereas the individual elements of which it is composed are completely lost. On the basis of demonstrations like this one, Ginsburg argued that *Gestalt* properties correspond to information in low spatial frequency channels of the human visual system.

Testing the Low Spatial Frequency Theory

Janez (1983) developed a particular model of Ginsburg's theory and applied it to the results of several of our early published experiments on perceived

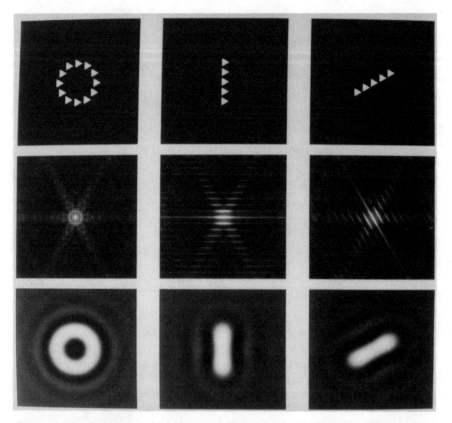

Figure 3.13   *Some examples of low-pass filtered images to illustrate the low spatial frequency theory of* Gestalt *phenomena. The top row shows images containing circular and linear configurations of triangles. The middle row shows their complete power spectra. The bottom row shows the images that result from using only the information in low spatial frequencies; these preserve the shape of the configuration, but not the individual elements of which they are composed.*

pointing of ambiguous triangles (Palmer and Bucher, 1981, 1982) and perceived shape of the ambiguous square/diamond (Palmer, 1985) with notable success. We have replicated his results in an independent computer simulation, obtaining correlation coefficients generally in excess of 0.90 for the data he modeled. Thus, the spatial frequency approach seems to be promising enough that direct experimental tests are needed. We have now performed several different tests, only one of which is presented here.

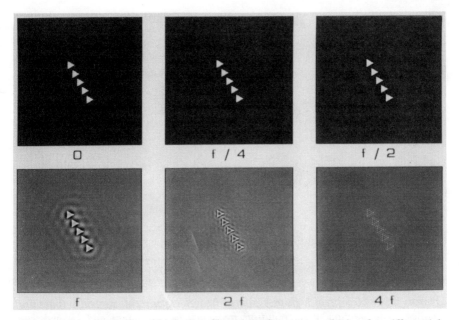

Figure 3.14 *Examples of high-pass filtered configurations of triangles. All spatial frequencies below the specified cut-off frequency (in cycles/side) have been removed from the spectrum before resynthesizing these images.*

High-pass Filtered Images

If the low spatial frequency channels are indeed responsible for *Gestalt* effects, then it should be possible to eliminate or greatly reduce them simply by taking out the information at low spatial frequencies. This operation is called "high-pass filtering." We can then use the behavioral techniques described above to compare these high-pass filtered stimuli with their unfiltered counterparts in order to determine experimentally how much of the configural effect remains after taking out the low frequencies. Figure 3.14 shows example stimuli that were filtered so that only frequencies above the specified cut-off frequency are present in the images: 0 (no filtering), 1/4, 1/2, 1, 2, and 4 cycles relative to the triangle's side. ("One cycle per side" would correspond to a sinusoidal grating that went through one complete light-dark cycle in the spatial interval equal to the length of the triangle's side.) The complete stimulus design in the experiment consisted of the independent combination of four factors: configural alignment (axis- versus base-aligned), configural bias (consistent versus two inconsistent orientations), high-pass filter cut-off frequency (0, 1/4, 1/2 1, 2, or 4 cycles per side), and direction of triangle pointing (left versus right).

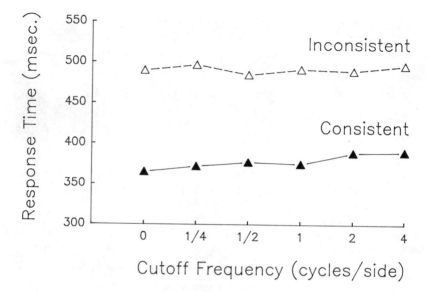

Figure 3.15   *Results of high-pass filtered images experiment. Response times are plotted as a function of filter cut-off frequency for consistent and inconsistent configurations of triangles.*

The results reveal absolutely no effect of filtering out low spatial frequencies (see figure 3.15). That is, the difference in reaction time between consistent and inconsistent conditions is just as large in the most radically filtered images (when all frequencies below 4 cycles per side were removed) as in the unfiltered images. In contrast, Janez's (1983) theory specifies that all configural effects should disappear by a cut-off of 2 cycles per side. These results thus constitute strong evidence that information in low spatial frequency channels – indeed, even in relatively high spatial frequencies – is not necessary for this *Gestalt* effect to occur. Still, it might be *sufficient* to produce such effects, and we are currently undertaking further experiments designed to test this possibility.

It is becoming increasingly clear from this and other experiments specifically designed to test the low spatial frequency theory of *Gestalt* effects that global spatial frequency models of this sort are not strong candidates for explaining the contextual effects we have examined in our experiments. While the symmetry theory has non-trivial support from several experiments and seems to fare better than spatial frequency models on several scores, by itself it does not seem to be entirely adequate either. We are now in the somewhat embarrassing position of having cast serious doubt on all the presently available models. The next step, therefore, should be to explore new theoretical directions.

Connectionist Theories of Frame Selection

Perhaps the most promising direction for new theoretical developments of *Gestalt* phenomena comes from "connectionist" or "parallel distributed processing (PDP)" or "neural network" models (McClelland and Rumelhart, 1986; Rumelhart and McClelland, 1986). They are relative newcomers among theories of complex perceptual phenomena, although neural networks have been previously proposed for a variety of low-level visual phenomena such as Mach bands and various contrast effects (cf. Cornsweet, 1970). The connectionist approach we are about to consider is quite different from the three theories we have just discussed in that it primarily concerns the *mechanisms* underlying perceptual phenomena, whereas the previous theories concerned the *stimulus structure* that was responsible for producing those phenomena. Naturally, both aspects need to be specified in order to reach a complete understanding of the phenomena to be modeled. My experience with network models has led me to believe that they will broaden our perspective on how to account for *Gestalt* phenomena in important ways that are not touched by theories of stimulus structure.

Connectionist models are based on the assumption that information is represented by patterns of activation over neuron-like *units*. Units are linked together by synapse-like *connections* which can be either excitatory or inhibitory, to varying degrees. Certain units – called *input units* – are excited directly by structure in the environment, and other units – called *output units* – directly represent responses of the system. In between there may be various levels of *hidden units* that perform the information processing required to map from input units to output units. Feedback loops among the units cause such systems to exhibit dynamic behavior in which the system "settles" into the pattern of activity that is most compatible with the strength of the connections among units.

The properties of these densely connected, parallel neural networks are hauntingly similar to certain ideas advanced many years ago by *Gestalt* theorists. The relation between *Gestalt* theory and dynamic connectionist networks is to be found in Kohler's (1920) abstract concept of "physical *Gestalts*." Recall that he identified a physical *Gestalt* as a dynamic system that settles into an equilibrium state of minimum energy, such as a soap bubble deforming into a perfect sphere or perhaps, as Kohler suggested, the brain forming an organized percept. His specific version of this abstract hypothesis was that the brain functioned by the interaction of complex electrical fields, but, as mentioned above, several experiments showed this not to be the case (Lashley et al., 1951; Sperry and Milner, 1955). Nevertheless, the foregoing discussion of dynamic connectionist networks suggests that Kohler may have been right in the abstract and wrong merely in the particular.

The proof that dynamic neural networks are modern examples of physical *Gestalts* is found in the analysis of their temporal behavior. They are initially activated by some external stimulus that affects some of the input units, and this activation is then propagated by excitatory and inhibitory connections throughout the network until it "settles down" into a state of equilibrium after which no further changes take place. John Hopfield (1982, 1984) proved mathematically that if the connections between units are symmetrical, the equilibrium state of the network can be characterized by a minimum in an explicit energy function defined over the whole network and that the system will inexorably converge toward this minimum energy state. The minimum energy state represents an optimal compromise between the information imposed on the network by external stimulation and the information encoded in the interconnections among the units. Although the "energy function" that is minimized in the convergence behavior of such networks is not *real* physical energy – it is merely analogous to physical energy – such dynamic connectionist networks are clearly within the spirit of Kohler's concept of physical *Gestalts*; they just hadn't been invented then!

Let us now consider how to construct a simple connectionist network that might account for some phenomena in the perceived pointing of equilateral triangles. To begin, let us suppose that a triangle is seen pointing in a particular direction when the perception of one of its three angles (vertices) dominates that of the other two. This can be modeled in a simple network as shown in figure 3.16. Units are represented as circles and their connections by line segments between them. Lines with arrows indicate excitatory connections and lines with dots at the end indicate inhibitory connections. In the network for a single ambiguous triangle, there are three "input" units representing the three sides of the triangle. These form excitatory connections to the units representing the angles of which they are part. Because these angle units mutually inhibit each other in the network, they produce something called "winner-takes-all" behavior: the more one angle unit is activated, the more it suppresses the activation of the other two angle units, so that eventually one of the three angle units will completely dominate the other two. Thus, there are just three stable states in which the angle network comes to equilibrium, each corresponding to domination by one of the three angle units over the other two. This would account for the three-way ambiguity in the perception of the triangle: the triangle seems to point in the direction of the bisector of the angle whose unit dominates the winner-takes-all network, and only one of the three will dominate at any given time.

The dynamic behavior of this simple network and its relation to "minimum energy" formulations can be understood more fully by considering the *state space* of the system consisting of the three angle units. If the activation of each angle unit can vary from 0 to 1, then the activation state of this three-unit system at a particular time can be represented by a single point in a three-dimensional unit cube (see figure 3.17A). The three stable states of the network are indicated in figure 3.17A by the three circles at the corners of the state space labelled (1,0,0), (0,1,0), and (0,0,1). The dynamics of the system can be represented by vectors at each point (represented as arrows in figure 3.17B) that show how the system's state – i.e. the activations of all three units – will change after some small amount of time has passed. To simplify the

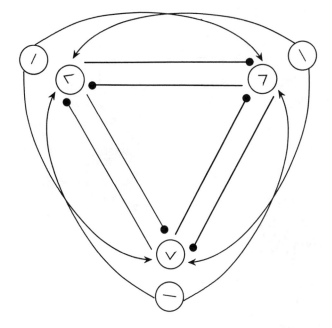

Figure 3.16 *A simple neural network that models perceived pointing of an ambiguous triangle. Circles with lines or angles inside them correspond to line and angle detector units of the specified orientation. Connections with arrows at the end are excitatory and those with dots are inhibitory.*

diagram sufficiently to be illustrated on a two-dimensional page, figure 3.17B only shows the dynamic vectors for states of the system that lie in the plane defined by the three points representing stable states. (This is equivalent to constraining the system so that its total activation is held constant at unity.) The vectors show that all states but the three equilibrium points on this plane are unstable in the sense that they will tend to change inexorably in the direction of the nearest equilibrium state: (1,0,0), (0,1,0), or (0,0,1). In the language of dynamic systems, these three stable states of equilibrium are "basins of attraction" toward which the system inevitably converges. The dynamic behavior of the system can thus be described by the "path" it takes over time through its state space, and all possible paths lead to one of the three stable states corresponding to seeing the triangle point in one of three possible directions.

The dynamics of this simple three-unit system can also be captured by plotting the global "energy" of each point in the state space. We will not be concerned here with the mathematical form of this energy function (see Hopfield, 1982, 1984) but, qualitatively speaking, high-energy states are unstable and tend to move toward adjacent lower-energy states, as with

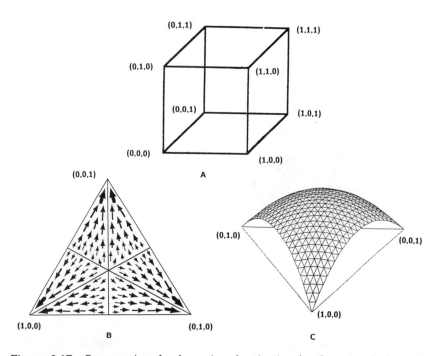

Figure 3.17   *Representing the dynamics of activation for the network shown in figure 3.16. The current activation of the three angle units defines the state of the system within its "state space" (a). How this state changes over time can be represented by vectors within the state space, as shown for a subspace in (b) and can be determined by an "energy surface" defined over the state space, as shown for a subspace in (c).*

thermodynamic systems, until the system reaches a stable state of minimum energy. If we again restrict the situation to a three-unit system whose total activation is fixed at unity, the energy surface describing the system's dynamics is plotted in figure 3.17C. The system's dynamic behavior can now be described roughly as that of a ball placed on this surface at the point corresponding to the system's initial state: the ball will roll downhill into the trough – that is, "basin of attraction" or "minimum energy state" – nearest its starting point. The analogy with minimum-seeking dynamic systems should now be perfectly clear: These networks are indeed examples of physical *Gestalten*.

An important property of the perception of ambiguous triangles is their multistability: their pointing tends to alternate over time from one direction to another. This can be modeled in the parallel connectionist network by assuming that the angle units, like neurons, *fatigue* when they are activated for an extended period, thereby decreasing their response rate over time. This reduction will eventually lower the dominant angle unit's activation enough that eventually one of the other units will come to dominate. The consequence is that if this connectionist network is composed of units that fatigue, it will generate the sort of multistable behavior that is observed in perception of ambiguous triangles.

How can more complex aspects of *Gestalt* phenomena be modeled within connectionist networks? If many triangles are present in the display, of course, there will be many corresponding networks, and the *Gestalt* effects could arise from interactions among these networks. For instance, consider the fact that randomly arranged triangles, such as those displayed in figure 3.1B, always point in the *same* direction rather than in random different ones. This would occur if the triangle networks were interconnected so that angle units were excitatorily connected to other angle units of the same direction and inhibitorily connected to other angle units of different directions. These interconnections might be either direct or mediated through some more central, orientationally selective units. In either case, the triangle networks would then interact in such a way that the whole *network-of-networks* will settle into a minimum energy solution. It turns out that there are three global minima in this larger state space, and they correspond to states in which all triangles point in the same direction. Thus, if the larger network-of-networks converges on one of these optimal solutions, it will mimic the perceptual coupling observed among a group of randomly positioned triangles.

Still more complex issues arise in modeling configural effects like the linear arrays shown in figure 3.1C and D. Indeed, they are too complex to be considered in detail here, but some interesting possibilities can be considered briefly. One is that the excitatory connections between angle units having the same direction would be stronger for those angles that point parallel or perpendicular to the configural line. Exactly why this might be the case is not entirely clear – it might be based on considerations such as local or global symmetry – but it would have the desired effect of biasing the network's dynamic behavior toward the single global minimum that corresponds to the perceptually biased direction. The state space of such a network would be vastly more complex than the one illustrated in figure 3.16, of course, and it would have many local minimums as well as the single global one. The *global* minimum would correspond to the state in which all triangles are seen to point in the direction parallel or perpendicular to the configural line. The most prominent *local* minimums would correspond to the other two states in which all triangles point in the same direction, but not in the direction parallel or perpendicular to the configural line. The energy difference between the global and local minimums should correspond to the magnitude of the configural interference effect as measured by the experimental procedures defined earlier in this chapter. The size of this energy difference should also vary with the kinds of factors explored in our experiments.

Nobody yet knows how well such a theory could account for the many known facts about contextual effects on perceived pointing of ambiguous triangles, or exactly how to go about testing it. One major problem with the particular model just described for multiple triangles is that it does not generalize to other, related forms of reference frame effects. As described, for example, it cannot readily account for either the influence of rectangular frames or textural stripes on perception of ambiguous triangles (see figure 3.1E to H); nor can it account for configural or frame effects with the ambiguous Y (see figure 3.1I to L). At least one problem is that it seems overly reliant upon "angle units" and their interactions. I doubt that this is a fundamental drawback to connectionist models of those phenomena, however, because very little of the system's overall behavior depends on the choice of these specific representational units. For example, the theory could easily be generalized by introducing "local symmetry detector" units that have interactions similar to those described above. Networks defined in this way would have dynamic behavior similar to that described as long as their energy surfaces in their respective state spaces were similar, because that is what determines their behavior. Thus, what ultimately matters is merely that there is a network-of-networks consisting of three-unit, winner-takes-all sub-networks that are interconnected in the appropriate ways. What remains is to get the basic units to respond to the right kind of spatial structure in the environment. This is not an easy problem, to be sure, but it is one that may be logically independent of the global structure of the network-of-networks.

Whether a connectionist theory along these lines will turn out to be consistent with all, or even most, of the known facts about these reference frame effects remains to be seen. Many problems have not yet been addressed, much less solved, within such network theories, and they are notoriously difficult models to use. The most that can be said at this point is that dynamic connectionist networks represent a promising direction for future theorizing about *Gestalt* phenomena such as we have been considering in this chapter.

Conclusion

We have now come almost full circle. We began our discussion of modern theories of *Gestalt* perception with a brief description of the now-discredited theory of cortical interaction due to electrical fields. We then described three recent computational theories of a particular *Gestalt* phenomenon that has been studied intensively in our laboratory: contextual effects on the perception of shape and orientation of simple geometric figures. The major differences among these three models lie in the nature of the stimulus structure proposed to drive the selection of perceptual reference frames: the orientation of maximal elongation, symmetry, or low spatial frequency power. Each theory initially seemed plausible and had some measure of empirical success, yet none survived experimental scrutiny of its critical predictions. In search of an alternative framework, we finally considered dynamic neural networks. We found strong evidence that they can be considered within the framework of *Gestalt* theory, particularly Kohler's abstract formulation of physical *Gestalts*. Finally, we demonstrated that many aspects of triangle pointing can be captured by relatively simple neural networks composed of fatiguing units, or by more complex interactions among many such networks. If the initial promise of these models can be realized, a new era of *Gestalt* theory may be unfolding in which the old notion of interaction through electrical fields is replaced by a new model of interaction through dynamic neural networks.

Acknowledgments

This research was supported in part by National Science Foundation Grants BNS-83-19630 and BNS-87-19934 to the author and by an Alfred P. Sloan Foundation Grant to the Institute of Cognitive Studies at the University of California, Berkeley. I wish to thank Nancy Bucher, John Kruschke, and Paul Kube for their numerous intellectual contributions to the research project described in this chapter. Ephram Cohen and Jack Gallant provided valuable programming assistance for the experiments, and Paul Kube single-handedly wrote all of the software to do Fourier analysis and synthesis of images, including the simulation of Janez's low spatial frequency model. I also thank Craig Fox for his useful comments on an earlier draft of this chapter.

Notes

1 One obvious objection to the symmetry hypothesis is that it applies only to geometrically symmetrical stimuli, and this is a very restricted set. However, the symmetry hypothesis concerns the *visual coding* of symmetry which, I would argue, should be viewed as a continuous dimension rather than a binary attribute. Geometrically speaking, a figure either is symmetrical about a given line or it is not. Perceptually speaking, however, there are undoubtedly degrees of symmetry. In fact, few things that we consider symmetrical – such as faces – are truly symmetrical in the strict geometrical sense. I presume that the perceptual system computes symmetry by a procedure that provides a continuous variable (or an approximation thereof) as output. When explicit judgments about symmetry are called for, this variable can then be thresholded at various criterial levels to determine binary outputs. However, I suspect that if the mechanism of reference frame selection uses symmetry as a basis, it works with the continuous representation of "degree of symmetry" rather than the binary representation one would report in a forced-choice task. However, the precise quantitative nature of such a continuous symmetry theory has not yet been formulated.

2 Members of the dihedral symmetry group, denoted generically as *Dn*, consist of the set of transformations that include central reflections about *n* equally spaced axes and central rotations through *360/n* degrees.

3 The images depicting the power spectrum are interpreted as follows. The

brightness of each point represents the amount of power present at the orientation and spatial frequency indicated by its polar coordinates (indicated by the direction and distance, respectively, of the point from the center). Thus, low spatial frequencies are near the center and high ones far from the center. Orientations are represented so that vertical gratings (gratings with vertical stripes) produce bright spots along the horizontal axis, and horizontal gratings produce bright spots along the vertical axis.

4

Thinking Visually

KRIS N. KIRBY AND STEPHEN M. KOSSLYN

It is often convenient to divide visual information-processing into two broad types. Low-level visual processes are driven solely by the stimulus input, and serve to detect edges, encode differences in wavelengths, establish depth using stereo disparity, and so on. In contrast, high-level visual processes involve the use of stored information. Such processes are utilized, for example, in the later stages of object recognition and identification and in navigation. In addition, high-level visual processes appear to underlie visual mental imagery (Kosslyn, 1987; Farah, 1988). In this chapter we explore some of the implications of the idea that visual mental imagery draws upon mechanisms used in visual perception. In particular, we consider visual thinking from the standpoint of high-level visual processing.

Speculation about the use of visual mental imagery in reasoning and problem-solving has a long and rocky history (e.g. Boring, 1950). The extreme views, represented by the British Associationists (who thought that all thought relied on imagery) and the Behaviorists (who scoffed at the idea that such a thing could be studied) are well known. Even when prevailing philosophical and psychological attitudes have been generally sanguine about the susceptibility of mental events to scientific study, imagery has not always been in favor. Most recently, although information-processing approaches to cognition made the study of mental events generally respectable, the role of imagery as a distinct form of cognition has been regarded with skepticism in some quarters (e.g. Anderson and Bower, 1973; Pylyshyn, 1973, 1981).

The skepticism about imagery seems to have three roots. First, some have doubted the coherence of the very idea (e.g. Pylyshyn, 1973; see Kosslyn and Pomerantz, 1977, for a summary and review of these issues). It seems fair to say that enough debate has now passed regarding these concerns to draw out the empirical issues and lay to rest the fundamental "in principle" objections. Secondly, mental imagery, even if not an incoherent idea, seemed beyond the reach of science; for many years it was unclear how one could such an ephemeral and ethereal creature in a rigorous way. However, methodologies were developed, which allowed us to learn a lot about the role of visual imagery in memory (e.g. Paivio, 1971, 1986), the similarities between images and like-modality percepts (e.g. Finke and Shepard, 1986; Kosslyn, 1987), and the properties of <u>images as repositories of information</u> (e.g. Kosslyn, 1980; Shepard and Cooper, 1982). Thirdly, and perhaps most basic, there has been skepticism about why a linguistic animal would need imagery, and what it is used for. Indeed, there are some who claim never to have had the experience of mental imagery, and yet they appear to function adequately in the world.

One way of thinking about the purposes of imagery is to consider how and why it emerged during the course of evolution. From this perspective, it is useful to consider the relations between imagery and like-modality perception; this link may provide clues about the phylogenetic development of imagery. If, for example, visual imagery actually plays an important role in visual object recognition, it is possible that imagery evolved primarily to serve this role. However, once a mechanism has developed for use in one domain, it can sometimes be taken over for use in other domains, a process called "exaptation" (Gould and Lewontin, 1979). For example, it is thought that the earliest development of wings in insects was through a process of exaptation of appendages that had previously been used to cool the insect through a fanning action. Although these "fans" evolved to help cool the insect, once they were in place new airborne niches became available, and mutations that allowed insects to exploit those niches were highly viable, which promoted the emergence of new species. Similarly, once visual imagery was available for use in high-level visual perception, it could then begin to be exapted for use in other domains, and ultimately in such sophisticated tasks as reasoning and problem-solving. The use of visual imagery in visual thinking, then, would be a by-product of its role in visual perception.

For example, consider a series of experiments reported by Cave and Kosslyn (1989). Cave and Kosslyn were impressed by the computer vision system developed by Lowe (1987a,b). Lowe noticed that once various bottom-up heuristics have been used to narrow down the <u>possible identity of a stimulus</u> to a few options, it is <u>useful to activate a stored "model" of a likely object and project an image</u> of it back to the input, comparing it with the stimulus. This process is particularly useful when the stimulus is partially occluded or otherwise obscured. To examine this idea, Cave and Kosslyn showed subjects rectangles and diamonds, and asked them to decide whether a form had sides of equal length. In some experiments two forms appeared overlapping, and the subjects were asked to evaluate the one drawn with light lines, whereas in other experiments only a single form was presented at a time.

One interesting result was that faster comparisons could be made when the same form appeared that had appeared on the previous trial, but this only occurred when it was embedded in a more complex stimulus configuration (containing another form or fragments of a form). Furthermore, Cave and Kosslyn varied the sizes of the stimuli, and found that more time was required when a stimulus appeared at a different size than the previous stimulus, with increasing amounts of time for greater disparities. This "size-scaling" function appeared both when the stimulus was the same as the one that appeared on the previous trial, and when the stimulus was different. However, when the target stimulus was embedded in a complex context – and only then – the slopes were very different in the two cases. When a form had to be recognized in a noisy environment, it appeared that subjects used an image of the previous form. Indeed, the size-scaling rates found by Cave and Kosslyn were very similar to those reported by Larsen and Bundesen (1978) for scaling attention versus imaged size, suggesting that there were two mechanisms at work in the task: one that alters the scope of an "attention window" (used when different figures appeared on successive trials) and one that alters the size of a mental image (used when the same figure appeared on successive trials). Cave and Kosslyn (1989) ruled out various different accounts for the results, and concluded that imagery does in fact play a special role in identifying objects in noisy environments, as predicted by Lowe's theory.

The notion that imagery emerged primarily in the service of perception leads to some interesting hypotheses about ways in which imagery might be most effective in visual thinking. When we ask about uses of visual imagery, we begin by asking what it is about imagery as part of the visual system that would make it suitable for use in various types of tasks. We then are led to ask about the kinds of tasks we would predict to benefit from its use. This chapter is an attempt to provide a theoretical framework for studying the use of visual imagery in domains other than object recognition *per se*, particularly in the domains of reasoning and problem-solving.

Thus, we begin by considering the properties of depictive representations, and how these properties make such representations useful in problem-solving tasks. We then turn to key properties of the human visual imagery system, and will consider how these properties help determine when this system would be useful in problem-solving. Finally, we discuss properties of classes of problems themselves, and how these properties of problems could help determine when imagery would profitably be used.

"Privileged Properties" of Depictive Representation

From a computational standpoint, perhaps the most salient characteristic of visual mental imagery is that it provides a mechanism for recalling and manipulating depictive representations.[1] Before we can explore the possible utility of depictive representations, we must briefly characterize them. Depictive representations differ from propositional representations in both their syntax and semantics (Kosslyn, 1984). Whereas the syntax of propositions allows for any number of symbols and classes of symbols to be combined according to a set of specific rules, depictive representations use "points" as their sole class of symbols, and these are combined simply by spatial juxtaposition. And whereas the semantics of propositional representations depend solely on interpretation of its symbols (or sentences; Quine, 1960), depictive representations convey meaning by visual resemblance. That is, each part of a depictive representation corresponds to part of the depicted object (or objects) such that relative "distances" among the parts of the representation correspond to those among the actual parts themselves (see Kosslyn, 1984).

The consequences of these properties of depictive representations will prove important for understanding the usefulness of visual imagery in a variety of domains. First, object shape properties are made explicit. All of the implicit local and global geometric relations among parts of the representation are accessible to varying degrees. For example, if asked to describe the shape of the empty enclosed space in an upper case letter A, one can generate an image and "see" the triangle as easily as one can "see" the shape of the lines. Or if one is asked "What shape are a Doberman's ears?", one might proceed to generate a visual image of the dog, "inspect" its ears, and respond something like "pointed." To answer such questions using a propositional representation, one would have required the foresight to store this shape information explicitly in one's list of letter or Doberman properties; the vast number of shape properties of parts of any normal object make it unlikely that one could have stored the explicit propositional information necessary to answer arbitrary questions such as these. Depictive representations make all of this spatial information available when needed.

A second, but closely related, consequence of using depictive representations is that spatial relations between objects are made explicit (this does not follow necessarily from the consideration just mentioned, for example if multiple objects could not be juxtaposed into the same array). This makes possible relative size judgments ("Was Hitler's moustache wider than Charlie Chaplin's?"), and relative position judgments ("Would President Bush be able to look an elephant in the eye while he 'shook hands' with its trunk?"). These judgments can be either categorical, as in the two previous examples, or coordinate: requiring absolute metric information, as in "Approximately how much longer is an American football than the diameter of a basketball?'

For present purposes there are two important implications of the above considerations: (a) depictive representations are likely to be particularly useful in any task requiring the assessment of shape or spatial information, and (b) depictive representations are an efficient way of storing spatial information. For any given object or scene, there is an enormous number of possible spatial relations that can be extracted, and it seems unlikely that a propositional representation large enough to store all of these relations explicitly could be managed, even if one had the foresight at the outset to encode all of the possible spatial relations. This is a clear example of a picture being worth a thousand words, if not more.

Key Properties of the Human Visual Imagery System

Our observations about distinctive properties of depictions are suggestive, but the implications of these observations cannot be developed further unless we tie them to the structures and processes underlying human visual mental imagery. To gain insight into the types of tasks that would be facilitated by using imagery, we must consider the constraints and limitations of depictive representations used in human cognition. Central to our line of thinking is the idea that the visual imagery system provides a mechanism for recalling and manipulating depictive representations, and establishing mappings between non-spatial and spatial relations. We will focus now on these functions.

Structure: A Working Memory Store

Given the evidence that imagery and like-modality perception share brain mechanisms (e.g. Farah, 1988), it is of interest that many visual areas in the brain are topographically mapped, and are capable of supporting depictive representations (Van Essen, 1985). Indeed, Farah (1988) summarizes much data indicating that the occipital lobe is involved in imagery, which is known to contain numerous topographically mapped areas. Thus, when visual mental images are generated, we assume that the image representations proper are depictive and are maintained in a buffer; this buffer represents spatial information by preserving distances between points. We will refer to the array used in imagery as the "visual buffer" to stress its connection with the visual system (Kosslyn, 1987).

The idea that images occur in perceptual structures has far-reaching implications. For one, during perception it is important that visual areas have the neurological equivalent of a "fast-fade phosphor" to avoid smearing of input during eye movements. The neural substrate does not "automatically" retain a state for very long once the source of stimulation is removed. Thus, it is no surprise that information in the imagery array decays rapidly over time. This property of imagery is of crucial importance when one considers possible uses of imagery. A primary constraint on the effective use of any memory store is its capacity limits, which determine the amount of information that can be held in the store at one time. The capacity limits of the visual buffer appear to have two sources.

First, because the neural substrate of the visual buffer does not automatically retain a state for very long after the input is removed, images decay very quickly. Hence, images can be maintained only through effort, by continually regenerating the input pattern (see Kosslyn, 1980). There is a limit to how many entities one can retain at once in an image. For example, in an unpublished study (Kirby and Kosslyn, 1990) eight subjects were asked to form a clear visual image of a brick, and to continue adding new bricks to the image until any of the bricks could no longer be seen clearly: on average, subjects reported being able to "see" 6.3 bricks, with individuals ranging from four to nine. Consider an analogy to the number of balls one can juggle simultaneously: the capacity limit here is defined by the speed with which one can throw balls, the height one can throw them, and the speed with which they fall.

A second class of limitations on processing in the visual buffer is associated with the depictive nature of its representations: the represented objects can have only a limited scope (the size of the room in which one is juggling). Kosslyn (1978) and Finke and Kosslyn (1980) showed that objects can subtend only a limited visual angle before their edges begin to blur, as is expected if topographically mapped areas used in vision proper are also used in imagery (these areas typically magnify the fovea, allocating more than a proportional amount of cortex to input from it, and have decreased resolution toward the periphery). Depending on the type of object, the actual angle at which such blur is noticed varies. For objects with sharp edges, only about 20° of visual angle can be used effectively.

A third kind of limitation also concerns spatial factors: the visual buffer appears to have a "grain." When imaged objects subtend too small a visual angle, their details are difficult to "see." Indeed, Kosslyn (1976) pitted size and association strength of parts of objects against each other, and found that the time to "see" a part of an imaged object was determined primarily by its size, whereas the time to recall a part not using imagery was determined by its association strength. (Kosslyn, 1980, summarizes much data pertaining to the scope and resolution of imaged objects.)

Although it has not yet been investigated, it seems likely that, just as in visual perception, one must trade off detail for scope (Eriksen and St James, 1986; Shulman and Wilson, 1987). By analogy to a video camera, as one zooms in to inspect finer details of the image, the portion of the image that remains in view must diminish. Conversely, for a given "image distance" there is a limit to the detail that can be discerned on the imaged object. Unlike visual perception (at least beyond one's minimal focal length) there is an upper bound to the detail that is available in an image; one can only image to the detail that was stored in the long-term image representation. For example, in perception one can inspect the detailed fur patterns on a Doberman by moving physically closer and closer (up to some courage limit), but this may not be possible with a mental image: if one has never been close enough to a Doberman to encode that visual information into memory, it cannot be included in a subsequent mental image.

Finally, if visual images do in fact occur in visual cortex, then a fourth limitation will exist. Images will compete for space with actual perceptual input. And, in fact, there is much evidence that imagery and like-modality perception interfere with one another (e.g. Kosslyn, 1980; Finke and Shepard, 1986). This limitation is often easily overcome simply by closing one's eyes. But for some types of problems, one may need to compare an image to an actual object; in these cases, the limitations posed by competition for representational resources may be severe.

The visual buffer, then, has limited capacity, as determined by how many objects or patterns can (a) be retained at the same time, (b) fit within its limited scope, (c) subtend a large enough angle to be "visible," and (d) be represented at the same time within the structure without interfering with each other. The limitations on amount, scope, and size are partially interdependent. To pursue our juggling analogy, one might have the ability to juggle a large number of objects but be limited to less than one's maximum because of the size of the room in which one is juggling. Similarly, if the objects are too big, they could not be tossed about in a relatively small room, but if they are too small they may be difficult to see. Thus, the two spatial constraints are clearly interdependent: imaged objects cannot subtend too large an angle or they will seem to overflow, but cannot subtend too small an angle or they will not be identifiable.

The limitations on the amount of material that can be retained at the same time appear to be best characterized in terms of shape units ("chunks"). It is clear that the time to form an image hinges on the number of perceptual units, not the actual physical properties of the stimulus. For example, if subjects are asked to see a Star of David as two overlapping triangles when studying it, they later can form a visual mental image of the star much faster than if they are asked to see it as a hexagon with six small triangles along its sides. Similarly, if subjects see an array as three rows of six letters, they later visualize it more quickly than if they see it as six columns of three letters (Kosslyn, 1980). We assume that this generation process is critical in maintaining images, given that the buffer itself does not retain patterns of activation. Thus, it is of interest to note that although only a handful of perceptual units can be maintained in an image at once (Weber and Harnish, 1974; Kosslyn et al., 1984), this limit does not have a simple relation to the number of spatial relations that can be maintained. Because the number of spatial relations among a set of units is not a simple function of the number of units, there is no direct limit on the representation of spatial relations *per se*, only on the number and complexity of the units being related. For example, with only two units (e.g. one unit two inches northwest of the other) one could encode the relations left-of, right-of, above, below, collinear, two inches from, northwest, and so on. The number of spatial relations increases exponentially with the addition of a third unit.

The level of performance of a task relying on imagery will decrease dramatically when a capacity limit is reached. This can occur when the information required to solve a problem exceeds the limit that one can maintain in an image at once, or when a concurrent memory load placed on the system by a secondary task effectively reduces the limit. For example, imagine trying to determine whether a race horse's knees are above the tip of its tail while concurrently imaging a route through a maze on a computer screen. To the extent that the latter information taxes the representational capacity of the visual buffer or diverts effort necessary to maintain the image of the horse, it will become increasingly difficult to use imagery to access the information relevant to the question.

The constraints imposed by the capacity limits of the visual buffer in some cases might be overcome by using a second, longer-term, memory store as a "swap-space," moving information in and out of the visual buffer as it is needed. The use of imagery in visual thinking can be thought of as an instance of the use of "working memory." Information in working memory corresponds to information that has been activated and is available for immediate use in problem-solving. Working memory typically is conceived as consisting of central executive and at least two independent stores, the visual/spatial and the articulatory/phonological (Baddeley, 1986). Each of the stores presumably has its own capacity limit. It is possible that when one of these stores, perhaps the one normally used in a given task, reaches its capacity limit the other store could be used as an additional temporary store, or "swap space" for the primary store. This conjecture apparently applies to memory *per se*; Kosslyn et al. (1976) showed that people could retain more words if they imaged some and verbalized some, rather than using only a single method for the entire list. Similarly, if one tries to retain both a telephone number and a street address long enough to cross the room and write them down, it may be necessary to rehearse the phone number in the articulatory store and "picture" the street address (the process of writing it down may interfere with the image, however, so write down the image information first!). This type of application does not appear to be widespread, and may depend on learning specific control strategies for coordinating the swapping. However, this process would take measurable time and increase the probability of error because the image generation process is not flawless.

Thus, the limited capacities of the visual buffer will affect the difficulty of tasks when either the amount of information needed to solve a problem exceeds capacity, or when part of this capacity is taken by a concurrent task. To the extent that the capacity limit can be circumvented by using another memory store as swap space, the time to solve the problem will be substantially lengthened and the probability of error increased. However, a "chunking" mechanism that forms new hierarchical relations within a depiction should functionally expand the limits on the visual buffer, grouping portions of the image into more abstract structures that can be refreshed as wholes. For example, if one tries to generate an image of the night-time sky it would be very difficult to generate or refresh images of a significant number of individual stars even though they represent the simplest possible chunks: single points. However, if one were to group stars into constellations these constellations would themselves become chunks and could be refreshed as wholes. These new chunks would be more abstract, in that the individual star information would no longer be explicit, but finer-grained information could be accessed by "zooming in" on a particular constellation. The chunking in this example is most likely to occur during visual perception, while one is actually looking at the sky, but a similar process could occur while one is "looking" at an image of a number of disparate items (Finke et al., 1989). This process would allow the imagery system itself to increase the amount of information it can work with within the confines of the spatial and te~~n~~poral limits on the visual buffer.

Processes: *Manipulating Chunks*

So far we have focused primarily on the usefulness of the visual imagery system in tasks requiring recall and inspection of visual and spatial information. Yet within the imagery system spatial relations and shapes can be manipulated and reinspected, and these functions greatly enhance the kinds of problems to which imagery can be applied. The various kinds of manipulations have received a great deal of attention in recent imagery research. Rather than simply recount well-known findings (for a review, see Shepard and Cooper, 1982), we will try rather to illustrate how some of the most well-documented kinds of image manipulations could play a role in some problem-solving tasks.

Rotation.   Suppose one were asked whether a lower case *p* is the same as an upside-down *b* or *d*. Many people report forming a mental image of a *p*, mentally rotating it 180°, and simply inspecting the image for the answer. This introspection receives support from the results of formal experimentation: rotation takes measurable time and has been much investigated by Roger Shepard and his colleagues. It is not difficult to describe more "ecologically valid" situations in which such an ability might be used. For example, suppose that you have just walked through a complex building for the first time, memorizing the floor plan of the path you took as you went, and now wish to return the way you came. One simple strategy is to generate an image of the floor plan and mentally rotate it 180°, using the inverted version to guide your walk back. Another example, if not everyday task, in which rotation would be useful is working jigsaw puzzles. One starts with a pattern and looks for its complement in a large array of scattered shapes. The task is eased if one can generate an image of the "missing" shape and rotate it to compare it with the available shapes, rather than picking up each piece and trying it out manually. A conceptually similar algorithm was used by Lowe (1987a) in a computer program that could pick out the individual disposable razors in a bucket of jumbled, partially overlapping razors.

Translations.   An object in an image can be translated from one position to another. This is an important property because it permits objects to be juxtaposed in different ways for comparison. For example, suppose that you were replacing the back on a broken wooden chair, where the back had pulled out of square holes in the seat. You measure the holes in which the original pieces had been inserted and determine that they are two inches across the diagonal. At the furniture store the clerk tells you that they no longer make those pieces, but now use dowels whose ends form two-inch diameter circles. Will these new pieces fit into the old seat? One strategy for answering this question is to generate an image of a two-inch diagonal square

ameter circle and juxtapose them so that their compatibility
d. By doing this one could readily "see" that the circle would
are at all four corners and therefore would not fit inside.
ample, suppose that you have repaired your chair and now
ge the furniture in the room. You want to know whether the
inst the wall. Rather than measuring the sofa and the wall,
or p   e sofa into place, one could generate an image of the sofa
against the wall and "see" whether it fits. This will only work to the degree
to which the veridical relative sizes of the sofa and wall can be preserved in
the image, and there is considerable room for error when the sizes are close.
However, this strategy would suffice in a great many situations and save one
considerable stress on the lower back.

Size Alteration.   When one generates an image of an object one is not stuck
with considering that object at the size evident in the image. Objects in an
image can be expanded or contracted. For example, when you determined
earlier that the two-inch diameter dowels would not fit into the two-inch
diagonal holes, you might wonder how much the dowels would need to be
cut down to make them fit. By keeping your image of the square constant
and shrinking the size of the circle you could get a rough estimate of how
small the circle would have to be to fit. Or suppose that you were buying a
T-shirt for a friend whose shirt size you did not know. You might hold up
one T-shirt and imagine it expanding or shrinking until it seemed to fit the
size of your friend in the image.

Some of us often buy shirts of the wrong size for our relatives and friends,
and the point of these examples is not to argue that imagery is a precise
method for making spatial comparisons. The value of imagery is that it offers
a low-cost heuristic for making such comparisons, and because of this feature, its use is pervasive in everyday situations.

Motion.   Perhaps the most intriguing, and least studied, property of the
imagery system is its ability to use sequences of the above three transformations to perform analog simulations of real motion. In these cases, images
represent metric spatial relations over time. This gives the organism the
ability to preview courses of action, or forecast outcomes of events currently
underway in its environment. We can distinguish among different cases
of this use of imagery, emphasizing the primary aspect of the tasks, but it
should be noted that each borrows from the others to some degree. They are
perhaps best illustrated by concrete examples.

1   Extrapolation of current movement. (a) Will I need to slow my car to
    allow another car on the entrance ramp to enter my lane? (b) In football,
    for a quaterback to properly "lead" a receiver when throwing a pass he
    needs to judge both the speed and course of the receiver (extrapolating
    his current movement) and see to it that the ball crosses that course at an
    appropriate time.

2 Extrapolation of size alteration. Can I carry this box through that door? One may (a) imagine oneself as though watching another person from behind, moving forward and trying to pass through the doorway with the box, or (b) simply imagine the doorway approaching, taking into account how the doorway would "grow" as it approached.

3 Process simulation. (a) What would happen if I were to push this rolling table down the hall into that stack of folding chairs on top of which the cat is sleeping who when startled always jumps out of the window with the flower pot on the sill? (b) When assembling or installing a new appliance, say an air conditioner, most of us have had the experience of finding that the line drawings in the instructions usually do not map precisely onto the pieces that actually come in the box. Before even holding the pieces up for comparison one might run a quick imagery simulation of a few steps to see if there is any chance of the pieces fitting together as desired. (c) People probably cannot solve the entire Tower of Hanoi problem in their heads, but they can work ahead a few steps, testing actual sequences of moves by simulating them using visual imagery. One might, in fact, be able to solve the "Missionaries and Cannibals" problem totally by imagery simulation if one has enough patience. Finally, there is some evidence that chess players use visual imagery to "think ahead" a few moves during play (Holding, 1985).

The ability to perform mental simulations of ongoing activities has important implications for skill acquisition. When the goal of skill learning is to string together a set of disparate movements, it is important to rehearse those particular movements in the correct order without intrusion from unwanted movements. If a mental simulation of the activity is being run slightly in advance of the actual behavior, one could test each move before actually making it, and thereby limit the actual behavior to only the desired, correct movements. This makes virtually error-free performance possible even on relatively unlearned tasks, and might significantly enhance the learning of a particular pattern of movement. And, in fact, there is much evidence that imagery can enhance such learning (e.g. Richardson, 1969).

Non-spatial to Spatial Mapping

The foregoing examples have primarily focused on the use of images of objects or scenes as they would be seen in visual perception. But the imagery system is much more versatile than this: correspondences between non-spatial information and spatial representations can often be established, and imagery can be used to solve non-spatial problems. Thus, symbols (letters, numbers, tokens, etc.) can be manipulated in the visual buffer in the same way that they are manipulated on paper. For example, try doing a simple three-digit addition problem (e.g. 479 + 187) in one's head by simulating the manner you would do it on paper. Although the addition of each pair of digits is a reflexive process for most of us, for the two rightmost columns one must "carry the ones" to the next column to the left. For most people, these new digits can be easily encoded into an image of the numbers above the appropriate columns. (By this point, some readers will have now discovered that individual differences in imagery are more relevant to personal concerns than had heretofore been realized.)

The most extensively studied application of this type of symbol manipulation is in the study of syllogistic reasoning. When solving transitive inference problems, or "three-term syllogisms," such as "Joe is smarter than Bill; Bill is smarter than Tom; who's smartest?", many people report that they image symbols representing each person in the problem (perhaps the first letter of each name, or simply a dot, for example) and arrange them in a linear visual array corresponding to their order on the "intelligence" dimension. Empirical data support these reports (Huttenlocher, 1968; Shaver et al., 1975; Ormrod, 1979). In particular, Huttenlocher (1968; Huttenlocher et al., 1970) showed that the relative difficulty of many of these problems corresponds to the relative difficulty of placing real objects in a linear array.

In a related paradigm, Johnson-Laird (1983) suggests that people solve classic syllogisms by concretizing the items in the premises and then manipulating these representations. For example, a person might represent "Some dogs are black" by generating representations ("tokens") that stand for particular black dogs, and then might manipulate the relations between these tokens and the tokens from another premise in order to determine whether a given conclusion is warranted. Johnson-Laird's experiments show that the order of problem difficulty can be predicted by the number of different relationship structures ("models") that must be made to test whether a given conclusion is consistent with a given pair of premises.

Although Johnson-Laird does not take this step, it is straightforward to suggest that many people perform this token manipulation by generating images of the tokens in the visual buffer, and represent relations among tokens by spatial position in the array. In fact, in his illustrations of this process, Johnson-Laird (1983) represents the relationships among tokens by spatial position on the page. Given the capacity limits of the system, one would expect that syllogisms would become more difficult when the number or complexity of the models required to solve them approached or exceeded these limits. This suggests that one's ability to solve syllogisms in one's head might be predicted by measures of imagery capacity.

Problem-Solving Tasks that Engender Imagery

We are now in a position to outline classes of problems in which visual imagery is likely to play a functional role. Such an analysis is useful because it can help us acquire a better understanding of the tasks themselves, and because of the empirical implications for the use of imagery in the tasks. In general, imagery should be useful when (a) a problem addresses (or can be made to address) visual properties that do not exceed the visual buffer's capacity limits, or (b) spatial relations are critical (or can be made critical) for deriving the solution. Depictive representations can be used in an abstract problem if a mapping can be achieved between the elements in the problem and objects in an image. If an effective mapping can be established between the problem and depictive representation, visual mental imagery should play a useful role.

Thus, the generality of imagery as a means of solving problems hinges on the ability to map problems into depictions. What follows are two classes of problems that are defined according to the principles that determine how they can be depicted. "Direct" mapping is the depiction of visual properties of an actual object or objects in the image (although perhaps in an abbreviated or idealized form). In contrast, "abstract" mappings require a second layer of interpretation: the depiction stands for something else (a dot for a person, a statue holding scales for justice, spatial proximity for class inclusion etc.). In cases of the latter type the complexity of the mapping rule adds another set of factors affecting the ease of using imagery. Thus, the challenge in these problems is to devise a depiction that is effective not only because it respects the capacity limits of the imagery system but because it is unambiguous and easy to interpret symbolically.

Direct Depiction

The class of problems most likely to command the use of the visual imagery system are those that require one to consider subtle spatial relations or visual properties of objects not present. Examples of this type were given above regarding Dobermans' ears, Hitler's moustache, and footballs. In each of these cases it is not likely that the required visual or spatial information was previously stored explicitly in one's long-term memory. Rather, the information was stored implicitly, and extracted from the image in the same way that it would be from the actual stimulus.

Problems of geometry are well suited for imagery, and fit in this class. For example, if asked what shape lies at the center of a Star of David, most people would need to form an image of the star and inspect the center. Geometry problems in two dimensions are subject to the capacity limits discussed above, and it is probably the case that the limit on three-dimensional problems is even more strict. Questions that require the use of subtle relations among purely visual properties are also likely to invoke imagery. For example, most people report using imagery when deciding whether a Christmas tree is a darker green than a frozen pea (Kosslyn, 1980; Kosslyn and Jolicoeur, 1981). (Note that whenever we consider a situation to be a "problem," we are assuming it has not been dealt with in the past by the person; if it has, the answer typically can be reproduced via rote memory, retrieving information stored propositionally.)

Abstract Mapping

A second class of problems does not require one to consider spatial or visual information *per se*, but recruits imagery by establishing a mapping between non-spatial information and spatial representations. There are two situations in which such a mapping would be useful. The first is when a depictive representation would be more concise than a verbal or propositional representation alone. For example, finding a representation that facilitates solution of the problem is the impetus behind setting up and working with "models" of syllogisms rather than carrying out a purely syntactical calculation. Just as Venn diagrams were developed to facilitate the solution of syllogisms on paper, people may spontaneously adopt depictive representational methods for reasoning problems performed "in the head." In these cases, the depictions should have a direct correspondence between spatial and conceptual properties. For example, putting one circle inside another corresponds directly to the idea that members of one class are also members of another class; similarly, having more of a visual dimension correspond to more of a quantity (e.g. increased height for increased intelligence) has such a direct correspondence. Thus, the depiction is useful not only because it is concise, having fewer "chunks" than would be required in a different format, but because there is a simple and direct way of decoding the depiction.

The second situation is when the imagery method of solution involves a simpler algorithm. For example, consider a problem in which one tries to "exclusive-or" (XOR) together two strings of binary digits. The exclusive-or takes a pair of digits (e.g. 1, 0) and yields a 1 if either the first *or* the second digit (but not both) is a 1, and yields a zero otherwise. To XOR together two strings, one must consider each pair of digits corresponding in serial position in the two strings, XOR them, and keep track of a third string containing the results of XORing these pairs. Now try XORing together the strings "10110" and "01110" without looking back at the strings while you work. This is a very difficult task to perform in one's head, but most of our pilot subjects found it tractable when they generated a visual image of the two strings, one above the other, and visualized the solution below. As the strings increase in length, a more efficient algorithm is to image the two strings, then inspect each pair of digits serially while subvocally rehearsing (acoustically imaging) the result string as it is produced. It is difficult to devise a plausible algorithm for this task that can be performed without external memory aids and avoids using a depictive representation.

Conclusions

If we assume that image representations are depictive, we are led to infer that three properties of imagery can be exploited to aid problem-solving. First, visual information can be effectively organized into "chunks." Thus, one can reason about a large configuration of stars if they are treated as a constellation, or can reason about complex geography if an imaged map is organized into neighborhoods. Such chunking is necessary to circumvent the notorious capacity limitations of imagery. Secondly, spatial relations are in a sense "free" in depictions. Unlike propositional representations, where such relations must be explicitly noted, in depictions spatial relations are an emergent property of sets of depicted perceptual units. Thus, to the extent that such relations can be used to represent key information, or manipulations of such relations can be used to solve problems, depictions will be useful. Finally, depictions need not be "literal." Depicted patterns can stand for other things. To the extent that the first two properties can be exploited, the effectiveness of imagery in these cases will be determined by the ease of using the decoding rules. If analogies can be exploited (e.g. "inside" conceptually depicted by a shape inside another), such rules can be easily learned and used.

What is missing here are precise and general rules for how to decide when it is a good idea to use imagery to solve any given problem. One major reason such rules are missing is that they probably are impossible to formulate, for two reasons. First, the range of individual differences in imagery abilities is very large. To the extent that effective imagery hinges on working within capacity limitations, we cannot prescribe imagery for any given problem: people differ widely in their imagery capacities (Kosslyn et al., 1984). Secondly, the same problem applies to decoding rules when nonspatial mappings are used: what is easy for one person will not be for another. One reason a rule is easy to use is that one's previous knowledge allows one to learn the rule quickly and to remember it easily. People differ widely in their knowledge, and hence we cannot expect a single dictum to apply universally.

Nevertheless, imagery has useful properties that might be exploited in ways currently overlooked. Our goal in this chapter has been to explicate the relevant variables, and point out ways in which properties of imagery lend themselves to certain types of problem-solving. We suspect that if it is possible to characterize the strengths and weaknesses of a given individual's imagery-processing system and to characterize his or her range of knowledge in an area, it may be possible to develop more precise rules for the use of effective imagery in that area. By realizing that imagery is part of the visual system we can show how some properties of the visual system make predictions about properties of imagery, and it will be interesting to see in the future how the study of imagery benefits from further discoveries about the visual system as a whole. It might seem only fitting if a full understanding of imagery required an understanding of broader areas of psychology; after all, imagery has not only often been viewed as at the fringe (or outside) of psychology, but also has often been viewed as at the very heart of psychology. In our view it probably is somewhere in between, and a full understanding of imagery will both draw from and inform other aspects of psychology.

Acknowledgment

This work was supported by a grant from the AFOSR (88-0012) to SMK.

Note

1   An "image," by definition, is depictive; the debate about imagery has hinged on whether the depictive properties of mental images that are evident to introspection are functional (see Kosslyn and Pomerantz, 1977); the present chapter rests on the assumption that images are depictive and that these depictive properties can be functional, and explores the ways in which such representations could be exploited.

5

Perceiving and Recognizing Faces

VICKI BRUCE

The human face provides important information which contributes to a number of distinct social activities. The unique configuration of the individual's face provides the most reliable visible key to their identity. Movements of this configuration help to specify the emotional state of the person, and movements of the lips and tongue help us to distinguish different speech sounds. As well as providing such information for an observer of a face, the perceiver's own face of course mediates these acts of observation. The face bears the eyes and ears in an arrangement conducive to distance perception, and so forth.

It is likely that because the face must subserve these diverse functions, faces must be very similar to one another in their overall configuration, and it is this similarity that makes our usual facility at recognizing faces appear so extraordinary. In this chapter, I will examine the approach taken by psychologists and computer scientists to the problems of face recognition, before suggesting directions for the future in which a more integrated "cognitive science" approach seems likely to prove fruitful.

Psychological Research into Face Recognition

Psychological research into face recognition was stimulated some 15 years or so ago by two, somewhat contradictory, sets of findings. The first set of findings concerned the apparent *fallibility* of an eye-witness to a crime when attempting to identify the criminal from a line-up or from photographs (see Devlin, 1976). Public concern over cases of mistaken identity rightly resulted in an enormous amount of applied research aimed at investigating the limits and limitations of human memory for briefly glimpsed events, and aimed at evaluating and improving the techniques available for probing a witness's memory for a face (see Shepherd et al., 1982).

The second set of findings stemmed from demonstrations of the remark-able *capacity and durability* of picture memory. Initial demonstrations (e.g. Nickerson, 1965; Shepard, 1967; Standing et al., 1970) showed that subjects could distinguish literally thousands of briefly studied pictures from novel ones. Subsequent research on this theme examined picture memory using more homogeneous stimuli, and faces were a much studied class of such stimuli. This research generally showed that recognition memory for pic-tures of faces was more accurate than recognition memory for such items as pictures of inkblots or snowflakes (Goldstein and Chance, 1971), dogs (Scapinello and Yarmey, 1970) or aeroplanes (Yin, 1969).

The observation that subjects could be remarkably accurate at recognizing which face they had previously studied was obviously at odds with the eye-witnessing literature. Some sense can be made of this discrepancy, however, now that research has given us a clear idea of the factors that reduce the accuracy of face-recognition memory (see Shapiro and Penrod, 1986, for a meta-analysis of factors affecting facial recognition). Accuracy of recognition memory is considerably affected by changes in view between study and test, even for portraits taken in the same session where paraphernalia and visible clothing remain constant (Bruce, 1982). Accuracy is affected by changing the study-test mode (from slides at study to film at test or vice versa: Patterson, 1978), or context (see Memon and Bruce, 1985 for a review). Disguising the face, even moderately, has a detrimental effect (Patterson and Baddeley, 1977). Memory for faces is generally higher given longer initial study times (e.g. Bruce and Valentine, 1988; though see Read et al. in press, who show that longer study time can be detrimental under certain circumstances), it is improved by elaborated semantic coding at study (Patterson and Baddeley, 1977) and better for members of one's own than of another race (see Shep-herd, 1981). Eye-witnesses who have briefly glimpsed a face may have made little attempt to encode it along elaborated semantic dimensions, and must then try to recognize the face in a different context, from a different view-point, wearing different clothes and quite possibly with a different hairstyle. Under these circumstances we should perhaps not expect them to be accu-rate at their task. Additionally, hit rates to single targets in recognition memory experiments decline dramatically with the number of distractor faces encountered prior to the target (Laughery et al., 1971). A witness who must search through a police "mugshot" file (which may comprise hundreds or even thousands of faces) has rather little chance of correctly spotting the criminal's face if it occurs late in the volume. At the same time, however, a witness searching a mugshot file may be exposed to the face of another person who may come under suspicion, and who could then appear familiar in a line-up due to such "mug-shot induced bias" (Brown et al., 1977). Re-search into factors influencing recognition memory for unfamiliar faces has thus allowed us a reasonable insight into problems inherent in eye-witness identification procedures. Such insight, in turn, allows these procedures to be improved (see Shepherd, 1986, for a description of a computer-aided mug-shot retrieval system which reduces the number of pictures a witness needs to inspect).

While obviously of major applied concern, the majority of work in the area of face recognition until about ten years ago was conducted in a theoretical vacuum. It is only in the past few years that psychologists, particularly those in the UK, have tired of asking, for example, "how *many* faces can be remembered?" and have turned to ask the question "*how* may faces be recognized?". My own early input to this was to suggest that most of the work on memory for unfamiliar faces was no more relevant to understanding face recognition than work on memory for nonsense syllables was relevant to understanding reading. This, I argued (Bruce, 1979) was because our everyday task is to derive an identity from a face, and unfamiliar faces do not have identities. Such arguments promoted a shift in empirical research on face recognition to include studies of factors affecting the speed with which highly familiar faces could be accurately recognized.

The argument that unfamiliar faces do not have identities is not to deny that unfamiliar faces are *meaningful*. However, it is important to distinguish the different uses made of the information from the face, and the different kinds of meaning that may be derived. I alluded to these different uses at the beginning of this chapter. Bruce and Young (1986) (cf. Bruce, 1982, 1983; Hay and Young, 1982) distinguished seven different information "codes" which are extracted in face processing to reflect these different uses. Expression codes and facial speech codes result from the analysis of expressions and phonemic lip movements respectively. Pictorial codes result from processing the particular pictorial pattern seen of a face, and are contrasted with structural codes which are a more abstract visual representation of the face. At the level of semantics, Bruce and Young (1986) distinguished *identity-specific* semantic codes, that can only be derived for known faces, and which specify their occupations, relations, nationalities, and so forth, from *visually derived* semantic codes, which can be produced for any face. Visually derived semantics include such things as deciding that a face looks old or young, male or female, looks like a filmstar or looks like a frog. Finally, known faces also have names, and these were considered the seventh kind of information that can be extracted.

Bruce and Young (1986) produced a functional model for face recognition to describe the sequence in which different codes could be derived to faces, and the independence of some processing routes from others (see also other similar models by Hay and Young, 1982; Rhodes, 1985; Ellis, 1986). The model is shown in figure 5.1, and was based upon evidence obtained from studies of normal subjects, studied in laboratory experiments and in real life using diary studies, and patterns of dissociation observed in neuropsychological studies. Space does not permit a review of this evidence (see Bruce and Young, 1986; Bruce, 1988; Young and Bruce, 1991, for further details), but I will here give a flavor of the kind of shift in paradigm which led to the specification of frameworks such as this one.

Figure 5.1 contains a description of the sequence of stages that allows a person to be identified by their face. This route (drawn to the right of figure 5.1) is shown as occurring in parallel to other routes whereby we analyze facial expressions, facial speech, or carry out "directed visual processing" to

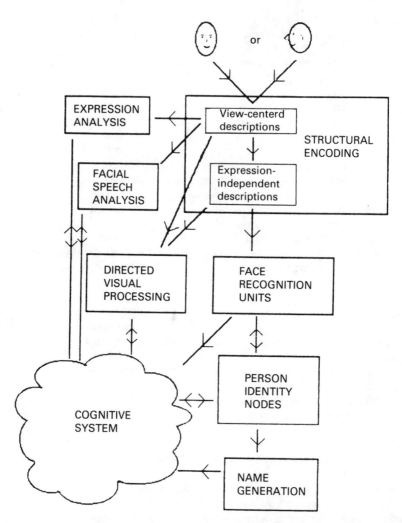

Figure 5.1 *A functional model for face recognition (Bruce and Young, 1986).*

particular aspects of a face (e.g. to look for a person with a moustache, or for a person with red hair). The independence of these routes from the mandatory face recognition route (see Young and Bruce, 1991, for a discussion) is suggested mostly by neuropsychological evidence. For example, the independence of expression analysis from identification is indicated by the observation that some prosopagnosic patients, who can no longer identify familiar faces, have preserved abilities to recognize emotional expressions (Bruyer et al., 1983). Other patients suffering from "organic brain syndrome" have been observed with impaired expression perception but with intact facial recognition (Kurucz and Feldmar, 1979; Kurucz et al., 1979). More striking still was the observation by Campbell et al. (1986) of a dissociation between lip-reading and expression analysis. One of the two patients they studied was prosopagnosic, had impaired expression analysis but normal lip-reading, while the other, alexic patient had no problems with recognizing facial identities or expressions but was impaired at tasks requiring lip-reading. Finally, the observation that some prosopagnosic patients are able to match views of unfamiliar faces supports the separation of "directed visual processing" from the identification route.

Experiments with normal subjects also suggest that expression analysis and face identification occur in parallel. For example, subjects are no quicker or more accurate to judge or to match pairs of expressions when shown the faces of familiar people than when shown unfamiliar faces (Bruce, 1986a; Young et al., 1986b). There is also evidence for the independence of "directed visual processing" from identification of faces (Bruce, 1979), though as yet the relationship between lip-reading and other analyses of faces remains unexplored with normal subjects.

The identification route shows how faces are initially categorized as familiar by the "face recognition units" – this is the stage at which perceptual classification is achieved so that different views of the same familiar face can be categorized in the same way. After access of the appropriate face recognition unit, identity-specific semantic information may be accessed from the "person identity nodes." This is the stage which is common to the recognition of people via faces, voices, clothing, or names. Finally, the name may be retrieved. Evidence for this three-stage identification route comes from studies of normal subjects in everyday situations (Young et al., 1985) and studies of speeded recognition in the laboratory (Young et al., 1986a; Johnston and Bruce, 1990).

The identification route of figure 5.1 is obviously and deliberately a derivative of a number of similar models in the area of word and object recognition (e.g. Morton, 1969, 1979; Seymour, 1979). This was because, once face recognition was probed using methods similar to those used to study word and object recognition, it seemed appropriate to propose similar mechanisms to accommodate basically similar patterns of finding. For example, Morton's (1969, 1979) "logogen" model of word recognition proposed variable threshold word detector units called logogens, whose thresholds could vary due to momentary expectations (the mechanism for "semantic priming") or due to longer-term repetitions ("identity" or "repetition" priming). Experiments demonstrating repetition and semantic priming of faces have made use of the face familiarity decision task, which is an analog of the lexical decision task, so that factors affecting speeded recognition of faces can be explored without the problem of naming blocks. In the face familiarity decision task, subjects are shown a series of faces of which about half should be familiar (those of celebrities or local teachers) while others should be unfamiliar, though of similar pictorial style (e.g. the faces of models may serve as unfamiliar items that are of similar style to pictures of familiar actors). The subject's task is to decide as quickly as possible whether each encountered face is familiar. This allows us to investigate factors affecting face recognition without requiring the much more variable and error-prone process of name retrieval.

Using this methodology, it has been shown that the recognition of familiar faces is speeded if the faces have been seen some time earlier in the same or different views, though not if the name or body have been studied earlier (Bruce and Valentine, 1985; Ellis et al., 1987), and that recognition of a familiar face is speeded if it is preceded by a closely associated face (e.g. Princess Diana's face preceded by Prince Charles) (Bruce and Valentine, 1986). The pattern of these semantic priming and identity priming effects found in face recognition is very similar to that found in analogous tasks of word and object recognition, and has thus sustained the "logogen" analogy which encouraged the experiments.

A functional model of the kind proposed in figure 5.1 provides a much needed *starting* point for the formulation of future research questions. Much psychological research on face recognition had been confused about the different components of face perception, and clarifying the relationships between, say, expression analysis and identification, and between identification and naming is obviously important. However, models of these kinds deliberately side-step the issues of *how* the different functional components operate. By postulating "face recognition units" which recognize a familiar face independent of its viewpoint, we have avoided the tricky problem of specifying the computational procedures and primitives that could underlie such an ability. Additionally, the proposal that priming effects are mediated by threshold changes at the level of face recognition units leads to the same problems as are encountered by analogous models of word recognition. For example, it has been shown both for word recognition (Dannenbring and Briand, 1982) and face recognition (Bruce, 1986a) that semantic priming effects are virtually abolished by an unrelated item intervening between the prime and target, whereas repetition priming effects are virtually abolished by an unrelated item intervening between the prime and target, whereas repetition priming effects persist indefinitely and are affected rather little over the course of minutes by intervening items or the passage of time. If both priming effects result from reduction of recognition unit thresholds, it is difficult to see why they should be differentially sensitive to subsequent items.

Clearly, we need to unpack the mechanism of "perceptual classification" in some way that can provide a proper explanation of the nature of facial encoding, while also enabling us to provide an account of factors influencing facial recognition. In fact, there has been other work within psychology aimed at specifying the perceptual stages underlying face recognition, but again, much of it has failed to understand how differing task demands may create different kinds of face processing.

One strand of psychological work on encoding processes in face recognition has reflected a particular psychophysical trend to investigate visual information-processing within different spatial frequency channels (see reviews and contributions to this field by Sergent, 1986, 1989). Sergent (1986), for example, suggests that different spatial frequencies can support different levels of analysis of identity. The age or sex of a face may be derived from low spatial frequency (coarse scale) information, while individual identification may require the derivation of higher spatial frequencies (finer scales). However, analysis of how different bands of spatial frequencies sustain different kinds of decision does not explain basic face recognition phenomena such as the disproportionate effect of inverting faces (Yin, 1969). It is essential to enquire *what* is encoded from these different bands of spatial frequencies.

When we turn to consider the dimensions along which faces are encoded, one much-asked question has been whether faces are processed as independent features or as *Gestalt* wholes which are more than the sum of their parts. Early research found scant evidence for the *Gestalt* position. For example, Bradshaw and Wallace (1971) found evidence for a process of serial, self-terminating feature comparison in a task where subjects had to decide whether pairs of Identikit faces were the same or different. However, both the task and the materials used encouraged such a strategy. The faces themselves could only differ in terms of one or more of the discrete features from which Identikit faces are made, and the subject's task was to examine faces to find such differences as quickly as possible. It would surely be a sensible strategy to compare each feature serially when given such a task, and so such experiments cannot really address the kind of facial analysis that normally underlies access to memory representations of known faces.

Despite such difficulties with "same–different" methodology, Sergent (1984b) nevertheless produced evidence for the interaction between different face features. She found that subjects could decide that two Photofit faces differed more quickly if they differed on two dimensions than if they differed on any individual dimension, i.e. decisions to faces with two changes were faster again relative to even the fastest performance when only one of the dimensions was changed. This suggests that the manipulated dimensions must be interacting in some way.

Young et al. (1987) reported further evidence for processing facial configurations. They made new composite faces from the top and bottom halves of different, famous faces. When the face halves were mis-aligned, people could easily name the top halves. But when the top and bottom halves were carefully aligned, "new" individuals emerged and subjects were much slower at naming the top halves. Interestingly, performance improved when the composite faces were inverted, suggesting that configural processing is affected by inversion. Sergent (1984b) likewise showed that the interaction between different face features was only apparent with upright faces.

In our laboratory, we have recently shown that subjects are extremely good at *remembering* facial configurations. Specifically, shown four slightly different configural variants of the same basic face produced with the Mac-a-Mug electronic composite system, subjects will remember having seen the prototype or average configuration, even if this was not studied. Subjects do this much more strongly for faces, than for pictures of houses whose configuration of internal windows alters (Bruce et al., 1991), but this ability also appears to be affected by inversion. Clearly, then, any account of the encoding of faces must explain how we encode facial configuration as well as independent features such as hair texture or hair or eye color.

A further set of observations that should influence future theories of face encoding comes from the effects of facial *distinctiveness* found by Tim Valentine and myself (Valentine and Bruce, 1986a, b). Effects of typicality already noted in recognition memory for unfamiliar faces (e.g. Light et al., 1979; Bartlett et al., 1984) are found also in the recognition of highly familiar faces: famous faces rated as distinctive in appearance are recognized as familiar more rapidly than those rated as more typical in appearance. If the task is changed, to one where subjects must decide whether each encountered item is a *face* (as opposed to a jumbled face), the effect reverses, and typical faces are responded to more accurately. Such findings suggest that faces are represented in memory in some way that captures their deviation from the "prototypical" or "average" face. Such a view helps explain why caricatures can promote better recognition than veridical line drawings, since caricatures exaggerate the relationship between a face and the prototype (Rhodes et al., 1987).

In summary, recent research into the psychology of face recognition has been directed more towards understanding how familiar faces are recognized. Functional models of this process provide a useful overall framework for developing research questions, but side-step the problem of *how* faces are encoded. Recent psychological research stressing the encoding of configurations, and the importance of the relationship between a configuration and the "norm" looks promising, but we remain some way from formulating *algorithms* which specify such processes in anything better than words. At this point then, it seems pertinent to explore the potential from explicit computer models of the face recognition process.

Computer Recognition of Faces

Space here does not permit any comprehensive review of attempts to automate face recognition, and the interested reader should consult Laughery et al. (1981) for a review of early systems and Bruce and Burton (1989) for an updated review. The systems which have been devised differ according to whether recognition proceeds via the generation of an explicit description of the face, or whether the system operates as a neural network within which strengths between connections are altered, rather than explicit memories stored.

The general procedure in systems which derive explicit descriptions of faces is to locate and measure certain crucial features or dimensions of the face, and then to look up this list of measurements or features in a store of known faces. If the "fit" is sufficiently close, then the face is recognized. Attempts to locate and measure face features have been reported by Craw et al. (1987) and by Sakai et al. (1972). In both cases, the location of different features is model-driven: the system expects to find certain features at certain locations. For example, in Craw et al.'s work, the outline of the head is first found by trying to fit a coarse scale version of the test image with an idealized outline head model. Having located the outline of the hair, the program then looks for elongated features at positions that should correspond to eyebrows, and so forth for other face features. Sakai et al.'s system was the more comprehensive and successful, and they reported that of 607 clean-shaven faces without spectacles, hats etc., the program correctly located the features of 552 of these. The program as designed, however, could not cope with any faces wearing spectacles or beards, presumably because the "models" used to drive feature location did not incorporate such paraphernalia as possibilities.

Baron's (1981) computer model of face recognition rather side-steps the issue of feature finding, and concentrates on building representations in memory for each of a set of training faces. Each face is standardized in size, and then represented as a coarse-quantized, low-resolution "whole" face. This is done by reducing the original image to only 15×16 pixels, with the grey level of each pixel representing the average intensity in that area of the original image. The whole face description is stored along with a set of four more detailed descriptions of parts of the face (e.g. an eye, mouth, nose, and hair). The "fudge" here is that the human observer decides which are the four distinctive feature regions to store for each face, thereby ensuring that the memory description contains distinctive rather than typical parts of that face. In selecting the parts to store, the problem of feature location is also avoided. The system can build representations of faces seen in more than one different picture. The different pictures may be blended together, so that the stored description reflects the "average" of the training instances, or if they differ too severely for blending, they are stored separately, so that the memory representation of a particular person could end up as a collection of different views of that person. We will return to consider the plausibility of such an approach to human face recognition later. At test, coarse-quantized descriptions of to-be-recognized faces are correlated against the whole-face representations stored. Where there is conflict on the basis of matches at the whole face level, the detailed features are examined to resolve the conflict. Recognition thus proceeds from coarse to fine scale.

Baron tested the system by training it on the faces of 42 different people (from a total of 89 photographs) and testing it on 150 face images. All the original 42 faces were recognized and all the novel faces were correctly rejected. It would clearly be interesting to combine this storage and comparison method with the automatic location of features to be stored.

A quite different approach to automating face recognition is seen in pattern associators such as WISARD (Wilkie, Stonham and Aleksander's Recognition Device, e.g. Aleksander, 1983; Stonham, 1986). WISARD is a general purpose pattern recognition device based on neural network principles. For each pattern category to be learned (e.g. Fred's face might be one such category), a "discriminator" is set up. The discriminator retains a memory of all the responses obtained from instances of its category when the brightness values of different pixels are sampled with "n-tuples." If $n = 2$, pairs of pixels are sampled; $n = 3$, triplets are sampled, and so forth. Suppose, for the sake of simplicity, that each pattern were displayed as an array of $3 \times 3 = 9$ pixels, each of which could be black or white only. If fixed triplets of these pixels were sampled, then the responses obtained for each triplet could fall into one of eight possibilities only (pixels 1, 2 and 3 could be black, black black; black, black, white and so forth to the eighth possibility white, white, white). Each discriminator contains an address for each possible result of sampling each triplet and a "one" is stored at every address which is accessed by training exemplars of this category. Because certain responses will occur frequently given a particular category, and others will never occur, discriminators dedicated to different categories will build up different patterns of response. For example, if we wished to discriminate a "T" from a "C" using the 9-pixel array described, a triplet sampling the bottom row of images containing Ts would never find all three black, while that same triplet would often contain three black pixels when exposed to instances of "C." Training thus results in a memory of past responses to the category being stored: the instances themselves are not stored at all. If a test pattern is given, the same pixel samples are taken and compared with those stored in the pattern discriminators. A pattern is classified as belonging to the category where there is the greatest overlap between the current and stored responses.

Stonham (1986) reported that a system of this sort could correctly discriminate between the faces of 16 different male individuals. Each face was presented on an array of 153×214 pixels, and sampled with n-tuples of size 4. Each of the 16 discriminators was trained on upwards of 200 different images of each person, as they varied their expression in front of the camera. The hardware implementation of the memory storage and access enabled such performance to occur in real time.

The WISARD demonstration (and others from the "connectionist" literature, e.g. Kohonen et al., 1981) is important because it shows how patterns such as faces may be discriminated with no explicit representation of their form. The faces are distinguished on purely statistical grounds, and it is instructive to see how much progress can be made on these terms alone. However, to provide a plausible model of human face recognition much more would be needed of such a system. It would need to be able to recognize the same face again despite a different background, or different size of image, i.e. some figure-ground and scaling problems would need to be tackled. Changes in the lighting on the face could be even more problematic, and yet human vision seems untroubled by this. There would have to be different discriminators for different viewpoints (full face and profile, for example), and so forth.

From this brief overview it can be seen that although the recognition of relatively small numbers of human faces has proved a tractable task for automation, none of the published systems approaches the capacity and flexibility of human visual recognition. However, there have been no explicit attempts to simulate human face recognition procedures among the systems I have mentioned.

Future Directions

The research we have reviewed shows that psychologists and computer scientists have in recent years made a promising start in trying to understand and automate the processes of face recognition. Here I will show how some of the most interesting current work reflects a more integrated position. We now find psychologists, neurophysiologists, and computer scientists beginning to converge upon a truly "computational" approach to face perception and recognition, which is in the spirit of Marr's (1982) thesis. Marr (1982) emphasized that vision could be understood at different levels of theory. The "computational" or "in principle" level involves understanding the nature of the input to the visual system, and of any constraints that might be relevant to the problem at hand. The level of "algorithm" and "representation" involves suggesting working solutions to the problem. The "implementation" level theory is concerned with how the nervous system actually achieves these solutions in terms of its own hardware. Marr argued that theories of algorithm and implementation should be guided by an understanding at the level of computational theory. Here, I will demonstrate how current work on aspects of facial image processing by people, monkeys, and machines is starting to achieve this goal in addressing issues at each of Marr's three levels.

Level 1: Computational Theory

The work of psychologists and computer scientists which has addressed the question of *which* dimensions are important to discriminate individuals, has construed the problem of face recognition as one of *pattern recognition*. The implicit, or explicit, suggestion is that faces are discriminated by means of some set of measurements made at the level of the picture plane. However, consideration of a different literature – from artists, orthodontists, and animators – makes us realize that the face is not a flat pattern, but a mobile, bumpy surface (Bruce, 1988, 1989). Furthermore, the face is appended to the skull, whose growth is constrained in a number of ways (see Enlow, 1982). Enlow suggests that the constraints of growth result in the emergence of different heads, and hence face types. He contrasts the two extremes of the leptoprosopic and the euryprosopic face. The former has long, narrow and protrusive features while the latter has broader, shorter, flatter features. Understanding the true nature of the input to a face recognition system may have important consequences in designing algorithms for specifying identity.

A good example of the importance of such a level 1 or computational theory comes from Pearson and his associates' work on designing video-phones for the deaf (Pearson and Robinson, 1985; Pearson et al., 1990). The problem was to design a way to automatically compress images of moving faces and hands, so that these images could be transmitted more econom-ically down telephone lines. An obvious way to compress grey-level images is to "sketch" them – to produce an animated cartoon film. Pearson and his colleagues found that applying standard line-finding routines to grey scale images of faces produced a hopelessly cluttered representation, unusable for their purposes. To design a better cartoon drawer, they considered the na-ture of the boundaries around which edges need to be drawn. In addition to high-contrast boundaries, like those between hair and forehead, Pearson and Robinson (1985) pointed out that the important contours are those formed where the *surface* of the face shifts sharply away from the line of sight. Such contours are signalled by luminance valleys in the image, and Pearson and Robinson devised a "valley-detecting" algorithm to pick up such shifts in surface orientation as well as the contrast boundaries. This algorithm pro-duces excellent sketches of faces, which are highly similar to those produced by human artists.

The videophone work illustrates how a proper understanding of the nature of facial structures may properly guide the design of algorithms for detecting such structures. Similarly, it is possible that understanding the ways in which facial features may be mutually constraining through growth may allow us to suggest algorithms for measuring individual faces which can in some way exploit any such redundancies. Our current projects in-clude one in which we are measuring a large number of adult male and female heads, taking both 2D and 3D measures, in order to explore possible covariation between face features, and to examine which measures best pre-dict psychological dimensions such as apparent age, sex, or distinctiveness. If there are redundancies among face features then this may go some way to explain the importance of global variants such as "face shape" and "age" in studies of factors accounting for perceived similarities between faces (Shepherd et al., 1981).

A further possibility, however, is that the human visual system actually represents the surface shapes of faces and heads when it represents such shapes for recognition. One project in which we are currently engaged exam-ines how global and local deformations to the facial surface may influence judgments made to that surface. The surface of a face is represented as a large data-base of xyz coordinate points obtained from laser-scanning. These points are linked together to form polygonal facets, and the resulting surface can be viewed by applying standard lighting models (Gouraud and Phong) to these facets (see figure 5.2). Using such materials we have shown that subjects can judge the relative age levels of two such surface models as readily when two different viewpoints are shown as when two coincident views are shown, suggesting that they can extract and compare the shapes of the surface rather than just the shapes of 2D occluding contours (Bruce

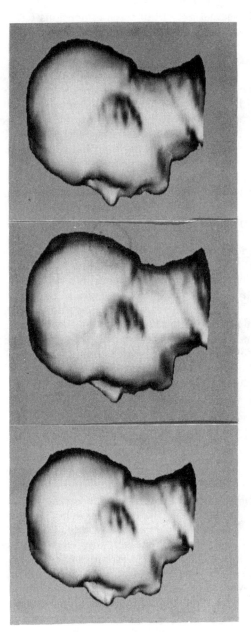

Figure 5.2 A representation of the surface of a human head (wearing a swimming cap). The left and right panels show the same head with the shape of the nose altered. Representations were obtained from measurements made by laser-scanning at University College, London.

et al., 1989). (In these experiments the "age" of the face surface has been manipulated by applying the cardioidal strain function, which models the changes produced by actual growth in three dimensions (cf. Pittenger and Shaw, 1975; Mark and Todd, 1983).

We have also been able to re-examine the role played by the nose in the individuation of faces. The "feature salience" literature in psychology suggested that the nose was the least important of internal features, and in some cases suggested that changes to the nose went virtually un-noticed (e.g. Haig, 1986). However, the invisibility of changes to the nose is hardly surprising given the full face images used in all such feature salience research, within which noses cannot be properly seen. Even so, Roberts and Bruce (1988) found that concealing the nose had a highly detrimental effect (much greater than that obtained by concealing eyes or mouths) on judging the sex of each face, when superficial cues from hairstyle and facial hair were minimized. This finding is consistent with Enlow's (1982) claim that an important difference between the shapes of male and female faces comes from the "muzzle" region. Male faces (on average) have more protruberant noses and brows while female faces have more retroussée noses. Using our 3D facial surfaces, with local manipulations made to the shape of the nose, we have confirmed that retroussée noses are seen as more female in appearance than hooked noses (Bruce et al., in press, describe this work in more detail).

I am here trying to suggest that a proper "level 1" understanding of the face can lead to a rather different research agenda from that we have been accustomed to in this field. Certainly, Pearson and Robinson's work illustrates the practical as well as theoretical benefits of such a change in direction. It is still early days for our own research efforts, but we feel certain that assessing the impact of the surface manipulations of faces will lead to important additional insights into the nature of facial encoding.

Level 2: Algorithmic Level

The computer models of face recognition outlined above clearly represent attempts to devise theories at the algorithmic level, but these attempts were not aimed at providing theories of human information-processing. Of those discussed, Baron's (1981) comes the closest to incorporating design principles that resemble human processing. Attempted matches proceed from coarse to fine (or global to local), which emulates aspects of human vision (e.g. Navon, 1977; Watt, 1988). Similarly, faces are stored as composite images where the instances differ a little, and as separate instances where they differ greatly. Such a mechanism would create separate representations for, say, full-face and profile views, and it has already been suggested (Bruce and Young, 1986; Perrett et al., 1986) that this might be a better model for face perception than the kind of object-centered (viewpoint invariant) representations suggested by Marr and Nishihara (1978) for basic level object categorization. However, the weakness of the Baron model is that it leaves the choice of face parts to be stored with the human operator, thus side-stepping critical issues of encoding.

The criticism of a "weak" perceptual interface applies even more strongly to attempts to use computer modeling to elaborate "paper" theories of human information-processing. We have recently produced a simulation of the Bruce and Young (1986) framework for face recognition, cast as an interactive activation system (Burton et al., 1990). It turns out that problems that appeared intractable when cast "on paper" can be reformulated and overcome quite naturally in interactive activation terms. In our simulation of the Bruce and Young (1986) framework, we have assumed that a number of different pools of units contribute to familiarity decisions. There are feature units, face units, person units, and semantic units. Units within a pool inhibit each other, while those corresponding to the same identity between pools excite each other. Within such a system we have been able to produce priming effects with different time courses as described earlier. In our system, repetition priming results from changing the weights on the connections between units, and thus its time course is limited by whatever decay parameter is put on such weight changes. Semantic priming results from alteration of the activation of particular units, as a consequence of shared semantic links, and thus its time course is affected by new faces (which will alter the pattern of activities in the system) as well as decay factors. By assuming that familiarity decisions are taken at the level of the person units (person identity nodes in figure 5.1) we have been able to simulate many of the basic phenomena of semantic and repetition priming, while also generating new predictions which are currently being tested.

However, in contrast to the computer models discussed above, our current algorithmic simulations are severely limited by the nature of the input which drives them. Like other demonstrations in the Parallel Distributed Processing (PDP) camp (e.g. McClelland and Rumelhart, 1985), our simulation works on hypothetical face patterns which are represented as values on a notional set of artificial feature dimensions. Further progress at the algorithmic level will require that such a system be interfaced with a perceptual "front end," and while the possibilities of using a WISARD-like system for such a front end are available now, it is hoped that the dimensions will be understood explicitly with the aid of the surface-based theories discussed in the preceding section.

It is important to note that these dimensions *must* be understood explicitly in order properly to simulate facial recognition, whether with conventional, symbolic descriptions or as a connectionist implementation of these. Pixel- or edge-based neural network models cannot provide a proper explanation of the way in which face configurations are encoded. As an example, consider the experiment by Young et al. (1987) which showed that the top halves of famous faces were very difficult to recognize when aligned with the wrong bottom halves. One of the attractive properties of auto-associative distributed memory networks (Kohonen et al., 1981) is their ability to complete "wholes" given "parts" of them. Trained on Margaret Thatcher's face, for example, such a net would recreate the activation associated with the whole pattern when later shown a part of it. Clearly, a pixel-based pattern associator should find it as easy to recreate the "whole" Thatcher from its top half whether it is closely aligned or mis-aligned with the wrong bottom half. The fact that the human visual system *is* sensitive to the alignment of the halves suggests that human vision creates "wrong" primitives at a level more abstract than pixels. The alignment means, for example, that a face shape and hairstyle can emerge which are not the face shape or hairstyle of the component "halves." But in order to understand why such emerging holistic properties interfere with perception of the parts requires that we understand, explicitly, how such properties are represented. Having understood the nature of the represented properties, we can then suggest algorithms for extracting these.

Level 3: Implementation Level

Understanding the neural mechanisms underlying face recognition has been considerably advanced by a computational perspective. It is now well established that particular cells in the superior temporal sulcus of the macaque temporal cortex respond selectively to faces (see Rolls, 1984, 1988, in press; Perrett et al., 1986, for reviews). Cells which are selective for faces respond more strongly to faces than to other arousing stimuli such as snakes or to other face-like stimuli such as clocks. However, within those cells which respond to faces, there is further selectivity in terms of viewpoint, identity, and so forth.

For example, Perrett's group (Perrett et al., 1986) found certain cells responding preferentially to particular facial features (e.g. there are cells which will only respond to a picture of a face in which the eyes or mouth are visible), though usually only when the configuration of the features is normal. Some cells respond strongly to particular viewpoints, such as full face and profile, and others respond more strongly to some facial identities than others. Some cells will respond to a particular individual in any viewpoint, while others respond selectively to a particular view of a particular individual (e.g. Dave Perrett's face in profile). Perrett has interpreted these selectivities as reflecting the implementation of progressively higher levels of perceptual identification. He suggests that faces are identified via a hierarchy in which features and configurations of features are first identified from the groups emerging at primal sketch level (Marr, 1976). These features then drive units selective for particular views of particular individuals, which in turn drive view-independent units selective for particular, individual identities (cf. Bruce and Young's "face recognition units.") These view-independent units then allow access to a "polymodal conceptual" level (cf. Bruce and Young's "person identity nodes.")

Similar results from single-cell recording obtained by Rolls' group in Oxford (Rolls, 1984, 1988) are interpreted rather differently. Rather than see individual cells as responding to identity in the manner of "grandmother cells,"

Rolls emphasizes that most cells show some generalization of their responses to different individuals. He thus suggests that identity is encoded by an ensemble of cells in a distributed fashion. There is probably little real conflict between these two approaches, since Perrett is not arguing against redundant coding in the scheme that he proposes. The advantage of Rolls' approach is that it encourages us to think about how such a network could have emerged through competitive learning, while the advantage of Perrett's is that it allows us to think more easily about what the neural machinery is actually accomplishing.

Whatever the ultimate fruitfulness of one or other perspective, the important point is that it is no longer sufficient to demonstrate that a certain set of cells is sensitive to a certain class of stimuli. As stressed by Marr, in order to understand what role such cells play in information-processing requires a much better understanding of the nature of the problem itself, and an explicit formulation of possible representations and algorithms for achieving solutions to this problem.

Concluding Remarks

This chapter has shown how the study of face perception and recognition has evolved over the past 10 to 15 years. From an initial, somewhat atheoretical, approach which emphasized memory for unfamiliar faces, a new framework has emerged which emphasizes the derivation of different kinds of meaning from facial patterns. Within such a framework it has become natural to work toward a more rigorous, computational approach to face processing.

Face processing is interesting in its own right, because of the range of different meanings conveyed by the face and its crucial role in social interaction. However, understanding facial recognition may reveal principles which extend to other kinds of visual object too. Most computational theories of object recognition are aimed at elucidating the recognition of basic level object categories. Marr and Nishihara's (1978) theory, for example, suggested a means of distinguishing a dog from a cat, or a horse from a giraffe. But we are also very good at discriminating within the same basic level category: we can tell Labradors from Retrievers, and can recognize our own Labradors playing with others in the park. Contemporary theories of object recognition have little to say about such abilities. It may be that the study of face recognition will suggest solutions to other kinds of recognition which seem to rely on sensitivity to configural variations on the same basic theme.

Acknowledgments

Research discussed in this chapter has been supported by grants from the Economic and Social Research Council, and the Science and Engineering Research Council.

6

The Breakdown Approach to Visual Perception: Neuropsychological Studies of Object Recognition

GLYN W. HUMPHREYS, M. JANE RIDDOCH, AND
MURIEL BOUCART

A major difficulty in understanding vision is that, normally, it is so very efficient. Even when given the briefest of glimpses we can recognize a known object, even when it has undergone a radical change from its normally depicted view (see, for example, Humphreys and Quinlan, 1987; and chapter 9 here). For humans, tasks such as visual object recognition are performed so rapidly that it is often difficult to explain to the lay person that many complex processes are involved. Yet many complex processes undoubtedly *are* involved, and tasks like object recognition, performed by the brain within a few hundred milliseconds, remain beyond the capabilities of any present-day computer vision systems.

Because of the sheer efficiency of vision, many steps have traditionally been taken to make the underlying processes falter, in the hope that we can learn about these processes by studying the kinds of errors made, or the kinds of judgments possible, under abnormal conditions. We term this the *breakdown approach* to understanding vision. The main theme of this chapter – the attempt to understand vision by studying its neuropsychological breakdown – represents one example of this approach. It is, however, by no means the only one. We will first consider two other such approaches: the study of visual illusions, and psychophysical studies of perception when all but certain visual cues are eliminated. The similarities and contrasts among the different approaches will serve to highlight their relative strengths and weaknesses.

Visual Illusions

A well-known example of the breakdown approach to vision is the study of visual illusions (see, for example, Gregory, 1970, 1980). Observers may be presented with a stimulus in a particular context (often one in which the redundancy normally present in the visual world – e.g. the elaboration of depth cues by means of texture, brightness gradients, binocular disparities, linear perspective, and so forth – is minimized) and asked to make a judgment. The judgment may be systematically distorted such that it does not accurately reflect the stimulus presented. By studying the kinds of distortion that occur, various proposals can be raised about the nature of the underlying perceptual processes.

Figure 6.1 shows two examples: the Müller–Lyer illusion and a Kanizsa figure. In the Müller–Lyer illusion, the central bar is typically judged as longer in the figure with outward-pointing fins than in the figure with inward-pointing fins. It can be suggested that this illusion occurs because angles and junctions are strong cues for the three-dimensional interpretation of scenes (e.g. Gregory, 1970; cf. Barrow and Tenenbaum, 1978), and the bar with outward-pointing fins is coded as being further away than the bar with inward-pointing fins. Despite this, the length of the bars on the retina is equal. In reality, bars at different depths only subtend the same angle on the retina if the bars are unequal in length, the bar that is further away being longer. Our perception, then, appears to follow this inference.

In the Kanizsa figure, we "perceive" illusory contours between the edges of the aligned pacmen, and we even see the surface of the enclosed square as differing in brightness from the surround (e.g. Prazdny, 1985). The perception of illusory contours such as this provides a strong constraint on any theory of visual perceptual organization and grouping: the processes which group aligned edges together (in our example, to form the central square) must be insensitive to the direction of the light contrasts which define the edges. This must be so because illusory contours are formed between edges of opposite contrast (light to dark versus dark to light). Such illusory effects have strongly influenced the development of computational models of perceptual organization, such as Grossberg's FACADE (see chapter 11), in which systems that group edges are functionally separated from those that define the surface details of shapes. The system that groups edges (the *boundary contour system* in Grossberg's terms) is not affected by the sign of the edges (i.e. the direction of light contrast), while the system that specifies surface detail (the *feature contour system*) is.

Unfortunately, there are several problems associated with using illusions to study vision. One is that many illusions are only generated from relatively impoverished visual stimuli. Studies of perception under this circumstance may illustrate the ability of the observer to "best guess" the nature of a stimulus, but this might be far from the processes involved in normal perception, when the observer faces a rich visual field, typically containing highly

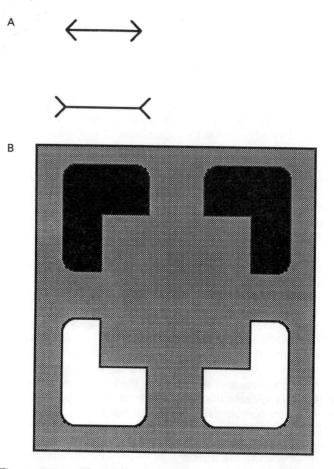

Figure 6.1   *a, The Müller–Lyer illusion. b, A Kanizsa figure.*

redundant information: objects whose 2D or 3D form can be specified by their contour, local texture, shading, type of motion, and so forth (see chapter 8 for a discussion of these different means of coding objects). Illusions may cast little light on the processes involved in more complex (and perhaps more common) situations.

An additional problem is that the study of illusions is very often "phenomenon driven." A systematic distortion in perception – the illusion – might be noted when observers are presented with certain stimuli. This then serves for demonstration purposes, but demonstrations alone do not greatly add to our understanding. Increasingly, we need to know details of the parameters of an effect (how it varies, under what conditions), in order to generate accurate computational models. Even when such detailed parametric investigations are undertaken, it remains the case that illusions are rarely derived on a purely theoretical basis. Starting from a phenomenon, and working backwards towards a model, can place a limitation on tests of theories, since the phenomenon may not be designed with theory-testing in mind. A consequence of this is that many different theories can often remain consistent with a particular illusion.[1]

Psychophysical Studies of Visual Modules

A somewhat different approach is to start out by systematically limiting the kinds of visual information presented to observers, and to generate measures of the perceptual performance achieved. An example of this is work with "random visual noise stimuli" (i.e. stimuli with the appearance of interference on a television screen). Random visual noise stimuli have proved useful in the study of visual perception because they minimize the pattern information present. Perceptual performance cannot then depend on the presence of pattern information in a display.

Perhaps one of the clearest examples of the use of such stimuli has been in the study of depth perception. Julesz (1971) created "random dot stereograms" in the following way. A visual noise display was created and then replicated. A central area was cut in one of the two displays and displaced slightly to one side (with the area uncovered being filled again with visual noise). Consequently, the two visual noise displays were identical in all but the displaced area. Julesz found that when each pattern is presented separately, one to the right eye and one to the left, people with normal binocular vision can have a clear impression of depth, with the displaced area seeming to be at a different depth relative to the area that remains identical in the two patterns. Since random noise displays lack pattern information, the perception of the two areas at different depths can only be achieved by the visual system responding to the disparities in the two images; binocular disparity alone is sufficient for the perception of forms in depth (see also chapter 1, for further discussion of depth perception via binocular disparity).

Visual noise stimuli have also been adopted in the study of motion perception. Here an equivalent experimental situation can be established to that used to study depth perception, with the difference being that instead of the two random noise displays being presented one to each eye, each display can be presented in an alternating sequence simultaneously to both eyes. Again, there will be an area in the two displays that is identical, and an area that is displaced. When there is a relatively short interval between the presentation of one display and its replacement with the next (e.g. under one-tenth of a second), observers see a moving surface (the area displaced in the displays) which oscillates as one display is replaced by the next (e.g. Braddick, 1973). Such stimuli, termed "random dot kinematograms," demonstrate that pattern displacement over time is sufficient for the perception of form in motion, even in the absence of static form information.

Investigations using stimuli such as random noise patterns differ from the study of visual illusions in that the stimulus properties determining performance are under strict experimental control from the outset. Hence such investigations can be directly related to theories concerned with how such stimulus properties are coded.

This approach has been particularly influential in the development of computational models of vision. By isolating and manipulating single stimulus properties (local displacement of random dots across time, in the case of motion perception, or across space, in the case of depth perception), algorithms for deriving the appropriate properties from the image can be developed. Furthermore, these algorithms can be developed independently for the separate image properties. This has the virtue of obeying the principle of modularity, as expressed by David Marr (1982): namely, that any complex information-processing task can be best achieved by a system composed of separate modules, in which modification to one module does not have consequent effects on other modules. That is, this approach emphasizes the utility of a modular architecture for vision, in which there are separate systems for computing the different image properties.

Consider the utility of the principle of modular design for the development of biological visual systems. As an observer grows, there will be large changes to properties of the visual system important for binocular depth perception – the distance between the eyes, for instance. Such changes may be relatively unimportant for motion perception, which can be computed on the basis of angular displacements taking place within one image (and so does not require the images in the two eyes to be related). Any changes to the algorithm for coding depth, as the observer grows, will not produce consequent changes in the algorithm for motion perception.

A problem with this approach is that, perhaps even more so than the study of visual illusions, it limits the use of complex, redundant stimuli. Studies show that particular stimulus properties are *sufficient* for particular aspects of perception (e.g. binocular disparities for deriving surfaces in depth, angular displacements over time for deriving surfaces in motion), but this is a long way from showing that, normally, the modules do not interact when images contain redundant properties. In such images, the changes in depth computed by the system concerned with binocular disparity will correlate with those computed by the motion system if an object moves away from or toward an observer; they will also correlate with the changes computed by the system concerned with the surface texture of objects in the environment, and with the changes computed by the system concerned with surface brightness, and so forth. There may be considerable computational gains to be had by a visual system that combines partial outputs from different processing modules in order to gain a better solution than is possible from any single module operating in isolation. At present we know very little about how different visual processing systems interact.

Neuropsychological Studies

Neuropsychological studies are also concerned with the performance of the visual system under restricted conditions, but in this case the restriction is typically induced by some form of organic brain damage, affecting some of the higher cortical processes mediating visual perception. As we shall discuss below, neurological damage can produce quite selective functional loss, affecting one aspect of visual perception more than others. Several consequences can follow.

One is that selective functional disturbances can be counter-intuitive, producing dissociations between different abilities which, *a priori*, one might imagine were closely intertwined. Studies of such dissociations can throw fresh light on the subject, suggesting the existence of different modules from those indicated by (for example) psychophysical studies.

A second consequence is that, even if a particular form of functional disturbance might be expected (e.g. from psychophysics, from studies of illusions), neuropsychological studies can begin to answer the important question of whether processes, in normality, interact. For example, let us suppose that a given behavior (e.g. the ability to judge the relative depths of the surfaces of objects) is based on the combined processing of more than one "visual module." From our discussion in the last section, it seems possible that judgments of surface depths might be based on both binocular disparity and texture information. Let us also suppose that a patient suffers damage which produces selective loss or even distortion of binocular depth perception. This could be detected by the patient showing inappropriate responses to random dot stereograms which, as we noted above, minimize depth cues other than binocular disparity. If the perception of surface depth normally depends on a contribution from the system that computes binocular disparities, then we would expect surface depth judgments to be compromised. This should occur even if the patient can be shown to have normal ability to judge surface texture, when texture but not depth is varied. The overriding point here is that, within a system that normally depends on interactions between processing modules, impairment of one module should influence behavior of the whole system. In this way neuropsychological studies can foster an understanding of "whole system" behavior in a way that other "breakdown approaches" to perception cannot.

Of course, neuropsychological studies are not without their problems, some of which are shared with other approaches to perception. For example, like the study of illusions, neuropsychological studies can be "phenomenon driven." Also the ways in which brain damage divides up the problems of vision will by and large be determined by the vagaries of anatomy rather than by theoretical questions. Damage to a particular area in the brain may happen to produce a constellation of associated deficits; however, this may simply be because a number of functionally separate processes happen to be closely located in the brain, rather than because the processes are functionally related. By studying the perceptual phenomena revealed by chance brain lesions, there is a danger that the investigator may be led down paths that do not lead to new theoretical developments.

In addition, selective losses of perceptual functions tend to be relatively rare. Of necessity, this means that theoretically interesting studies will often be carried out on single patients. We are then, of course, left with the question of whether any single case can tell us about the perceptual functions instantiated in the majority of normal observers. Are we dealing with someone who premorbidly had an idiosyncratic perceptual system? For instance, in cases of long-standing epilepsy it is possible that there may have been some form of re-allocation of function to different neural loci; and, indeed, even some change to the functional processes themselves. Questions concerning the validity of generalizing from individuals to whole populations are particularly pertinent to neuropsychology because of the danger that the processing system of the individual studied has undergone some form of singular change. Valid inferences from neurologically impaired individuals to normal performance are based around the notion of *transparency* – the idea that brain damage can selectively reduce the normal processing system, so that in studying brain-damaged individuals we witness a processing system operating normally apart from the loss of certain processing functions (see Caramazza and McCloskey, 1988). Clearly, the validity of this notion must be addressed if neuropsychological studies are to be of theoretical value. We will return to attempt some answers at the close of the chapter.

In the meantime, we can also note one further virtue of neuropsychological studies. Although many studies begin by being "phenomenon driven" (it is often the striking behavior presented by a patient that initially drives an investigation), they may not end so providing the investigation can be directly related to functional models of behavior. Increasingly this is becoming possible, as more detailed models of visual perception develop. Indeed, data from patients can also serve to constrain model development, since any model of normal visual perception must have the property that it can degrade in a way consistent with neuropsychological data. We will attempt to illustrate this point by reference to our own work with a single patient with a very profound impairment in the normally effortless task of recognizing visually presented common objects.

Case Study

The patient, HJA, was an executive in charge of the European end of an American business. In 1981, when aged 61, he suffered a stroke that produced a small bilateral lesion in the occipito-temporal region of the brain. The occipital lobes, in the left and right cerebral hemispheres, are the primary site of projections from the retina to the cortex, and are likely to be involved in computing sensory aspects of visual signals. One main visual pathway within the cortex projects from the occipital lobes to the temporal lobes, where there is physiological evidence suggesting that visual memories are stored (e.g. Ungerleider and Mishkin, 1982). For instance, while cells in the occipital lobe respond selectively to simple properties of images, such as edges at particular orientations (Hubel and Wiesel, 1962), some cells in the temporal lobe respond selectively to images as complex as individual faces (Perrett et al., 1985). Lesions to the occipito-temporal pathway are thus likely to impair the ability to link incoming images to stored object memories, and thus they can lead to marked problems in visual object recognition.

Following his stroke, HJA had difficulty recognizing many common objects by sight, though his recognition of the same objects presented tactilely was relatively normal (Riddoch and Humphreys, 1987a). He was unable to recognize any familiar faces, including his wife's. He had difficulty reading (reading was reduced to operating on one letter at a time). He was poor at both naming and matching colors, and he reported seeing the world in black, white, and gray. He failed to recognize known buildings (including his own house), and became lost and disoriented when trying to find his way around the environment. There was a profound impairment to a number of putatively separate visual functions. Given the variety and severity of these different impairments, what can be learned about the processes normally mediating visual object recognition?

Object Recognition

Intact Performance

An important starting point within any case study is to establish the existence of intact aspects of performance. Tests of a given ability can be failed for many reasons – patients may be selectively impaired at the functions tapped by the tests, they may fail to understand the instructions, they may fail to concentrate during a given test session, and so forth. Tests showing intact performance provide a framework for interpreting performance impairments. If a patient can be shown to understand the instructions for a task similar to the one they subsequently fail, it may be safe to infer that the difficulty is not just in following task instructions. Indeed, it may even be possible to show that one patient who is intact on one test but impaired at another, shows exactly the opposite pattern of performance to a second patient (who is impaired at the "good" task for the former patient, and intact at the "bad" task). This would demonstrate a strong *double dissociation* (see Shallice, 1988). Such strong double dissociations are useful because they suggest that any impairments are not simply because a particular task is difficult; if that were the case, then another patient (showing a deficit on some other task) should not show intact levels of performance. Strong double dissociations are based on the contrast between some impaired and some intact abilities.

In HJA's case, we were able to show that several perceptual functions remained intact (see figure 6.2). Most of these functions concern what we

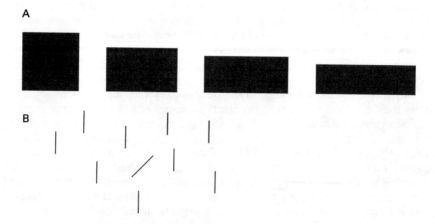

Figure 6.2   *a, Figures from the Efron task. Observers have to discriminate between squares and rectangles matched for illumination. This is often used as a clinical test of shape perception. b, A search task requiring the discrimination of a target line differing in orientation from the background.*

might think of as "early" stages of the object recognition process; for instance, with stages concerned with computing simple perceptual attributes based on edge orientations, with computing surfaces in depth from binocular disparities, and surfaces in motion from angular disparities over time.

For example, HJA was able to perceive surfaces at different depths when presented with random dot stereograms. He was similarly able to see surfaces in motion from random dot kinematograms. As far as the processing of visual form is concerned, HJA was able to copy objects that he failed to recognize. He was also able to judge whether shapes matched for brightness were squares or rectangles (the Efron test; see Efron, 1968), and he showed normal performance when asked to detect the presence of a target line differing in orientation from the background. In the latter task, his mean reaction times (RTs) to detect targets differing in orientation from the background were of the order of 425 ms, and they did not vary as a function of the number of background items present. His performance was at least as good as that of normal (non-brain-damaged) age-matched controls, and the lack of an effect of the number of background items indicates that he was able to perform the task "at a glance", without having to scan to find the target (if he had had to scan, we would then expect there to be effects of the number of background items he had to scan).

Impaired Access to Stored Knowledge

In contrast to this good performance on tasks requiring judgments of simple properties of forms, HJA was severely impaired at any tasks requiring stored

Figure 6.3   An "unreal" object used to test whether HJA could judge the familiarity
of visually presented objects.

knowledge of objects to be accessed from vision. For instance, he typically
named only about 60 percent of common objects correctly, and even this
performance level decreased considerably when the objects appeared in more
complex situations; for instance, when multiple objects overlapped one another (Humphreys and Riddoch, 1987a; Riddoch and Humphreys, 1987a).
This was not just a problem in finding the correct name; HJA was unable to
demonstrate any specific knowledge about objects he failed to identify (e.g.
he could not demonstrate how an object might be used, although this should
be possible were the problem one of naming). He was poor at pointing to
which two of three objects could be used to perform the same function (e.g.
when shown two types of umbrella and a walking stick; see Warrington,
1982), and he was also unable to discriminate between pictures of real objects
and pictures of "unreal" objects we constructed by interchanging the parts
of two common objects (see figure 6.3). In order to perform the last task, it
may be sufficient to judge whether an object looks familiar; such a task can
be performed by patients with severe deficits in retrieving the names of
objects (see Riddoch and Humphreys, 1987b).

Impaired Memories for Objects?

The contrast between apparently good early perceptual abilities, and poor
access to stored knowledge of objects from vision, could arise for several
reasons. One possibility is that the patient suffers from an impaired long-
term memory for objects. For instance, HJA may perform poorly on tasks
requiring access to stored knowledge from vision because his stored knowledge of objects has been disrupted.

We think that this is unlikely in HJA's case. One reason for arguing against
such an account is that HJA is able to give very precise definitions of objects
he typically fails to recognize visually. When asked to tell us what a lettuce
is, HJA replied:

[It is] a quick growing annual plant – cultivated for human consumption of its crisp green succulent leaves which grow during the young state of the plant, tightly formed together in a ball-shaped mass. It is widely cultivated and of many varieties and of absolutely no value as a food. They do however enable one to eat delicious mayonnaise when using a knife and fork in polite places . . .

Judging from this definition, HJA retains knowledge about several visual properties of lettuces: their colour and general shape, for instance. He also retains his sense of humor!

HJA was not only able to give precise verbal definitions about objects, he also retained a quite remarkable ability to draw objects from memory (see figure 6.4). Such drawings suggest that HJA does have good stored knowledge about the visual properties of objects. He fails to recognize objects from vision because he cannot access his stored knowledge appropriately.

Impaired Intermediate Vision

We have proposed that HJA has good processing of simple properties of single shapes (in the Efron test) and of multiple line orientations (in search tasks); in addition, he has good long-term knowledge about visual properties of objects. However, object recognition undoubtedly involves more than the matching of representations coded in terms of line orientations and single shapes against stored knowledge. Objects are differentiated on the basis of the relations among line orientations and among the component parts making up the objects. Also, in complex images, the correct parts of objects need to be coded and segmented from irrelevant "background" stimuli, so that only appropriate relationships are coded. These points were recognized by the *Gestalt* psychologists, who argued that the relations between the parts of objects could give rise to whole perceptual structures with emergent characteristics different from those of the individual parts they contain (see chapter 3). They also noted the fundamental role of coding figure–ground relationships for object recognition.

Coding the relations among the component parts of objects seems particularly important for recognizing some objects. For instance, the component parts of faces (noses, eyes, ears, mouths), taken individually, do not serve for efficient face recognition, and there is good evidence that face processing is normally based on perceptual relationships among component parts (e.g. Sergent, 1984). Tasks such as face recognition may also prove difficult if faces are encoded into the wrong parts because (for example) a shadow is taken as the boundary differentiating two facial regions. Thus the segmentation of figures into the correct parts, and the encoding of perceptual relations among parts, are closely interlocked processes.

Might HJA's problems in visual object recognition be caused by impaired intermediate visual processes, concerned with figure–ground segmentation and perceptual grouping? Several pieces of research suggest that this is the

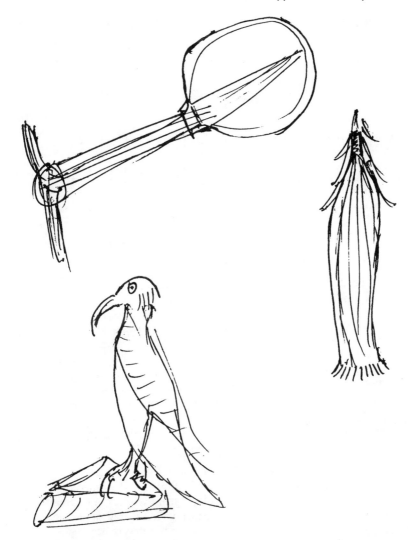

Figure 6.4   *HJA's drawing of objects from memory: a guitar, celery, and an eagle. Note that HJA was unable to identify any of these objects by sight.*

case. For instance, HJA and groups of normal observers were given stimuli such as those shown in figure 6.5, and asked to judge whether pairs of stimuli were in the same orientation or whether they were in mirror reversed orientations. Three types of stimuli were used: outline forms, "structured" fragmented forms, and "unstructured" fragmented forms. The difference between the "structured" and "unstructured" fragmented forms was that, in

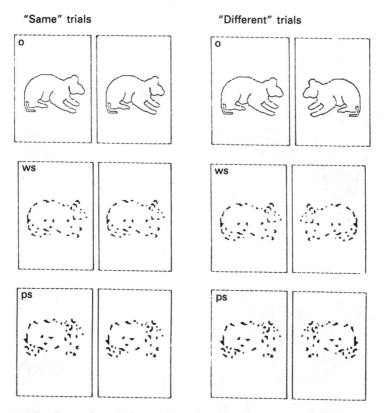

Figure 6.5 *Examples of the outline drawings (o), "structured" (ws) and "unstructured" (ps) fragmented drawings used in the orientation discrimination task with HJA.*

the structured forms, the fragments were collinear and aligned on the virtual contour of the outline drawing of the object from which the fragmented form was derived. In the unstructured forms, individual fragments were rotated so that they were no longer collinear. Normal subjects are fastest to match the outlines, then the structured forms, and they are slowest to match the unstructured forms. This is because judgments about the orientation of such stimuli are based on the encoding of perceptual groups, which lie either on the same or on opposite sides of the stimuli when they are respectively in the same or in opposite orientations; the coding of perceptual groups is facilitated by the presence of particular relationships among the line contours, such as collinearity.

HJA, on the other hand, showed no difference between the three types of stimuli: there was no advantage for forms having perceptual structure over those lacking such structure. HJA seemed insensitive to the presence of

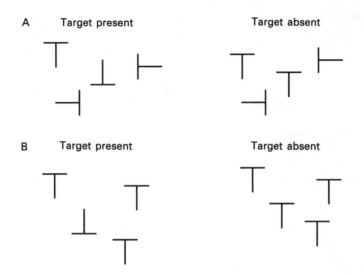

Figure 6.6 *Examples of displays in which targets and background elements differ only in the way in which their component line orientations combine. a, Heterogeneous background elements; b, homogeneous background elements.*

collinearity among line segments. From this we take it that HJA is impaired at encoding an important relationship between edge segments – collinearity – and thus he is impaired at an intermediate stage of processing between the initial coding of edge orientations and the accessing of stored object knowledge (Boucart and Humphreys, in press).

We can also contrast HJA's good ability to discriminate differences in line orientation "at a glance" with his ability to discriminate targets and background stimuli differing in their combination of two or more orientations. For instance, consider a task such as finding an inverted T target against a background of upright and 90 degree rotated T distractors (see figure 6.6). All the items in this case have the same component horizontal and vertical line orientations; they differ only in the way in which the component orientations combine. Search of such displays is normally very inefficient; it is slow and strongly affected by the number of distractors present (Humphreys et al., 1989). However, this result is critically dependent on the nature of the background items. If homogeneous rather than heterogeneous background items are used (all upright Ts rather than Ts in three different orientations; see figure 6.6), performance is little affected by the number of distractors in the displays. That is, observers can tell "at a glance" whether the target differs from the homogeneous distractor group. Thus this result tells us about some of the parallel grouping procedures mediating visual object recognition which, in normality, seems based on combinations of line orientations.

HJA performs relatively poorly on this task when homogeneous distractors are used: he shows abnormally slow reaction times, a high error rate, and marked effects of the number of distractors. Apparently, he has an impaired ability to group items containing even simple combinations of line orientations. Note that this task, requiring the grouping of line combinations in parallel across the visual field, differs from the Efron shape-matching task, which only requires the processing of one shape at a time. Interestingly, when presented with heterogeneous distractors in the search task HJA performs quite normally. Like normal subjects, HJA shows strong effects of the number of distractors present, but his overall reaction times and his rate of search do not differ from those of controls. This suggests that HJA is able to scan and search for a single form perfectly well, but he does this by treating each element in the display as a separate object; hence there are strong effects of the number of distractors on his search time. His problem is revealed only when displays normally give rise to grouping, so that individual background elements are not treated as separate perceptual objects (i.e. with homogeneous background items). HJA is impaired at carrying out parallel grouping with complex displays, where elements differ in the combinations of their line orientations (see Humphreys et al., 1992c).

Because of his problem in grouping stimuli containing combinations of line orientations, HJA's visual object recognition may break down. For instance, he may be unable to form appropriate intermediate visual representations, based on the relations between line orientations, which are important for object recognition and for figure-ground segmentation. This would account for his difficulty in forming appropriate figure-ground relationships, when presented with complex displays with multiple overlapping objects. His case supports the distinction between early visual processes, concerned with the initial coding of edge orientations, and intermediate vision, concerned with coding the relations between those edge orientations. HJA has a selective deficit of intermediate vision.

A Simulation

As we discussed at the outset, there are certain problems associated with single case studies, no matter how interesting the patient. These problems primarily concern making inferences from an individual to the population at large, and from a case of pathology (and possibly altered function) to normality. Nevertheless, increased confidence in the relevance of the case study may follow if it can be shown that the pattern of behavior shown by the patient emerges naturally from a working cognitive model with a simulated lesion.

The study of cognition through the "lesioning" of working models has recently been taken some way by the development of connectionist processing systems. Connectionist systems typically contain computationally simple processing units, which sum incoming activity from units to which they are connected, with the incoming activation weighted as a function of the strength of the connection between the units (see Rumelhart and McClelland, 1986). Computational power is created by using massive numbers of interconnected processing units. Such models can simulate the effects of a brain lesion in several ways. Units may be zeroed so they can no longer be activated, connections between units can be lost or their weights altered, random noise can be added to activation functions and so forth. "Lesioning" has been used to examine models of word naming (e.g. Patterson et al., 1989), word comprehension (Hinton and Shallice, 1991) and visual attention in reading (Mozer and Behrmann, 1990).

We (Humphreys and Müller, 1992) have been involved in developing a connectionist model of visual search, in order to simulate the way in which grouping between background elements determines search efficiency. Within the model, termed SERR (for SEarch via Recursive Rejection), elements in the visual field interact to produce perceptual groups. As elements support one another, disparate elements compete with one another. Hence stable, self-supporting groups tend only to be formed between like elements. "Templates" coded for specific target or background elements are activated according to the amount of evidence for particular items in the field. When a target template reaches its threshold a response can be made ("target present"). Alternatively, when a template for a background element reaches threshold, that element can be rejected and search continues until the target is detected; hence search can proceed via the recursive rejection of background elements. Usually, the first template to reach threshold will conform to the largest group, and if all the background elements form a single group, search is very efficient. Search efficiency is dependent on perceptual grouping.

SERR can be run in real time to mimic human reaction time studies, with the number of iterations required for SERR to reach a decision serving as the reaction time measure. SERR accurately simulates the pattern of performance demonstrated by human subjects when the target and background differ in the combination of their line orientations. Search is efficient and little affected by the number of background elements when the background items are identical. Search is inefficient and affected by the number of background elements when the background items are heterogeneous (Humphreys and Müller, 1992) Search with heterogeneous background elements is inefficient because there is competition between disparate elements in the field, and stable grouping is difficult to achieve.

We have also examined SERR's performance under conditions where random noise is added to the activation functions. When there is a moderate increase in the amount of noise present, an interesting result emerges: search is more affected when the background elements are homogeneous than when they are heterogeneous (Humphreys et al., 1992a). This is illustrated in figure 6.7. An effect of increasing the noise present is to hinder grouping, since like elements may be coded as being different and so compete instead of supporting one another. This exerts a deleterious effect with homogeneous background elements, which are normally coded and rejected from the search process as a single group.

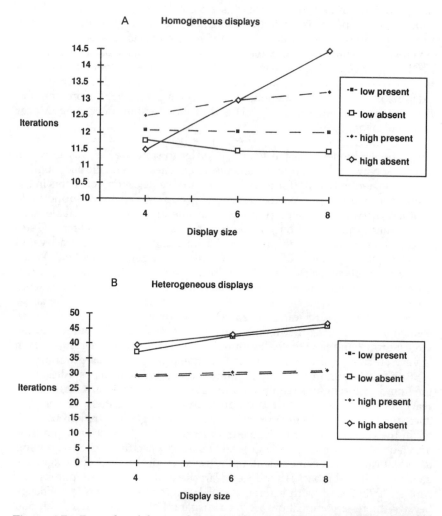

Figure 6.7   *Examples of the search functions generated by the connectionist model of visual search, SERR, with (a) homogeneous and (b) heterogeneous background elements. The amount of noise within the activation functions of the model is determined by a parameter termed the "temperature": the higher the temperature, the more noise there is. Search functions are shown here for when the target is either present or absent, when the temperature is either high (with relatively noisy activation functions) or low (with relatively noiseless activation functions). Increasing the temperature has a selective effect on search for targets against homogeneous backgrounds relative to those against heterogeneous backgrounds. Search efficiency in the model is measured in terms of the number of iterations required for the model to decide whether the target is present or absent.*

The performance of SERR under conditions of increased noise in its activation functions bears a striking resemblance to the pattern of HJA's performance with similar displays (in which targets and backgrounds differ in the way in which their component orientations combine). Like SERR under noisy activation conditions, HJA is selectively impaired when the background elements are homogeneous and he performs relatively well when the background elements are heterogeneous. This abnormal pattern of search performance across the different search tasks can emerge naturally from a model with raised noise levels in its activation functions. It is even possible to conceptualize that, in HJA's case, brain damage has had an equivalent effect of raising the internal noise within the system that normally groups simple pattern elements in the visual field.

Impaired Face Recognition (Prosopagnosia)

One valuable attribute of neuropsychological studies is that they can address questions concerning how processes interact. In a case such as that of HJA, several questions can be asked about the relations between his impaired object recognition and his ability to process faces. If face and object recognition were served by two quite separate processing systems, it should be possible for face recognition to be spared when object recognition is affected, and vice versa. That is, double dissociations should arise between patients with impaired face recognition and those with impaired object recognition.

Double dissociations between object and face recognition have indeed been reported. De Renzi (1986) reported a patient whose problems were only apparent with faces; McCarthy and Warrington (1986) reported a patient with problems in visual object recognition but not face recognition. Double dissociations such as this tell us that object and face recognition differ in some respects, so that each can be selectively impaired without affecting the other. Unfortunately, they do not tell us which processes are independent and which (if any) shared. To understand this, we need to study object and face processing in relation to one another. For instance, having isolated a particular deficit in object processing in a patient such as HJA, we need to go on to examine whether his face processing is affected at a similar processing stage. If it is, and if the processing of faces and objects is affected in qualitatively similar ways, the evidence would be consistent with the idea that the affected processing stage is common to both tasks.

We proposed above that HJA is impaired at an intermediate stage of visual processing so that he fails to group and segment objects appropriately. Nevertheless, his long-term memory for objects seems relatively preserved. Does the same hold for his face processing?

We examined HJA's memory for faces by asking him questions about facial characteristics of well-known people. For example, he might be asked to decide whether Joseph Stalin or Winston Churchill sported a moustache, whether Gerald Ford or Jimmy Carter was bald, whether Marilyn Monroe or

Sophia Loren had blonde hair. He did very well on this test, scoring at the same level as age-matched control subjects. Despite his apparently good memory for facial features, HJA is markedly prosopagnosic. When tested some ten years after his stroke, he still failed to identify a photograph of his wife. He is unable to name any famous faces we have tested him with, and performs at chance level on tests just requiring him to judge whether a face is familiar or not.

Other tests suggest that there is a perceptual locus to HJA's prosopagnosia. In one study we presented HJA with schematic drawings of faces, and he was required to match the internal features present in such faces (either the eyes, nose, or mouth) with a set of five possible features. HJA showed marked and abnormal effects of stimulus exposure on this discrimination task.

In another task, we presented two faces simultaneously, and HJA was required to judge whether the faces were identical or not. When different, faces had contrasting chins, eyes, and/or hairstyles. In addition, we used either line drawings of faces or photographs. HJA found it harder to match photographs than line drawings, though other prosopagnosics we have tested find photographs easier. That is, there are abnormal effects of photographic detail, as well as exposure duration, on HJA's ability to process faces.

These effects of photographic detail and of exposure duration are consistent with the proposed account of HJA's agnosia for objects: namely, impaired grouping and segmentation. Reduced exposure durations limit the time for grouping to operate, highlighting any deficit in this process (indeed, similar effects on HJA's object identification were reported by Riddoch and Humphreys, 1987a). Photographic details may provide extra cues to segment and parse faces into appropriate features for subsequent grouping and recognition (e.g. based on regions of the same contrast and the same surface orientation). Although these extra cues will often reinforce the features specified by changes in 2D edge intensities, this is unlikely always to be the case. For example, surface texture may specify extra contours which define faces as 3D surfaces rather than as 2D patterns (e.g. contours indicating the slope of a person's nose away from the line of sight; Pearson and Robinson, 1985; Pearson, 1986). Such 3D representations may be particularly important for face recognition (see chapter 5). Problems in grouping and segmentation will be exacerbated by the addition of photographic details that compete for grouping with 2D image features.

Our comparisons of object and face processing in HJA point to there being a common deficit affecting both tasks: impaired grouping and segmentation processes. It follows from this that intermediate visual processes concerned with the segmentation of objects into appropriate parts, and the grouping of those parts to form appropriate object descriptions, are fundamentally the same for objects and faces. To be sure, faces and objects will typically differ in many important ways, not least in the differential similarity between a given image and other images of the same general type (faces on the whole being very similar). Such differences undoubtedly place contrasting burdens on intermediate visual processing, and this may explain why HJA is somewhat worse at identifying faces than objects (failing to identify any faces, whilst many common objects are identified correctly). Nevertheless, we suggest that the nature of intermediate visual processing is fundamentally the same for faces and objects.

Some General Points

Selective brain lesions can impair visual perception in a number of different ways, and this chapter has been concerned with only one of what we believe are several different types of object recognition impairment (Humphreys and Riddoch, 1987b; Humphreys et al., 1992b). Selective impairments of depth, motion, and color processing also exist (e.g. Danta et al., 1978; Zihl et al., 1983; Heywood et al., 1987, respectively). Hence visual object processing can be fractionated into various selective components, one of which we suggest is concerned with the intermediate segmentation and grouping of local edge contours in images.

Cases such as HJA can provide striking insights into such normally hidden components, not least because his impairments stand in contrast to several islets of impressively spared abilities. For instance, in his case visual processing has been profoundly disturbed without impairments of intellect. The disturbance is also particular to processing visual forms, and leaves undisturbed many aspects of depth and motion perception. This supports a "modular" view of vision, at least in so far as the processing of independently specifiable image properties is concerned (e.g. depth and motion being separated from the processing of form).

There are also some correlated deficits. We have pointed to some of the correlations between HJA's processing of objects and that of faces. If our interpretation of such correlated deficits is correct, then the modularity of vision may not extend to there being independent early and intermediate processing of objects and faces. Thus such cases can help pinpoint the boundaries of modular organization in vision.

We have also argued that some of the inherent problems of neuropsychological research of this type can be reduced by relating the pattern of impairments to fully specified computational models of human performance. If the research carries any theoretical validity, investigators must generalize from single cases to whole populations, and from pathological cases to normality. Some researchers have argued that such generalizations do not present any theoretical problems because cognitive processes are universally organized in the same way, and because cognitive deficits reflect reduced as opposed to altered cognitive systems (Caramazza and McCloskey, 1988). In vision, the argument for there being a universal processing structure can perhaps be pushed further than in many other cognitive domains, since many early and intermediate visual processes are likely to be innate (e.g. Kellman, 1984; Slater and Morrison, 1985). However, even if this argument is not taken up, we suggest that confidence can be gained in generalizations from single cases of pathology to normal populations, if the pathological pattern of performance emerges naturally out of a processing model when "damaged." To the extent that the same model, in its undamaged state, accurately simulates normal performance, we can achieve a two-way mapping: from human pathology to normality, and from simulated normality to pathology. In HJA's case, we are able to simulate his pattern of performance in some visual search tasks by increasing the noise in the activation functions within the SERR model of visual search: a model in which search is determined by the perceptual grouping of background elements. This concurs with our argument that HJA's perceptual grouping is impaired.

There remain at least some difficulties that are linked to this form of research. One concerns our interpretation of associated patterns of impairments. We have pointed out that *dissociations* can indicate functional independence between components of the perceptual system. Our arguments about the relations between face and object processing, however, are based on a pattern of *associated* deficits. Such arguments are necessarily weak, since they can be refuted by even a single patient who does not show the proposed association. For instance, our argument for common intermediate visual processes in face and object recognition would be refuted if a patient could be found with: (a) impairments to segmentation and grouping procedures in object recognition that are at least as severe as the impairments found in HJA, and (b) intact face recognition.

Nevertheless, though they are weak, we believe inferences concerning common processing stages can be accurate, providing they are based on tests that selectively tap the common stages. Some confidence can also be derived if the associations are predicted by existing computational models. Finally, because such inferences depend on an accurate specification of the processing stages in common, and because they are clearly testable, they can also guide empirical research.

In conclusion, the "breakdown approach" to visual perception, exemplified by neuropsychological studies of selective perceptual disorders, has, like all approaches to visual perception, strengths and weaknesses. Its virtues concern its ability to reveal unexpected patterns of deficit and of spared islets of performance, its ability to reveal something of the interactions between processing modules and of the stages in common in the processing of different stimuli, and in the fact that neuropsychological studies can be related to explicit computational models of performance. For valid theoretical inferences to be made, it is vital that there is converging interdisciplinary work among studies of normal perceptual performance, cognitive modeling, and neuropsychological studies of vision.

Acknowledgments

The work reported in this chapter was supported by grants from the Medical Research Council and the Wolfson Foundation of Great Britain to GWH and MJR, by a grant from the Fondation Fyssen to MB, and from a European grant from the Ministre de la Recherche et de la Technologie, France, to GWH and MB.

Note

1 For example, a very different account of the Müller–Lyer illusion to the one offered above is as follows. Suppose that, when judging line length, observers pool information together from local areas. The outward-pointing fins, when pooled with the central bar, will create a longer line than will the pooled inward-pointing fins and bar; see Robinson (1972).

7

Mechanisms which Mediate Discrimination of 2D Spatial Patterns in Distributed Images

KEITH H. RUDDOCK

The visual recognition of objects and scenes rests upon their representation in the light evoked activity of the visual pathways. Specification of a complex scene in terms of its physical attributes, such as the spatial and spectral distributions of its component objects, requires a very large data set and it seems likely that visual processing involves the construction of a simplified representation or description of the physical image. The representation of spectral information in terms of three independent variables is well understood, and has been extensively exploited in the various technologies of color reproduction (Wright, 1946, 1964). An equivalent understanding has not, however, been achieved in the case of visual processing of spatial patterns, despite intensive study involving a variety of experimental and analytical techniques.

Color vision is trivariant because there are just three spectral classes of cone photoreceptor, and the spatial characteristics of neuronal responses should, correspondingly, provide some indication of the strategy employed by the visual system in the processing of spatial patterns. Electrophysiological studies in cat and primate have established that single neurones in the visual pathways have well-defined spatial responses (receptive fields), the majority of which fall into one of two classes. Most neurones of the peripheral pathways, such as retinal ganglion cells, have radially symmetrical receptive fields, which are center-surround antagonistic (Kuffler, 1953) and may be either excited ("on-center") or inhibited ("off-center") by light stimulation of the receptive field center (figure 7.1a). In contrast, many neurones of the striate and pre-striate cortex have elongated receptive fields and are stimulated selectively by bars or edges of a given orientation (Hubel and Wiesel, 1962, 1968). The on-center/off-center dichotomy is observed in the responses of bar-sensitive simple cells, as is illustrated in figure 7.1b. Receptive fields

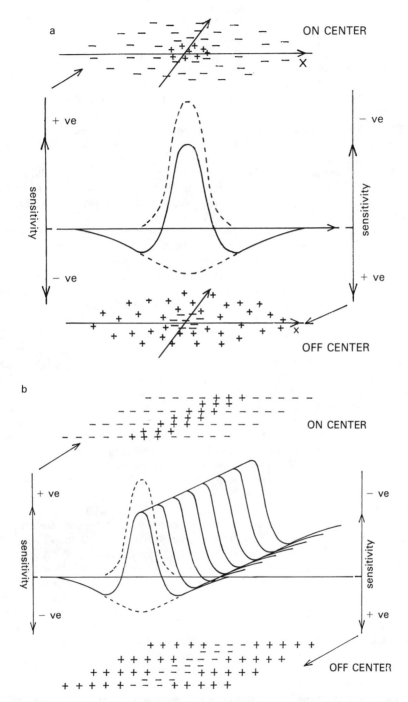

Figure 7.1 *a, Receptive field organization of concentrically organized ganglion cells, which are on-center (positive response centrally) or off-center (negative response centrally). The receptive field distribution of sensitivity can be derived from a combination of two Gaussian distributions, which is illustrated for a single radial direction, x. b, As (a) but for orientation–selective neurones of the striate cortex.*

of the kind shown in figure 7.1 can be represented mathematically by a combination of two Gaussian distributions of opposite sign, i.e. a difference of Gaussians or DOG function, varying in two dimensions for radially symmetrical fields (Rodieck, 1965; figure 7.1a) or in one dimension for orientation-sensitive fields (Hawken and Parker, 1987; figure 7.1b). Psychophysical experiments on human subjects have provided independent evidence for the activity of both classes of spatial response mechanisms, those with radially symmetrical, center-surround antagonistic organization being described by Wilson and Bergen (1979), Barbur and Ruddock (1980), and Holliday and Ruddock (1983), and those with orientation-sensitive response characteristics by Gilinsky (1968), Pantle and Sekuler (1968), and Blakemore and Campbell (1969).

Many analyses of spatial vision have employed filters with spatial properties similar to those discussed above, although for computational purposes a Laplacian of a Gaussian function ($\nabla^2 G$) is frequently employed instead of a DOG function. In most studies, the visual response is obtained by convolution of the retinal image with a set of $\nabla^2 G$ filters, and the resulting convolution signals are characterized by a restricted set of parameters (e.g. Marr, 1980; Marr and Hildreth, 1980; Watt and Morgan, 1985; Voorhees and Poggio, 1988). The various authors select different parameters with which the visual response is specified, but none has succeeded in obtaining significant generalization of spatial vision equivalent to that provided by the trichromatic representation of spectral information for color vision.

A quite different approach to the problem of spatial vision rests upon the construction of symbolic descriptions of an image in terms of both discrete and continuous parameters (see review by Foster, 1984). These encode parameters such as local features (e.g. the curvature of line elements), spatial relations (e.g. "to the left of"), and global features (e.g. pattern orientation and symmetry), thereby forming an internal representation of the image. It is proposed that internal representations are compared by internal operations governed by well-defined rules. Experimental studies, based on the ability to discriminate between briefly presented stimuli, have led, for example, to the identification of internal representations based on broad categories such as the collinearity and non-collinearity of points (Foster, 1980) and the degree of line curvature, categorized as "straight," "just curved," and "more than just curved" (Foster, 1983). It is apparent that representation of a complex image in such terms will result in a very extensive list of descriptions.

Experiments designed to derive simpler representations of spatial patterns, based on fewer features, have explored visual discriminations between images presented transiently, for durations too brief to permit exploration of the visual field by scanning eye movements. Julesz and his colleagues have provided a theoretical basis for the construction of multi-element texture fields and have proposed that their discrimination, in this so-called preattentive mode of vision, utilizes certain primitive features, or textons, such as the orientation and termination of line elements (Caelli and Julesz, 1978; Julesz, 1980, 1981; Bergen and Julesz, 1983). An alternative analysis of such experiments based on the output of $\nabla^2 G$ filters has been proposed by Bergen and Adelson (1988) and Voorhees and Poggio (1988).

The study to be presented in this chapter employs multi-element stimuli, but examines visual detection of a single target element, rather than of texture differences involving multiple elements. Early experiments employing a similar experimental design were concerned with the division of attention between foveal and peripheral vision (e.g. Engel, 1971, 1974; Ikeda and Takeuchi, 1975), but subsequent studies (e.g. Treisman, 1983, 1988) have analyzed the parametric conditions under which the visual system can detect a target, without scanning of the visual field (the so-called "pop-out" condition). In this chapter, I review the results of experiments in which my colleagues and I have attempted to establish the parametric limits at which a target can no longer be detected without scanning of the field (see also Treisman and Gormican, 1988). As is customary in such studies, we distinguish between target detection achieved by parallel processing, in which search time for detection of the target is independent of the number of background (or distractor) elements, and detection by serial processing which requires scanning of the field, characterized by search times which increase as the number of background elements increases (though see Duncan and Humphreys, 1989, for an interpretation which does not rely on serial and parallel modes of function). We have found that with a field of identical background elements, a target distinguished by magnification or orientation can be detected by parallel processing except for very small differences between its spatial parameters and those of the background elements (Javadnia and Ruddock, 1988a). If the reference field consists of two classes of background element, however, target detection usually requires serial processing (Alkhateeb et al., 1990b). The introduction of two classes of background element has enabled us to examine the response characteristics of those visual mechanisms which mediate detection of the different target parameters, such as color, orientation, and magnification (Alkhateeb et al., 1990a). I propose that the results of such experiments provide a basis for the simplification of complex spatial stimuli into a restricted set of images, characterized by discrete parametric values. I argue further that groups of physically non-identical images which can be reduced to the same member of this set provide equivalent information for the planning of voluntary saccadic eye movements.

Methods

The experiments were performed with a computer-generated visual display, consisting of a selected number of spatial patterns, or elements. The elements were in the form of simple geometrical patterns such as lines, equilateral triangles, and squares, which were distributed randomly over the screen (the field size of the screen was 8.6×6.3 degrees, elements were side length 0.45 degrees). In the first set of experiments, a single target differed from the other identical elements in a single feature, such as orientation or magnification. The target was drawn from one of four elements, three of which differed from the background elements by a different value of the parameter under investigation e.g. orientation, whilst the fourth was identical with the background elements and acted as a null target (see figure 7.2a). Subjects simply made a manual response according to whether a target was present or absent. The display was cleared as soon as a response was made and replaced by a new random array. The response for a given target is characterized by $\tau_{1/2}$, the time required to achieve detection of the target on 50 percent of the presentations. Values of $\tau_{1/2}$ include the dead time required for the pressing of the button, equal to about 200 ms (Ike et al., 1987).

In the later experiments, the background contained two classes of element, presented in equal numbers. For example, in the measurement of orientation discrimination, the two classes of background element differed in orientation, and the targets differed in orientation from each of the two classes, with the null target matched to one or other (see figure 7.2b).

$\tau_{1/2}$ was measured as a function of N, the number of background elements. As discussed at the beginning of the chapter, two kinds of response are distinguished; in one, $\tau_{1/2}$ is independent of N, which implies that no visual scanning of the elements is required for target detection; while in the other, $\tau_{1/2}$ increases significantly as N increases, implying that scanning of the elements is required for detection of the target. These two response patterns are designated "parallel" and "serial" respectively (Javadnia and Ruddock, 1988a).

Observers

Data are given for a number of normal, young observers. In the Discussion section below, reference is made to data obtained for a single subject, HJA, who suffered visual form agnosia, including prosopagnosia. His condition is associated with bilateral lesions of the pre-striate cortex, and has been described at length by Humphreys and Riddoch (1984, 1987a) (see also chapter 6).

Results

The data presented are illustrative of more extensive measurements reported by Javadnia and Ruddock (1988a,b) and by Alkhateeb et al. (1990a,b).

Discrimination of Target Orientation or Magnification with simple background fields (figure 7.3). Plots of $\tau_{1/2}$ against N, the number of background elements, show that both orientation and magnification can be discriminated by parallel processing, with $\tau_{1/2}$ essentially independent of N (figure 7.3b, c, d). Under limiting conditions, however, discrimination becomes serial. For

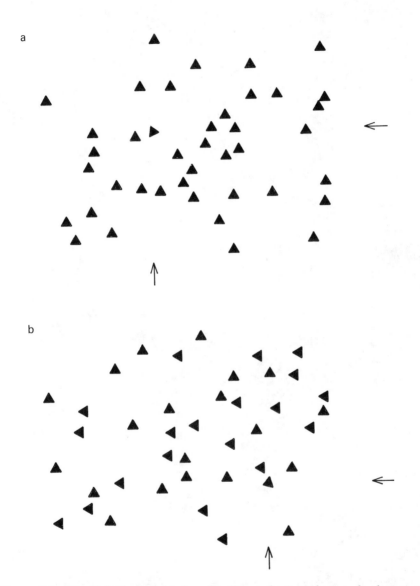

Figure 7.2 *Visual fields of the kind used in this study. In each example, the target is distinguished by its orientation, and its location is denoted by two arrows. a, A simple background field, consisting of triangles pointing upwards. b, A complex background field, consisting of triangles pointing upwards and oriented at 30 degrees relative to the upright triangles.*

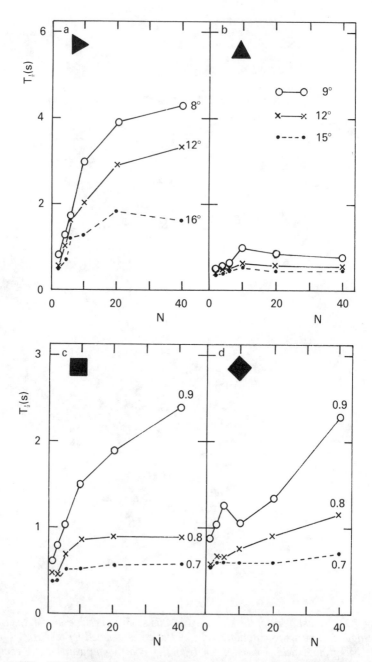

Figure 7.3 *Discrimination data for simple reference fields. a and b, Orientation discrimination. The background elements were oriented as indicated in the inset, and the targets were oriented relative to the background elements at the angle indicated with the data. c and d, Magnification discrimination. The background elements, of relative linear magnification 1.0, were oriented as indicated, and the relative linear magnification of the target elements is indicated with the data.*

orientation, this occurs with targets orientated 5° to 8° for reference elements oriented upright (figure 7.3b) but at significantly larger target orientations for reference elements of other orientations (figure 7.3a). For magnification, the limit for parallel processing occurs when the target magnification differs from that of the background elements by between 20 and 30 percent (figure 7.3c, d). There is an important difference between discrimination of orientation and that of magnification. In the former case, values of $\tau_{1/2}$ are markedly dependent on the orientation of the background elements. In contrast, discrimination of magnification differences is independent of the orientation of the background elements. This was first noted by Ike et al. (1987), who discussed possible reasons for the effect, without finding any persuasive explanation.

It should be noted that for certain combinations of target and background elements, e.g. background ▲ and target ▼, orientation discrimination is based on the change in symmetry of the whole element, rather than on differences in orientation of the edges. Javadnia and Ruddock (1988a) have shown that certain changes in symmetry can be detected by parallel processing, as in the case for the example cited above.

Discrimination of Target Orientation or Magnification with complex background fields. The experiments with simple background fields examine spatial discriminations under the simplest conditions, in which the background elements are identical. In real images, however, objects have to be differentiated from a complex background which contains a range of object magnifications and orientations. Use of complex fields, with two classes of element (figure 7.2b), simulates more closely natural viewing conditions. In such circumstances, discrimination of neither orientation nor magnification is achieved by parallel processing, except when the orientation or magnification of the target is clearly outside the range encompassed by the two classes of background element (figures 7.4 and 7.5) (Alkhateeb et al., 1990b).

Parallel processing is not observed even when measurements with either class of background element individually yield parallel processing, as is demonstrated by the data of figures 7.4 and 7.5. Thus, the visual mechanisms which mediate these spatial discriminations must be sensitive to both parametric values present in the background. In the case of line elements, it was possible to determine the range of orientations over which interference occurs between the classes of reference element. When the two classes are orthogonal, there is no interference with discrimination of target orientation, and parallel processing occurs. When the two classes have 60 degrees relative orientation, there is weak interaction for some observers, leading to a small increase of $\tau_{1/2}$ with N, but when the relative orientation is reduced to 40 degrees, there is strong interaction leading to serial processing. Thus, the mechanisms which mediate discrimination of line orientation must have a sensitivity range of some ± 20–30 degrees, approximately that found by the psychophysical adaptation experiments and the electrophysiological studies on orientation discrimination mechanisms (see above). This value is much

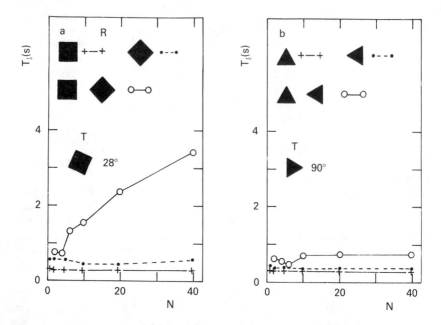

Figure 7.4   *Orientation discrimination data for complex background fields. The background elements (R) are indicated in the figure and the target (T) orientation angle is also defined.*

greater than the discrimination limit of some ± 5 degrees obtained with a simple background and the presence of two classes of background element, with different orientations, therefore impairs performance of orientation discrimination. Foster and Ward (1991) have proposed that early processing of lines is dominated by just two classes of orientation-sensitive filter, one tuned to vertical and one to horizontal lines, each with a tuning half-width of 30 degrees. Visual judgment of line orientation is also influenced by the presence of lines which differ in orientation from each other, and such effects are usually attributed to inhibitory interactions between channels tuned to respond maximally to the orientations of the different stimulus lines (Blakemore et al., 1970; Thomas and Shimamura, 1975). Such inhibitory interactions may contribute to the effects reported here.

Effect of Orientation Differences on Discrimination of Magnification.   In the experiments described previously, magnification and orientation have been treated as separate variables. The question is now asked, are the mechanisms which mediate discrimination of magnification sensitive to the orientation of the elements? The background contained two classes of element, which differed in both orientation and magnification, while the target elements had

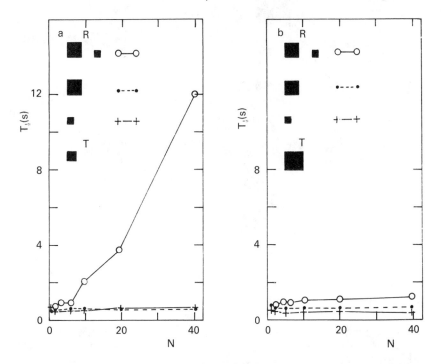

Figure 7.5 *Magnification discrimination data for complex background fields. a, The linear magnifications of the background elements (R) were 0.72 and 0.35, and of the target (T), 0.5. b, The linear magnifications of the background elements (R) were 0.72 and 0.35, and of the target (T), 1.0.*

the same orientation as one class of background element, and differed from both in magnification (see inset, figure 7.6a). The data of figure 7.6a demonstrate that rotation of one of the two classes of background element has little effect on $\tau_{1/2}$ values, and the data of figure 6b show more precisely that as the orientation changes, there is little variation in $\tau_{1/2}$. It is concluded that mechanisms for magnification discrimination are not significantly sensitive to the orientation of the elements.

Effect of Magnification Differences on Discrimination of Orientation. Given that magnification discrimination is independent of background orientation, we now ask whether orientation discrimination is independent of background magnification. The background again contained two classes of element, which differed in both orientation and magnification, with the target elements matched in magnification to one class of background element, and different from both in orientation (see inset, figure 7.7a). Both sets of data presented in figure 7.7 show that change in magnification of one of the two classes of

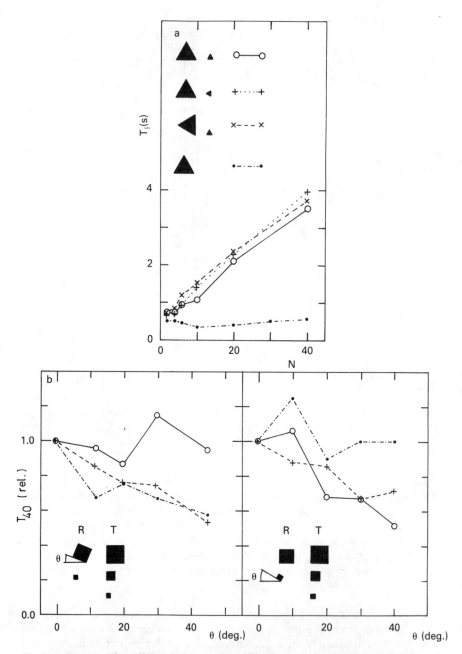

Figure 7.6 *a, The effect of orientation differences on discrimination of target magnification. The inset shows the background elements, which were of linear magnification 0.8 and 0.33, and the target was of linear magnification 1.0. The orientations of the background elements are indicated on the figure, and the target was oriented upright. b, τ_{40}, relative values of the response time ($\tau_{1/2}$), measured for 40 background elements, plotted against Θ, the angle at which one of the two classes of background element was oriented (see inset). The background elements, R, were of relative size 0.8 and 0.33, and the three targets, T, were of relative size 1.0, 0.5, and 0.25, oriented upright.*

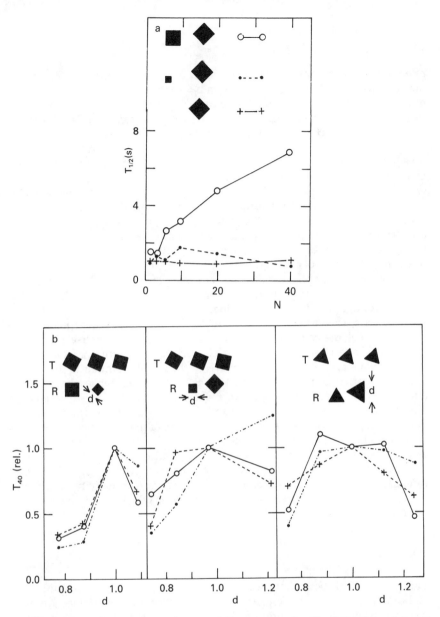

Figure 7.7 *a, Effect of magnification differences on the discrimination of target orientation. The background elements were of relative linear magnification 0.8 and 0.33, and the target of relative linear magnification 0.8, rotated clockwise through 28 degrees relative to the upright. The orientation of the background elements is indicated in the figure. b, τ_{40}, values of the response time $\tau_{1/2}$ measured for 40 background elements, plotted against the linear size, d, of one of the two classes of background element. The square background elements were of relative orientation 0 degrees and 45 degrees, and one class was of fixed linear magnification 0.8. The square target elements, T, were rotated clockwise through 8 degrees, 16 degrees, and 28 degrees relative to the upright orientation, and were of linear magnification 0.8. The triangular background elements, R, were of relative orientations 0 degrees and 30 degrees, and one class was of fixed magnification 0.8; the triangular elements were rotated clockwise through 7 degrees, 10 degrees, and 17 degrees relative to the upright position, and were of linear magnification 0.8.*

reference element leads to a reduction in $\tau_{1/2}$ values, and those of figure 7.7b indicate that there is quite a sharp fall in $\tau_{1/2}$ as the magnification of one class of reference element is changed systematically from that of the other. This result implies that the mechanisms which mediate discrimination of orientation *are* sensitive to change in the magnification of the elements.

Sensitivity to Contrast Polarity and Color Differences.   The methods described above have also been applied in the investigation of target detection, with two classes of background element which differ not only in orientation or magnification, but also in contrast polarity or color. For example, the two classes of background element illustrated in figure 7.4, which differ from each other in orientation, were presented against a uniform display field, and the contrast of one class was reversed relative to that of the other, and of the target. The experimental data (Alkhateeb et al., 1990a) reveal that the responses are effectively parallel (i.e. $\tau_{1/2}$ independent of N), in contrast to the serial responses ($\tau_{1/2}$ dependent on N) observed in figure 7.4, and a similar result is found for discrimination of magnification. The detection processes are, therefore, selective in their response to contrast polarity, responding to elements of one polarity and not to those of reverse polarity. If the color of one class of background element (e.g. red) differs from that of the other class and of the target (e.g. green) the result is similar to that found with reversal of contrast polarity, that is, the red reference elements are effectively ignored. Similar data were obtained for either a red–green or a blue–yellow combination of background elements, presented either on a dark field or at equiluminance (i.e. with the brightness of the field and the elements equated; Alkhateeb et al., 1990a). It was concluded that the detection processes are selective in their response to color, and effectively discount those background elements which are not matched in color to the target. In further recent experiments we have established the range of chromaticity coordinates for the different colors, such as red or green, over which response selectivity occurs.

Discussion

This paper pdeals essentially with the detection of changes in magnification and orientation in multi-element visual fields. These two variables are basic parameters in the description of 2D spatial images, and understanding of their processing by the visual pathways is an essential step in the analysis of pattern recognition. The data illustrated in figure 7.3 demonstrate that with a set of identical background elements, detection of changes in these variables is achieved by parallel processing, except when the target differs from the background by relatively small amounts (less than 5–10 degrees in orientation, and by less than 20–30 percent in linear dimension). The data also illustrate an asymmetry in detection of orientation, which is more finely tuned for some orientations than for others (e.g. for upward pointing as compared to sideward pointing background triangles, figure 7.3; see also Ike et al., 1987). Visual search asymmetries in the detection of line orientation have been reported previously by Treisman and Souther (1985) and Treisman and Gormican (1988).

Detection of a target against a set of identical background elements is an artificial task, because natural scenes contain elements which vary in scale and orientation, from which objects of interest must be identified. Nonetheless, man-made environments do sometimes exhibit great uniformity in the size and orientation of their sub-structures, e.g. tiled surfaces, and the data of figure 7.3 demonstrate how sensitive the visual system is in detecting irregularity in such structures. It is, however, the experiments with two classes of background element which correspond more closely to normal stimulus conditions.

The experimental results for such fields (Alkhateeb et al., 1990a) are exemplified by the data of figures 7.4 and 7.5, and demonstrate that target detection requires serial processing, the only exceptions occurring when the orientation or magnification of the target lies outside the range of values covered by the two classes of background element. It is important to note that serial processing occurs even when target detection is achieved by parallel processing for either class of background element alone. This implies that the sensitivities of the detection mechanisms extend over a much broader range of orientations and magnifications than is implied by the data obtained with identical background elements. The visual system, therefore, has very restricted capacity for parallel processing when analysing a complex image, the elements of which are distinguished only by their spatial distributions. As discussed in the Results section, orientation discrimination for line elements is serial when the two classes of background element are at 40 degrees relative orientation, and square elements orientated at 45 degrees to each other prevent parallel processing of target orientation (figure 7.4a). Thus targets which differ significantly in their orientations (or magnifications) relative to the background are treated as equivalent by the mechanisms which mediate parallel processing of multi-element stimuli; that is, under these particular conditions, sets of physically different stimuli are visually equivalent. In principle, a similar approach could be undertaken for real images composed of continuous rather than discrete components, but the requirement that the images remain continuous with changes in orientation and magnification of their components complicates the analysis. We are currently attempting to implement an experimental study, similar to that described here, but employing continuous rather than multi-element patterns.

The experiments in which the two classes of reference element differ in two parameters, such as color and orientation, establish a hierarchy of discriminations. For example, Alkhateeb et al.'s (1990a) finding that background elements which differ in color from the target are effectively ignored implies that discrimination of orientation or magnification is performed

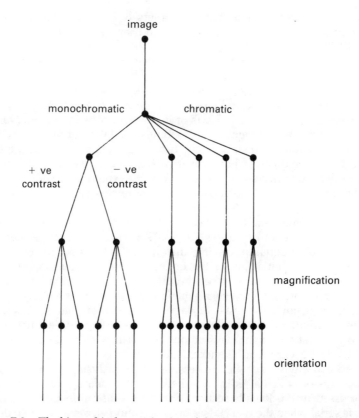

image

monochromatic   chromatic

+ ve
contrast

− ve
contrast

magnification

orientation

Figure 7.8   *The hierarchical organization of the discrimination processes examined in this chapter. The image is processed along parallel pathways which deal with monochrome or colored images, and the former subdivides into two pathways, which deal with the image components of positive and negative contrast polarity. Subsequent subdivisions indicate the activity of multiple channels for magnification and orientation discriminations. Weak interactions, e.g. between channels for different colors or different contrast polarities, are not indicated in the scheme.*

separately for differently colored elements. Similarly, for monochromatic images, elements with reversed contrast are neglected (Alkhateeb et al., 1990a), thus detection proceeds separately for the two contrast polarities. The experiments in which both magnification and orientation of the background elements were varied establish that discrimination of differences in magnification are relatively insensitive to the orientation of the elements (figures 7.6 and 7.7). This implies that magnification discrimination occurs prior to orientation discrimination, and, as would be expected from this sequential arrangement, orientation discrimination is strongly influenced by the magnification of elements (figure 7.7). A schematic representation of the hierarchical organization of the visual discriminations, derived from the data discussed here, is given in figure 7.8.

What visual function is served by the parallel processing mechanisms, the response characteristics of which have been examined in this study? I propose that they provide sensory control of saccadic eye movements, with which objects of interest are fixated for closer examination. In performing the experiments, observers noted that under conditions which permitted parallel processing, they automatically fixated the target after detection, and not until fixation was achieved could they identify the target. Ability to saccade to the target occurs, therefore, without detailed recognition, although some discrimination of features such as orientation, magnification, and color must be made, in order to perform the saccade. It is instructive at this point to consider residual vision in those patients with cortical lesions, who retain the capacity to locate by eye-movements, or otherwise, transient stimuli presented within "blind" areas of the visual field. These patients can be subdivided into two groups, those who report a sensation associated with the stimulus, and those who do not, thereby exhibiting "blindsight" (Weiskrantz et al., 1974). Some patients are able to discriminate between stimuli on the basis of differences in spectral or spatial parameters (e.g. Weiskrantz et al., 1974; Weiskrantz, 1986; Stoerig and Cowey, 1989), but others retain only the ability to distinguish the location and state of movement of the stimulus (e.g. Perenin and Jeannerod, 1975, 1978; Barbur et al., 1980). None however, displays the full range of sensory discriminations achieved with normal vision (Ruddock, 1991) and none appears capable of performing detection tasks of the kind described in this chapter, although no direct experiments have been reported. Residual function in such patients is usually attributed to activity in those retinal pathways which project via the superior colliculus, and I conclude, therefore, that the detection mechanisms studied in this chapter involve the striate projection pathways. Some features of the experimental data, such as the angular range of interaction for detection of line orientation and selectivity for contrast polarity, are consistent with the responses of single striate neurones (Hubel and Wiesel, 1962, 1968).

In this chapter, I have proposed a method for partitioning spatial patterns in groups which provide equivalent information for the generation of foveating eye movements. We have also had opportunity to test an agnosic patient, HJA, who has marked problems in identifying visual patterns. His data, illustrated in figure 7.9 (see also Bromley et al., 1986), suggest that an inability to perform parallel processing of spatial patterns may be a factor in the loss of pattern recognition in visual agnosia. Such a conclusion is consistent with a number of reports that agnosic patients are able to identify single rather than multiple objects, and are able to recognize local features of the visual image, without being capable of integrating local features in order to interpret the whole image (Godwin-Austen, 1965; Levine, 1978; Wapner et al., 1978; Karpov et al., 1979; Gomori and Hawryluk, 1984; Humphreys and Riddoch, 1984, 1987a; Larrabee et al., 1985).

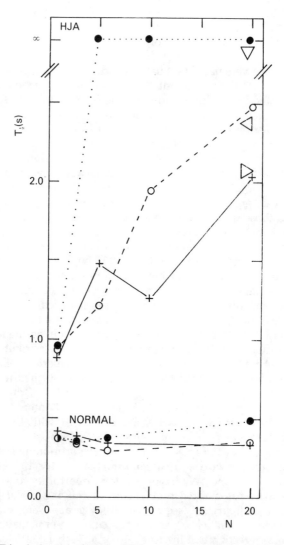

Figure 7.9 *Discrimination data for HJA, a patient suffering visual form agnosia. The response time, $\tau_{1/2}$, is plotted against N, the number of background elements. The background elements were oriented in an upright position, Δ, and comparison data are given for a normal subject. $\tau_{1/2}$ equal to ∞ denotes that HJA failed to detect the target on 50 percent of presentations.*

8

The Analysis of 3D Shape: Psychophysical Principles and Neural Mechanisms

ANDREW J. PARKER, CHRIS CHRISTOU,
BRUCE G. CUMMING, ELIZABETH B. JOHNSTON,
MICHAEL J. HAWKEN, AND ANDREW ZISSERMAN

Perhaps the most profound and lasting influence of the present exchange of ideas between the study of computer vision and of biological visual systems may be through descriptions of the natural environment. One of the main goals of work in computer vision has been to provide an accurate and faithful description of the physical processes by which the interaction of light and objects gives rise to images. From the viewpoint of artificial intelligence, such descriptions could then be used to equip the artificial system with knowledge about the environment in which it will have to operate – taking the term "knowledge" to have its widest possible scope. From the point of view of biological systems, accurate descriptions of the natural world would constitute a specification for the optimal functional form that an organism's visual system should acquire, either as a consequence of Darwinian evolutionary forces or through learning over the lifetime of the individual organism.

Descriptions of image formation in the natural world, however accurate or sophisticated, do not lead inevitably to a unique specification of an optimal procedure for extracting information from images. The diversity of proposals for computational schemes in machine vision, as well as the richness and variability of the organization of biological visual systems, are practical evidence of this. Moreover, in the case of biological systems, it is not obvious that the system has to be optimized in an absolute sense. All that is required is for one gene type, or alternatively a learning strategy, to lead to a phenotypic selective advantage over a competitor.

Representations

What kinds of internal representation are used by the nervous system to store and manipulate information about the shape of objects? It is reasonable to conjecture that one of the goals of vision is to acquire knowledge of the 3D shape of objects and their spatial relationships within the 3D scene. The image projected by the eye's optics on to the retina is inadequate and unsuited to this task, unless some further process of interpretation is carried out. The nature of a representation for carrying out this task must be constrained in two ways. First, there are constraints that arise from the nature of the information sources that signal 3D shape to the human visual system. Classically, these information sources are termed *cues* in perceptual psychology. Secondly, there are constraints on the representation that arise from the needs that it is required to fulfill. The needs might be simple to state, such as knowing the absolute distance to an obstruction in the 3D visual scene. But there are also more complex forms of knowledge about 3D structure, such as understanding how the surface features will move relative to one another as an object rotates dynamically in the field of view.

Generally, recent computational studies have examined the utility of two types of representation for 3D shape. One is a surface-based description of 3D objects. This arises naturally from processing various cues to depth (see below). The surface-based representation is basically a description of the depths or distances to the array of objects within the scene as measured from a particular vantage point. This representation does not explicitly incorporate knowledge about what will be seen from a different vantage point. By contrast, a volumetric representation does incorporate this knowledge. Here the 3D shape or objects in the scene are considered in a fully 3-dimensional form. Even though the representation could be quite simplistic, such as attempting to represent all solid bodies as being constructed of generalized cylinders (basically cylinders and cones, possibly with smooth bends in them), it is still completely 3D. The visual system could infer how the scene will look from another vantage point based on the representation alone.

Cues to Depth

How could a visual system recover information about the third spatial dimension of depth? This is often felt to have some special status compared with the other two spatial dimensions because height and breadth seem to correspond naturally with the projection of the scene onto the 2D retinal image. In reality, this is naïve, for even the interpretation of something as apparently simple as a silhouette leads to a number of complex problems in 3D projective geometry (Marr, 1982; Koenderink, 1984). In a natural scene, there are always several potential sources of information about the depth dimension. These sources of information rarely lead directly to a measure of depth or 3D shape. Typically, the information needs to be processed in some way, taking account of conflicting or consistent information from other sources.

Generally speaking, psychophysical experiments have often been concerned to isolate just one source of information in order to study it in detail. Probably, the most well-known example of this is the cue of binocular stereopsis, which exploits the fact that the left and right eyes obtain slightly different views of the world owing to their lateral separation in the head (Wheatstone, 1838, 1852). If the visual system can match up the features of the left and right eye's images so that the correspondence between these two views can be discovered, then the relative depths of objects can be recovered, essentially by triangulation of the sort done in land-surveying. The study of stereo depth in isolation from other cues was greatly facilitated by the construction of the random dot stereogram (Julesz, 1971; see below figure 8.2b). Other cues also lead readily to the perception of depth. A collection of moving points on a video display screen can convey a vivid percept of depth, if their 2D motion gives rise to images on the retina similar to those arising from the motion of a solid 3D shape. The value of shading and texture cues in conveying depth is, of course, often exploited by artists.

What these cues have in common is that they arise naturally from inspecting opaque objects, where the range of surface markings and properties typically causes one or more of these cues to be available at nearly every point across the surface of the object. For this reason, Marr (1982) classed these various cues together as *dense depth cues*. The idea is that some form of common representation of this information from different sources might be one of the useful intermediate stages in visual processing. Much of the interest in this arises from Marr and Nishihara's description of the $2\frac{1}{2}$D sketch as a possible intermediate processing stage, incorporating a surface-based description in viewer-centered coordinates (Marr and Nishihara, 1978). This was intended to provide a description of depth relationships in the visual world as seen from a particular vantage point. The sources of information that can feed this description are the well-known list of "depth cues": stereo, motion parallax, shading, texture gradients, etc. The point is that each of these cues can be thought of as providing some information about the local behavior of a small surface patch on the object. Exactly the same point was made about human stereo vision by Koenderink and van Doorn (1976a).

It was also argued that this intermediate representation might cater for a process whereby missing information could be filled in. To take a specific example, the random dot stereogram in figure 8.2b below still gives a powerful percept of a continuous cylindrical surface, even when the density of dots is very low. Marr (1982) attributed this to a specific process of *interpolation*, in which the gaps between individual items of information are filled in. This is generally done on the basis that the surface is expected to be smooth (Grimson, 1982; but see also Blake and Zisserman, 1987). However, there are important cues for 3D shape that are extremely sparse by their very nature. Examples are outline contour from a line drawing or cues that arise when one object occludes another.

Geometry

The accumulation of evidence from surface patches or features over the visible aspect of the object can provide extremely useful information about the overall (global) shape of the object (Koenderink and van Doorn, 1980; Brady et al., 1985; Besl and Jain, 1986). At a purely mathematical level, the importance of 3D geometry for the description of shape is readily apparent. For solid 3D objects, one mathematical description that has been of considerable value in computational vision is by means of the differential geometry of surfaces. (A helpful and pragmatic introduction to this topic is given in Faux and Pratt, 1979, while an intuitive, yet authoritative, account is given in Hilbert and Cohn-Vossen, 1932). The particular value of differential geometry is the way in which it specifies the relationships between local surface geometry and global 3D descriptions of solid objects. In order to see how this might work in practice, it is necessary to introduce in an informal way some mathematical descriptions of the behavior of surface patches. The simplest invariant properties for shape specification are linked to properties of curves and surfaces that are described mathematically by second-order derivative characteristics.

The tangent plane at a point on the surface can be characterized as the plane formed by a pair of (non-parallel) tangent lines to curves forming the surface at the point of interest (see figure 8.1a). The slope and attitude of the tangent plane summarize the gradient behavior of the surface (a first-order derivative characteristic). Consider then any plane normal to the tangent plane. Such a plane meets the surface in a curved line, and the curvature of this line is the local curvature of the surface in a particular direction (see figure 8.1a). It is a remarkable geometrical fact that, for each point on the surface (provided it is smooth and differentiable), these curvatures have just one maximum and one minimum value – or are identical in all directions, as in a portion of a sphere or a flat plane. The maximum and minimum values are termed the principal values of curvature and the directions of the surface normal where the curvature is maximum or minimum are the principal axes of curvature. The significance of these principal curvatures is that they summarize the local shape behavior of the surface (Hilbert and Cohn-Vossen, 1932; Besl and Jain, 1986).

For local shape behavior, one of the most important parameters, which is derived by taking the product of the principal curvatures, is the Gaussian curvature. The Gaussian curvature is positive if both principal curvatures have the same sign, which means that the surface is wholly convex or wholly concave. In other words, like the surface in figure 8.1a, a surface of positive Gaussian curvature would be only on one side of the tangent plane. When the Gaussian curvature is negative, the surface is locally saddle-shaped and actually cuts through the tangent plane. When the Gaussian curvature is zero, this means that the principal curvature is zero in at least one direction and so the surface region is locally cylindrical – or planar, if both principal curvatures are zero.

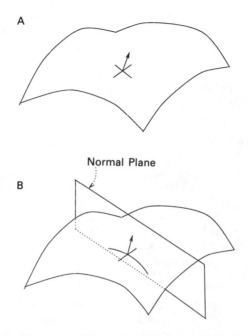

Figure 8.1 *a, A tangent plane to a surface at a point. The arms of the cross lie in the tangent plane and the arrow indicates the direction of the surface normal. b, The measurement of curvature in a particular direction at the same point on the surface. A normal plane passing through the surface normal is selected and the curve in which the original surface meets the normal plane is treated as a plane 2D curve. The curvature of this plane curve is the curvature of the surface in the direction defined by the normal plane.*

Exactly how information from depth cues can be processed to yield these local descriptions of surfaces is partly a question of understanding how depth information is specified within the raw 2D images on the retinas. Marr (1982, p. 276) provided a list of cues and proposals for the information that they might specify. One of the goals of computational analysis, in Marr's view, is to formalize information like this and to suggest possible means of analysis. For human observers, understanding how information from depth cues might specify 3D shape also requires experimental measures of how these cues are treated perceptually. The next section of this chapter covers the perception of 3D shape by humans, when they are presented with images of simple geometric solid objects. These images incorporate monocular cues to shape, such as texture and shading, and the binocular cue of stereo disparity. The following section presents extensions of this work involving more complex illumination models that allow for mutual illumination effects (Forsyth and Zisserman, 1989, 1990); the present development of techniques for exploring these cues is discussed. A further section provides a brief review of the present state of knowledge about physiological mechanisms that might underly the analysis of 2D and 3D shape.

3D Shape Judgments

Types of Shape Judgment

Visual psychophysics provides a number of classic paradigms for the experimental investigation of perceptual processing. In one type of experiment, observers are asked to discriminate between two stimuli, using any means possible, and the experimenter measures the minimum difference required to support a statistically consistent discrimination performance. In another type of experiment, observers are required to adjust a comparison stimulus until it appears to match perceptually another test stimulus in some significant parameter. An example of this might be to adjust a comparison stimulus – a small, readily visible point target, for example – until its binocular stereo depth appears to match the depth of a monocularly viewed, shaded figure (Bülthoff and Mallot, 1988).

Neither of these approaches was entirely suitable for the questions investigated here. The judgment required for the shape task is concerned with the intrinsic configuration of a single target. A discrimination method only tells us how easily the observer sees the differences between stimuli. It cannot tell us how the observer perceives the absolute shape of the 3D object. In the case of a depth-matching technique, perhaps with a stereo depth probe, the experimental design rather begs the question of exactly what impression of depth is conveyed by the comparison stimulus itself. Similarly, asking subjects to match an impression of depth by adjusting the length of a line laterally extended in the fronto-parallel plane raises many questions about the comparability of distance judgments in different dimensions, and even about how the observer perceives the length of the reference line itself. Accordingly, a shape judgment task was devised in which observers were asked to decide whether a single object deviated in configuration from a canonical or ideal form.

Binocular Stereo Cues to Depth

Suppose the observer is presented with a 3D cylindrical shape whose axis lies in the horizontal meridian. The cylinder is formed as a stereo depth impression from a pair of Julesz-type random dot figures (see figure 8.2). The task of the observer is to report whether the cylinder is stretched in depth relative to height or vice versa. For a cylinder with a cross-section that is perceptually elliptical, this is equivalent to discriminating and identifying the major and minor axes of the ellipse. In order to solve this task, the human visual system must extract the depth values from stereo disparities and

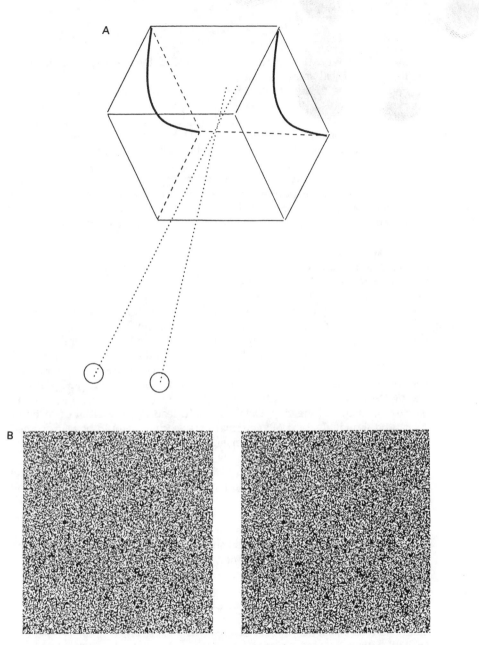

Figure 8.2 *a, The shape judgment task with binocular viewing in schematic form. A cylindrical shape is depicted by the stereo disparity information from the left and right images. The observer is asked to judge whether the cylinder is either* stretched *or* compressed *in depth relative to height. The 50 percent point of this judgment corresponds to a cylinder that is* perceptually *circular in cross-section. b, A sample random dot stereogram depicting a cylindrical surface in depth. The figure is built by creating a pair of identical fields of dots, each dot randomly black or white. These form images to be inspected by the right and left eyes. Because the essence of binocular stereo disparity is that objects at different depths have slightly different relative*

compare them with the height values provided by the visual angles subtending the vertical spatial extent.

The initial clue to the problem faced by the visual system arose from an informal observation on the perceived shape of cylinders that were geometrically circular. The positions of the dots in the random dot pair, and therefore the binocular stereo disparities in the target, had been carefully calculated (in accordance with 3D Cartesian coordinate geometry for a cylinder of circular cross-section at a viewing distance of 200 cm). Yet, the cylinder did not actually appear circular, but appeared flattened in depth. Recalculation of the disparities and inspection of the resulting cylinders at other viewing distances showed that, at near viewing distances (ca. 50 cm), the depth was exaggerated. At this viewing distance, geometrically circular cylinders appeared to have a stretched elliptical cross-section in the depth axis. Subsequent quantitative measurements confirmed this pattern of perceptual distortions and showed that perception was veridical at about 80 cm: at this distance, geometrically circular cylinders actually look circular (Johnston, 1988, 1991; Parker et al., 1991).

Consideration of the information required by the human visual system to solve the task suggested an explanation. As shown in figure 8.3, the relationship between disparity and depth is scaled by $1/D^2$, whereas the relationship between the visual angle subtended at the eye and height is scaled by $1/D$ (where D is the viewing distance). Thus, if observers attempt to solve the task by measuring first stereo disparities and visual angles and then by scaling the two measures with an estimate of viewing distance, the use of an *incorrect* measure of viewing distance would lead to perceptual distortions. As can be shown algebraically, circular cross-sections would be transformed into elliptical cross-sections – either enhanced or flattened in depth according to the error in estimating viewing distance.

Quantitatively, the overall pattern of results is consistent with the notion that observers recover correctly all the angular relationships, including stereo disparities, between points in the visual fields, but they then scale those angular measures with an incorrect estimate of absolute viewing distance (Johnston, 1988, 1991; Parker et al., 1991), which we call the *scaling distance*. Specifically, the observer's estimate of viewing distance changes in proportion with true viewing distance, but the constant of proportionality is less than one. Such a pattern of responses is what von Kries termed *proportionate depth perception* (see Helmholtz, 1910).

Figure 8.2 (cont.)
horizontal positions in the two eyes (see figure 8.3), stereo disparity can be simulated by shifting the relative positions of corresponding dots in the left and right images. Any gaps left are filled in with extra random dots. Even though the 3D shape cannot be seen in either eye's image, when the two image halves are combined binocularly and inspected for a while, a vivid perception of depth is obtained. The image pair is arranged to be inspected by crossing the eyes: that is, the left image on the page should be inspected by the right and vice versa.

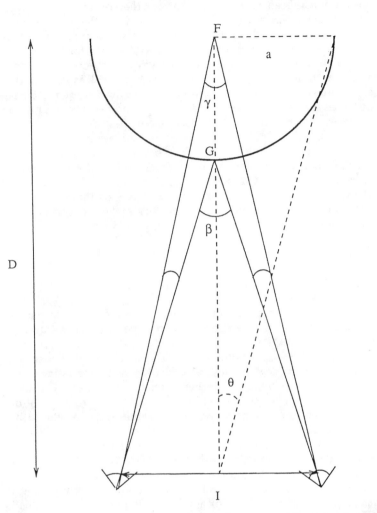

Figure 8.3 *The geometrical relationships between angular measures (visual angle and stereo disparity) and distance measures (lateral extent and depth) when an observer is viewing a segment of cylindrical surface with symmetrical convergence in the midline. The relationship between lateral extent (a) and visual angle (θ) scales with $1/D$, where D is the absolute viewing distance, while the relationship between depth (δ, which equals a for a circle) and stereo disparity (μ) scales with $1/D^2$. In detail (using small angle approximations in which interocular separation (I) and depth (δ) are assumed to be small relative to D) $\theta = a/D$ and*

$$\mu = \beta - \gamma = I/(D-\delta) - I/D \approx I\delta/D^2.$$

This same idea has been invoked to explain other results in binocular spatial vision (summarized by Foley, 1980). In these tasks, the observer may be given a set of widely spaced vertical rods to be inspected binocularly. The observer is requested to align the rods in depth so that they form a vertical flat plane parallel to the line joining the two eyes (equivalent to standing square on in front of a wall and deciding whether the wall is flat). In this task, observers make judgments that are systematically distorted. At near viewing distances, the rods are set into a slightly concave form, and at far viewing distances a slightly convex form is selected. These distortions can be accounted for in the same way as the distortions of perceived shape, by arguing that the observer applies an incorrect estimate of viewing distance to the binocular information from the eyes. Traditionally, these perceptual distortions have been thought to give information about the relationships between the dispositions of separate points or objects as they occupy 3D space. The newer results in the cylinder shape task make it clear that even single, perceptually solid and continuous objects are subject to 3D shape distortions.

More Generalized Shape Judgments

How might the results with pure stereo relate to the inspection of natural objects? The task developed here is an absolute type of judgment and requires the observer to compare the external sample shape against an internal model of the canonical shape of the object. The first part of this section outlined a number of practical and logical difficulties in investigating shape perception using more conventional forms of relative judgment. The absolute shape judgment proves to be an easy task for observers. Analysis of the statistical reliability of the observer's responses within the task shows that they are performing close to the limits imposed by their acuity for delineating 2D spatial position (Johnston, 1991). Acuity for small changes in 2D spatial configuration has been extensively studied (see Westheimer 1981, on *hyperacuity*) and it is known that human observers can reliably detect changes in 2D position that correspond on the retina to a positional change whose size is smaller than the dimensions of a single cone photoreceptor. This is discussed further below.

There is no reason to restrict the task to cylindrical shapes. In practice, any shape can be used, provided that the observer has a notion of its canonical 3D form. Figure 8.4 shows a stereo pair depicting a textured sphere that was made using techniques described (in the next section). Figure 8.5 illustrates results from two observers, who were asked to make shape-configuration judgments with a variety of 3D forms. The results are expressed in terms of the *scaling distance* (as defined above for the cylinder experiment) at two physical viewing distances. The results are essentially similar for each shape tested, meaning that a single value of scaling distance can apply to all shapes. Thus, observers make consistent depth/height judgments across different

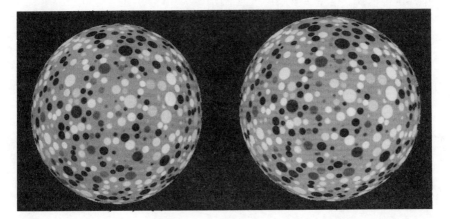

Figure 8.4 *A stereo pair depicting a spherical surface covered with texture and generated using techniques described in text below. The shape judgment task can be equally well carried out with shapes other than cylinders. Spherical shapes transform into ellipsoids if the observer applies an incorrect estimate of absolute viewing distance.*

3D configurations, and this suggests that the principle of proportional depth perception holds generally in 3D shape perception.

The straightforward interpretation of proportionate depth perception is that the observer uses information other than that available in the retinal image for interpreting the pattern of stereo disparities. This interpretation is at odds with the view expressed elsewhere that it might be possible to recover true physical 3D shape from the purely visual information in the stereo disparity field without recourse to any other sort of information (Mayhew, 1982; Mayhew and Longuet-Higgins, 1982).

Rather than scaling disparities directly, there are a number of ways that the human system could solve this 3D task, particularly if there are multiple cues as in the natural world. One obvious strategy is to assess the surface properties of the object in terms of the surface gradients or surface curvatures or both (Brady et al., 1985; Besl and Jain, 1986; Rogers and Cagenello, 1989). For example, the cylinder judgments could be represented as a task in which the observer is required to adjust the surface properties until the curvature is perceptually identical over the whole of the visible surface; of course, for an ellipse the curvature would be changing over the surface.

For pure stereo cues, Rogers and Cagenello (1989) suggested that a measure closely related to curvature might in fact be used for shape judgments. This is based on directly measuring the properties of the pattern of stereo disparities from an object rather than the actual values of depth or distance – recall that stereo disparity must be scaled appropriately to obtain depth. Rogers and Cagenello (1989) argue that differentiating twice the values of stereo disparity is a sufficiently useful approximation to object curvature in

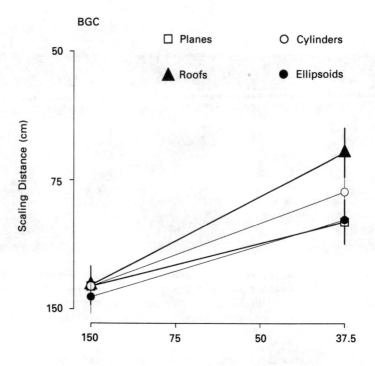

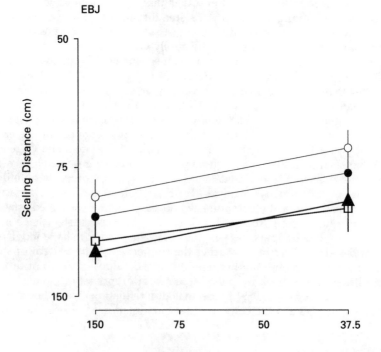

depth coordinates. What this means is that shape judgments would be consistent across viewing distances if the human system could exploit the measure proposed by them. However, the persistence of shape distortions indicates that this cue is not very useful for human observers in these shape judgment tasks.

For a natural object, computational studies have shown that, under some assumptions, cues such as shading and texture gradients can be processed to recover the surface gradients directly (Horn, 1986). So it is possible that adding these cues in conjunction with stereo would produce perceptual judgments that are closer to physical reality. Moreover, the conventional random dot stereogram in figure 8.2b has a strong texture cue signalling a planar surface, a cue which is in conflict with any depth variations signalled by stereo disparities. One may therefore suggest three possibilities for under-standing shape judgments with stereo alone:

1   Stereo disparities are recovered in raw form and scaled with an estimate of viewing distance: the estimate might be derived from knowledge about the positions of the eyes, notably their degree of convergence when they view a nearby as opposed to a distant object, or it might come from purely visual sources (e.g. Mayhew and Longuet-Higgins, 1982) or from a mixture of cues.
2   Some perceptually invariant property of the disparity field is extracted and used for shape judgments: examples of this might be the proposal of Rogers and Cagenello (1989) mentioned above or measures that arise from treating the pattern of stereo disparities mathematically as a vector field over the whole scene and then applying the tools of vector calculus – Koenderink and van Doorn (1976a) specifically propose the use of *def*, the deformation operator.
3   The distortions of shape from stereo reflect the fact that, under natural viewing with multiple cues, information from stereo is vetoed or receives a smaller weighting as a consequence of information from other cues.

These considerations suggested that we should extend the shape judgment task in two ways. The first would be to pay much closer attention to the

Figure 8.5   *Results from a stereo shape judgment task in which four different 3D shapes were judged in terms of whether their perceived depth was equal to their perceived vertical extent. The results are expressed in terms of "scaling distance" on the ordinate versus true physical viewing distance on the abscissa. The scaling distance is the distance at which the pattern of stereo disparities judged by the subject to be equal in depth and vertical extent (e.g. perceptually a sphere or a circular cylinder) would give rise to a geometrically correct shape. At the physical viewing distance used for this experiment, the pattern of stereo disparities judged as equal in depth and vertical extent corresponds to a geometrically distorted pattern. The estimated scaling distance is reasonably consistent across different shapes, suggesting that a single scaling factor may account for nearly all shape changes.*

exact form of the pattern of stereo disparities that would arise from a real object, so as to represent naturalistically cues such as vertical disparities and the higher-order derivatives of the disparity field. The second would be to include other cues to depth and surface shape in the visual images presented to the observer. To combine these goals, it was necessary to implement several techniques based on recent developments in computer graphics.

Creating Naturalistic Stimuli

The influence of computers and computational theory on ways of thinking about biological visual systems has already been mentioned. It is equally significant that the improved technology of computing machinery has provided methods and techniques for generating visual stimuli and carrying out experiments that were impossible even ten years ago. At that time, work with visual stimuli was forced into a compromise. On the one hand, computer-based methods offered sophistication and control but they provided only a limited range of visual patterns. On the other hand, more naturalistic visual targets could be generated by using genuine solid objects, but at the expense of flexibility and ability to control each cue separately. While the element of compromise has not been eliminated, it has been greatly reduced by purely technological advances which are likely to continue.

Ray Tracing to a Visible Surface

The main aim of implementing new techniques was to be able to reproduce more faithfully on a computer graphics screen the optic array that would be received by each eye when looking at a true 3D solid object. This can be achieved by selecting each gray level or color value on the graphics screen to correspond to what would be received by the left or right eye via a perspective projection from a 3D object (figure 8.6). Bülthoff and Mallot (1988) present a discussion of the basic geometry of imaging that underlies this technique and demonstrate some applications in human vision.

In our earliest attempts to use this approach, the starting point was a geometrical description of the surface of a cylinder, onto which a black and white chequer-board pattern was mapped. Within the computer's model of the scene, the cylindrical surface was illuminated by a single light source positioned above the observer's head and the chequer-board pattern was used to define the diffuse reflectances of the matt surface (see Horn, 1986, for a discussion of surface properties). The perspective projection was determined, using a limited form of the computer graphics technique known as ray tracing (Bülthoff and Mallot, 1988; Foley et al., 1990). In this procedure, the light path for each ray arriving at the eye is followed from the focal point of the eye back through to the image plane from the notional 3D object (see figure 8.6). Unlike some of the more sophisticated ray tracing that has been carried out, the software used here only dealt with a single opaque object

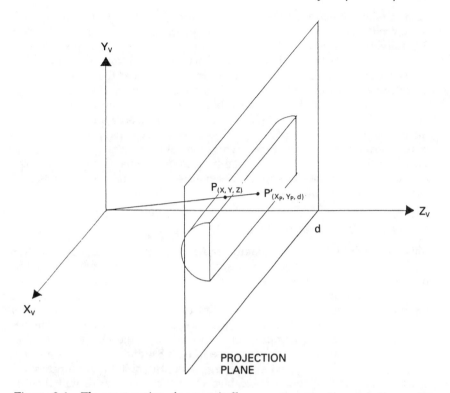

Figure 8.6 *The construction of geometrically accurate perspective projections using the technique of ray tracing (see Foley et al., 1990). The eye is placed at the origin of the coordinate system and rays are traced from the origin to the required pixel in the image plane and then back to the 3D shape to determine the brightness value for the selected pixel.*

and did not follow rays through multiple reflections around the scene (see Foley et al., 1990). This technique is also termed "image rendering" in computer graphics. The resulting images, traced separately for left and right eyes, contained stereo, texture gradient, and shading information. Somewhat surprisingly, adding these extra sources of information did not greatly change the pattern of perceptual distortions experienced by the observers (Johnston, 1988, 1989; Parker et al., 1991).[1]

This method of producing images has several limitations, most of which relate to the use of a surface-based description of the 3D shape rather than a true volumetric representation and to the fact that rays were traced to only one depth of iteration. First, the illumination model is limited in the kinds of illumination effects that can be present in the scene: there are no shadows, no surface highlights that arise from specular (mirror-like) reflections, and no mutual illumination of the sort that arises when two brightly lit surfaces of different orientation meet each other (Forsyth and Zisserman, 1989, 1990). Secondly, the texture model is limited in that planar samples of texture, such as a chequer-board, can only be mapped without distortion onto a restricted mathematical class of surfaces, namely those that have the same Gaussian curvature as a plane, which is zero. While the distortion of surface patches may be a valid model for the generation of surface texture in some cases – notably zebra stripes (Bard, 1977) – it is not the only possibility. Essentially, the problem is that when planar patches of surface are mapped onto a patch of non-zero Gaussian curvature, such as part of a spherical surface, some of the original planar patch must be compressed or eliminated. Such a manipulation would alter the statistics of the texture as measured locally on the 3D surface, even before any perspective projection is carried out.

Volumetric Texture Representation

This approach to producing images begins with a volumetric representation of the 3D shape to be imaged. In order to include high-quality texture information, the initial step is to produce a computer representation of a solid cube of 3D textured material, as if it were granite, marble, or wood. The required shape is then "sculpted" out of the solid block by the computer program. The result is that when the shape is inspected from a particular viewpoint, the texture compression expected from the change in surface gradient is automatically included (see figures 8.4 and 8.7). At the present stage, the 3D shape is treated as if it were an emitter of light, but future work will include lighting sources (see below) so that the texture will then be treated as a pattern of reflectances.

However, the present stimuli have the desired property of being covered with a richly textured surface. This provides good binocular stereo information in which the texture cue for surface orientation is *concordant* with the stereo cues. This is different from a conventional random dot stereogram (as shown in figure 8.2b), where the uniform texture signals a flat, uniform surface with no change in depth. Thus, wherever the stereo cues indicate a change in depth, the random dot stereogram in the form devised by Julesz (1971) actually provides conflicting cues. In the methods devised here, it is possible to provide stimuli with geometrically consistent information from both stereo and texture cues and, if desired, to vary independently the information available from each (see below).

Obtaining Accurate Geometry

The pair of stereo images are produced by tracing rays from each eye's viewpoint to the 3D shape that has been carved out of the block. With this approach to image generation, the resulting images contain the physically correct pattern of geometric cues for stereo disparity.[2] The pattern of higher-order derivatives of the disparity field (Koenderink and van Doorn, 1976a;

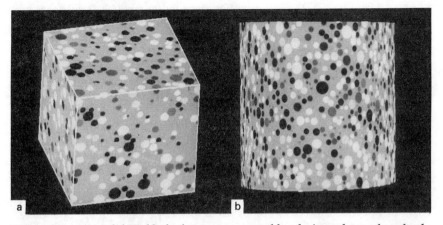

Figure 8.7 *a, A solid 3D block of texture generated by placing spheres of randomly selected size, position, and gray-level intensity within the confines of the block subject to the constraint that spheres do not overlap. The 3D shape required for the shape judgment task is "carved out" of the block and then used as the object to which rays are traced during the production of the pair of stereo images. b, A single view of a cylindrical shape; the ability of this volumetric method to depict texture gradients can be readily appreciated. Controlling the statistics and properties of spheres in the block is used to set the texture characteristics for the final stereo pair.*

see section on Geometry above) is identical to that obtained by inspecting a natural target. Thus, stimuli such as these can be used to evaluate the role of these geometrical cues for depth and 3D shape.

The pattern of vertical disparities (Mayhew and Longuet-Higgins, 1982) is another source of geometrical information that could be used to assist the interpretation of 3D shape. The usefulness of vertical disparities is that they might provide a technique for recovering the absolute distance to an object. As discussed in the preceding section, this would then be a purely visual method of solving the problem of calibrating stereo disparities. The easiest way to appreciate intuitively the potential usefulness of vertical disparities is to consider viewing the following scene. Imagine that the observer is look-ing straight ahead with both eyes open and that a pen is held vertically at a distance of about 50 cm and a little way off to the right. Because the pen is nearer the right eye than the left eye, it will subtend a slightly larger angle at the right eye than the left. Suppose also that there is a telegraph pole in the far distance. For the telegraph pole, the difference in the vertical angles subtended at the left and right eyes will be minimal – in fact, zero at an infinite distance – because the differences in the distances to the left and right eyes will be very small too. By monitoring the vertical disparities, it is therefore possible to recover information related to viewing distance. For a fuller account, the reader is referred to the original papers (Mayhew and

Longuet-Higgins, 1982) or the recent account by Rogers (1991), where it will be seen that vertical disparities also depend on the angle of gaze of the eyes and that some mathematical analysis is required to isolate the terms that relate solely to viewing distance.

Even with the more accurate depiction of stereo disparities provided by our revised graphical methods, there are still perceptual distortions of solid shape that are dependent on viewing distance (Cumming et al., 1991). If vertical disparity were a cue to viewing distance, observers should be able to extract viewing distance as a parameter from the pattern of vertical disparities and thereby avoid the perceptual distortions of solid shape. In fact, manipulating vertical disparities directly in a way that simulates changes of viewing distance does not lead to changes in the observer's estimate of viewing distance used for interpreting stereo disparity information (Cumming et al., 1991). By contrast, changes in convergence of the eyes do lead to changes in the interpretation of the disparity field, as originally mentioned by Wheatstone (1838, 1852).

Independent Control of Shape Cues

The statistics of the texture in the block can be manipulated to control the shape cues available from texture gradients of various types. In figure 8.8, the texture in the original block has been either stretched or compressed more in one axis than another, but the block itself is still cubic. Compressing the texture in the axis corresponding to the depth dimension results in an increased number of texture elements that are transected when the shape is sculpted from the block. Consequently, there is a change in local texture density. The texture cue to local surface orientation essentially depends upon the variations in texture density across a small patch of surface. Cylindrical shapes carved from these blocks of stretched or compressed texture thus have artificially decreased or enhanced depth from texture when a pair of stereo images is traced from the shape. It is important to appreciate that the depth signal available from point to point matching of stereo correspondences is unaffected by these manipulations of texture.

In the extreme, if the front plane of the original block is extended and replicated throughout the whole cube, so that the cube consists of a pile of gray rods viewed end on, then this corresponds to constructing a classic Julesz-type random dot stereogram. Because this configuration corresponds to a planar patch of texture, it can be regarded as having *zero* depth from texture. Other images are placed on a ratio scale compared with the canonical form of the textured block, whose texture density is uniform in all three dimensions. As a specific example, compressing the texture by a factor of 2 in depth dimension results in a texture : stereo (T : S) ratio of 2 : 1.

Figure 8.9 shows some results for two observers who were asked to judge whether horizontally oriented cylindrical shapes of elliptical cross-section (depicted by stereo pairs) had a larger radius in the depth dimension than in the vertical height dimension. The experiment was set up as a forced-

Figure 8.8 *Example of a different form of 3D textured block, which consists of a low-pass filtered 3D random noise pattern. The upper block is isotropic. The lower two blocks are stretched and compressed in one axis to make anisotropic textures. The stretching or compression takes place in the z-axis direction (depth direction along the primary cyclopean line of sight), so that depth from texture in the final images is either enhanced or diminished relative to the isotropic form of the block. Variations in the depth from texture lead to changes in the perceived shape (see figure 8.9).*

choice judgment, so that a set of elliptical cylinders was used and the 50 percent probability corresponds to finding the physical shape that is *perceptually* circular in cross-section. At the viewing distance selected (ca. 100 cm), shape judgments using stereo alone are approximately veridical (see above). Adding artificially enhanced depth by means of the texture cue alters the subjects' behavior and they respond by setting the physical shape of the cylinder to be somewhat flattened in depth as a compensation. Interestingly, this actually biases their results away from veridical, so that the relationship between texture and stereo may be roughly additive, rather than one vetoing the other.

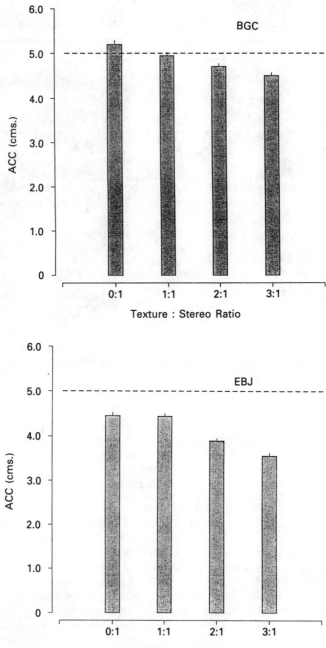

Naturalistic Images

Clearly, one of the major open questions is whether the perceptual distortions of solid shape persist when truly solid, natural objects are inspected. A related question that is often raised is how many observers experience these perceptual distortions and to what degree. It is possible to examine these questions using real 3D objects. For example, to examine the perception of solid shape, we have constructed a set of solid wooden cylinders, which have been accurately machined to the required shapes and mounted so that they protrude halfway out of a window formed within a large piece of flat card. Informal observations suggest that the distortions of perceived shape persist, notably at far viewing distances. We are presently investigating this question with a larger group of naïve observers.

Some interesting insights into the use of multiple cues by human observers are available simply from inspecting and adjusting these shapes. First, careful control of the illumination conditions is necessary so that the overall outline shape is not revealed through the shapes of shadows. This has led us to investigate the role of shadows' shapes in controlling perceived 3D shape under the more precisely controlled conditions of computer-generated displays. Secondly, control of the vantage point is needed to avoid seeing the flat ends of the cylindrical block. The 2D shape cues that are available from being able to see the contours forming the cylinder (so-called *shape from contour*) affect significantly the interpretation of the shape cues of stereo, texture, and shading by human observers. A similar point concerning the interaction of 2D contour information and 3D shape information from motion flow has been made by Aloimonos and Liuqing Huang (1990).

The only currently satisfactory way to gain independent control over each of these cues and others is by means of computer graphics displays. For example, one topic of current interest is the way in which shading should be represented within a computer graphics display. There is widespread use of

---

Figure 8.9 *Results of an experiment to investigate the interaction of texture and stereo cues to depth. Subjects carried out the shape judgment task shown in figure 8.2, and described in text, with horizontally aligned cylindrical shapes which were at a viewing distance of 100 cm and had a radius in the height dimension of 5 cm. The shapes were taken from blocks of texture similar to those illustrated in figure 8.6. The texture : stereo (T : S) ratio expresses the relative distortion of the texture cue in the cyclopean depth axis. The ordinate shows the value of depth at the 50 percent point on the forced-choice psychometric function. Colloquially, this is referred to as the "apparently circular cylinder" (ACC) because this depth value corresponds to a cylinder that appears circular in cross-section. Enhancing the depth cue from texture by increasing the T : S ratio causes both subjects to compensate by reducing the actual amount of physical depth required to produce an ACC. The small ticks at the top of each bar indicate the upper 95 percent fiducial limit and the horizontal dashed line shows the physically correct match.*

shading in these displays and the usual approach is extremely straight-forward. Typically, the scene is assumed to contain a single-point light source. The light arriving at the observer's eye is calculated from a knowledge of the 3D geometry of the light source, the patch of illuminated surface, and the observer's vantage point. This is an entirely "local" calculation in the sense that each surface patch is dealt with independently from all others. Often in addition, an "ambient" illumination is added: this is wholly non-specific in that it simulates the illumination that would arise from a completely non-directional source, such as the light from a completely cloudy and overcast sky. The combination of these two terms (a simple directional light source and a diffuse one) can produce images whose 3D shape can be interpreted by human observers.

However, in the real world, the interactions of light are more complicated. Light will bounce from one surface to another before it reaches the observer's eye and the nature of these interactions cannot be satisfactorily modeled by a non-specific ambient illumination. For example, a large white area will reflect light very well onto nearby objects and thus the white area will act as a secondary source of illumination.[3] Of course, if there are two such surfaces, then the illumination is mutual, that is from one surface to another and back again. Some of these subtleties were well appreciated by the Impressionist painters. For example, Renoir pointed out insistently, "Shadows are not black; no shadow is black. It always has a colour." And, in criticism of another painter, he said: "You admit that you have a sky above that snow. Your sky is blue. That blue must also show up in the snow" (Rewald, 1973, p. 210). This indicates an appreciation of the fact that illumination within shadowed areas has been transformed as a consequence of its reflection from nearby surfaces.

The particular interest of mutual illumination from the present point of view is that many of the simpler algorithms for recovering shape from shading (Horn, 1986, 1989) are easily upset by its effects. For example, as two surfaces approach one another to form a cleft, fold, or crease, the illumination of one surface by light reflected from the other (and vice versa) increases according to the usual inverse square law relationship as the surfaces approach. The consequence is that if the primary source of illumination should happen to be directed into the concave feature, even surface regions that are highly slanted with respect to the observer's vantage point and the light source may have relatively high radiance values and thereby direct a lot of light towards the observer's eye. This would confound any attempt to relate the amount of light leaving the surface patch to the 3D orientation of its surface normal (see above), which is the basis of many current algorithms for shape from shading.

On the other hand, mutual illumination can be particularly effective in revealing detail about the shapes of boundaries within shadowed regions (see figure 8.10). Recent analysis (Forsyth and Zisserman, 1990) has shown that mutual illumination generates discontinuities in the radiance only at points where the first derivative of the surface (i.e. the surface slant) is discontinuous

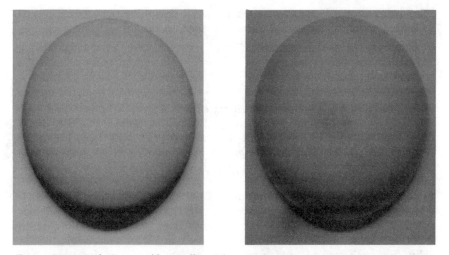

Fgure 8.10   *Left, Image of hemi-ellipsoid resting on plane with simple shading and no mutual illumination. Right, Image of hemi-ellipsoid resting on plane incorporating mutual illumination effects. Note, in particular, the bright boundary enhancement on the hemi-ellipsoid caused by the reflected light from the background plane. This bright boundary feature marks very well the junction between hemi-ellipsoid and plane, whereas in the simple shaded figure the self-shadow and the cast shadow are indistinguishable. The mutually illuminated image was created by an implementation of the radiosity method (Foley et al., 1990). Calculations for radiosity involved subdividing the 3D scene into a set of triangular surface patches and specifying for each patch the radiant energy flow in and out of the surface, starting from a description of the light sources and surface reflectances in the scene. Fortunately, this scene is simple enough to be dissected into relatively coarse triangular patches. Using a low number of triangles keeps the computational overhead much lower but, even so, high-quality images take several hours to compute.*

or at discontinuities in surface reflectance. Moreover, these new discontinuities are linked to surface features. Mutual illumination may also be effective in disambiguating concave versus convex surface patches, since within a concavity the effects of mutual illumination are particularly marked.

Neural Mechanisms for Analyzing Shape

If we now turn our attention to what kinds of mechanisms within the brain are used to analyze "naturalistic" visual cues to 3D shape, it must be admitted that much of our knowledge is sketchy and conjectural. This is particularly so if we think in terms of mechanisms for which there is evidence from both psychophysical studies and neurophysiological studies. It may be helpful to review briefly the elementary studies of visual receptive field properties in the primary visual cortex, as a preliminary to discussing the current state of knowledge about 2D and 3D shape analysis. A reasonably leisurely approach to this elementary material has been presented by Hubel (1988) who, together with Wiesel (Hubel and Wiesel, 1962), was responsible for nearly all of our initial understanding of this problem.

Receptive Fields of the Primary Visual Cortex

Hubel and Wiesel (1962) took the idea of a receptive field as it had been applied to the cells of the retina and showed how the idea could be developed and applied to the cells of cortical visual area V1 (also known as primary visual cortex, striate cortex, or Brodmann's cortical area 17). The essence of the receptive field concept is that light falling in a circumscribed spatial region of the total visual field is sufficient to cause electrical activity in one or more nerve cells in the form of nerve impulses, classically termed action potentials. It was also discovered in the retina that some of these spatial regions are selectively excited by any increment in light falling within them, whereas other regions are selectively excited by a decrement. Typically, two such regions, which are more or less circular in form, are combined to make a single receptive field in which a central zone is selective for increments and a larger surround zone is selective for decrements (or vice versa). The essential characteristic of this combination is that the responses of the center and surround zones oppose each other, and this gives the receptive field some important spatial properties. A large diffuse field of light (either increment or decrement) is not very effective in exciting the nerve cell, whereas any light pattern with a transition between bright and dark positioned near the boundary between center and surround zones will be very effective. What this means is that even retinal cells, through their sensitivity to contrast, contribute to the analysis and detection of contours formed by a difference in luminance.

Hubel and Wiesel (1962) found that cells in the cat's cortical area V1 take the analysis of contours somewhat further. Two main kinds of cell were identified in the initial study. Both kinds of cell had elongated zones within their receptive fields. These zones mean that the cells are especially well excited by an elongated bar or edge stimulus of the appropriate orientation. Cells with *simple* receptive fields have subregions that are selective for increments or decrements of light. These subregions are also antagonistic, like the center and surrounds of retinal cells, but each subregion is spatially elongated. Cells with *complex* receptive fields do not have identifiable zones in which increments and decrements are selectively effective in exciting the cell. Indeed, often they respond about equally well to bright and dark bars at several locations within their receptive fields (Movshon et al., 1978b), provided that the orientation of the bar is correct for the receptive field.

Varieties of Receptive Field Selectivity

Most work since Hubel and Wiesel (1962) has developed and tested the concept of receptive field selectivity in more and more elaborate form. Thus, it is now standard to think of nerve cell receptive fields as a means of analyzing any of the visual cues explored earlier in psychophysical experiments. Most of this section is devoted to evaluating the possibility that some receptive fields are especially equipped to detect 2D line curvature. However, to highlight the current problems and areas of ignorance in bringing forward evidence about other cues, a very brief overall summary will be presented.

Texture. In the case of extracting shape from texture cues, there is no systematic study of how visual neurones might respond to a naturalistic texture gradient cue. This is despite the fact that it has been repeatedly suggested that complex receptive fields (Hubel and Wiesel, 1962), even at an early a stage as cortical area V1, might be involved in the processing of texture (Hammond and MacKay, 1977; Robson, 1980). The sensitivity to texture in complex cells may well arise because they would be well excited by patterns comprising both local increments and decrements in light (see above).

Shading. Shading is a reasonably powerful cue to object shape, although the human visual system is easily deceived by some configurations of shading and illumination. There are specific proposals that the receptive fields of simple cells in V1 may be appropriately organized for processing shading information (Lehky and Sejnowski, 1988, 1990; Pentland, 1989). However, there are no experimental studies, especially with physically realistic distributions of luminance as input stimuli, that could support or test these proposals adequately. Moreover, there is at least one deficit in the proposals that needs to be sorted out, since it is unclear what might be the significance for the shape extraction algorithms of the adaptive gain control mechanisms in the retina, since these mechanisms cause a local, contrast signal, rather than a luminance signal, to emerge from the retina (Shapley and Enroth-Cugell, 1984).

Motion. For motion, rather more is known about the early detection and signalling of motion by nerve cells (e.g. Hildreth and Koch, 1987). There are also suggestions for how some higher-order processing of motion might proceed (Movshon et al., 1985) and how local motion signals might be combined to give information about the 3D trajectory of moving objects (Cynader and Regan, 1978), the observer's motion through the environment, and the control of pursuit eye movements (Lisberger et al., 1987; see also chapter 10). Recently, there have been observations on the responses of neurones to motion flow patterns that correspond to simple differential forms of the optic flow field (Saito et al., 1986). But, there is little or nothing to indicate how local motion signals might be used to extract the 3D shape of objects by analysis of the information in the motion flow field (Horn, 1986).

Stereo. The basis of disparity detection in V1 has been well studied (Barlow et al., 1967; Poggio and Fischer, 1977), and in more recent work the structural basis of disparity selectivity has been examined quantitatively (Ferster, 1981;

Freeman and Ohzawa, 1990). It has been proposed that single cells (and indeed psychophysical mechanisms) might be specifically sensitive to local differences in orientation or spatial frequency or both (Blakemore et al., 1972). Cells with such a sensitivity would be ideal for carrying out preliminary analyses of the differential forms of the stereo disparity field (Koenderink and van Doorn, 1976a). In the specific case of receptive fields that differ in orientation preference between the two eyes, Nelson et al. (1977) have argued that the sensitivity of cells for binocular orientation differences is rarely sufficient to cope with the sizes of orientation difference found in natural scenes. By contrast, the sensitivity of cells to horizontal positional disparity is often sufficient to deal with naturalistic stereo cues. The whole matter will only be resolved with more objective 2D measures of receptive field structures (see, for example, Freeman and Ohzawa, 1990), and by closer attention to the statistical criteria for detection by single neurones. Beyond these relatively low-level issues, much remains obscure about the neurophysiology of stereo. There is little neurophysiological evidence on many of the problems of current interest in stereo vision: the role of interpolation in stereo vision, the role of disparity gradients and the correspondence problem, and the extraction of 3D shape from stereo.

Receptive Fields and Contour Analysis

The importance of outline contour for giving information about 3D is evident in the effectiveness of line drawings in conveying 3D structure. Attneave (1954), in particular, pointed out that much of the critical information is encapsulated at the points of high curvature in a line figure. For these reasons, architects of machine vision systems have generally found it advantageous to supplement a stage of edge detection on the gray-level image with a structured description of the local organization of contours in the image. Terminators (Marr, 1976), blobs (Marr, 1976), discontinuities of orientation (Binford, 1981), intersections (Waltz, 1975; Marr, 1976; Barrow and Tenenbaum, 1981; Binford, 1981) and curvature (Binford, 1981; Brady and Asada, 1983) have all been tried. These kinds of feature are crucial for object segregation and 3D shape analysis because they can disambiguate the depth relationships within a scene, especially with occlusion cues. For example, certain forms of intersection guarantee that an extremal boundary exists (Barrow and Tenenbaum, 1981) and local measures of curvature give clues to global organization (Hoffman and Richards, 1984). All these kinds of descriptor can also be considered dynamically in moving objects or stereoscopically in binocular vision as well as over a range of spatial scales.

What kinds of neural receptive field organization would support computationally useful contour analysis with a high degree of precision? One preliminary observation is that many of the required forms of visual information can be computed locally from the image. This agrees well with what is known of the physiological properties of cells in the various striate and extrastriate visual cortical areas of the monkey. The most striking gap in current understanding of this system is between cortical area V1, where at least the basic properties of the receptive fields are well characterized (Hubel and Wiesel, 1962; Movshon et al., 1978a,b), and the higher-order areas in the superior temporal sulcus (STS) or inferotemporal cortex (IT), where cells respond to whole objects or complex visual patterns (e.g. Miyashita, 1988) and may have visuomotor related signals as well as purely visual ones (Komatsu and Wurtz, 1988a,b; Newsome et al., 1988). It is remarkable that neuroanatomy suggests that there are only a few synaptic stages, possibly 5 or 6, between V1 and these higher-order areas (Van Essen and Maunsell, 1983), although of course there are many branches and reciprocal interconnections.

Discrimination of Spatial Configuration by Single Nerve Cells

Psychophysical studies show that many 2D geometrical features in line configurations can be located with very high precision: often the observer is sensitive to a change in the position of a contour or feature, when the spatial change on the retina is smaller than the diameter of a single cone photoreceptor (so-called *hyperacuity*, Westheimer, 1981). Although there may be some interesting and informative exceptions, cases where hyperacuity fails are something of a rarity. Curvature discrimination performance is also in the hyperacuity range (Watt and Andrews, 1982). In order to localize any relevant feature in the luminance distribution of an image, a detector (either a man-made device or a neural receptive field) must be highly sensitive to small changes in the distribution of luminance. The neurone's performance at discriminating small differences in spatial configuration is thus closely linked to the sensitivity of the cell's receptive field to local differences in luminance, i.e. contrast (Parker and Hawken, 1985; Hawken and Parker, 1990).

This kind of result only tells us about the precision of discrimination. It does not show how a particular feature can be correctly and unambiguously identified. A cortical simple cell will change its output as a consequence of any of a number of changes in the stimulus applied: orientation, spatial position, spatial frequency content, temporal waveform of stimulation, contrast or luminance, and so on. Thus, at first sight, since the cell has only one form of output, namely its production of action potentials, there is no way of labelling any change in the stimulus without ambiguity. It is possible that subtle differences in the exact temporal pattern of action potentials from the cell are induced by different types of change in the stimulus (Richmond and Optican, 1990). This might allow resolution of some of these ambiguities. However, the straightforward interpretation of current evidence is that these small differences in temporal pattern are no less ambiguous than any other aspect of the cell's firing pattern. So, the information required for detailed contour analysis is available with high precision from changes in the firing of individual cells, but the code for pattern identification must be distributed across at least a number of cortical cells in V1. It is reasonable to consider the possibility that there are other receptive fields, perhaps in higher visual areas, whose stimulus requirements are more elaborate and specific.

End-stopped Cells

After the earliest studies of cat cortex, Hubel and Wiesel (1965) went on to identify a class of cells called *hypercomplex*, which had an even more elaborate selectivity for the shape of contours. These cells were thought to resemble complex cells in many properties (orientation selectivity, binocularity, and spatial summation behavior), but had the additional requirement that the lines or edges stimulating their receptive fields needed to be restricted in length to give an optimal response. Subsequently, cells were identified, which had the property of length selectivity but were similar to simple cells in other respects. Indeed, there may be a continuum of cell types ranging from extreme complex-type to classic simple types (as suggested for non-end-stopped cells by Dean and Tolhurst, 1983). The whole class of these cells is nowadays generally termed "end-stopped" and such neurones are found in V1, V2, and other cortical areas of Old World monkeys: indeed, one recent estimate put the fraction of end-stopped cells in V2 as high as one-third (Burkhalter and Van Essen, 1986).

An example of the behavior of a cell of this type is shown in figure 8.11. The cell, which had complex-like spatial summation properties (Movshon et al., 1978b), was recorded in layer two of primate visual cortex (V1) during experiments described in detail elsewhere (Hawken and Parker, 1987). The receptive field was stimulated with drifting grating patterns (sets of bright and dark bars), which had a sinusoidal luminance profile in which the spatial frequency (in cycles per degree of visual angle) describes the widths of the bars. The bars were of optimal orientation and were displayed on the CRT screen within a window (of rectangular profile) to restrict the length of the bars forming the grating. As the length of the bars was increased from 0.5 degrees of visual angle to a full height grating (greater than 3 degrees), the response of the cell at its preferred spatial frequency dropped by a factor of about 4. Interestingly, with a full-height grating, the response of the cell was depressed proportionately at all spatial frequencies, which implies that the effect of lengthening the bars cannot be modeled by a simple subtractive process.

Most of the detailed quantitative measurements of end-stopped cells come from the work of Bishop and collaborators in cat V1 (Kato et al., 1978; Orban et al., 1979a,b) and more recently Dobbins et al. (1987, 1989). The most striking features of these receptive fields found in V1 are:

1 With stimuli of restricted length, the receptive field seems to possess a center-zone whose characteristics (orientation selectivity and so on) are fairly similar to the ordinary sort of simple or complex cell.
2 The receptive fields seem to possess end-zones which can be explored by using a longer line of the same orientation and which seem to be

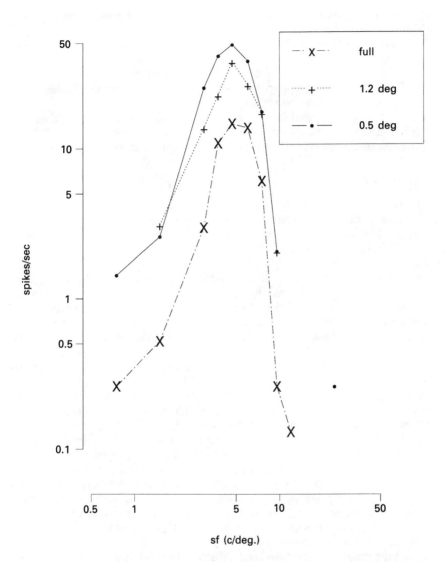

Figure 8.11 *Responses of an end-stopped neurone in primate visual cortex V1 to drifting sinusoidal grating targets as a function of spatial frequency at different bar lengths. The grating was of optimal orientation, and was drifted for two complete temporal cycles across the receptive field. The cell showed complex-like spatial summation properties (Movshon et al., 1978b). It can be seen that as the length of the bars is increased the response of the cell declines by a factor of almost 4. See Hawken and Parker (1987) for details of recording methods.*

exclusively involved in suppressing the response normally arising from the center-zone.

3 Stimulation of the end-zone is most effective in suppressing the firing of the cell when the stimulus in the end-zone is aligned with the most sensitive region of the center-zone of the receptive field.

4 Nearly every end-stopped cell has inhibitory end-zones of roughly equal size at each end of the receptive field.

5 The inhibitory region in the end-zone is itself orientation selective.

6 The end-zone confers on the cell some selectivity for curvature.

7 Many end-stopped cells are binocular or direction selective or both.

Models of End-stopped Cells

The potential role of end-stopped neurones in signalling the curvature of contours in the visual scene was appreciated clearly by Hubel and Wiesel (1965): "The hypercomplex cell can, in a sense, serve to measure curvature." Recent work (Dobbins et al., 1987, 1989; Koenderink and van Doorn, 1987; Koenderink and Richards, 1988) has highlighted this proposal. These authors present different, but quite specific, models for the receptive field organization of end-stopped cells having simple receptive fields.

Koenderink and van Doorn (1987) developed the concept of detecting curvature by means of a set of 2D mathematical functions, whose profile resembles approximately the receptive field structures identified in the visual cortex. The mathematical form of these functions is actually a nested family. The lowest-order member has a 2D Gaussian profile (see figure 8.12). Applying this function to an image will simply blur the image, smearing out the fine detail to a degree dependent on the size of the Gaussian profile. The next members of the family are constructed by differentiating the original Gaussian in the x or y direction once (first derivative: $\partial/\partial x$ or $\partial/\partial y$) or twice (second derivative: $\partial^2/\partial x^2$ or $\partial^2/\partial y^2$). These members of the family resemble qualitatively the detectors for oriented bars and edges discovered by Hubel and Wiesel (1962). More elaborate members arise from taking first or second derivatives in both directions (see figure 8.12). These members of the series may provide a model for the behavior of end-stopped cortical cells. Combinations of these outputs of local operators can be exploited to compute the curvatures of lines or edge boundaries at specific points in the image.

Koenderink and Richards (1988) express these ideas in terms of specific structural models for end-stopped cells. An important point is the need to use different combinations of receptive field structures to overcome potential ambiguities in labeling curved contours. Although a curved boundary edge (between a bright region and a dark region of the image) and a thin, curved line (either bright or dark) may have the same shape and curvature geometrically, they will produce very different responses within a single member of the Gaussian derivative family. Specifically, consider the model receptive field G_{xxyy} in figure 8.12. A curved bright line falling in three of the positive regions will excite the receptive field very well. However, if the line were replaced by a curved boundary edge in the same location, the stimulus would then also invade negative zones of the receptive field, with a consequent decrease in net excitation. Indeed, no single member can unambiguously identify even the straightforward classes of stimulus (line vs. boundary edge, convex vs. concave curvature; bright vs. dark). Combinations of receptive fields would be essential under this scheme.

It is actually questionable whether the Gaussian derivative shapes depicted in figure 8.12 are a genuinely accurate description of cortical cell receptive fields in V1 (Hawken and Parker, 1987). On the other hand, any deviations of the true receptive field profile from this theoretical ideal of the Gaussian derivative model may be inconsequential, in the sense that actual receptive fields may be sufficiently like a Gaussian derivative so as to permit them to analyze curvature at least crudely. The proposals of Koenderink and Richards (1988) do make one critical prediction concerning the receptive field organization of end-stopped cells. There ought to be evidence for simple summation (or antagonism) between stimuli presented simultaneously in any two zones of the receptive field. More formally, the two zones should show linear spatial pooling such that the output from stimulating both zones should be predictable from a knowledge of the responses obtained from each zone stimulated independently. (See Enroth-Cugell and Robson, 1984, for a tutorial introduction to this concept and its application to the responses of retinal ganglion cells.) Hence, this model makes a clear prediction of linear spatial pooling between the end-zones of the end-stopped receptive field and the center-zone.

The model of Dobbins et al. (1987, 1989) differs by including non-linearities in the structural organization. The output of a typical non-end-stopped simple cell in the visual cortex is limited by the fact that its firing rate cannot drop below zero. This means that if the sum of the positive and negative influences on the output of the cell should be negative overall, then the actual measured output will be zero. A formal analysis of this point has been made by Movshon et al. (1978a), who conclude that, by analogy with electrical devices, the simple cell can be thought of as *half-wave rectified* – that is, it allows a positive-going signal through but it fixes all other signals at zero. The actual level of input signal at which rectification occurs may vary from cell to cell.

Dobbins et al. (1987, 1989) build an end-stopped cell from the outputs of two non-end-stopped simple cells, each of which is modeled by a linear summation followed by half-wave rectification. In the model, the two simple cells have different length-summation zones, one short and one long. Subtraction of the (rectified) output of the "long" cell from the "short" cell results in an end-stopped cell that is sensitive to short lines or highly curved lines, but is insensitive to elongated lines. Because of the rectification prior to subtraction, this model does not predict complete linear spatial pooling between the end-zones and the center-zone of the receptive field. But, under conditions where center and end-zones are both stimulated above their thresholds, then linear pooling should be observed.

The most comprehensive tests of the interaction between the central region

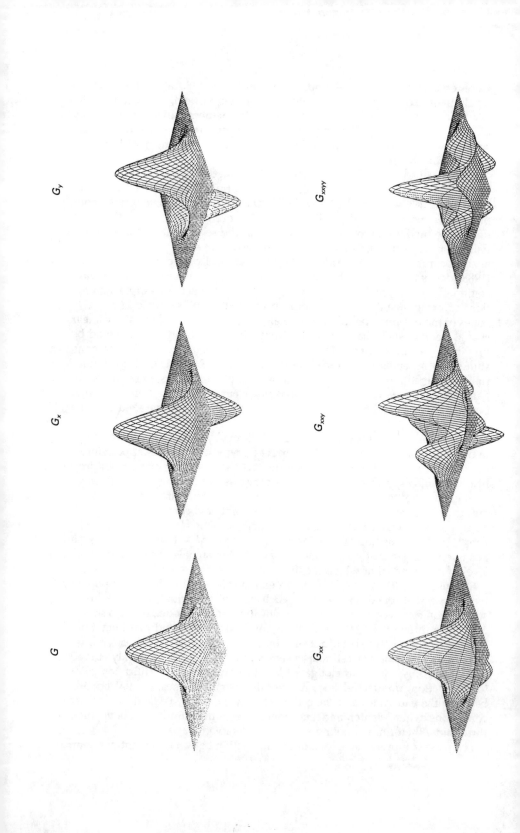

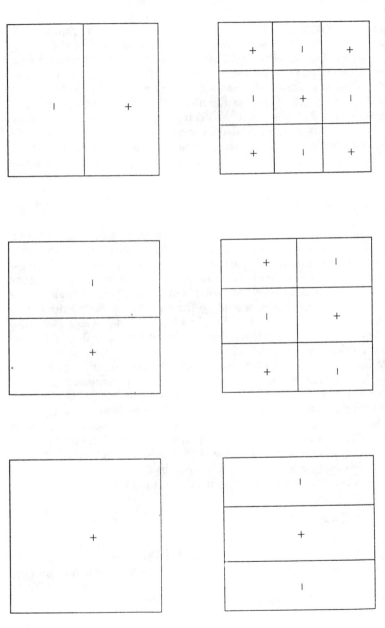

Figure 8.12 Above, A two-dimensional Gaussian function G and some of the functions created by taking its derivative in the x and y directions. Thus, G_{xy} is the original Gaussian function differentiated twice in the x direction and once in the y direction; the result has been rescaled vertically. Below, Receptive field maps in the style of Hubel and Wiesel (1962) that could correspond to the functions shown above. Regions marked + indicate where an increment of light would excite the receptive field and regions marked − show where a decrement of light would excite the receptive field.

and end-zones in end-stopped cells are due to Orban et al. (1979a,b) in cat V1. Summation along the length of the central region – corresponding to the central "+" region in receptive field model G_{xxyy} in figure 8.12 – was found to be approximately linear. The end-zones also seemed to summate independently, but then have a suppressive effect on excitation of the center-zone. It is notable that, in their work, the only effect of a bar in the end-zone is suppressive and it never enhances the response to a bar in the center-zone. According to the Koenderink and Richards (1988) model, a bright bar placed in one of the corner "+" regions of the model G_{xxyy} should add to the excitation created by a bar placed in the central "+" region (see figure 8.12). Unfortunately, it could be argued that the expected strength of the enhancement may be rather too weak to measure easily. So, although the Koenderink and Richards (1988) model is unlikely to be adequate, better data are really required.

Curvature Identification

It is important to distinguish between receptive field structures that give reliably different responses to curved and straight lines and those that might allow unambiguous labeling of a particular class of features within an image. If we are concerned with the *identification* of image features useful for contour analysis (as opposed to the detection of curvature changes), then a more interesting receptive field type would be the hypercomplex "corner detectors" found in cat areas 18 and 19 by Hubel and Wiesel (1965). Recently, Peterhans and von der Heydt (1991) have reported finding cells of this type in primate cortical visual areas, V2 and V3. The better characterized end-stopped cells found in cat V1 (Kato et al., 1978; Orban et al., 1979a,b) give the same response regardless of whether a line is curved leftwards or rightwards. Because they have end-zone inhibition at both ends, this gives the receptive field a degree of spatial symmetry, which entails an insensitivity to the sign of curvature. As mentioned previously, combinations of receptive field types (e.g. both G_{xxyy} and G_{xxy}) are needed to resolve these ambiguities. It would be very interesting to know if "corner-detecting" cells are constructed in this way, but, unfortunately, they have not yet been found in sufficient numbers to allow their full characterization.

Integration of Contour Analysis with Motion, Stereo, and Texture

One possible clue to the function of end-inhibition in cortical cells is the observation that end-stopped cells are often direction selective (particularly, end-stopped simple cells: Orban et al., 1979a) or binocular or both. Indeed, in the case of end-stopped direction selective cells in cat V1, Bolz and Gilbert (1986) have proposed that an inhibitory connection from cells with highly elongated receptive fields (found in the lowest of the six layers of the visual cortex) is responsible for the end-stopping observed in direction selective cells in layer 4 in the middle of the cortex layers. In monkey V1 there are direction selective, end-stopped cells in cortical layer 4b (Hawken et al., 1988), which is known to project to another visual area of the cortex (V5 or MT), which is particularly concerned with analyzing visual motion. However, the details of the intrinsic cortical projections and lamination patterns are different in cat and monkey V1 and receptive fields in layer 6 of the monkey do not appear as elongated as those in the cat.

Nonetheless, the primary feature in common with motion analysis and stereo analysis is the measurement of small spatial differences between two visual images, either in time or in disparity or both. It is arguable that the precise spatial organization of end-stopped receptive fields may be useful in this task. For example, Maske et al. (1987) propose that end-stopped receptive fields with a preference for short horizontal bars could be used in binocular matching and stereo detection. Furthermore, it has long been suspected that the non-linear type of spatial summation found in complex cells may reflect the fact that some of these cells are involved in measurements of textured elements in the visual scene (e.g. Graham et al., 1989). It is reasonable to conjecture that cells having both non-linear spatial summation *and* end-stopping might be involved in tasks such as the analysis of texture boundaries.

Outline Contour, Dense Depth Maps, and 3D Shape

Computing Shape

The rapid progress in computational studies of vision made over the past 10–15 years has resulted in a consistent view of 3D vision, in which various cues to depth are processed and re-represented in a viewer-centered description of the visual surfaces within the scene (Barrow and Tenenbaum, 1978; Marr and Nishihara, 1978; Marr, 1982; Brady et al., 1985; Besl and Jain, 1986). This surface-based description is used as a basis for a full 3D volumetric description of objects. The information to specify the surface-based description derives from so-called "dense depth cues", such as stereo, shading, motion, and texture. In this chapter and elsewhere (Johnston, 1988, 1989; Cumming et al., 1991; Parker et al., 1991), we have shown that there are systematic metrical errors in the perception of 3D shape by human observers. These errors persist even when the stimuli are very rich in cues to 3D shape. Such distortions would seem to provide a serious difficulty for a model of human object identification that is constructed around the outputs of different modules for extracting visual surfaces from depth cues, since the information from those modules seems to be subject to large absolute inaccuracies.

It is worth considering the following point. If a person were handed a cylindrical rod and asked to assess whether it was elliptical or truly circular, then the natural strategy, prior to using a measuring device, would be to inspect the rod end-on. This suggests that better information about 3D shape may be acquired from a careful selection of viewpoints, perhaps particularly if they contain powerful cues to outline shape. However, this proposal also raises the problem of how to integrate information over changes in viewpoint. Again, viewer-centered, surface-based descriptions of the scene seem rather cumbersome for solving this problem.

There seem to be two obvious lines of development for taking our understanding of 3D shape perception further. The first is to push still further toward an increased "degree of realism" in the information content of the visual stimuli. This would not only involve improved models for illumination and scene geometry of the sort discussed above, but would necessitate the study of shape perception in more complex scenes, so that cues such as classic linear perspective could be effectively specified. The second is to shift the emphasis away from what Marr (1982) termed the dense depth map and consider instead the shape information available from cues that are sparsely distributed over the visual scene. These cues arise from 3D object boundaries that project into specific 2D contour configurations in the retinal image. In particular, we know from common experience and many demonstrations in visual psychology how effective line drawings can be at conveying a qualitatively correct sense of 3D shape. It is also apparent that outline shape can often dominate shape information from dense depth cues (Barrow and Tenenbaum, 1981; Aloimonos and Liuqing Huang, 1990). This suggests that certain features within the image can be crucial for determining the interpretation of the remaining information.

Computing with Neurones

The possibility of using neural mechanisms to compute outline shape highlights a general deficiency in our understanding of visual processing within the nervous system. All methods of recovering global 3D shape will require some technique for linking local measurements of line or surface curvature, which are available as a consequence of the receptive field characteristics of single neurones early in the visual pathways. For example, Barrow and Tenenbaum (1981) use an interpolation method, based on local measures of curvature of line segments plus some global constraints on the Gaussian curvature of surfaces, to derive 3D shape from line figures. Whatever the details of the schemes used by biological visual systems, it is clear that information must be collated over significant distances within the topographical neural representation. This collation must be rather precise and yet the distances involved are much larger than the receptive field sizes of neurones early in the visual pathway. Receptive fields of much larger size are found at higher levels in the visual pathways, yet we have no very exact knowledge of the abilities of such receptive fields in processing the necessary types of geometrical information. Equally problematic is the fact that we cannot yet identify how the responses of local shape detectors might be modified dynamically by the global context in which their output is to be interpreted. The sparse nature of the information available from outline shape makes it especially puzzling how such information can be flexibly and efficiently communicated across significant distances within the "neural image" of the visual scene.

Acknowledgments

This research was supported by the Science and Engineering Research Council (GR/D/64193, GR/F/35043) and by The Wellcome Trust.

Notes

1 It is worth commenting briefly on the computational overheads incurred by this kind of work. Even with the restricted "degree of realism" in the images, the computing time required to produce one stereo pair was about 20 min on a reasonably powerful computer workstation (SUN Microsystems 3).
2 In practice, this also requires some care over the alignment of the mirrors forming the stereoscope, which is used to inspect the stereo pairs. It is important to consider carefully exactly how the light rays travel from the computer display via the mirrors to the eyes, in order to be sure that no distortions of the intended perspective projection have been introduced via the mirror geometry.
3 Those familiar with photography will be aware of these techniques for creating "softer" semi-directional illumination by means of a large reflector.

9

Identification of Disoriented Objects: A Dual-systems Theory

PIERRE JOLICOEUR

How do we do it? Normal humans, even at a young age, can recognize thousands of objects seen from a myriad of viewing angles, distances, illumination conditions, and background scenes. How is it that we can single out the internal representation that corresponds with such widely different retinal images? This question has been central for researchers interested in human pattern perception and recognition for over a century (e.g. Mach, 1886/1959; Dearborn, 1899; Gibson and Robinson, 1935; Arnoult, 1954). In many cases, we "see" patterns as being "the same object" despite differences in retinal stimulation. In most cases, however, we can also "see" the differences between the two stimuli – we perceive their orientation, size, location, and other "incidental" properties. That is, we do not factor out what is different, but the differences often do not obscure the identity of the underlying object or pattern, both objectively in terms of performance measures, or subjectively in terms of phenomenal appearance. This ability to perceive the identity of objects or patterns despite various transformations of the retinal image is sometimes referred to as *object constancy*, and in the case of changes in orientation across images as *orientation invariance* or *size invariance* in the case of changes in image size.

Much of the laboratory research on object constancy has focused on orientation invariance. There are many reasons for this focus, one of which is that it is relatively easy to manipulate the orientation of visual stimuli by rotating them in the image plane (e.g. Dearborn, 1899). The use of computers has, in fact, tended to make rotation a more difficult transformation to use than in the halcyon days of tachistoscopes[1] and index cards! But, this is not the only reason. Changes in pattern orientation create global transformations of the retinal image while leaving many properties of that image unchanged: the size is the same; the contrast is the same; the distance between any two points on the image is the same; and so on. Furthermore, the effects of a rotation are sometimes dramatic, as when we have difficulty recognizing

Marilyn Monroe in an upside-down picture (Rock, 1974); sometimes traumatic, as when exposed to Margaret Thatcher in the Thatcher Illusion (Thompson, 1980); yet sometimes hardly noticeable, as when we seemingly effortlessly see that NZ consists of disoriented versions of familiar characters.[2] In addition to an interesting mixture of empirical results, work on orientation effects has generated a number of theoretical positions, some of which have led to lively debate. For example, the manipulation of stimulus orientation has been fundamental to research in "mental rotation," which helped fuel the imagery proposition debate (see Kosslyn, 1981; Pylyshyn, 1981). Thus, the orientation transformation provides interesting and well-controlled stimuli for psychological experimentation, the associated research has produced results that include a rich set of observations and phenomena, and it has generated a range of hotly debated theoretical positions.

In this chapter, I review selectively some of the recent empirical and theoretical work that has focused on the effects of stimulus orientation. The next three sections review studies that have looked for effects of orientation on stimulus identification. A number of studies has revealed strong and systematic effects of orientation in various identification tasks. These studies are reviewed in the first section. In contrast, a number of studies have found small or non-significant orientation effects. These studies are reviewed in the second section. The third section examines results that provide some resolution to the apparent contradictions between the first two sets of studies. Following these sections, I review very briefly some evidence from brain-damaged subjects. In the last sections I describe a dual-systems theory and discuss how the theory can be used to integrate a wide range of empirical and theoretical work pertaining to the perception of disoriented forms.

Effects of Orientation on Identification and Memory

Effects on Memory

Much of the early work examined orientation effects on people's ability to remember visual shapes. In a typical experiment, subjects were shown visual stimuli in a learning or study phase, and their memory for these stimuli was tested later in a recognition phase. Often, the "old" previously seen stimuli were embedded in a set of "new" stimuli that had not been seen before (e.g. Rock, 1973). The typical finding in this type of experiment is that recognition memory is best when the stimuli are shown at the same orientation in the recognition phase as that used in the learning phase. In addition, recognition is often worse as the stimuli are rotated further from the orientation used in the learning phase. This result is especially robust when subjects are not informed that the orientation of the stimuli can change from the learning phase to the recognition phase (Rock, 1973; see also, Dearborn, 1899; Gibson and Robinson, 1935; Wiser, 1980; Jolicoeur and Rak, 1985).

Effects on Identification

More recently, several researchers have measured the effects of rotating patterns from their usual orientation on the time taken to identify them. For example, Jolicoeur (1985) asked subjects to name disoriented drawings of objects aloud as quickly as possible with the first name that came to mind. A millisecond clock was started with the onset of the object and was stopped when a voice key was triggered by the subject's vocal response. Figure 9.1 displays the mean time to name line drawings depending on the orientation of the depicted object.[3] Upright objects are labeled 0° and larger orientations represent clockwise rotations of the stimulus; the results shown for 360° are the same as those for 0°. As can be seen in figure 9.1, the time to name rotated objects increased sharply with increasing departure from upright and did so linearly from 0° to 120°. In contrast with the sharp increase in naming time from 0° to 120°, however, naming time was faster at 180° than at 120°. For expository convenience, I will refer to these results as M-shaped. Such M-shaped identification time results as a function of orientation have been reported elsewhere and seem quite common (e.g. Corballis et al., 1978; Jolicoeur et al., 1987; Jolicoeur, 1988; Jolicoeur and Milliken, 1989; McMullen and Jolicoeur, 1990).

Both the shape and the magnitude of the effects of orientation on naming time are noteworthy. First, consider the magnitude of the effects. These effects are substantial and are in the range usually accepted for mental rotation if we consider the results for stimuli within 120° of upright. This claim is corroborated further by experiments designed to compare the size of the effects directly across tasks. Subjects judged whether a disoriented drawing would face left or right if it had been presented upright, as quickly as possible while keeping errors to a minimum. In one study, using a between-subjects design, the slope of the orientation effect in the left–right task was not statistically different from the slope of the effect in the naming task, when orientations between 0° and 120° were considered (Jolicoeur, 1985, experiment 4). In another study, which used a within-subjects design, although the slope in the naming task was slightly (and significantly) shallower in naming than in mental rotation, the difference was quite small (see Jolicoeur, 1988, for details). In addition, the within-subjects design meant that there was an estimate of the slope of the orientation effect in both tasks for each subject. Thus, it was possible to compute a correlation on these scores to discover whether subjects displaying large orientation effects in the left–right task, presumably because they are slow mental rotaters, would also tend to display large orientation effects in the naming task. If the orientation effects in these two tasks share common processing mechanisms, such as mental rotation, and if the speed of execution and/or the efficiency of these mechanisms vary from individual to individual, then we should find a positive correlation between the slopes of the orientation effects in the two tasks. This correlation was $\tau = 0.35$ when the slopes were computed using the results ±

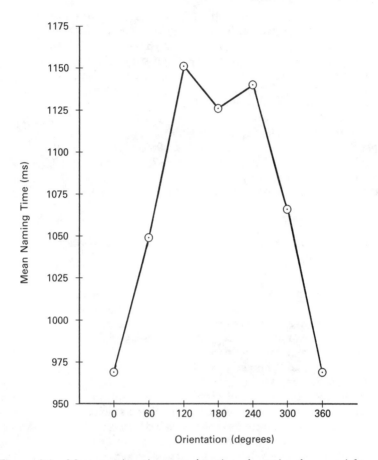

Figure 9.1   *Mean naming time as a function of rotation from upright.*

120° from upright. The small correlation was probably due to the counterbalancing techniques used to control for item and learning effects across orientations and subjects, which required that different items be seen in the different orientation conditions by any given subject (see Jolicoeur, 1985, or 1988). Thus, the naming time estimates for any particular subject would be partly confounded by item-specific effects such as the word frequency of the names of the items, which is known to have substantial effects on object naming times (Wingfield, 1968). I find it impressive that the slopes of the orientation effects still produced a significant correlation despite the built-in noise in the naming data at the subject-by-subject level. These two studies demonstrate that orientation effects on object identification are substantial and suggest that a mental rotation process could be the underlying cause.

The second major aspect of the naming results – the M-shape of the orientation effects – however, is quite unlike what is usually found in mental rotation experiments. Such non-monotonicity in the effects of a variable – orientation in the present case – has often been taken as a tell-tale sign for the operation of more than one underlying mechanism. This aspect of the results, however, will be discussed later in the chapter.

In general, the above results and those of several other studies show that human pattern perception and recognition is often quite sensitive to the orientation of the stimuli (see also Rock, 1956; Rock and Heimer, 1957; Ghent, 1960; Braine, 1965; Kolers and Perkins, 1969a,b; Yin, 1969, 1970; Shinar and Owen, 1973; Cavanagh, 1977; Navon, 1978; Pylyshyn, 1979; Jolicoeur and Kosslyn, 1983; Humphreys, 1984; Koriat and Norman, 1985; Maki, 1986; Humphrey and Jolicoeur, 1988; Tarr and Pinker, 1989; Jolicoeur, 1990).

Studies Finding Small or Nil Effects of Orientation on Identification

In contrast to the studies described and/or cited in the previous section, there have been a number of papers in which orientation effects on pattern identification have been very small and in some cases not statistically significant. Take, for example, the elegant experiments of Corballis et al. (1978). In their experiment 1, subjects named the upper-case letters, G, J, and R, and the digits 2, 5, and 7, shown in various orientations and in normal and left–right mirror-imaged versions. In the first block of trials, mirrored characters produced a sizable M-shaped orientation effect, although these effects were not as large as in studies in which subjects must make left–right decisions. Characters in normal format were associated with smaller orientation effects. In the second block of trials, the magnitude of the orientation effect for mirrored characters was reduced compared with that found in the first block. Each one of these blocks of trials involved 12 presentations of each character and the two experimental blocks had been preceded by an additional 12 presentations of each character in an unspeeded practice block.

Perhaps the most striking results in Corballis et al. (1978) came in their second experiment. In that experiment, each subject was assigned a single target character (G, J, R, 2, 5, or 7). The task was to press one of two keys as quickly as possible if the target was displayed in any orientation or version, and to press the other key if any of the other five characters was displayed. Response times were completely independent of the orientation of the characters. The results averaged response times from 60 presentations of the target character and 12 presentations for each of the other five characters.

Similar small or nil effects of orientation have been reported by a number of other researchers in identification and matching tasks (e.g. Corballis and Nagourney, 1978; White, 1980; Eley, 1982; Simion et al., 1982; Corballis, 1988; Koriat and Norman, 1989).

Resolutions of the Apparently Contradictory Results

Practice Effects

A number of studies have reported that the effects of stimulus orientation sometimes diminish over the course of testing with a particular subject and a particular stimulus set. For example, Shinar and Owen (1973) reported that, in the first part of an experiment, orientation had a substantial effect on the time to match a shape to a set of shapes in memory, in a memory-scanning paradigm (Sternberg, 1966). In later parts of the experiment, using the same shapes, the magnitude of the orientation effect on matching time was greatly reduced.

Similar practice effects have been obtained in later studies that required subjects to name objects as quickly as possible. Large effects of orientation are typically found in the early parts of these experiments. With repeated exposure to the same objects over the course of several blocks of trials, however, the orientation effects often become attenuated (Corballis et al., 1978; Jolicoeur, 1985, 1988; Maki, 1986; Jolicoeur et al., 1987; Jolicoeur and Milliken, 1989). What is perhaps more interesting is that the learning that takes place that allows subjects to be less sensitive to orientation effects appears confined to the particular stimuli that have undergone repeated testing – the "old" items. The attenuated orientation effects do not transfer to "new" items (Jolicoeur, 1985, 1988; Jolicoeur and Milliken, 1989). These results suggest that what is learned is not a general ability to perceive disoriented objects, which could have been the case because identifying disoriented objects may not be a very frequent activity (Biederman, 1985). Rather, it appears that subjects learn something over the course of these experiments that enables them to become increasingly insensitive to variations in stimulus orientation. In fact, it would have been rather surprising if such a general ability could be learned. If this were possible, one might expect that subjects would have done so over the course of their life prior to becoming subjects in these experiments; in which case we should not have observed any orientation effects at all – not even in the first blocks of trials.

Such practice effects may provide a partial resolution of the apparent discrepancies between studies that have found large orientation effects on pattern identification and those that have found small or nil effects. All the experiments that have reported nil effects had practice trials using the same stimuli used in "experimental" trials, they used a small number of stimulus patterns, and thus exposed the stimuli many times during the experiment (Corballis et al., 1978; Corballis and Nagourney, 1978; White, 1980; Eley, 1982). If just a few exposures can reduce the magnitude of orientation effects on identification time, as demonstrated in Jolicoeur (1985), for example, then one might expect that the magnitude of orientation effects would tend to be smaller for very familiar stimuli such as letters and digits, especially when they are repeated throughout an experiment (see Jolicoeur et al., 1987). In fact, it is possible to obtain sizable orientation effects on the time to name typical disoriented upper-case letters. Jolicoeur et al. (1987) have done so by recording responses to the first two trials in which any particular character was shown. In the next two trials, the orientation effects were already significantly reduced. Does this produce *a psychology of the first trial*?[4] To this charge, I plead guilty and innocent! Indeed, I believe that, in this particular case, there is a very interesting *psychology of the first trial* that needs to be explored further. The initial studies reveal that the pattern identification, which presumably requires one to find a match to stored representations in long-term visual memory, is quite sensitive to the orientation of the pattern. This is rather contrary to what one might expect from reading the chapter on pattern recognition in many introductory books on cognitive psychology (e.g. Lindsay and Norman, 1972). Apparently, in part, studies that have reported nil orientation effects may have inadvertently missed the first trial and formulated a psychology based mainly (sometimes only) on the *n*th trial. What we need, of course, is a formulation that considers both kinds of processing and that can account for the transition from the early trials (with large orientation effects) to the later trials (with smaller and sometimes nil orientation effects).

Two Routes

Another piece in the orientation puzzle concerns the frequently found M-shaped function relating identification time and orientation, when large orientation effects are found. Such non-monotonic functions have often been taken as evidence for the operation of more than one underlying process. In fact, I suspect that the M-shaped orientation effects on identification may be due to the operation of two underlying processing systems subserving pattern recognition.

The notion that the identification of objects that have undergone changes in orientation may be subserved by two underlying routes has been proposed by Humphreys and Riddoch (1984, 1985; Riddoch and Humphreys, 1986). Their evidence came from the study of five subjects with brain damage. The most important results, for present purposes, were obtained using three types of stimuli, all of which were photographs of familiar objects: prototypical views, foreshortened views, and minimal feature views. The prototypical views were photographed from a direction that did not strongly foreshorten the principal axis of the object, but the direction was slightly off-axis in order to show as many of the important attributes of the object as possible (see Palmer et al., 1981). The foreshortened views were taken from a direction that strongly foreshortened the principal axis of the object. Finally, the minimal feature views tended to display the objects rotated in the image plane and sometimes rotated about the principal axis in such a way as to reduce the salience of visual attributes usually associated with the depicted object, but without foreshortening along the principal axis.

The task of principal interest here was to match a prototypical view of an object with either a foreshortened view or with a minimal feature view. A visually similar distractor object was also used, and the subject's task was to choose which of two pictures matched the object in the prototypical view (the distractor or the foreshortened view). Several of their subjects' object-matching performance was very poor when matching prototypical views with foreshortened views, but had relatively good performance matching prototypical with minimal feature views. In contrast, one of the subjects had great difficulty matching minimal views but had relatively good performance with the foreshortened views.

The above pattern of results suggested to Humphreys and Riddoch that there may be two separate routes that could enable a subject to match different views of the same object: two routes to object constancy. One route would be dependent on an analysis of local features; the other route would depend on a more global form of processing that could somehow relate object parts to an intrinsic frame of reference defined by the object's main axis (Marr and Nishihara, 1978). Ratings by a separate group of normal subjects indicated that the salience of important attributes of the objects was greater in the foreshortened views than in the minimal feature views. In contrast, the rated figural goodness was higher for minimal feature views than for foreshortened views. A subject with damage to the local feature route should display better matching performance with foreshortened views than with minimal feature views – one subject exhibited this pattern of results. In contrast, a subject with damage to the global/axis route should be impaired on foreshortened views relative to minimal feature views, which was the case in four of Humphreys and Riddoch's five subjects. The patients who had difficulty with foreshortened views all had damage to the right hemisphere (see also Warrington and Taylor, 1973; Warrington and James, 1986). In contrast, the patient who had difficulty with minimal feature views (but not foreshortening) had bilateral occipital damage.

Multiple Orientation-specific Representations plus Transformations

My colleagues and I have suggested that the reduced orientation effects with practice could reflect one or both of two possible mechanisms (see Jolicoeur, 1985, 1988; Jolicoeur et al., 1987; Jolicoeur and Milliken, 1989; Murray et al., 1990). One mechanism could be based on attributes that are essentially orientation invariant such as texture, color, simple shape attributes, or relations between simple attributes. The other mechanism would involve the storage of several orientation-specific representations, and matching of incoming patterns to one of the multiple representations. In order for a recognition system to reduce the magnitude of orientation effects, the system would need to match the incoming stimulus with a representation corresponding with an orientation that was closer to the orientation of the depicted object than was the representation that corresponded with the upright object. It would be most efficient if the system somehow could find the stored representation with the orientation that was nearest to that of the stimulus. This scheme requires that the system be capable of storing multiple representations of the same object, as seen from different orientations, each representation corresponding with a specific orientation. Furthermore, the system must be capable of transforming the representation of an incoming pattern in such a way as to find a match with memory when the incoming pattern has an orientation that does not correspond with that of any of the stored representations. We suggested that the transformation that allows for these latter matches to take place could be mental rotation (as described in Shepard and Cooper, 1982). This possibility would account for orientation effects that are similar in magnitude to that found in "mental rotation experiments," and for the reduction in the magnitude of the orientation effect following exposure to views of the object in multiple orientations (Jolicoeur, 1985, 1988).

But, what evidence is there that people do in fact use a mental rotation process to match incoming patterns to stored representations when they *identify* disoriented patterns? Interestingly, Tarr and Pinker (1989) have provided strong evidence that human subjects sometimes do just that. A number of researchers had proposed previously that mental rotation was only used when the task required a left–right discrimination or a discrimination between mirror-imaged stimuli (effectively also a left–right discrimination: Hinton and Parsons, 1981; Corballis and McLaren, 1984). However, Tarr and Pinker's study demonstrated that subjects used mental rotation in an identification task that did not require discriminations between mirror-imaged stimuli. The representation of incoming patterns were apparently mentally rotated to match the stored representation with the nearest orientation. Tarr and Pinker argue that the ability to store a small number of orientation-specific representations, plus the ability to transform incoming patterns to match the nearest stored representation, overcomes one of the major traditional objections to "template" models or, more generally, to models in which patterns are stored in an orientation-specific format (Neisser, 1967). By storing a small number of well-chosen representations that span the range of possible views, the system can avoid both the cost of storing an excessively large number of representations and reduce the time spent performing costly transformations on the input pattern.

The results of Tarr and Pinker (1989) provide further support for my suggestion that mental rotation could underly the strong orientation effects found in the initial trials of experiments requiring subjects to identify disoriented patterns. However, do they explain the reduced orientation effects following multiple presentations of common objects (e.g. Jolicoeur, 1985; 1988; Maki, 1986; Jolicoeur and Milliken, 1989; McMullen and Jolicoeur, 1990)? The results at hand suggest not and seem to favor the claim that, in the case of natural objects, the reduction in the magnitude of orientation effects depends on the use of orientation-invariant attributes rather than on orientation-specific representations. The evidence supporting this claim comes from two studies in which identification performance following the previous viewing of upright objects produced as much reduction in the magnitude of orientation effects as the previous viewing of disoriented views (Jolicoeur and Milliken, 1989; Murray et al., 1990). Although it is possible that subjects could have mentally rotated images of the objects presented upright, which would have allowed them to store multiple orientation-specific representations of the objects, this possibility seems unlikely. It seems more plausible that the line drawings used (from Snodgrass and Vanderwart, 1980) are sufficiently rich in visual attributes and sufficiently diverse that subjects are able to isolate attributes of objects that are partially or completely orientation invariant and capable of discriminating among the objects in the stimulus set.

Orientation-specific and Orientation-invariant Information

A distinction between orientation-invariant object attributes and orientation-specific attributes has often been made in models and theories of pattern recognition (e.g. Sutherland, 1968; Milner, 1974; Corballis et al., 1978; White, 1980; Eley, 1982; Humphreys and Riddoch, 1984; Jolicoeur, 1985, 1988; Jolicoeur et al., 1987; Jolicoeur and Milliken, 1989; Tarr and Pinker, 1989). My colleagues and I have argued that the presence of strong orientation effects on identification in the early trials of an experiment suggest that the use of orientation-invariant attributes is not the default type of information used for pattern recognition. If objects were stored in representations that made exclusive use of orientation-invariant attributes, then we would not expect orientation effects during any part of these experiments. However, it appears that subjects do rapidly come to encode and use such attributes, which would account for the reduced orientation effects with practice, and for the fact that such reduced effects can follow the presentation of upright views only. Takano (1989, experiment 2) provided a nice demonstration that the encoding of orientation-invariant[5] attributes is an optional strategy and that subjects sometimes need to be coaxed into using it even when the stimuli are simple and few in number. This demonstration converges nicely with earlier results suggesting that the use of orientation-invariant attributes is not the default processing mode, but suggesting also that it is a processing mode that can be used efficiently when required. The strong effects of orientation on the initial attempts to identify disoriented objects suggest that the human visual system opts not to represent objects using only orientation-invariant attributes, although it is perhaps conceivable that it could do so. Takano's results provide good support for this point of view.

Object Constancy without Mental Rotation?

Farah and Hammond (1988) present an interesting case study of a patient, RT, whose performance in mental rotation tasks was very poor, but who could identify the majority of a set of upside-down objects presented to him (his performance on upright objects was significantly better than on upside-down objects). Farah and Hammond claimed that their patient's preserved ability to recognize misoriented objects despite his inability to perform mental rotation disconfirmed the hypothesis that orientation invariance is accomplished by mental rotation. This conclusion does not follow. Farah and Hammond have implicitly assumed that orientation invariance can be accomplished by only one system or route. However, there is good evidence that the identification of disoriented objects can be accomplished in at least two different ways or using two different systems (e.g. Humphreys and Riddoch, 1984; Jolicoeur, 1988). There is good laboratory evidence that mental rotation can be used by normal subjects to identify disoriented patterns (Tarr and Pinker, 1989) and that this mechanism may be one of at least two optional strategies available to subjects (Takano, 1989). In short, the dissociation between mental rotation and identification reported by Farah and Hammond is just what we would expect if orientation invariance can be achieved via two distinct systems, one of which was intact in RT.

Orientation Effects in Free-viewing and in Brief-masked Presentations

Empirical and theoretical reasons lead me to believe that very brief and masked presentations of stimuli may prevent the use of mental rotation for the purpose of identifying disoriented patterns. One consideration is that the time required to imagine a pattern rotating can easily take more than 100 ms for even modest amounts of disorientation (e.g. Jolicoeur, 1985, experiment 4). In the Jolicoeur and Landau (1984) experiments, however, the characters were exposed for much shorter durations before the onset of a pattern mask (see also Jolicoeur, 1990). The imagined rotation could involve a representation of the pattern, however, if there was enough time to encode the spatial structure of the stimulus. However, brief-masked presentations may allow one to encode simple shape attributes while making the encoding of spatial relations relatively difficult (e.g. see Mewhort et al., 1981). Encoding the relations between attributes is critical in constructing a spatial representation of the stimulus, which presumably is required in order to perform mental rotation. This possibility could explain some differences between Jolicoeur and Landau's (1984) results and those of Jolicoeur et al. (1987). Jolicoeur and Landau (1984) found no evidence for a reduction in the size of the effects of orientation on subjects' ability to identify briefly exposed and masked disoriented letters and the orientation effects were strikingly linear. In contrast, Jolicoeur et al. (1987) found clear-cut evidence for a reduction in the size of orientation effects with practice and some of the results suggested M-shaped orientation effects on the time to name upper-case letters that were in view until the subject's verbal response. It was argued in an earlier section that the M-shaped orientation effects could reflect the operation of two underlying systems and that the practice effects could reflect a shift from an initial use of mental rotation to an increasing use of orientation-invariant attributes. If these hypotheses are correct, then preventing mental rotation would likely change the shape of the function to something other than M-shaped and practice effects should be much less pronounced or eliminated, on the assumption that practice effects usually reflect a shift from mental rotation to feature extraction. The orientation effects revealed by this paradigm would be those associated with the non-rotational route to object constancy. Any orientation effects would suggest that even the non-rotational route makes use of attributes and/or spatial relations that are not orientation invariant (e.g. Jolicoeur and Landau, 1984). Additional evidence that orientation invariance observed following tachistoscopic presentations does not rely on mental rotation can be found in Farah and Hammond (1988). They reported that the effects of orientation on the responses of normal subjects following tachistoscopic presentations of rotated objects was similar to those of their patient (RT) who has difficulty performing mental rotation.

Where is the Top?

An important issue for anyone postulating that some form of mental rotation is involved in the process of identifying a disoriented object concerns how the system knows which way to rotate. Orientation effects are symmetric about 180° (upside-down), which suggests that, somehow, the system knows which rotation path is shorter (clockwise or counter-clockwise). A possibility usually dismissed on intuitive grounds (e.g. Corballis et al., 1978) is that patterns are somehow rotated in both directions simultaneously and that the representation that becomes upright first allows the system to find a match to memory. If this hypothesis is correct, the system does not need to know the location of the top of the object. However, most researchers do not seem to take this possibility seriously.

Three points of view have evolved concerning the relationship between the top-bottom directions of an object (more generally, orientation) and pattern recognition. Some have argued that information about the orientation of the object is derived first and used during the identification process (e.g. Rock, 1973; Marr and Nishihara, 1978; Marr, 1982). Some have argued that both orientation and identity information are extracted simultaneously, in parallel (e.g. Hinton, 1981). The third point of view, espoused by Corballis (1988), is that identity information is extracted first with little or no effects of orientation (except in special circumstances, such as when one tries to identify a particular person from an inverted image of their face). According to Corballis, shapes may be encoded in a frame-free description consisting mainly of orientation-invariant shape attributes. Orientation information about the pattern would be established following its identification and might be used occasionally merely to verify the identity of an already identified pattern. The studies that have investigated this issue have not been conclusive (e.g. Corballis et al., 1978; Braine et al., 1981; Corballis and Cullen, 1986; Maki, 1986).

McMullen and Jolicoeur (1989) examined this issue in some detail in the case of the identification of disoriented objects. In these experiments, a dot was presented either near the top or near the bottom of a disoriented object. The task was to decide as quickly as possible whether the dot was near the top or near the bottom of the object. The three most important results were as follows. First, the initial effects of orientation on top-bottom decisions were M-shaped, and in fact were indistinguishable from the initial effects of orientation on naming time (i.e. in the first block of each task). Secondly, orientation effects did not diminish over the course of six blocks of trials in which each object was shown in each block, unlike the findings in the naming task. Thirdly, the effects of orientation on naming time were not smaller when the subject was pre-cued with the orientation of an upcoming disoriented object (by displaying a dot near the top of the upcoming object) compared with a condition in which orientation was not cued (see also Braine, 1965).

The first result – highly similar orientation effects on naming and on top-bottom decisions – are consistent with Rock's (1973) intuitions concerning the intimate relationship between knowledge of top-bottom directions and knowledge about identity. But, there seems to be more required to make top-bottom decisions after practice than for identification. This claim is supported by the second result, the differential effects of practice in the two tasks. One account of the relatively persistent orientation effects on top-bottom decisions is that top-bottom decisions cannot be performed by extracting orientation-invariant attributes, whereas identification can. Consider an experiment in which the only stimulus with black and white stripes is a zebra. Upon detecting the presence of stripes the object's identity can be inferred, the object has been identified. It seems likely that the stripes would be perceived with only minimal effects of orientation on response time (e.g. Appelle, 1972). But, is the dot near the top or the bottom of the zebra? More generally, what is the orientation of the zebra? Clearly, knowledge about identity and orientation are independent in this situation. The results suggest that extracting orientation information requires a more detailed analysis of the visual stimulus than is required for naming after several repetitions of the stimulus set. McMullen and Jolicoeur (1989) argued that top-bottom decisions require the continued extraction of the spatial relations between shape attributes, whereas naming, in some circumstances, may proceed without the extraction of these relations.

The absence of a benefit on identification performance from advance orientation cues suggests that the time to find the top of a disoriented object is not the principal time-consuming operation that produces orientation effects on naming time, as has sometimes been suggested (e.g. Biederman, 1987; see also Rock, 1973). These results also seem particularly damaging to the Marr and Nishihara (1978) model. Shapes are represented in this model using object-centered representations that are effectively orientation free. One account of the observed orientation effects found in naming tasks would be to locate these effects in the stage that finds the main axis of the object and to suppose that axis-fitting might be faster for upright objects than for disoriented ones because it takes longer to find the top of disoriented objects. That account is untenable given the absence of benefit from advance orientation cues.

Huttenlocher and Ullman (1987) have proposed a scheme for building a recognition system capable of recognizing disoriented objects. Their approach is to store a small number of local features (at least three) and the spatial relations among these features. In addition, the spatial relations between the set of "key" local features and a fuller description of the objects is also encoded. The important idea in their approach is to use the small set of features to compute how the object presented for recognition needs to be transformed in order to align it with a stored representation. The small set of key features is used to find matches in a memory bank of stored sets of keys. Once a match to one or more sets of keys is found, these matches can be used to compute how the input pattern should be transformed so as to match the more complete stored representation. The system then performs a series of confirmatory checks to verify that the located representation and the transformation derived from the feature keys does indeed provide an account of the visual data input to the system.

In a system with the representational complexity comparable to that of a human adult, it seems likely that most objects, on initial viewing, would contact several sets of keys. Nonetheless, the size of the search space would be reduced considerably compared with the task of searching through the entire set of representations. Once a key is selected, the stored spatial information can be used to compute a transformation that will align the stored representation with the input image. In the human visual system, the alignment process could well be mental rotation. The interesting possibility suggested by the work of Huttenlocher and Ullman is that the human perceptual system might use a similar scheme. Landmark features (e.g. Hochberg and Gellman, 1977) could be used initially to help determine the direction of rotation required to put a pattern upright and enable a complete match to be found. Later, depending on the experimental context (see Jolicoeur and Milliken, 1989), the landmark features themselves and probably some additional shape attributes may be sufficient to discriminate one object from the others in the stimulus set, which could allow the system to reduce the need to perform a full transformation in order to identify an object and would produce a reduced orientation effect with practice. Huttenlocher and Ullman's (1987) approach could provide an answer to the issue of how subjects seem to know which way to rotate a disoriented object in order to put it upright with the minimum amount of rotation. Note also the relationship between the claims of Corballis (1988) and the alignment approach proposed by Huttenlocher and Ullman. If Corballis's frame-free representations correspond with Huttenlocher and Ullman's keys, then the transformation process in Huttenlocher and Ullman's model might correspond with Corballis's notion of a check or verification of the detailed identity of the object. Where I tend to disagree with Corballis, however, is that he suggests that the transformation process is optional and unnecessary in most cases, whereas I believe that the transformation process is required for identification initially, and only later becomes less important. As discussed earlier, this difference of opinion may be a matter of what one chooses to emphasize (the first trial, the nth trial, or the change from trial 1 to trial n).

Conclusions

The main focus in this chapter has been on how people identify known visual objects despite changes in their orientation across different exposures. The fact that people can often do this is a special case of the more general problem – object constancy – of how we can identify objects despite numerous potential changes in the pattern of retinal stimulation. The fact that we can do this at all suggests either that the representations and processes used by the visual system are capable of transforming diverse patterns of retinal stimulation so as to compensate for the changes in stimulation resulting from rotation, or that the attributes that are represented in visual memories of objects are relatively stable across the different views, or both. I believe that the weight of the evidence suggests that the human visual system can and does use both approaches to overcome the changes in retinal stimulation produced by rotations of objects, and I present a dual-systems theory of identification process below. First, the main empirical and theoretical points that have emerged from the review are summarized briefly:

- Changing the orientation of a pattern between the learning and test phase of a memory experiment usually impairs recognition (Rock, 1973).
- The time to name disoriented line drawings of objects is sharply affected by orientation; the effects are usually linear between 0° and 120° with a slope comparable to that obtained in classic mental rotation experiments (Jolicoeur, 1985, 1988).
- The overall shape of the orientation function, however, often has a dip at 180°, which gives rise to an M-shaped function (Jolicoeur, 1988).
- The magnitude of orientation effects on identification time often decreases with practice if the same stimuli are repeated several times over the course of an experiment (Jolicoeur, 1985, 1988; Jolicoeur et al., 1987; Jolicoeur and Milliken, 1989).
- Studies in which there have been minimal orientation effects have used a small stimulus set consisting of simple patterns that have been repeated several times (Corballis et al., 1978; White, 1980; see also Koriat and Norman, 1989). Thus, practice effects could have reduced the size of orientation effects on the identification of these stimuli.
- The presence of strong orientation effects in some cases and their absence in others, plus neurological dissociations suggesting the existence of two underlying routes to object constancy (Humphreys and Riddoch, 1984; Farah and Hammond, 1988), plus the non-monotonic (M-shaped) orientation effects in normal subjects, all provide good and converging evidence for at least two underlying mechanisms supporting orientation constancy.
- Evidence for the use of both postulated systems has been found in elegant laboratory studies. Tarr and Pinker (1989) have shown that subjects sometimes use mental rotation to identify disoriented patterns even when

there is no need to discriminate between mirror images. Takano (1989) has shown that subjects often use mental rotation to identify objects, but that they can also make use of what he calls orientation-free information if required to do so.

- Results from several studies suggest that mental rotation is used in the initial stages of identification experiments and that there is a gradual shift from a mental-rotation strategy to a strategy based on the extraction of shape attributes that are less orientation sensitive (Jolicoeur, 1985, 1988; Jolicoeur et al., 1987; Jolicoeur and Milliken, 1989; Murray et al., 1990).
- Orientation effects in brief-masked displays tend to be linear and resistent to practice (Jolicoeur and Landau, 1984; see also Jolicoeur, 1990) and may not be subsumed by mental rotation (Farah and Hammond, 1988).
- The time to decide whether a dot is near the top or bottom of a disoriented object is affected by orientation in the same way as the time to name the object, initially. With repeated presentations, however, top-bottom decisions are not attenuated as they are in naming (McMullen and Jolicoeur, 1989).
- Pre-cueing with the orientation of a disoriented object does not reduce the magnitude of the orientation effect on the time to name the object (Braine, 1965; McMullen and Jolicoeur, 1989).
- The alignment model of Huttenlocher and Ullman (1987) provides a potential solution to the problem of how the visual system might know which way to rotate a disoriented pattern in the most efficient way without knowing the identity of the pattern.

A Dual-systems Theory

The dual-systems theory I propose has been developed throughout the chapter and can be summarized as follows. The theory borrows many ideas from other researchers and theorists in the area, and in particular from Humphreys and Riddoch (1984). I hope that I can stand on their shoulders and provide a coherent overview of the many empirical results that need to be explained.

First, it is assumed that there are at least two functionally separate systems that can be used to identify disoriented patterns: a mental-rotation system and a feature-based system. The mental-rotation system uses mental rotation to transform disoriented patterns by aligning them to the retinal upright (McMullen and Jolicoeur, 1990), at which point contact can be made with stored orientation-specific representations that are also referenced to the retinal upright. The feature-based system is postulated to rely on the extraction of shape attributes and surface attributes of objects (Price and Humphreys, 1989; cf. Biederman and Ju, 1988), some (but not all) of which are orientation invariant. In normal subjects these two systems operate in parallel and either one can achieve a match to memory representations. The time taken for the first system to find a match will determine the time taken to identify the object.

Somehow, the mental-rotation system is able to compute which way to rotate the input image along the shortest path, at least on a substantial fraction of the trials. The decision about how to rotate the object could be guided by an alignment scheme such as the one proposed by Huttenlocher and Ullman (1987). In the case of the human visual system, however, the alignment process could be supported by additional general heuristics. For example, the "natural" orientation of most elongated objects is either vertical or horizontal (a constraint imposed by the physics of gravity). Very few objects are balanced on a long thin point and if a thin protrusion is found on an object, there is a high probability that this part of the object does not belong on the ground. Another heuristic might be that most animals have their feet closer to the ground than to the sky. If, for example, the recognition system had partial evidence for the presence of "feet" on one side of an object, that evidence could be used to rotate the postulated feet towards the bottom of the retinal reference frame, through the shortest rotation path. Note that detecting the presence of feet and using this attribute to rotate the object and then identify it is quite different from Corballis's (1988) suggestion that the system already knows what the object is and only uses mental rotation to confirm this knowledge. In the present case, all that could be decided from a knowledge that the object had feet is that it has a good likelihood of being an animal. If it turns out to be an animal, however, and if the system is able to pinpoint which animal, then the system would have been able to rotate the image through the shortest path without knowing what the object actually was until the uprighting process terminated – no small feat! This in turn suggests that there may be some top-down involvement in the identification process especially when the top of the object is at the bottom of the frame of reference.[6]

The feature-based system does not use mental rotation. Instead, this system uses sets of shape attributes and matches these attributes to representations that map such attributes onto more complete representations of the object. The attributes could be orientation sensitive or orientation invariant. The feature-based system does not necessarily need to preserve detailed spatial relations between the extracted shape attributes in order to achieve a match to memory. In contrast, the representations contacted by the mental-rotation system are postulated to be functionally spatially isomorphic to the stimuli (see Shepard, 1981).

It is likely that the feature-based system, like the mental-rotation system, is also sensitive to the orientation of the pattern, but for different reasons. The features themselves are likely, in general, to be somewhat sensitive to orientation, but the effects on performance should be much smaller than those associated with mental rotation. For example, the presence of bilateral symmetry could be such an attribute or feature. Symmetry is detected most quickly when the axis of symmetry is vertical and tends to be detected more slowly at oblique orientations (±45°, for example). Suppose that an upright object, such as a vase, is also symmetrical about the vertical axis. The presence of symmetry would be detected most quickly when the object was upright or upside-down and would be detected more slowly at all other orientations. If the feature-based system can make use of this attribute to narrow down the set of possible objects to consider, we would expect some orientation sensitivity even if mental rotation was not used.

When identification is possible from the extraction of isolated features, that is, without a full set of spatial relations linking that attribute to others in the representation of the object, the effects of orientation are expected to be especially small. The attributes that are orientation invariant include texture, color, size, particular types of line intersections and angles, global properties such as complexity, jaggedness, smoothness, and so on. In addition, however, the system may use spatial relations, especially ones that are categorical in nature, such as "next to" or "connected to." These relations are less sensitive to changes in orientation than metric relations, but may be affected by orientation changes nonetheless (see Kosslyn, 1987).

The fact that the extraction of the features themselves may be sensitive to orientation can be used to explain why robust orientation effects are found in studies using brief-masked stimuli even though the mental rotation system may have been prevented from operating effectively by the brief-masked presentations. If the feature-based system was completely orientation-invariant, it would be difficult to account for results such as those of Jolicoeur and Landau (1984; Jolicoeur, 1990). In addition, the theory may account for these results because masking may increase the positional uncertainty associated with shape attributes (e.g. Mewhort et al., 1981) and make the recovery of categorical spatial relations more difficult to perceive than in normal viewing (see Koriat and Norman, 1989).

The theory can provide two accounts of the decreased effects of orientation that follow repeated exposures of the stimuli. One account is that subjects can store multiple orientation-specific representations of the objects, one for each orientation in which the object has been seen previously. On a subsequent presentation, the mental-rotation system need only rotate an input pattern to the representation with the least discrepant orientation. My colleagues and I suggested this possibility (Jolicoeur, 1985, 1988; Jolicoeur et al., 1987) and recently Tarr and Pinker (1989) have provided strong evidence that subjects can store multiple orientation-specific representations of objects and in fact use mental rotation to identify patterns by rotating to the nearest orientation neighbor of the input pattern. The other account is that the initially large effects of orientation reflect the operation of the mental-rotation system. With repeated exposures the subject builds up or strengthens representations suitable for the feature-based system. The gradual decrease in the magnitude of orientation effects with practice would reflect the gradual shift from identification mediated by the mental-rotation system to identification mediated by the feature-based system. In the case of natural objects, the present evidence supports the latter account (Jolicoeur and Milliken, 1989; Murray et al., 1990).

The theory can also account for the greater resistance to practice of orientation effects in the top-bottom task and in the left–right (or normal–mirror) task than for naming. The observation here is that although naming can sometimes be mediated by the feature-based system without the use of any relational information (for example, saying "canary" upon seeing yellow in a stimulus once the subject knows that the only yellow object in the stimulus set is a canary), top-bottom and left–right decisions cannot be carried without the extraction of more detailed relational information.

The theory accounts for the M-shaped orientation effects on initial identification because both systems operate in parallel. It must be supposed that the feature-based system has some advantage over the mental-rotation system when objects are shown at 180° or near 180°. One possible reason is that some categorical relations and/or some isolated attributes are relatively unaffected by a 180° rotation (e.g. symmetry). In this view, the M-shaped effects reflect a mixture of identifications resulting from the mental-rotation system and from the feature-based system. The studies that report minimal or nil orientation effects have used situations in which identification could be mediated by the feature-based system, according to the theory. This could have been due either to effects of practice or to the use of stimuli that were easily discriminable using orientation-invariant stimuli (see Koriat and Norman, 1989; Takano, 1989).

Finally, if, as theorized, large initial effects of orientation on the identification of natural objects are due to mental rotation, then pre-cueing with the orientation of the stimulus should not reduce the magnitude of these orientation effects (see Cooper and Shepard, 1973), which is what was found by McMullen and Jolicoeur (1989).

Notes

1   A device much used in the past to display stimuli briefly to human subjects.
2   No disrespectful allusions to our New Zealand friends intended.
3   These means were computed by averaging the mean naming times for objects seen for the first time across experiments 1, 2, and 3 in Jolicoeur (1985).
4   I thank Lee Brooks for pointing this out.
5   Takano (1989) uses the labels "orientation-free" and "orientation-bound" information.
6   This is not to deny that much of the processing is bottom-up.

10
Surface Layout from Retinal Flow

MIKE HARRIS, TOM FREEMAN, AND GLEN WILLIAMS

As an observer moves around the world, the retinal image changes smoothly over time. J. J. Gibson (e.g. 1950, 1979) was the first to emphasize that, rather than making vision more difficult, this smooth change might actually be very useful because it provides a great deal of information about the observer's movement and about the three-dimensional structure of the world. He pointed out, for example, that as we approach an object, its image gradually expands so that each point moves steadily away from a unique "focus of expansion." As long as we keep our eyes still, this focus coincides exactly with the direction in which we are moving, and so provides a simple cue for sensing and controlling our locomotory heading. Similarly, as we move about, the rate of the resulting image change depends systematically upon our distance from objects in the world. This is particularly noticeable if you look out of the side window of a moving car or train: things which are close to you flash past, while those further away maintain a relatively stately progress. Gibson realized that, because of this, movement relative to a rigid surface will generally produce a smooth gradient of speed in the image, and that this gradient can tell us about the three-dimensional layout of the surface.

During the past 15 years or so, several mathematical treatments have been developed (e.g. Koenderink and van Doorn, 1975, 1976b, 1981; Clocksin, 1980; Longuet-Higgins and Prazdny, 1980; Prazdny, 1983a; Koenderink, 1985, 1986; Rieger and Lawton, 1985; Waxman and Wohn, 1988) which formalize Gibson's inspired insights into the potential uses of retinal motion in guiding locomotion and in specifying three-dimensional surface layout. These analyses have so far had a much greater impact upon the computational community than upon psychologists and, perhaps because of Gibson's own lack of interest in such questions, they have directly inspired rather little psychophysical or neurophysiological work into the kinds of processes which encode retinal motion in the human visual system. As a result, although we have several ideas about how people *might* make use of retinal motion, we have yet to develop a coherent model of how, and even whether, they actually do so.

In this chapter we outline a very simple interdisciplinary approach to the analysis of retinal motion in the human visual system. Our goal is to use existing mathematical descriptions to identify the kinds of processes that might be involved in the analysis of retinal motion, and then to outline psychophysical and neurophysiological techniques which are relevant to their study.

The Optic Array and Optic Flow

One of Gibson's most important contributions was actually to shift emphasis away from the retinal image as the effective stimulus for vision, to think instead in terms of the optic array and, more importantly, of the smooth changes or transformations of this array which we experience as we move about. The optic array is simply the bundle of light rays which impinges from all directions upon each point in the environment. Objects in the world can be thought of as labelling specific rays, so allowing us to keep track of the changes in the optic array as we move from one position to another. This concept is illustrated in figure 10.1, which shows a 2D fragment of the optic array associated with just two different positions in the same simple world. An observer who moves smoothly from point A to point B has access to an optic array which gradually transforms from that shown in figure 10.1a to that shown in figure 10.1b. Notice that, in this example, the observer moves directly towards object O2, and that the ray associated with this object is the only one which does not change its position. The rays associated with all the other objects move smoothly away from this ray in a way that clearly depends partly upon the direction of the objects relative to the direction of observer movement (compare the rays associated with objects O1 and O3), and partly upon their distance from the observer (compare the rays associated with objects O4 and O5).

Of course, since light generally impinges upon each point in space from all directions, the optic array is really three-dimensional, rather than two-dimensional as depicted in figure 10.1. A more generally useful representation is therefore to imagine a sphere centered upon the viewpoint. The smooth transformation of the optic array produced by movement of the observer is termed optic flow, and can be thought of as the overall pattern of paths which the rays draw out upon the surface of this sphere. This representation is illustrated in figure 10.2, which shows a fragment of the optic flow patterns produced by movement of the observer relative to an evenly textured vertical surface. Each line represents the path traced out by the ray associated with a single texture element. Of course, because this figure should really be drawn upon the surface of a sphere, any representation on a flat piece of paper inevitably distorts the pattern. However, for small sections of the pattern, the distortion is small and we can, for the moment, safely ignore it.

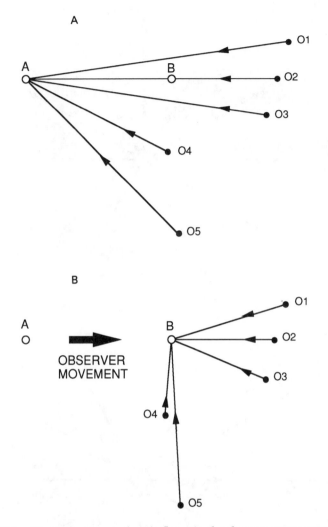

Figure 10.1 *The optic array and optic flow. As the observer moves smoothly from point A to point B, the light rays coming from objects in the world smoothly change in angle.*

Figure 10.2a shows the optic flow pattern that results when the vertical surface is at right angles to the observer's direction of movement. As we would expect from figure 10.1, the ray which coincides with direction of movement remains stationary, and all the other rays move smoothly away from it. Figure 10.2b shows the flow pattern when the vertical surface is at an angle to the direction of movement. Again, the ray coinciding with the

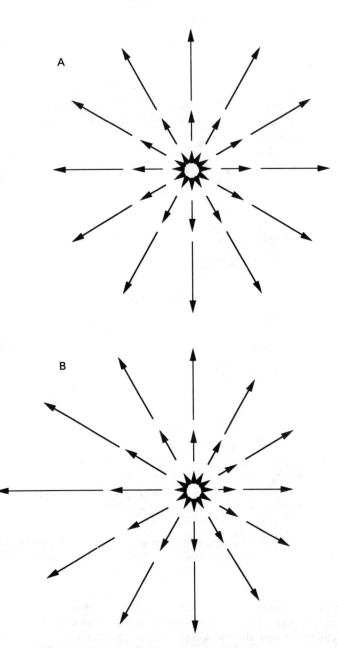

Figure 10.2   *Typical optic flow patterns. a, Movement toward a vertical surface at right angles to the angle of approach. b, Movement toward a vertical surface tilted relative to the angle of approach so that the left side is nearer the observer.*

direction of movement remains stationary and all the other rays move smoothly away from it, although this time the pattern is rather different.

A comparison of figure 10.2a and b makes clear two important points about the optic flow pattern. First, the direction of motion of each ray is determined entirely by the observer's direction of movement. Both figures show the same basic radial pattern and so this aspect of the flow is unaffected by variations in the 3D layout of surfaces in the world. This simple property provides the basis for Gibson's idea that the focus of expansion may be useful in determining locomotory heading. All the observer has to do to work out which way he or she is moving is to locate the focus of expansion or, more generally, to extrapolate the paths of any two elements back to the point at which they intersect. This simple strategy will always work because the directional aspects of the optic flow pattern are unaffected by the structure of the external world.

Secondly, optic flow patterns are characterized by smooth gradients of speed both in the direction of the flow and at right angles to it. In figure 10.2a and b, for example, speed increases smoothly along each radial line, i.e. in the direction of the flow. In figure 10.2a, the flow pattern is symmetrical so that speed is constant around any circle centered upon the focus of expansion. Thus, in this case, there is no speed gradient at right angles to the direction of flow. In figure 10.2b, however, there is a clear speed gradient at right angles to the direction of flow so that, at any given distance from the focus of expansion, speed is greater on the left of the figure than on the right. This follows simply from the fact that the surface in figure 10.2b is not at right angles to the direction of locomotion, so that elements on the left-hand side of the figure are closer to the observer. The important point to note is that, while a given movement of the observer always produces the same *directional* pattern of optic flow, the *speed* of flow is affected by the 3D structure of the world. In figure 10.2b, for example, the speed gradient at right angles to the direction of flow clearly carries information about the angle of the surface relative to the direction of locomotion.

From the above simple illustrations it should be clear that the informative aspects of optic flow lie not in how individual elements change their *position*, but in how they change their *relationships* to each other. If we use optic flow to guide locomotion or to inform us about the layout of the world, then, in addition to a "classic" motion system which is capable of signalling the speed and direction of motion of each element in the flow pattern, we also need a "relative" motion system that combines the outputs of these individual classic motion encoders to produce mechanisms sensitive to particular *spatial patterns* of flow. Relative motion mechanisms capable of signalling information about the direction of observer locomotion need only be sensitive to the directional aspects of the pattern. Those capable of signalling information about the structure of the world must also be sensitive to speed gradients. Before considering these relative motion mechanisms any further, however, we need to introduce the important distinction between optic and retinal flow.

Retinal Flow

The optic array is a very convenient mathematical abstraction but, if we wish to relate our account to human vision, we need to shift our attention back to the retinal image. Since the eye is roughly a sphere centered upon the viewpoint, it may at first seem that the actual pattern of retinal flow which the observer experiences is, to all intents and purposes, the same as the optic flow pattern which we have described. In fact, this is more or less the case when the observer moves from one position to another *while maintaining a fixed angle of view* but this is obviously fairly unrealistic in that people generally move their eyes about to fixate different things in the world as they move around it. In other words, rather than thinking of observer movement as a simple linear *translation* from one position to another, we need to think of this movement as a combination of a translation and a *rotation* about the viewpoint. The rotational component of the movement results from eye movements and rotations of the head about the line of sight.

Rotational movements will clearly have no effect upon the optic array itself, because this is just a description of the structure of the light that impinges upon each point in space. In these terms, we can think of eye movements simply as a way to bring different portions of the optic array into the retinal image. However, rotations do have a profound effect upon the retinal image, shifting the whole pattern in the opposite direction to the rotation. To illustrate this important point, figure 10.3 depicts the same situation as in figure 10.2a but shows what happens to the retinal flow pattern when the observer smoothly tracks one of the elements in the flow pattern. The important points to emerge from a comparison of figures 10.2 and 10.3 are that the actual retinal flow pattern is not generally the same as the theoretical optic flow pattern, and that simple features of the optic flow, such as the focus of expansion, are not necessarily available directly from the retinal flow. Note that a given rotation will always produce precisely the same pattern of flow upon the retina and so it provides no information whatsoever about the observer's locomotory heading or about the structure of the external world. Since the observer has direct access to retinal flow rather than optic flow, the relative motion system must somehow disentangle the informative aspects of the pattern, produced by translation, from the uninformative aspects, produced by rotation.

Differential Invariants: Div and Curl

How might the relative motion system recover the informative aspects of retinal flow? A promising first step would be to identify a set of fundamental components into which any flow pattern could by decomposed. One such set has been proposed by Koenderink and van Doorn (1976b) who, using vector calculus, confirmed that optic flow could be decomposed into just the three

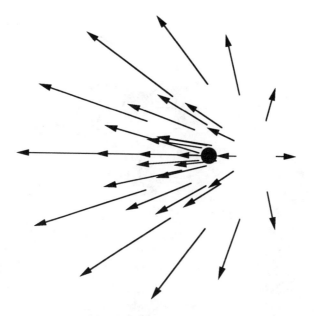

Figure 10.3   *Retinal flow. The optic flow pattern shown in figure 10.2a distorted by a rightward eye rotation. The small dot in the center of the figure shows the point toward which the observer is heading.*

components of *curl* (local rotation), *div* (local expansion), and *def* (local deformation). These components are called differential invariants. They are all based upon spatial derivatives, simply measuring the rate of change of speed in different directions, and so they look a particularly promising way to capture both the directional aspects of the pattern and its speed gradients. Although *def* is often regarded as the simplest of these components to use (e.g. Koenderink, 1985), we shall concentrate here upon *div* and *curl* because *curl*, especially, has been largely neglected. We shall begin by outlining their basic properties then go on, following Koenderink and van Doorn's work, to describe how they might be used to recover useful information about locomotory heading and 3D surface layout.

   The value of *curl* at each point in a flow field is a measure of the local rotation at that point, while *div* is the equivalent measure of local expansion. Both are derived from localized estimates repeated everywhere, so each component gives rise to a 2D function defined over the whole field. We can therefore think of a 2D *div* function and a 2D *curl* function which respectively describe the overall patterns of local expansion and rotation in the flow field. *Div* and *curl* are both scalars, even though they are derived from vectors, so these 2D functions are decribed by single value at each point in the field.

   Figure 10.4 shows the kind of physiological mechanisms which might

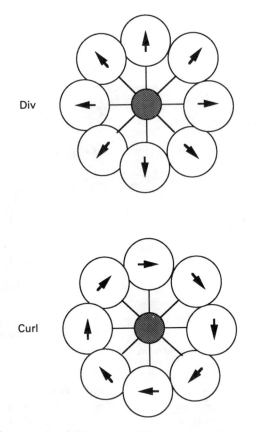

Figure 10.4   *The receptive fields of plausible neural mechanisms for estimating local rotation (curl) and local expansion (div).*

plausibly be used to estimate *div* and *curl* at each point in the retinal flow field and which are therefore candidate elements of our putative relative motion system. Each mechanism simply adds together the outputs from a set of velocity sensors with appropriate directional selectivity and spatial position. These models illustrate how *div* and *curl* act as differential operators. In both cases, the opposed directional selectivity of the pairs of velocity sensors on opposite sides of the circle effectively turns the addition into a subtraction, so that each pair computes the change in speed at a particular orientation. Because of the particular choice of individual velocity sensors, the opposing pairs making up the *div* mechanism actually compute the change in speed *along* each direction, whilst those of the *curl* mechanism compute the change in speed *at right angles* to each direction. This again looks promising, because we have already seen (figure 10.2) that retinal flow fields are

On-center

Off center

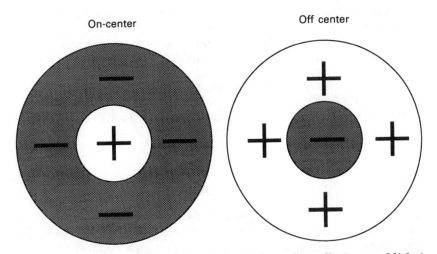

Figure 10.5 *The receptive fields of typical retinal ganglion cells. Increased light in a + area produces an increase in response, increased light in a − area produces a decrease in response.*

characterized by speed gradients both along and at right angles to the direction of flow.

The possible usage of *div* and *curl* may be made clearer by analogy with the more familiar example of luminance encoding by retinal ganglion cells. Retinal ganglion cells have luminance receptive fields made up from concentric, antagonistic regions, like the ones shown in figure 10.5. In effect, each cell compares the luminance of the image at adjacent positions and thus performs a differential operation, signalling the luminance gradient in the image at one position. Because the receptive fields are circular-symmetric, each cell simply sums the luminance gradients over all orientations. This is clearly analogous to the operations performed on motion, rather than luminance, by the *div* and *curl* encoders shown in figure 10.4. Each *div* or *curl* mechanism signals the speed gradient either along or at right angles to each orientation at one position in the flow field. Again, because the receptive fields are circular-symmetric, the appropriate speed gradients are summed over all orientations.

Returning to the case of luminance encoding, the output of a single retinal ganglion cell is of little use. However, the 2D response function provided by an array of retinal ganglion cells, one at each position in the image, is an extremely efficient way of extracting the useful information from the spatial pattern of image luminance. In this case, the 2D function accentuates the places where luminance changes abruptly and these tend to correlate with object boundaries in the external world. By analogy, the output of a single *div* or *curl* encoder would be of very little use. But the 2D functions produced by computing *div* and *curl* at every position in the flow field is potentially very useful. In this case, rather than simply accentuating rapid abrupt spatial changes, they also provide useful spatial maps of the smooth speed gradients typical of retinal flow patterns. To see how these maps would be useful in guiding locomotion and recovering surface layout, we need to consider the 2D *div* and *curl* functions produced by movements of the observer about the world. Fortunately, this has already been done for us by Koenderink and van Doorn (1976b). As before, we shall begin with the simple case of translational movements, where optic flow and retinal flow are roughly equivalent, and then go on to consider the effects of introducing rotational movements.

Some Possible Uses of the 2D Div and Curl Functions

The scheme which we describe is based upon Koenderink and van Doorn's (1976b) mathematical analysis of the simple situation depicted in figure 10.6, which defines the coordinates of the optic array. The bundle of light rays which impinges upon the point P at distance z_0 from a flat surface can be described in terms of the angles ϕ and θ, relative to the surface normal projected through point P. The angle ϕ defines a half-meridian in this optic array, while angle θ defines the eccentricity around it.

What happens to the optic array when point P moves in a horizontal plane at speed v and an angle α relative to the surface normal? We already know, from figure 10.1, that each ray swings outward by a varying amount as P moves directly towards the surface (i.e. along the surface normal, with angle $\alpha = 0°$). Figure 10.7 simply replots figure 10.2a, with the coordinate system superimposed to show how each ray moves as a function of ϕ and θ. Koenderink and van Doorn (1976b) showed that optic flow fields, like the one depicted in figure 10.7, can be decomposed into the orthogonal components *div*, *curl*, and *def* and they derived formal expressions for each of these components. The formal expressions for *div* and *curl* form the starting point for our own approach and so we quote them here direct:

$$div = (v/2z_0) \ [3\sin\alpha\cos\phi\sin2\theta + \cos\alpha(3\cos2\theta + 1)] \tag{1}$$

$$curl = -(v/z_0) \ \sin\alpha\sin\phi\sin\theta \tag{2}$$

Curl

The expression for *curl* is clearly the simpler of the two, and so we shall begin by examining some of the implications of equation 2. The first thing to note about the 2D *curl* function is that the angle of approach to the surface (determined by α) has no effect upon the form of the function, but only upon its amplitude. The *curl* function is always the same simple 2D function, which vanishes as one heads straight towards the surface ($\alpha = 0°$) and becomes progressively larger as one moves more obliquely, reaching a maximum

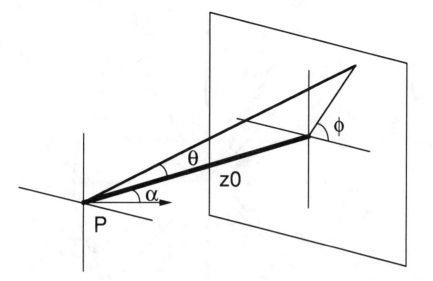

Figure 10.6 *The coordinates of the optic array. Angles are measured relative to the surface normal: the line at right angles to the surface which projects through the viewpoint, P.*

when one is moving at right angles to the surface ($\alpha = 90°$, which occurs, for example, when moving across level ground). The effect of angle of approach upon amplitude can readily be confirmed by inspecting figure 10.2, which shows fragments of the flow patterns produced by different angles of approach. For direct approach ($\alpha = 0°$, figure 10.2a), the flow pattern is a pure expansion: there is no speed gradient at right angles to the direction of flow, and hence no *curl*. For other angles (e.g. figure 10.2b), there is a speed gradient at right angles to the flow and clear *curl* in addition to the expansion. (A good trick for obtaining a more accurate impression is to imagine putting a tiny windmill, with its axis at right angles to the page, into the flow field at a given position. If the windmill would rotate, then there is some *curl* at that point: the direction of rotation gives the sign and the speed of rotation gives the amplitude of *curl*.)

The first implication of this finding has to do with navigation. There are many accounts of the guidance of locomotion which are based upon the expanding component (*div*) of the retinal flow field, but it is clear that *curl* offers an extremely simple alternative: all one has to do to move directly towards a surface is to adjust ones direction until *curl* disappears. It is not difficult to envisage a control system which could make use of this.

The second implication has to do with the recovery of information about the structure of the world, and it is this which we want to develop here. Since the form of the *curl* function is independent of the direction of

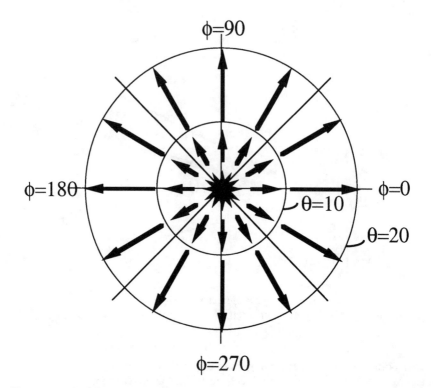

Figure 10.7   *The optic flow pattern shown in figure 10.2a with coordinates superimposed.*

movement, can we use it to recover information about surface layout without worrying about how we are moving? In fact, we can, in a fairly straightforward way. To understand this, we need to think about the origin of our coordinate system (i.e. the point where both ϕ and $\theta = 0°$). We already know, from figures 10.1 and 10.2, that the focus of the *flow pattern* lies in the direction of locomotion. However, from figure 10.6 and equation 2, it is clear that the origin of the *curl function* lies in the direction of the surface normal. When the observer moves straight towards the surface, with $\alpha = 0°$ as in figure 10.2a, the directions of locomotion and the surface normal coincide and our coordinate system lines up with the flow pattern, as shown in figure 10.7. However, for any other angle of approach, the coordinate system slides away from the focus of the flow pattern to remain centered upon the direction of the surface normal. At any point in the flow pattern we can gain an intuitive estimate of the amount and direction of *curl* simply by examining the speed gradient at right angles to the direction of flow. However, to understand the overall pattern of *curl*, we need to think in terms of a coordinate system centered upon the surface normal rather than the flow pattern itself. In fact,

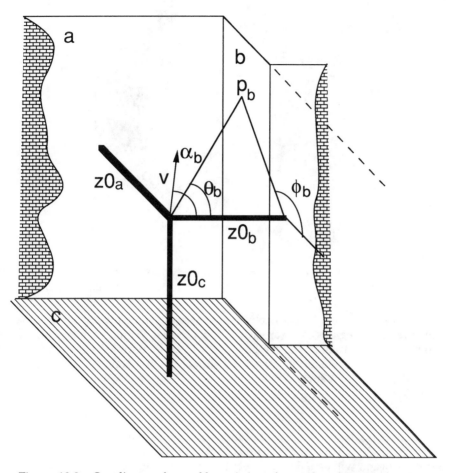

Figure 10.8 *Coordinates of a world consisting of several surfaces. Each point on a surface is defined in relation to the surface normal of that surface.*

recovering the direction of the surface normal, and hence the 3D layout of the surface, simply amounts to recovering the origin of the coordinate system from the 2D *curl* function. We term the origin of the coordinate system for a given surface, the *surface origin*.

For a given direction of locomotion, the *curl* function is just the separable product of two sinusoids of known period and the same amplitude, $(\sin\phi\sin\theta)$, so it is not difficult to recover the direction of the surface origin. In fact, for the simple case we have considered of a world containing only a single surface, the task is trivial, since there is only one origin and it is actually present in the *curl* function. This may not always be so, however, as is shown in figure 10.8, which depicts a more realistic world containing several surfaces.

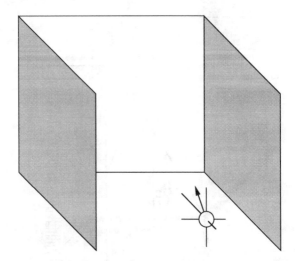

Figure 10.9   *A simple world consisting of three vertical surfaces. In the example described in the text, these surfaces extend upwards and downwards to infinity.*

The *curl* function produced by observer movement in this world will consist of several 2D regions, one for each of the surfaces. Within each region, the form and amplitude of the *curl* function will be determined with reference to the surface normal of the associated surface. So, for example, the value of *curl* at point P_b, on surface b, will be:

$$curl = -(v/z_{0b})\ \sin\alpha_b \sin\phi_b \sin\theta_b$$

Recovering the surface layout of this world simply amounts to finding the surface origin of each of the regions of the *curl* function. In some cases, the surface origin will actually be present within the region but in others, as in the case of surface b in figure 10.8, it will not. The general usage of *curl* may thus require some extrapolation, rather than the simple location of existing origins. Such extrapolation is quite plausible, given the simplicity and 2D separability of the *curl* function.

As a practical example, figure 10.9 shows a simple world consisting of three vertical surfaces at right angles to each other. The most obvious first step towards recovering surface layout would be to segment the *curl* function into the distinct regions associated with the three surfaces. One could do this, for example, by locating discontinuities either in the speed of the flow pattern or in the amplitude of the *curl* function. These really amount to the same thing and the latter technique is rather simpler because *curl* simultaneously takes into account all directions of movement. Having segmented the *curl* function, all the values of *curl* within each region could then be used to produce a single estimate of the surface origin of that region. This technique

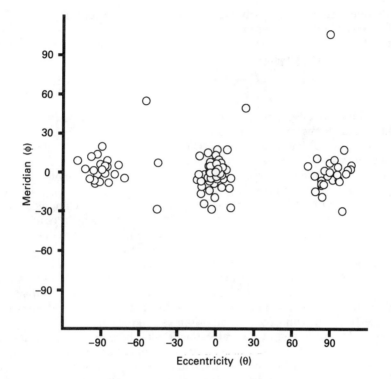

Figure 10.10 *Results of a simple segmentation scheme based on the world depicted in figure 10.9. See text for details.*

ought to be insensitive to noise, and to be quite suitable in sparsely textured worlds where the *curl* function may be rather poorly defined. An alternative technique would be to leave the segmentation process until after the estimation of surface origin. One can simply derive many local estimates of surface origin from different fragments of the *curl* function, and then segment the resulting clusters of estimates into surfaces. Figure 10.10 demonstrates the plausibility of this approach, showing the local estimates of surface origin derived from 100 fragments selected at random from the *curl* function associated with the world depicted in figure 10.9. Each fragment used the value of *curl* at 1 degree intervals on a 5×5 regular grid. To make the exercise more realistic, 10 percent Gaussian noise was added to the *curl* function. (This is really quite a substantial amount when one remembers that the estimation of *curl* pools the outputs of many individual velocity sensors and is thus inherently a fairly noise resistant process.) The clustering of points in figure 10.10 around the true surface origins at $\phi = 0°$, $\theta = -90, 0,$ and $+90°$, is quite clear. The occasional outliers result mainly from fragments which spanned the boundaries between segments in the *curl* function.

Although this alternative scheme may seem rather cumbersome, we believe it to be worthwhile because it has the potential to deal with complex, multi-faceted worlds and with surface curvature, which should show up as statistical trends in the clusters of local estimates.

Div

Fortunately, we do not need to consider the possible usage of *div* in quite so much detail. Some of its advantages and disadvantages have been discussed elsewhere (e.g. Priest and Cutting 1985; Regan, 1985; Torrey, 1985) and only a few points are directly relevant here. From equation 1 we can see that, along each meridian (i.e. constant ϕ), the value of *div* is the sum of a sinusoidal and a cosinusoidal term and is thus a sinusoid of a specific phase. This phase varies both with the meridian (ϕ) and with the direction of movement (α) relative to a surface. Obviously, the 2D *div* function is much less amenable to the kind of simple extrapolation techniques which we have described for *curl*. Nonetheless, it does have some informative features. In particular, the positions of the maximum and minimum values tell us about the direction of movement. For horizontal movement, these extremes will always occur along the meridian $\phi = 0, 180°$, and will always be 90° apart. The maximum will occur at $\theta = \alpha/2$ so that, for instance, for movement straight toward the surface the peak will occur at the origin ($\phi = 0°, \theta = 0°$).

In worlds consisting of several surfaces, like the one illustrated in figure 10.8, if either a minimum or maximum value of *div* exists within any of the regions of the flow field, then it is trivial to work out the direction of movement relative to the corresponding surface provided we also know, perhaps from *curl*, the direction of the surface normal. However, unlike the surface origins in the *curl* function, if the extreme values of *div* are not actually present, then they would be difficult to recover by simple extrapolation. This clearly limits the general usefulness of *div*, although we should remember that we can alter our direction of locomotion to manipulate the information which the optic array provides.

In summary, *div* and *curl* are well suited to providing complementary types of information. The surface layout of the environment can be conveniently recovered from the *curl* function in a way that is largely independent of the precise direction of movement relative to the surfaces. Information useful in guiding our movements relative to the surfaces is also provided by *curl*, although a more complete picture can be obtained from *div* if we also have some knowledge of surface layout.

The Effects of Eye Movements and Head Rotations

Our analysis, so far, takes no account of eye movements. It applies only to the translational movement of an observer with a fixed eye and head moving in a straight line. We already know that introducing a rotational component

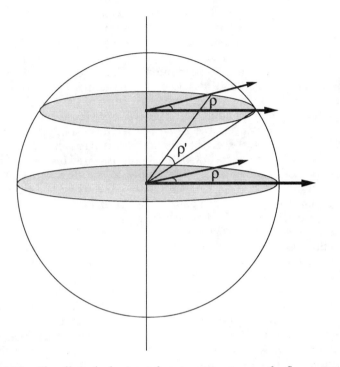

Figure 10.11   *The effect of a horizontal eye movement upon the flow pattern. Each point on the retina rotates horizontally through ρ degrees. However, note that using the origin of the optic array (at the center of the sphere), the angle of change (ρ') varies with vertical position.*

to the movement, to take account of eye and head movements, will distort the retinal flow patterns – but will it also affect our simple interpretation of *div* and *curl*?

Figure 10.11 illustrates the effect of a horizontal eye movement upon the retinal flow pattern. Each ray sweeps across the retina in the opposite direction to the eye movement, and the distance moved varies systematically with retinal position. Eye movements do not introduce any speed gradient along the direction of flow and they have no effect upon *div*. But they do introduce a speed gradient at right angles to the direction of flow, and they do affect the *curl* function. This complicates our simple model because the overall pattern of *curl* will potentially be the sum of two different functions: one caused by translation of the observer with respect to the world, and the other caused by rotations of the eye or, equivalently, rotations of the head about the line of sight. Moreover, we cannot simply ignore the component due to eye movement or head rotation because this will generally distort any estimation of the position of the surface origins and hence the layout of the world. There are several possible solutions to this problem.

The first, and most general, solution is to decompose the flow pattern into its rotational and translational components, so that the uninformative rotational component can be discounted. Unlike the retinal flow patterns associated with translation of the observer, the retinal flow associated with rotation is completely unaffected by the structure of the world. So the flow pattern (and the corresponding *curl* function) produced by a rotation in a given direction always has the same spatial form and simply varies in amplitude with the speed of the rotation. Moreover, any rotation can be decomposed into component rotations about just three orthogonal axes: for example, vertical, horizontal at right angles to the direction of gaze, and horizontal in the direction of gaze. The first two correspond to eye movements, the last to rotations of the head about the line of sight. In principle, then, one can envisage a system involving just three types of sensor, each with a receptive field covering the entire retina, and each tuned to the flow pattern (or *curl* function) associated with rotation about one of these orthogonal axes. Such a system could encode both the direction and speed of rotation and thus allow the recovery of the informative translational component of the flow. This suggestion, of course, is very similar to the idea that eye movements are somehow "subtracted from the percept" in order to maintain the stability of the visual world (von Holst, 1975). In that case, the rotation parameters are given by eye movement commands rather than being sensed from the retinal flow and this offers another plausible way to achieve the same result.

The second solution is rather less general and simply makes use of features which are not distorted by rotational movement. The *div* function, for example, is unaffected by rotations and the extreme values provide information about locomotory heading. However, as we have seen, the extreme values are not always available, may be difficult to recover, and may only be interpretable given additional information about surface orientation. An alternative scheme, which relies directly upon the retinal flow pattern rather than differential invariants, has been proposed by Longuet-Higgins and Prazdny (1980). This again relies upon the fact that rotational movements will affect the whole retinal flow pattern. Thus, elements which are close together in the flow but which are associated with objects at different depths (e.g. elements on either side of a 3D edge) will have the same rotational component but different translational components. Subtraction of the vectors drawn out by these elements in the retinal flow pattern will cancel out the rotational component, leaving pure translational information which could be used, for example, to locate the focus of expansion of the optic array and thus the direction of locomotory heading. A final scheme in this category can be more directly related to the differential invariants described above. During rotational movements, the *curl* function associated with each region of the image will consist of two components: one due to the rotational movement and the other due to translational movement. The component due to rotation will be the same for all regions, while the component due to translation will differ from region to region, depending upon the 3D arrangement of the associated surfaces. Thus, the surface origin of each region can be estimated as outlined above and the *relative* layout of any two surfaces is preserved by these estimates because they both contain the same rotational component.

The third solution is the least general but by far the simplest, requiring only an appropriate strategy of eye fixation. In flow patterns associated with translation of the observer, there is usually a stationary point even if, in the presence of rotational movements, this does not coincide with the direction of movement. Fixation of the stationary point will simply remove the effects of eye movements from the retinal flow pattern and so allow more or less direct access to the optic flow information. Under these circumstances, we could, for example, adopt the simple scheme of *curl* interpretation which we have outlined above. We should not be put off this idea by the fact that observers do commonly track elements of the flow pattern during movement; after all, our eyes have many other functions to perform in addition to extracting surface layout. All that is required is that the observer sometimes fixates the stationary point. During these, possibly brief, periods there will be no eye movement and the 2D *curl* function could be used to extract or check surface layout.

A Brief Review of Some Relevant Studies

In general, if the human visual system is to make use of the information provided by retinal flow patterns, then it must solve a number of basic problems. First, it must be equipped to recover the relevant features of the optic flow pattern from the retinal flow pattern with which it is actually presented. That is, it must be able to extract the informative aspects of flow, produced by translation of the observer, from the uninformative distortions introduced by rotational movements about the viewpoint. Having recovered the optic flow pattern, information about locomotory heading could be extracted by mechanisms which are sensitive only to the directional pattern of optic flow. However, information about 3D surface layout requires mechanisms which are also sensitive to spatial speed gradients. One convenient way to encode these speed gradients is to estimate the local expansion (*div*) and local rotation (*curl*) at each point in the flow pattern. In the case of *div*, at least, this strategy would automatically remove the effects of rotational movement.

In the following review, we shall mainly consider the specific question of whether the visual system is equipped to perform an analysis based upon the estimation of *div* and *curl*, because this is the scheme that we have described most fully. However, as we shall see, the relevant work inevitably also touches upon the other, more general, issues mentioned above. In fact, as we have already stated, the evidence is rather sparse and circumstantial, particularly in the case of *curl*, because very few studies seem to have considered that information about local rotation might in fact be useful. We shall look first at the psychophysical and neurophysiological evidence for expansion and rotation encoders, and then go on to look at the kinds of task that observers can perform with flow patterns.

Psychophysical Evidence for Rotation and Expansion Encoders

Any scheme based upon the extraction of *div* and *curl* has at least three minimum requirements. First, the visual system must contain localized mechanisms with small receptive fields, capable of encoding local expansion and rotation. Secondly, the system must be able to interpret the resulting 2D patterns of *div* and *curl* and so should also be sensitive to the large-scale, 2D patterns which occur in natural retinal flow patterns. Finally, the processes involved must be capable of analyzing complex patterns into their *div* and *curl* components.

Small-scale processes   The most compelling evidence for the existence of specialized, localized expansion and rotation encoders within the human visual system comes from a series of psychophysical studies by Regan and Beverley. They made use of a standard adaptation technique in which the observer views a suitable stimulus – the adapting pattern – for a few minutes. The basic idea of this technique is that the adapting pattern "fatigues" only those mechanisms that respond to it, so that one can "probe" for selective mechanisms by measuring post-adapt sensitivities to a range of suitable test stimuli. Regan and Beverley (1978a), for example, found that adaptation to a small, expanding and contracting square depresses sensitivity to a similar test stimulus much more than does adaptation to a square oscillating from side to side with the same amount of linear movement. Moreover, expanding squares produce an after-effect of movement in depth which has a quite different time course from the conventional motion after-effect produced by adaptation to simple linear motion (Regan and Beverley, 1978b). These results are difficult to explain solely in terms of conventional directionally tuned classic motion encoders, and provide strong evidence for relative motion mechanisms which are selective for expansion and contraction. These mechanisms appear to have very localized receptive fields, since the effects of adaptation are confined to the region of the retina which has been directly adapted (Regan and Beverley, 1979).

The evidence for similar small-scale rotation mechanisms is much more fragmentary. However, Regan and Beverley (1985) have shown that adaptation to a small rotating field of random dots does selectively impair sensitivity to rotation. Using a rather different technique, we have also obtained indirect evidence that some rotation encoders have fairly localized receptive fields, and that larger scale mechanisms also exist. Nakayama and Tyler (1981) used dense random dot patterns in which all the dots drifted in the same direction, but with dot speed varying sinusoidally at right angles to the drift direction, as shown in figure 10.12. Although these "shearing"

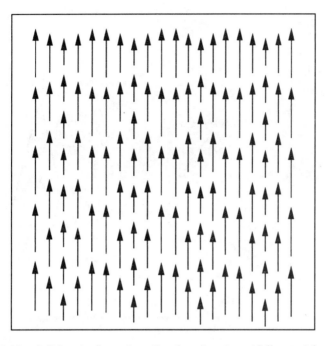

Figure 10.12 *A "shearing" grating. Speed varies sinusoidally at right angles to the direction of flow.*

movements are one-dimensional, they would provide a strong stimulus for rotation mechanisms of the type outlined in figure 10.4, because they are characterized by a continuously varying speed gradient at right angles to the direction of flow.

Nakayama et al. (1984) investigated sensitivity to speed gradients of different spatial scales by varying the spatial frequency of the sinusoidal modulation: low spatial frequencies produce wide gradients, whilst high spatial frequencies produce narrow gradients. They found that human sensitivity remained high at low spatial frequencies and declined rapidly at spatial frequencies above about 0.5 c/degree. If these results are indeed mediated by rotation encoders, they suggest that their receptive fields are no smaller that 2° in size and that they are likely to be much bigger than that.

Our own results (Williams, 1989) suggest that, in fact, a range of sizes exists. We used a simultaneous masking paradigm in which the observer had to detect a target stimulus in the presence of a masking stimulus. Rather like adaptation, this technique provides a probe for selective mechanisms because the detectability of the test stimulus should only be affected when the mask and the target are detected by the same mechanism. In this case the mask consisted of a single "shearing grating" of fixed contrast and spatial frequency and the target was a similar grating of the same or a different spatial frequency. We found that the presence of the mask enhanced the

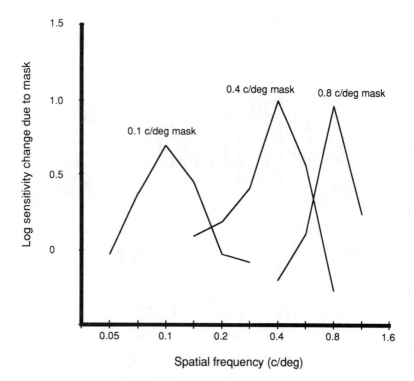

Figure 10.13   *The effect of masking upon the detection of a "shearing grating." The effect is narrow and is centered upon the spatial frequency of the mask.*

detectability of the target, but only when the spatial frequencies of the mask and target were very similar (figure 10.13). These results suggest that the mechanisms that detect speed gradients respond only over a narrow range of spatial scales, and that there are separate mechanisms selective for different scales. We take them as indirect support for rotation encoders with different sized receptive fields.

Large-scale processes   There is also psychophysical evidence for specialized processes which are sensitive to the overall patterns of rotation and expansion to be found in large-scale retinal flow patterns. Regan and Beverley (1979) provide circumstantial evidence that their small-scale expansion encoders are also involved in the encoding of large-scale retinal flow patterns, since adaptation to an expanding flow pattern does produce the expected reduction in sensitivity to a small expanding square, providing the flow pattern actually includes the focus of expansion (Beverley and Regan, 1982). Unfortunately, the flow patterns used by Regan and Beverley seem to have contained a uniform rate of radial expansion, with *div* present only at and near the focus,

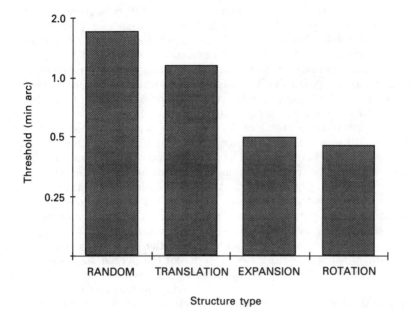

Figure 10.14   *Sensitivity to random dot patterns undergoing random, translating, expanding, or rotating motion.*

so it is not yet clear how their expansion encoders would respond to other regions of more natural flow patterns.

We have recently obtained rather more direct evidence for large-scale rotation and expansion processes, simply by comparing sensitivities to random dot patterns containing different types of motion. Our stimulus consisted of 128 dots randomly positioned within an annulus with an inner diameter of 2.4° and an outer diameter of 10°. All the dots moved at the same speed, but their directions were arranged so that the overall pattern of motion was random, translating, rotating, or expanding. Subjects were presented with two stimuli, one containing a static pattern of random dots and the other containing dots moving in one of the ways described above. They were simply asked to indicate which of the two stimuli contained motion. Our results, summarized in figure 10.14 show that sensitivity, defined in terms of the slowest detectable speed of dot motion, is significantly greater for rotating and expanding patterns than for linear or random patterns. These results suggest mechanisms specialized to deal with large-scale patterns of rotation and expansion because, if detection were mediated by mechanisms responding only to individual dots, sensitivity should be the same for all the different types of motion. The finding that sensitivity is greater for expansion and rotation suggests that responses to individual dots are combined for these stimuli more than they are for the others.

Analysis of complex patterns   The motion after-effect produced by a rotating spiral is often explained in terms of the adaptation of separate processes which independently encode the global rotation and expansion of the stimulus (e.g. Cavanagh and Favreau, 1980; Hershenson, 1984, 1987). We have obtained evidence for a similar decomposition of random dot flow patterns using a simple masking paradigm. We used random dot annular flow patterns, like the ones described above, in which the direction of motion of individual dots could be manipulated to produce an overall pattern of pure expansion, pure rotation, or a combination of the two. The pure expansion pattern corresponded to movement of the observer straight toward a vertical surface and contained *div* but no *curl*. The pure rotation corresponded to rotation of the head about the line of sight and contained *curl* but no *div*. The task was simply to detect global expansion in the presence of a rotating mask, or global rotation in the presence of an expanding mask. Figure 10.15 shows that masking had no significant effect on the detectability of orthogonal motion, but it significantly affected performance when masks were of the same type as the target. The detection of the expanding targets in this experiment cannot be explained in terms of the overall size change of the stimulus because the expanding targets were "windowed" to maintain a constant size. Nor is there any need to suppose that our results might be explained by conventional unidirectional classic motion sensors decomposing the motion of individual dots, because we found that sensitivity to pure expansion or rotation is significantly higher than sensitivity to destructured stimuli, which preserve the overall distribution of speeds but destroy the directional pattern by randomly rotating the trajectory of each element. The decomposition of complex flow patterns does seem to be mediated by mechanisms which are genuinely sensitive to specific overall directional patterns of motion in the stimuli.

Neurophysiological Evidence for Expansion and Rotation Encoders

Although by no means conclusive, the psychophysical evidence generally supports the existence of specific mechanisms, perhaps like those outlined in figure 10.4, which would be capable of measuring the local expansion and rotation present in natural retinal flow patterns. There is also psychophysical evidence for the existence of specialized processes sensitive to the overall patterns of rotation and expansion found in typical retinal flow patterns and that these processes can analyze complex patterns into simpler components. Unfortunately, however, the existing psychophysical work does not establish any clear linkage between these local and global processes: it is not yet clear whether large-scale mechanisms depend upon the 2D patterns of *div* and *curl* which the small-scale mechanisms could provide, or whether they are based upon simple directional templates, sensitive to specific large-scale patterns of expansion or rotation. Recent neurophysiological work provides some important clues to this crucial distinction.

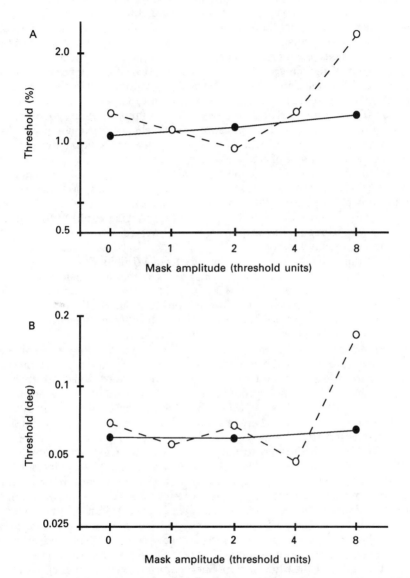

Figure 10.15   *Effects of masking upon the detection of rotating or expanding random dot patterns. a, Expanding target. Solid symbols: rotating mask; open symbols: expanding mask. b, Rotating target. Solid symbols: expanding mask; open symbols: rotating mask.*

There is at least one report of units in Area 18 of the cat which respond selectively to the expansion or contraction of a small 2° slit of light (Regan and Cynader, 1979), but there appears to be no evidence yet for small-scale rotation-selective units at this early stage in the visual pathway. Most of the relevant evidence comes from later stages of the pathway, particularly from two regions of the superior temporal sulcus (STS) of monkeys: the middle temporal (MT) area and the medial superior temporal (MST) area to which it projects. Both regions contain units sensitive to large-field unidirectional motion (D cells), and MST seems also to contain units which respond preferentially to rotations (R cells) or expansions (S cells), irrespective of whether the stimulus is a large oriented bar, a large square, or a random dot pattern. The receptive field size of MST cells is typically very large, ranging from 20 to 100° (Bruce et al., 1981; Sakata et al., 1985), but is rather smaller (less than 20°) in MT (Saito et al., 1986). In fact, receptive field size in MT varies with retinal eccentricity and, in the fovea, may be less than 1° (Tanaka et al., 1986). These findings have led to the suggestion (e.g. Tanaka et al., 1989) that the units in MST combine the outputs of several MT cells with receptive fields in different retinal positions.

If MST units do indeed combine the outputs of MT units, then it is important to know how the combination is arranged. Do the large-field MST units simply combine the outputs of MT units with appropriate preferred directions and retinal positions? This would produce simple large-scale directional templates which would signal only the directional aspects of the flow pattern. Alternatively, do the contributing MT units also have appropriate speed preferences, so that the resulting MST units would also be sensitive to the speed gradients in the flow pattern? Or are MT units first connected together to produce local rotation or expansion encoders which are then, in turn, connected together to produce large-scale rotation or expansion units? This could be regarded as one way to build a mechanism which encodes the 2D pattern of *curl* or *div*. There is some indirect support for this last model from the observation by Saito et al. (1986) that cells with large receptive fields in MST will respond to patches of rotation or expansion anywhere within the receptive field, although Tanaka and Saito (1989) point out that these patches must be at least 20° in diameter in order to elicit any response. In fact, however, the balance of the current evidence supports the simple directional template model. In a crucial experiment, Tanaka et al. (1989) showed that large-scale MST units continued to respond strongly to expanding or rotating stimuli from which the normal speed gradients had been removed (e.g. for expanding stimuli, all elements of the stimulus moved away from the center at the same speed). Such patterns contain *div* or *curl* only at the center, and so should be relatively ineffective stimuli for units which are based on contributions from local expansion or expansion encoders, or which are important in signalling speed gradients. Rather more circumstantial evidence for the directional template model also comes from the observation by Albright (1989) that the majority of unidirectional units in MT prefer motion away from the fovea rather than toward it. Wiring up such units into large-scale expansion and contraction templates would account quite simply for the common finding that there are more expansion- than contraction-sensitive units in MST.

Thus far, it seems that there is very little direct neurophysiological support, at least in MST, for the kind of scheme which we have outlined for the interpretation of local rotation. There is some evidence that expansion detectors with the required, reasonably small, receptive fields exist in the early stages of the visual pathway and these might form an early neural stage of such a process. But the kind of large-scale rotation and expansion encoders found in MST do not seem suited to the next stage, which involves encoding the 2D pattern of *div* or *curl*. Large-scale expansion templates might be involved in the guidance of locomotion, perhaps by encoding the location of the focus of expansion, but it is much more difficult to envisage how large-scale rotation templates could be involved in the recovery of surface layout because the relevant mechanisms do not seem to have the necessary sensitivity to speed gradients. It seems far more likely that the MST rotation-selective units which have so far been identified are more concerned with rotations of the head about the line of sight. Indeed, it may also be the case that the equivalent large-field unidirectional cells are concerned with rotations of the eyes, and the combination of all three types of cells (direction, expansion, and rotation) might form the neural basis for a strategy concerned with encoding eye movements and head rotations, and thus with the separation of the flow pattern into its rotational and translational components.

The current lack of direct neurophysiological support need not, of course, be taken as evidence against our scheme. Indeed, one main aim of this account is to try to identify the kinds of stimulus which might be useful in future neurophysiological studies. At the moment, one important puzzle concerns the neurophysiological basis of the relatively small-scale rotation and expansion detectors suggested by some of the psychophysical work. Thus far, there has been only a single report of small-scale expansion units and no reports of rotation units. Moreover, the putative expansion units were not found in the area of the cortex which has received most of the relevant attention. It remains possible that appropriate units do exist, though probably not in MT or MST, and have yet to be revealed. After all, mechanisms of the type shown in figure 10.4, with small receptive fields, could very easily look like ordinary directionally unselective motion cells when stimulated by bars of light or rigidly translating random dot patterns. Their true properties would only be revealed by the careful use of appropriate stimuli.

A second puzzle concerns the functional role of the large-scale rotation and expansion cells in MST. Since they seem insensitive to speed gradients, it seems more likely that they are concerned with analyzing eye rotations and, possibly, locomotory heading than with recovering surface layout. However, it is worth pointing out that cells concerned with encoding the overall 2D *curl* function would not necessarily respond to the types of whole-field rotation which have typically been used so far. They ought, in fact, to respond to flow patterns derived from movements of the observer relative to a surface with a specific slant, irrespective of large variations in the overall pattern of rotation in the flow pattern. Neither psychophysics nor neurophysiology has yet directly addressed this possibility.

The Use of Information in Retinal Flow Patterns

There have been many studies of the information that human and animal observers can extract from retinal flow patterns. Perhaps the majority of them have been concerned with expanding motion and have considered its use in such tasks as estimation of time to collision (Schiff, 1965; Schiff and Detwiler, 1979; Lee and Reddish, 1981; McLeod and Ross, 1983), the regulation of posture and gait (Lee et al., 1982; Stoffregen et al., 1987), and the perception of locomotory heading (Llewellyn, 1971; Johnston et al., 1973; Cutting, 1986) and speed (Evans, 1970). However, there is also a growing body of work on the role of retinal motion in recovering 3D object form (e.g. Rogers and Graham, 1979; Braunstein and Andersen, 1984; Hildreth et al., 1990; Treue et al., 1991), distinguishing between convex and concave edges (e.g. Farber and McConkie, 1979; Braunstein and Andersen, 1981; Braunstein and Tittle, 1988), and in estimating surface slant (e.g. Braunstein, 1968). This work has shown, for example, that the presence of speed gradients is crucial to the perception of 3D structure from motion (e.g. Braunstein and Andersen, 1981, 1984) and that speed gradients in the absence of texture gradients produce a compelling impression of 3D form (e.g. Braunstein, 1968; Rogers and Graham, 1979). We shall consider just three examples, which are particularly relevant to our theme because they have attempted, more or less directly, to investigate the possible role of *div* and *curl*: studies of image segmentation, of the perception of heading and distance, and of the perception of surface rigidity.

Segmentation   The instantaneous rigid translation of a small square of dots in the middle of a large random pattern provides a powerful cue to image segmentation. Our own observations confirm that a similar effect occurs when a disk of dots is subjected to an instantaneous rigid rotation. This is not surprising, given that Bell and Lappin (1979) have shown that the detection of the rigid rotation of a whole random dot pattern shows very similar properties to the detection of a rigid translation (Lappin and Bell, 1976). But is this segmentation based upon estimates of local rotation, or upon a global directional template?

Using a dense field of rotating needles, Julesz and Hesse (1970) showed that observers were quite unable to pick out a region in which the needles rotated in the opposite direction, even under free viewing conditions. Since the individual rotating needles should provide a strong stimulus for *curl* encoders, this is often taken as evidence that *curl* is not involved in segmentation. However, since regions of the flow field associated with a single surface frequently produce values of *curl* with opposite sign, it is not at all obvious that the sign of *curl* should provide an ecologically valid cue for segmentation. More generally, if segmentation occurred after a series of local estimates of surface origin, as considered in our scheme, occasionally deviant estimates are only to be expected (figure 10.10). A better test of the role of *curl* would be to arrange the rotations of the individual elements so that they depicted the smoothly varying 2D *curl* functions produced by translation of the observer in a world consisting of several surfaces. Regions of the field associated with surfaces at different orientations should then stand out. Unfortunately, such an experiment is impractical because of a second problem with this type of local element display. Although each element can be arranged to produce the required value of local rotation, the spaces between elements will always produce a conflicting value of local rotation in the opposite direction. In fact, Julesz and Hesse's observers had to detect one element rotating in a given direction in a field which contained a substantial amount of local rotation in both directions.

Angle of heading and surface distance   Using random dot flow patterns depicting movement across a horizontal surface, Warren et al. (1988) showed that human observers can very accurately report whether the display was consistent with a locomotory heading to the left or right of a fixed reference mark. Does this ability depend upon locating the maximum value of local expansion which, in this situation, would occur exactly along the direction of motion? In a second experiment, Warren et al. (1988) presented dot patterns depicting movement at various angles toward a flat vertical surface, and showed that observers were just as accurate at detecting heading. Warren et al. took this as evidence against the use of the maximum value of local expansion (*div*) because, as the angle of approach to the surface (α) increases, the position of the maximum deviates progressively from the direction of movement, so observers ought to become progressively less accurate if they are using this cue. But this conclusion assumes that the observers simply took the position of the maximum as indicating the direction of heading. As we discussed above, the position of the maximum value of local expansion varies simply and systematically with the angle of approach to the surface: it is always located at $\alpha/2$, halfway between the angle of heading and the surface normal. So observers might well have located the maximum value of local expansion and then interpreted this in conjunction with the surface origin defined by *curl*, which, of course, is also present in such displays.

A stronger argument against a scheme based upon the estimation of local expansion comes from the finding that judgments of heading remain accurate even with very sparse flow patterns containing only a few dots (Warren et al., 1988). In our own studies on the detection of large-scale patterns, described above, we have also found that the preferential sensitivity to rotation or expansion over "destructured" motion declines with decreasing dot density but persists at least down to 8 dots distributed at roughly even intervals around a circle subtending 10°. Similarly, De Bruyn and Orban (1990a) have reported that observers can reliably detect rotation or expansion in randomly perturbed patterns so long as just a few dots move in the correct directions. All of these findings suggest that comparisons between individual elements can occur at much greater spatial intervals than can comfortably be decribed as measures of local expansion or rotation.

De Bruyn and Orban's (1990a) result is particulary interesting because it shows that observers can detect coherent rotation or expansion from the trajectories of just a few dots, even when they are buried amongst a sea of elements moving in random directions. This sort of performance can be explained by fixed directional templates, which would simply filter out the directional noise, but it is much more difficult to explain by any simple system of local expansion or rotation encoders. Such mechanisms would simply perform comparisons between the dots in each local neighborhood and so produce an incoherent 2D pattern of response. A similar point has been made by Andersen (1989). He presented random dot patterns depicting movement directly toward or at right angles to a series of transparent, parallel surfaces at different distances from the observer. The dots corresponding to different surfaces were thus jumbled together in the resulting flow pattern. Nonetheless, observers could distinguish up to three coherent surfaces and, in two surface displays, could make reasonably accurate judgments of their relative distance. Andersen argues that this could only be accomplished by local expansion and rotation encoders if the dots were first segmented into their corresponding surfaces, perhaps on the basis of speed of movement (dots corresponding to a more distant surface will move more slowly in the flow pattern). Andersen dismisses this as unlikely because, in the expanding patterns depicting direct approach, the dots corresponding to each surface move at a considerable range of speeds. While this is true, it is worth emphasizing that speed only varies radially in expanding displays, so that segmentation could still be accomplished within annular regions.

In any event, there is an alternative explanation of these findings which is much more compatible with our simple scheme. The surfaces in Andersen's display were apparently represented by the same number of dots and, since the surfaces were at different distances, would presumably project into the flow pattern with different dot densities. Suppose local expansion and rotation were measured simultaneously at a range of different scales. Although the superimposition of two flow patterns would inevitably introduce considerable noise, the encoders tuned to the appropriate dot densities ought still to pick out the 2D functions corresponding to the different surfaces. It would obviously be interesting to know whether Andersen's task could be accomplished when the texture densities of each surface are equated in the flow pattern. Our own findings with shearing gratings, described above, suggest that rotation, at least, may be encoded by mechanisms with a range of receptive field sizes. Such mechanisms may function to estimate (relatively) local rotation and expansion in the sparse flow fields produced by surfaces with different texture densities. They may also assist in performing the natural equivalent of Andersen's task. Although our simple scheme has been developed to deal with carpentered worlds consisting of a few regular surfaces, the natural world is considerably more complex. Many natural objects, like trees, have a statistically regular 3D spatial structure and produce flow patterns like much more complex versions of Andersen's display. A scheme based upon the estimation of pure *curl* and *div* could never deal with such patterns, but a scheme capable of measuring expansion and rotation at a range of different spatial scales might well be able to pick out overall 3D structure.

Finally, it is worth pointing out that none of the tasks described in this section *requires* mechanisms which are sensitive to speed gradients. Locomotory heading, for example, can be recovered using only the directional information in the optic flow patttern. Consequently, the finding that these tasks do not provide direct evidence for the existence of *div* and *curl* encoders should not be taken as evidence that such mechanisms do not exist.

Surface rigidity The direction of motion of each point in the retinal flow pattern is determined entirely by the movements of the observer and is completely unaffected by the layout of surfaces in the world. So long as one is only interested in recovering information about observer movement, rigid templates sensitive to particular directional patterns of flow are really quite adequate. To recover information about surface layout, however, one needs to look at the speed gradients as well as directions of retinal flow. This is one way in which measures of local expansion and rotation are worthwhile, because they specifically capture the relevant information about change in speed in a particularly convenient form. Demonstrations that human observers can make use of the speed gradients in natural flow patterns thus provide fairly compelling evidence against simple directional templates and at least indirect support for schemes based on *div* and *curl*.

De Bruyn and Orban (1990b) have recently provided evidence that human observers can indeed make use of the speed gradients present in expanding flow patterns, not just in estimating surface slant (e.g. Braunstein, 1968) but also in more subtle tasks. When the observer heads straight towards a vertical surface, the speed of each element in the resulting flow pattern is directly proportional to its eccentricity (θ). Removal of this speed gradient, so that the speed of all elements is the same, would be compatible with movement towards a distorting surface. De Bruyn and Orban (1990b) manipulated the speed gradient in expanding flow patterns and showed that human observers did indeed perceive a distorting surface when presented with this latter type of flow pattern. Such performance cannot depend upon simple directional templates of the kind studied by Tanaka et al. (1989), because these seem to be insensitive to the pattern of speeds in the stimulus.

Concluding Remarks

Like all work on relatively low-level vision, the study of retinal flow clearly requires an interdisciplinary approach linking formal mathematical descriptions through psychophysical studies of human abilities to neuroscience. One of our aims in this chapter has been to show that, while the required interdisciplinary framework already exists, several crucial questions remain unanswered.

We began by using existing mathematical work to develop a simple scheme for the extraction of information about surface layout from rotational motion. One of the crucial questions to emerge at this stage concerned the problems of dealing with eye movements and head rotations, which distort the optic flow pattern. While more or less sophisticated computational strategies are required to deal with this once the distortion is introduced, a simple strategy of eye fixation would remove the complication at source. It thus becomes important to know what human observers actually do with their eyes as they move about the world. It ought not to be difficult to confront this question directly, simply by attaching an eye movement recorder and a camera to a moving observer's head, and studying pattern of eye fixations as the observer moves about to see whether there is any systematic usage of the stationary points in the flow pattern. The resulting data would obviously be much more useful than, for example, studying whether human performance declines when the effects of simulated eye movements are added to random dot displays. Given that eye movements have long been recognized as a potential problem for any account of retinal flow, this seems an important line for future research.

The basic requirement of our simple scheme is that the visual system should contain mechanisms which are capable of encoding and interpreting the 2D *curl* function. One crucial question here is whether the visual system contains mechanisms which can derive useful estimates of local rotation. Although the existing neurophysiological data are equivocal, psychophysical evidence suggests that it does, and that the estimation of local rotation may possibly occur simultaneously at a number of different spatial scales. Such a multi-scale system would be well suited to dealing with surfaces with different texture densities, and might also be useful in making sense of complex natural objects rather than simple surfaces. Of course, the larger the spatial scale at which the measurement is done, the less good is the approximation to the true value of *curl*. But that is not necessarily important. An understanding of the Fourier transform, for example, has helped us to describe and understand the properties of low-level luminance encoders, but it is almost certainly a mistake to claim that these mechanisms actually perform a Fourier analysis. Similarly, an understanding of the properties of the 2D *curl* function is useful, even if the actual mechanisms involved do not accurately compute *curl*. In fact, the *curl* function varies very slowly and smoothly across the retina, so a useful description could well be derived even by mechanisms which estimate local rotation at a fairly coarse spatial scale. According to our simple scheme, the coarseness of the scale would effectively be constrained by the size of the regions in the flow pattern which correspond to surfaces in the world. Computational analyses of natural flow patterns are likely to shed the most light on this constraint, while further neurophysiological and psychophysical studies of human processes are also clearly needed.

Ultimately, of course, the validity of any model depends not just upon showing that the visual system is equipped to implement it, but upon some clear demonstration that it actually does so. Our scheme makes clear predictions about the type of information that observers ought to be able to recover from random dot flow patterns: they ought, for example, to be able to make accurate judgments about the 3D layout of surfaces, this ability ought to depend to some extent upon angle of approach (since the magnitude of the *curl* function increases with more oblique approach), and it ought to depend upon the size of the surface and how it projects into the optic array (since the slope of the *curl* function will clearly influence the accuracy with which the surface origin can be located). Although recent studies have begun to emphasize more relevant tasks such as the ability to judge surface slant and surface rigidity, the majority of work so far has been concentrated upon the expanding component of retinal flow and its role in the judgment of heading and time to collision. While these tasks are important, they by no means exhaust the possible usages of retinal flow. The required psychophysical techniques are well established and we hope to see more comprehensive studies emerge over the next few years.

Acknowledgments

Our experimental work described here was supported by SERC studentships to TF and GW. Some of these results have been previously reported at the British Telecom Symposium Applying Visual Psychophysics to User Interface Design, Lavenham, 1990.

11

Neural Facades: Visual Representations of Static and Moving Form-and-Color-and-Depth

STEPHEN GROSSBERG

The Inadequacy of Visual Modules

This chapter discusses some implications for understanding vision of recent theoretical results concerning the neural architectures that subserve visual perception in humans and other mammals (Cohen and Grossberg, 1984; Grossberg, 1984, 1987a,b, 1988; Grossberg and Mingolla, 1985a,b, 1987; Grossberg and Todorović, 1988; Grossberg and Marshall, 1989; Grossberg and Rudd, 1989; Grossberg et al., 1989). In addition, a new result is stated concerning differences between the neural mechanisms for perception of static visual forms and moving visual forms; indeed, why both types of mechanisms exist.

These results contribute to the development of a neural theory of preattentive vision, called FACADE theory. FACADE theory clarifies that, whereas specialization of function surely exists during visual perception, it is not the type of specialization that may adequately be described by separate neural modules for the processing (say) of edges, textures, shading, stereo, and color information. In particular, the present theory provides an explanation of many data that do not support the modular approach described by Marr (1982).

A basic conceptual problem faced by a modular approach may be described as follows. Suppose that specialized modules capable of processing edges, or textures, or shading, etc. are available. Typically, each of these modules is described using different mathematical rules that are not easily combined into a unified theory. Correspondingly, the modules do not respond well to visual data other than the type of data which they were designed to process. In order to function well, either the visual world which such a module is allowed to process must be restricted, whence the module could not be used to process realistic scenes; or a smart preprocessor is needed to sort scenes into parts according to the type of data that each module can process well, and to expose a module only to that part of a scene for which it was designed. Such a smart preprocessor would, however, embody a more powerful vision model than the modules themselves; hence, it would render the modules obsolete. In either case, modular algorithms do not provide a viable approach to the study of real-world vision.

The task of such a smart preprocessor is, in any case, more difficult than one of sorting scenes into parts which contain only one type of visual information. This is because each part of a visual scene often contains locally ambiguous information about edges, textures, shading, stereo, motion, and color, all overlaid together. Humans are capable of using these multiple types of visual information cooperatively to generate an unambiguous 3D representation of Form-And-Color-And-Depth; hence the term FACADE representation. The hyphens in "form-and-color-and-depth" emphasize the well-known fact that changes in perceived color can cause changes in perceived depth and form, changes in perceived depth can cause changes in perceived brightness and form, and so on. Every stage of visual processing *multiplexes* together several key properties of the scenic representation. It is a central task of biological vision theories to understand how the organization of visual information processing regulates which properties are multiplexed together at each processing stage, and how the stages interact to generate these properties.

Hierarchical Resolution of Uncertainty using Interactions between Complementary Systems

FACADE theory became possible through the discovery of several new uncertainty principles; that is, principles which show what combinations of visual properties cannot, in principle, be computed at a single processing stage (Grossberg and Mingolla, 1985b; Grossberg, 1987a). The theory describes how to design parallel and hierarchical interactions that can resolve these uncertainties using several processing stages. These interactions occur within and between two subsystems whose properties are computationally complementary. These complementary subsystems are called the boundary contour system (BCS) and the feature contour system (FCS).

Issues concerning uncertainty principles and complementarity lie at the foundations of quantum mechanics. Mammalian vision systems are also quantum systems in the sense that they can generate visual percepts in response to just a few light quanta. How the types of uncertainty and complementarity that are resolved by biological vision systems for purposes of macroscopic perception may be related to concepts of uncertainty and complementarity in quantum mechanics is a theme of considerable importance for future research.

For present purposes, the themes of uncertainty and complementarity show the inadequacy of the modular approach from a deeper information theoretic perspective. Although the BCS, FCS, and their individual processing stages are computationally specialized, their *interactions* overcome computational uncertainties and complementary deficiences to generate useful visual representations, rather than properties that may be computed by independent processing modules.

Such an interactive theory also precludes the sharp separation between formal algorithm and mechanistic realization that Marr (1982) proposed. How computational uncertainties can be overcome, how particular combinations of multiplexed properties can be achieved, and how complementary processing properties can be interactively synthesized, are properties of particular classes of mechanistic realizations. Many workers in the field of neural networks summarize this state of affairs by saying that "the architecture is the algorithm."

Generating Invariant Boundary Structures and Surface Colors

FACADE theory clarifies how our visual systems are designed to detect relatively invariant surface colors under variable illumination conditions, to detect relatively invariant object boundary structures amid noise caused by the eyes' own optics or occluding objects, and to recognize familiar objects or events in the environment. These three principle functions are performed by the FCS, the BCS, and by an object recognition system (ORS), respectively, as indicated in the macrocircuit of figure 11.1.

The computational demands placed on a system that is designed to detect invariant surface colors are, in many respects, complementary to the demands placed on a system that is designed to detect invariant boundary structures. That is why the FCS and BCS in figure 11.1 process the signals from each monocular preprocessing (MP) stage in parallel. The FCS and BCS are not, however, independent modules. Figure 11.2 depicts in greater detail how levels of the FCS and BCS interact through multiple feedforward and feedback pathways to generate a FACADE representation at the final level of the FCS.

In addition to the complementary relationship between the FCS and the BCS, there also exist informational uncertainties at processing levels within each of these systems. In particular, the filtering computations within the FCS which reduce uncertainty due to variable illumination conditions create new uncertainties about surface brightnesses and colors that are resolved at a higher FCS level by a process of featural filling-in. The filtering computations within the BCS which reduce uncertainty about boundary orientation create new uncertainties about boundary position that are resolved at a higher BCS level by a process of boundary completion.

The division of labor between BCS and FCS is not simply a partitioning for simplicity or convenience. Rather, BCS dynamics require oriented filtering operations followed by oriented cooperative-competitive feedback

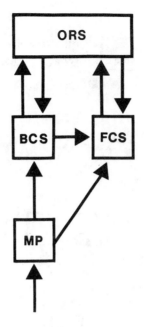

Figure 11.1 *A macrocircuit of processing stages. Monocular preprocessed signals (MP) are sent independently to both the boundary contour system (BCS) and the feature contour system (FCS). The BCS preattentively generates coherent boundary structures from these MP signals. These structures send outputs to both the FCS and the object recognition system (ORS). The ORS, in turn, rapidly sends top-down learned template signals, or expectations, to the BCS. These template signals can modify the preattentively completed boundary structures using learned, attentive information. The BCS passes these modifications along to the FCS. The signals from the BCS organize the FCS into perceptual regions wherein filling-in of visible brightnesses and colors can occur. This filling-in process is activated by signals from the MP stage. The completed FCS representation, in turn, also interacts with the ORS.*

interactions, because such an architecture can rapidly and in a context-sensitive manner perform the requisite boundary segmentations that the FCS itself needs in order to pool, or fill-in, its estimates of surface color among regions belonging to the same perceived objects. That pooling is a type of unoriented spatial averaging performed by a diffusion process. Were a diffusion of signals employed within the BCS itself, however, it could blur the very boundaries that it seeks to sharpen and thereby defeat both the BCS and FCS system goals. Accordingly, as shown in figure 11.1, the BCS processes occur separately of, and in parallel with, FCS processes, but send topographically matched signals to the FCS to organize the spatial structuring of the FCS filling-in process.

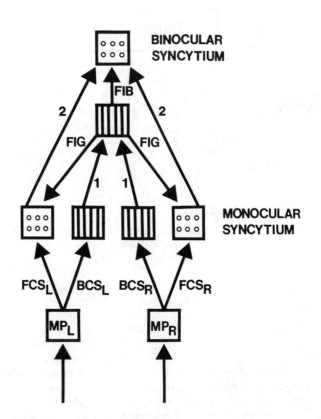

Figure 11.2   *Macrocircuit of monocular and binocular interactions within the boundary contour system (BCS) and the feature contour system (FCS). Left and right monocular preprocessing stages (MP$_L$ and MP$_R$) send parallel monocular inputs to the BCS (boxes with vertical lines) and the FCS (boxes with three pairs of circles). The monocular BCS$_L$ and BCS$_R$ interact via bottom-up pathways labeled 1 to generate a coherent binocular boundary segmentation. This segmentation generates output signals called filling-in generators (FIGs) and filling-in barriers (FIBs). The FIGs input to the monocular filling-in domains, or syncytia, of the FCS. The FIBs input to the binocular filling-in domains, or syncytia, of the FCS. Inputs from the MP stages interact with FIGs at the monocular syncytia where they select those monocular FC signals that are binocularly consistent. The selected FC signals are carried by the pathways labeled 2 to the binocular syncytia, where they interact with FIB signals from the BCS to generate a multiple scale representation of form-and-color-and-depth within the binocular syncytia. This chapter describes some monocular properties of the interactions from an MP stage through the first few BCS and FCS stages, namely those symbolized by the pathways labeled 1 and FIG.*

Preattentive Visual Processing by the BCS and FCS

The theory's general-purpose capabilities depend upon its decomposition into BCS, FCS, and ORS subsystems. Both the BCS and FCS operate preattentively and automatically upon all images, whether or not these images have been experienced before. The BCS is a general-purpose device in the sense that it can generate an emergent 3D boundary segmentation in response to a wide variety of image properties. For example, it is capable of detecting, sharpening, and completing image edges; of grouping textures; of generating a boundary web of boundary compartments that conform to the shape of smoothly shaded regions; and of carrying out a disparity-sensitive and scale-sensitive binocular matching process that generates fused binocular structures from disparate pairs of monocular images. The outcome of this 3D boundary segmentation process is perceptually invisible within the BCS. Visible percepts are a property of the FCS.

A completed segmentation within the BCS elicits topographically organized output signals to the FCS. These completed BC signals regulate the hierarchical processing of color and brightness signals by the FCS (figure 11.2). Notable among FCS processes are the automatic extraction from many different types of images of color and brightness signals that are relatively uncontaminated by changes in illumination conditions – again a general-purpose property. These feature contour signals interact within the FCS with the output signals from the BCS to control featural filling-in processes. These filling-in processes lead to visible percepts of form-and-color-and-depth at the final stage of the FCS, which is called the binocular syncytium (figure 11.2).

Such a theoretical decomposition of the vision process conforms to, and has in fact predicted, properties of a similar decomposition that governs the design of the mammalian visual cortex. For example, in the theory's analyses and predictions of neurobiological data, the Monocular preprocessor stage (MP_L, MP_R) of figures 11.1 and 11.2 is compared with opponent cells of the lateral geniculate nucleus, the first stage of the BCS is compared with simple cells of the hypercolumns in area V1 of striate cortex, the first stage of the FCS is compared with cells of the cytochrome oxydase staining blobs of area V1 of striate cortex, the binocular syncytium is compared with cells of area V4 of the prestriate cortex, and the intervening BCS and FCS stages are compared with complex, hypercomplex, double opponent, and related cell types in areas V1, V2, and V4 of striate and prestriate cortex (Grossberg and Mingolla, 1985a; Grossberg, 1987a).

Interactions between Preattentive Vision and Attentive Learned Object Recognition

The processes summarized in figures 11.1 and 11.2 are preattentive and automatic. These preattentive processes may, however, influence and be

Figure 11.3   *A Glass pattern: the emergent circular pattern is "recognized," although it is not "seen," as a pattern of differing contrasts. The text suggests how this happens.*

influenced by attentive, learned object recognition processes. The macrocircuit depicted in figure 11.1 suggests, for example, that a preattentively completed boundary segmentation within the BCS can directly activate an object recognition system (ORS), whether or not this segmentation supports visible contrast differences within the FCS. In the Glass pattern of figure 11.3. for example, the circular groupings can be recognized by the ORS even though they do not support visible contrast differences within the FCS.

The ORS can, in turn, read-out attentive learned priming, or expectation, signals to the BCS. Why the ORS needs to read-out learned top-down attentive feedback signals is clarified elsewhere by results form adaptive resonance theory, which has demonstrated that learned top-down expectations help to stabilize the self-organization of object recognition codes in response to complex and unpredictable input environments (Carpenter and Grossberg, 1987a,b, 1988). Learned top-down expectations seem to be a computational universal in all self-organizing cognitive systems, including systems for speech and language processing (Grossberg, 1978, 1980, 1982, 1986, 1987c; McClelland and Rumelhart, 1981; Rumelhart and McClelland, 1982; Cohen and Grossberg, 1986, 1987; Dell, 1986; Grossberg and Stone, 1986; Cohen et al., 1988; Ratcliff and McKoon, 1988).

In response to familiar objects in a scene, the final 3D boundary segmentation within the BCS may thus be *doubly* completed, first by automatic preattentive segmentation processes and then by attentive learned expectation processes. This doubly completed segmentation regulates the featural filling-in processes within the FCS that lead to a percept of visible form. The

FCS also interacts with the ORS in order to generate recognitions of color and surface properties.

The feedback interactions between the preattentive BCS and FCS and the attentive, adaptive ORS emphasize that these subsystems are not independent modules, and clarify why the distinction between preattentive and attentive visul processing has been so controversial and elusive in the vision literature. Indeed, while seminal workers such as Jacob Beck and Bela Julesz have probed the preattentive aspects of textural grouping, other scientists have emphasized the attentive and cognitive aspects of vision, as in the "unconscious inferences" of Helmholtz and the "cognitive contours" of Richard Gregory. The possibility that emergent segmentations within the BCS can be doubly completed, both by preattentive emergent segmentations and attentive learned expectations, helps to unify these parallel lines of inquiry, and cautions against ignoring the influence of attentive feedback upon the "preattentive" BCS and FCS. The rules whereby such parallel inputs from the BCS and the FCS are combined within the ORS have recently been the subject of active experimental investigation, especially due to the excitement surrounding the discovery of "illusory conjunctions" (Treisman and Schmidt, 1982), whereby form and color information may be improperly joined under suitable experimental conditions.

The functional distinction between the attentive learned ORS and the "preattentive" BCS and FCS also has a neural analog in the functional architecture of mammalian neocortex. Whereas the BCS and FCS are neurally interpreted in terms of data about areas V1, V2, and V4 of visual cortex (Zeki, 1983a,b; Desimone et al., 1985), the ORS is interpreted in terms of data concerning inferotemporal cortex and related brain regions (Mishkin, 1982; Schwartz et al., 1983; Mishkin and Appenzeller, 1987).

The complementarity that exists between BCS and FCS computations is illustrated by example in the next two sections.

Discounting the Illuminant and Filling-in

One form of uncertainty with which the nervous system deals is due to the fact that the visual world is viewed under variable lighting conditions. When an object reflects light to an observer's eyes, the amount of light energy within a given wavelength that reaches the eye from each object location is determined by a product of two factors. One factor is a fixed ratio, or reflectance, which determines the fraction of incident light that is reflected by that object location to the eye. The other factor is the variable intensity of the light which illuminates the object location. Two object locations with equal reflectances can reflect different amounts of light to the eye if they are illuminated by different light intensities. Spatial gradients of light across a scene are the rule, rather than the exception, during perception, and wavelengths of light that illuminate a scene can vary widely during a single day. If the nervous system directly coded into percepts the light energies which it received, it would compute false measures of object colors and brightnesses, as well as false measures of object shapes.

Land (1977) and his colleagues have sharpened contemporary understanding of this issue by carrying out a series of remarkable experiments. In these experiments, a picture constructed from overlapping patches of colored paper, called a McCann Mondrian, is viewed under different lighting conditions. If red, green, and blue lights simultaneously illuminate the picture, then an observer perceives surprisingly little color change as the intensities of illumination are chosen to vary within wide limits. The stability of perceived colors obtains despite the fact that the intensity of light at each wavelength that is reflected to the eye varies linearly with the incident illumination intensity at that wavelength. This property of color stability indicates that the nervous system "discounts the illuminant," or suppresses the "extra" amount of light in each wavelength, in order to extract a color percept that is invariant under many lighting conditions.

In another experiment, non-homogeneous lighting conditions were devised such that spectrophotometric readings from positions within the interiors of two color patches were the same, yet the two patches appeared to have different colors. The perceived colors were, moreover, close to the colors that would be perceived when viewed in a homogeneous source of white light.

These results show that the signals from within the interiors of the colored patches are significantly attenuated in order to discount the illuminant. This property makes ecological sense, since even a gradual change in illumination level could cause a large cumulative distortion in perceived color or brightness if it were allowed to influence the percept of a large scenic region. In contrast, illuminant intensities typically do not vary much across a scenic edge. Thus the ratio of light signals reflected from the two sides of a scenic edge can provide an accurate local estimate of the relative reflectances of the scene at the corresponding positions. We have called the color and brightness signals which remain unattenuated near scenic edges FC signals.

The neural mechanisms which "discount the illuminant" overcome a fundamental uncertainty in the retinal pick-up of visual information. In so doing, however, they create a new problem of uncertain measurement, which illustrates one of the classic uncertainty principles of visual perception. If color and brightness signals are suppressed except near scenic edges, then why do we not see just a world of colored edges? How are these local FC signals used by later processing stages to synthesize global percepts of continuous color fields and of smoothly varying surfaces?

FC signals activate a process of lateral spreading, or filling-in, of color and brightness signals within the FCS. This filling-in process is contained by topographically organized output signals from the BCS to the FCS (figure 11.2). Where no BC signals obstruct the filling-in process, its strength is attenuated with distance, since it is governed by a non-linear diffusion process.

Many examples of featural filling-in and its containment by BC signals can be cited. A classic example of this phenomenon is described in figure 11.4. The image in figure 11.4 was used by Yarbus (1967) in a stabilized image

Figure 11.4 *A classic example of featural filling-in. When the edges of the large circle and the vertical line are stabilized on the retina, the red color (dots) outside the large circle envelopes the black and white hemidisks except within the small red circles whose edges are not stabilized. The red inside the left circle looks brighter and the red inside the right circle looks darker than the enveloping red.*

experiment. Normally the eye jitters rapidly in its orbit, and thereby is in continual relative motion with respect to a scene. In a stabilized image experiment, prescribed regions in an image are kept stabilized, or do not move with respect to the retina. Stabilization is accomplished by the use of a contact lens or an electronic feedback circuit. Stabilizing an image with respect to the retina can cause the perception of the image to fade. The adaptive utility of this property can be partially understood by noting that, in humans, light passes through retinal veins before it reaches the photosensitive retina. The veins form stabilized images with respect to the retina, hence are fortunately not visible under ordinary viewing conditions.

In the Yarbus display shown in figure 11.4, the large circular edge and the vertical edge are stabilized with respect to the retina. As these edge percepts fade, the red color outside the large circle is perceived to flow over and envelop the black and white hemidisks until it reaches the small red circles whose edges are not stabilized. This percept illustrates how FC signals can spread across, or fill-in, a scenic percept until they hit perceptually significant boundaries. Our neural network model of this process explains how filling-in occurs within the black and white regions, and why the left red disk appears lighter and the right red disk appears darker than the surrounding red region that envelops the remainder of the percept. The model has, in addition, been used to simulate a wide range of classic and recent phenomena concerning brightness perception which have not heretofore been explained by a single theory (Cohen and Grossberg, 1984; Grossberg and Todorović, 1988).

The Yarbus percept illustrates three properties of the FCS that are complementary to properties of the BCS (figure 11.5); namely, filling-in is an *outward* flowing process that is *unoriented*, and FCS computations are *sensitive to direction-of-contrast*, or contrast polarity, since otherwise the FCS could not represent different brightnesses or colors.

In summary, the uncertainty of variable lighting conditions is resolved by discounting the illuminant and extracting contour-sensitive FC signals. The uncertainty created within the discounted regions is resolved at a later processing stage via a featural filling-in process that is activated by the FC signals and contained within boundaries defined by BC signals.

Oriented Boundary Filtering and Emergent Segmentation: BCS/FCS Complementarity

The corresponding complementary properties of the BCS may be seen by inspecting a reverse-contrast Kanizsa square in figure 11.6. The photographic reproduction process may have weakened the percept of this "illusory" square. The critical percept is that of the square's vertical boundaries. The black-gray vertical edge of the top-left pacman figure is a dark-light vertical edge. The white-gray vertical edge of the bottom-left pacman figure is a light-dark vertical edge. These two vertical edges possess the same orientation but opposite directions-of-contrast. The percept of the vertical boundary that spans these opposite direction-of-contrast edges shows that the BCS is sensitive to boundary orientation but is indifferent to direction-of-contrast. Moreover, the horizontal boundaries of the square, which connect edges of like direction-of-contrast, group together with the vertical boundaries to generate a unitary percept of a square. Opposite direction-of-contrast and same direction-of-contrast boundaries both input to the same BCS in order to achieve broad-band boundary detection. In contrast, the FCS maintains its sensitivity to direction-of-contrast and elaborates it into a double-opponent color and brightness perception system.

The BCS and the FCS differ in their spatial interaction rules in addition to their rules of contrast. Indeed, their spatial interaction rules exhibit complementary properties. For example, in figure 11.6, a vertical illusory boundary forms between the boundary contours generated by a pair of vertically oriented and spatially aligned pacman edges. Thus the process of boundary completion is due to an *inwardly* directed and *oriented* interaction whereby

BCS: FCS:

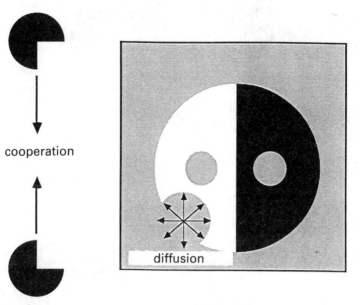

cooperation

inward   outward
propagation   propagation

orientation   not orientation
sensitive   sensitive

not sensitive to   sensitive to
contrast polarity   contrast polarity

Figure 11.5 *Computationally complementary properties of the BCS and FCS. The outcome of a BCS interaction is independent of direction-of-contrast, oriented and induced by pairs, or larger numbers, of oriented inducers. The outcome of an FCS interaction is dependent upon direction-of-contrast, unoriented, and generated by individual inducers.*

pairs of inducing BC signals can trigger the formation of an intervening boundary of similar orientation. In contrast, in the filling-in reactions of figure 11.4, featural quality can flow from each FC signal in all directions until it hits a boundary contour or is attenuated by its own spatial spread. Thus featural filling-in is an *outwardly* directed and *unoriented* interaction that is triggered by *individual* FC signals. These complementary properties of the BCS and FCS interaction rules are summarized in figure 11.5.

Figure 11.6   *A reverse-contrast Kanizsa square. An illusory square is induced by two black and two white pacman figures on a gray background. Illusory contours can thus join edges with opposite directions-of-contrast. (This effect may be weakened by the photographic reproduction process.)*

Cognitive Impenetrability of Neural Computations

An analysis of how the BCS implements the types of properties summarized in figure 11.5 illustrates the cognitive impenetrability of neural computations. In other words, we are designed so that our neural mechanisms and the organizational principles that govern their design are hidden from the direct introspective evidence of daily experience. The behavioral level can thus concern itself with percepts, feelings, ideas, and plans rather than with neurons, ions, and chemical transmitters.

In particular, early stages of BCS design include a circuit that contains formal analogs of cortical simple cells, complex cells, and hypercomplex cells, but the computational constraints that are predicted to govern this circuit's neural design are not obvious on the behavioral level. This fact may be highlighted by a personal anecdote. I did not notice the, now obvious, neurophysiological interpretation of the model hypercomplex cells until at least two years after the circuit was derived from perceptual considerations.

One of the hardest things to understand about neural modeling is how a modeler can discover a behavioral analysis from which neural mechanisms can be derived, despite the fact that these neural mechanisms are not obvious from our daily experiences, and the behavioral significance of the neural mechanisms may not at first be clear from direct neural measurements. In the present instance, at least two stumbling blocks to understanding can be identified:

1 The activities of BCS cells do not themselves become perceptually visible; they control properties of visibility that develop within the FCS.
2 The output stage (the hypercomplex cells) of the circuit in question is designed to overcome a computational uncertainty that is created at the input stage (the simple cells). Thus the circuit hides its perceptual function, except during perceptual anomalies, such as visual illusions.

In particular, the model simple cells, complex cells, and hypercomplex cells are predicted to be part of a circuit module that overcomes, through its hierarchical intercellular interactions, a computational uncertainty in processing image line ends and corners that is due to simple cells' oriented receptive fields. This compensatory process also generates properties of hyperacuity that have since been psychophysically reported (Badcock and Westheimer, 1985a,b). Thus the perceptual analysis of the computational limitations of oriented receptive fields predicts why simple cells, complex cells, and hypercomplex cells exist and, as an additional surprise, suggests a new understanding of hyperacuity. Some of these considerations will be discussed next.

Oriented Receptive Fields Imply Positional Uncertainty at Line Ends and Corners

In order to effectively build up boundaries, the BCS must be able to determine the orientation of a boundary at every position. To accomplish this, the cells at the first stage of the BCS possess orientationally tuned receptive fields, or oriented masks. Such a cell, or cell population, is selectively responsive to orientations that activate a prescribed small region of the retina, and whose orientations lie within a prescribed band of orientations with respect to the retina. A collection of such orientationally tuned cells is assumed to exist at every network position, such that each cell type is sensitive to a different band of oriented contrasts within its prescribed small region of the scene, as in the hypercolumn model, which was developed to explain the responses of simple cells in area V1 of the striate cortex (Hubel and Wiesel, 1977).

These oriented receptive fields are oriented *local contrast* detectors, rather than edge detectors. This property enables them to fire in response to a wide variety of spatially non-uniform image contrasts including edges, spatially non-uniform densities of unoriented textural elements, and spatially non-uniform densities of surface gradients. Thus, by sacrificing a certain amount of spatial resolution in order to detect oriented local contrasts, these masks achieve a general detection characteristic which can respond to edges, textures, and surfaces.

The fact that the receptive fields of the BCS are *oriented* greatly reduces the number of possible groupings into which their target cells can enter. On the other hand, in order to detect oriented local contrasts, the receptive fields must be elongated along their preferred axis of symmetry. Then the cells can preferentially detect differences of average contrast across this axis of symmetry, yet can remain silent in response to differences of average contrast that are perpendicular to the axis of symmetry. Such receptive field elongation creates greater positional uncertainty about the exact locations within the receptive field of the image contrasts which fire the cell. This positional uncertainty becomes acute during the processing of image line ends and corners.

Oriented receptive fields cannot easily detect the ends of thin scenic lines (Grossberg and Mingolla, 1985b) whose widths fall within a certain range: wider than lines which generate a continuous band of vertically oriented receptive field responses, and narrower than lines which generate a band of horizontally oriented receptive field responses throughout their lowest extremity. Such a choice of lines always exists if the receptive field is elongated by a sufficient amount in a preferred orientation. This property illustrates a basic uncertainty principle which says: orientational "certainty" implies positional "uncertainty" at the ends of scenic lines whose widths are neither too small nor too large with respect to the dimensions of the oriented receptive field. If no BC signals are elicited at the ends of lines, however, then in the absence of further processing within the BCS, boundary contours will not be synthesized to prevent featural quality from flowing out of line ends within the FCS. Many percepts would hereby become badly degraded by featural flow.

Thus basic constraints upon visual processing seem to be at odds with each other. The need to discount the illuminant leads to the need for featural filling-in. The need for featural filling-in leads to the need to synthesize boundaries capable of restricting featural filling-in to appropriate perceptual domains. The need to synthesize boundaries leads to the need for orientation-sensitive receptive fields. Such receptive fields are, however, unable to restrict featural filling-in at scenic line ends or sharp corners. Thus, orientational certainty implies a type of positional uncertainty, which is unacceptable from the perspective of featural filling-in requirements.

Later processing stages are needed to recover both the positional and orientational information that are lost in this way. We have called the process which completes the boundary at a line end an *end cut*. End cuts actively reconstruct the line end at a processing stage higher than the oriented receptive field much as they do to form an Ehrenstein figure (figure 11.7). In order to emphasize the paradoxical nature of this process, we say that *all line ends are illusory*.

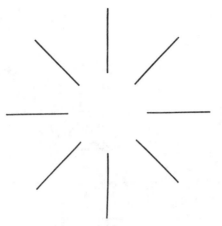

Figure 11.7   *An Ehrenstein figure. A bright circular disk is perceived even though all white areas are equally luminant. The text suggests how this happens.*

The OC Filter: Simple, Complex, and Hypercomplex Cells

The processing stages that are hypothesized to generate end cuts are summarized in figure 11.8. First, oriented simple cell receptive fields of like position and orientation, but opposite direction-of-contrast, generate rectified output signals. These output signals summate at the next processing stage to activate complex cells whose receptive fields are sensitive to the same position and orientation as themselves, but are insensitive to direction-of-contrast. These complex cells are sensitive to *amount* of oriented contrast, but not to the *direction* of this oriented contrast, as in our explanation of figure 11.6. They pool inputs from receptive fields with opposite directions-of-contrast in order to generate boundary detectors which can detect the broadest possible range of luminance or chromatic contrasts (De Valois et al., 1982; Spitzer and Hochstein, 1985).

The rectified output from the complex cells activates a second filter which is composed of two successive stages of spatially short-range competitive interaction whose net effect is to generate end cuts (figure 11.8). First, a cell of prescribed orientation excites like-oriented cells corresponding to its location and inhibits like-oriented cells corresponding to nearby locations at the next processing stage. In other words, an on-center off-surround organization of like-oriented cell interactions exists around each perceptual location. This mechanism is analogous to the neurophysiological process of *end stopping*, whereby hypercomplex cell receptive fields are fashioned from interactions of complex cell output signals (Hubel and Wiesel, 1965; Orban et al., 1979b). The outputs from this competitive mechanism interact with the second competitive mechanism. Here, cells compete that represent different

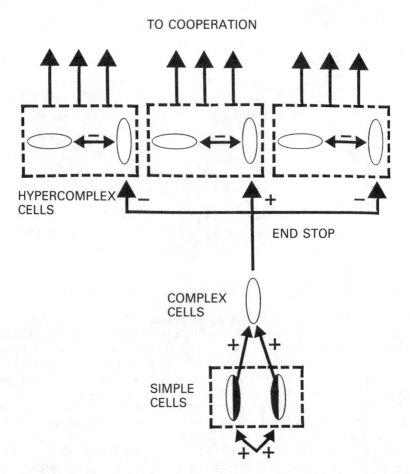

Figure 11.8 *Early stages of boundary contour processing. At each position exist cells with elongated receptive fields (simple cells) of various sizes which are sensitive to orientation, amount-of-contrast, and direction-of-contrast. Pairs of such cells sensitive to like orientation but opposite directions-of-contrast (lower dashed box) input to cells (complex cells) that are sensitive to orientation and amount-of-contrast but not to direction-of-contrast (white ellipses). These cells, in turn, excite like-oriented cells (hypercomplex cells) corresponding to the same position and inhibit like-oriented cells corresponding to nearby positions at the first competitive stage. At the second competitive stage, cells corresponding to the same position but different orientations (higher-order hypercomplex cells) inhibit each other via a push–pull competitive interaction.*

orientations, notably perpendicular orientations, at the same perceptual location. This competition defines a push–pull opponent process. If a given orientation is excited, then its perpendicular orientation is inhibited. If a given orientation is inhibited, then its perpendicular orientation is excited via disinhibiton.

The combined effect of these two competitive interactions generates end cuts as follows. The strong vertical activations along the edges of a scenic line inhibit the weak vertical activations near the line end. These inhibited vertical activations, in turn, disinhibit horizontal activations near the line end. Thus, the positional uncertainty generated by orientational certainty is eliminated at a subsequent processing level by the interaction of two spatially short-range competitive mechanisms which convert complex cells into two distinct populations of hypercomplex cells.

The properties of these competitive mechanisms have successfully predicted and helped to explain a variety of neural and perceptual data. For example, the prediction of the theory summarized in figure 11.8 anticipated the report by von der Heydt et al. (1984) that cells in prestriate visual cortex respond to perpendicular line ends, whereas cells in striate visual cortex do not. These cell properties also help to explain why color is sometimes perceived to spread across a scene, as in the phenomenon of neon color spreading (Redies and Spillmann, 1981; Grossberg and Mingolla, 1985a; Grossberg, 1987a) by showing how some BC signals are inhibited by boundary contour processes. The end-cut process also exhibits properties of hyperacuity which have been used (Grossberg, 1987a) to explain psychophysical data about spatial localization and hyperacuity (Badcock and Westheimer, 1985a,b; Watt and Campbell, 1985). A version of the double filter in figure 11.8 was also derived from data about texture segregation (Graham and Beck, 1988) in a way that supports the texture analyses of Grossberg and Mingolla (1985b). These analyses also utilize the cooperative-competitive feedback interactions, indicated in figure 11.9, to generate emergent boundary segmentations, such as the circular groupings generated in response to the Glass pattern in figure 11.3 and the Kanizsa square generated in response to the four pacman figures in figure 11.6. These feedback interactions between bipole cells and hypercomplex cells have properties akin to those discovered experimentally in visual cortex by von der Heydt et al. (1984) and Peterhans and von der Heydt (1989) during the formation of illusory contours, and by Eckhorn et al. (1988) and Gray et al. (1989) during long-range cooperative linking operations among assemblies of similarly coded visual features. The process of emergent boundary segmentation will not be further discussed herein. Instead, I will indicate how further analysis of this hierarchical network leads to explanations of data about motion perception.

Why is a Motion Boundary Contour System Needed?

It is well known that some regions of visual cortex are specialized for motion processing, notably region MT (Zeki, 1974a,b; Maunsell and van Essen, 1983;

BOUNDARY CONTOUR SYSTEM (BCS)

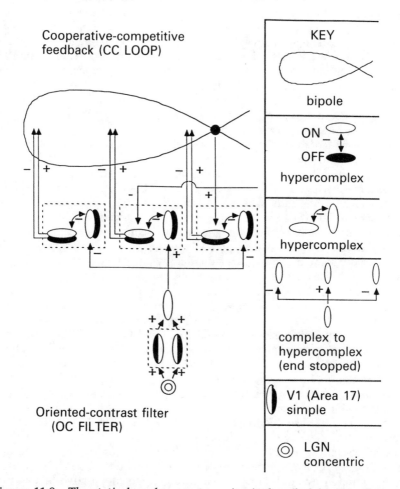

Figure 11.9 *The static boundary contour circuit described by Grossberg and Mingolla (1985b). The circuit is divided into an oriented contrast-sensitive filter (OC filter) followed by a cooperative-competitive feedback network (CC loop). Multiple copies of this circuit are used, one corresponding to each receptive field size of the OC filter. The depicted circuit has been used to analyze data about monocular vision. A binocular generalization of the circuit has also been described (Grossberg, 1987b; Grossberg and Marshall, 1989).*

Newsome et al., 1983; Albright et al., 1984). On the other hand, even the earliest stages of visual cortex processing, such as the simple cells in V1 (figure 11.8), require stimuli that change through time for their maximal activation and are direction-sensitive (Hubel and Wiesel, 1962, 1968, 1977; Heggelund, 1981; De Valois et al., 1982; Tanaka et al., 1983). Why has evolution gone to the trouble to generate regions such as MT, when even V1 is change-sensitive and direction-sensitive? What computational properties are achieved by MT that are not already available in V1?

As indicated above, the monocular BCS theory of Grossberg and Mingolla (1985a,b), schematized in figure 11.9, and its binocular generalization (Grossberg, 1987b; Grossberg and Marshall, 1989), has successfully modeled many boundary segmentation properties of V1 and its prestriate projections. This BCS model has thus far been used to analyze data generated in response to static visual images. Henceforth we therefore call such a BCS a static BCS model. The cells of the static BCS model can easily be gated by cells sensitive to image transients, such as Y cells (Enroth-Cugell and Robson, 1966; Stone, 1972; Hoffmann, 1973; Stone and Dreher, 1973; Tolhurst, 1973; Sekuler, 1975), to generate receptive fields sensitive to image transients. How does a motion BCS differ from a static BCS whose cells are sensitive to image transients? The answer to this question that is suggested by Grossberg and Rudd (1989) illustrates once again the importance of BCS/FCS complementarity in understanding preattentive vision, and the inadequacy of a modeling approach based on independent processing modules.

Joining Sensitivity to Direction-of-motion with Insensitivity to Direction-of-contrast

As shown in figure 11.8, although the simple cells of the BCS are sensitive to direction-of-contrast, or contrast polarity, the complex cells of the BCS are rendered insensitive to direction-of-contrast by receiving inputs from pairs of simple cells with opposite direction-of-contrast. Such a property is also true of the simple cells and complex cells in area V1 (De Valois et al., 1982; Thorell et al., 1984; Poggio et al., 1985).

This property is useful for extracting boundaries along contrast reversals in the image. As a result, however, the output of the OC filter is unable to differentiate direction-of-motion. For example, the complex cell in figure 11.8 can respond to a vertical light-dark contrast moving to the right, and to a vertical dark-light contrast moving to the left. Because the complex cell can respond to image contrasts that move in opposite directions, it is insensitive to direction-of-motion. A key property of the motion BCS model of Grossberg and Rudd (1989) is that it possesses a modified OC filter that multiplexes the property of insensitivity to direction-of-contrast, which is equally useful for the processing of static and moving forms, with sensitivity to direction-of-motion. The properties of this motion OC filter, or MOC filter, mirror many properties of motion perception, including percepts of apparent motion. When the MOC filter is connected to a CC loop, as in figure 11.9, a much larger body of data, including coherent global motion percepts such as induced motion and motion capture, can also be analyzed.

This model suggests that a fundamental computational property achieved by a motion segmentation system, such as MT, is to generate output signals that maintain insensitivity to direction-of-contrast without sacrificing sensitivity to direction-of-motion. The fact that such a modest change of the static OC filter enables us to define a motion BCS that is useful to analyze a large body of data concerning motion segmentation provides additional support for both the static BCS model and the motion BCS model by showing that both models may be considered variations on a single neural architectural theme.

The property of insensitivity to direction-of-contrast in the static BCS reflects one of the fundamental new insights of the FACADE theory of preattentive vision. Insensitivity to direction-of-contrast is possible within the BCS because all boundary segmentations within the BCS are perceptually invisible. Visibility is a property of the complementary FCS, whose computations are sensitive to direction-of-contrast. Thus a vision theory built up from independent processing modules could not articulate the heuristics of the motion BCS because it could not understand BCS/FCS complementarity.

Once the MOC filter was defined, its properties clarified a new set of issues that also argue against the existence of independent modules. One issue concerns why parallel systems exist for the processing of static visual forms and moving visual forms. Why is not a motion system sufficient, given that objects typically move with respect to an observer's eye movements in a natural environment? We link the existence of these parallel systems to a symmetry principle that is predicted to govern the development of visual cortex (see below), with the static and motion systems as two interdependent parts of its overall design. A second issue concerns how orientational tuning in the static form system is replaced by directional tuning in the motion form system (see later), with the same direction-of-motion being computed from more than one orientation of a moving figure. As we will see in the next section, both short-range and long-range spatial interactions are needed to define an MOC filter whose output signals are insensitive to direction-of-contrast but sensitive to direction-of-motion. The extra degree of freedom provided by the long-range interaction permits merging of many static orientations in the service of a single direction-of-motion.

Design of an MOC Filter

An MOC filter is mathematically defined in Grossberg and Rudd (1989). Its five processing stages are qualitatively summarized in Figure 11.10 and described below.

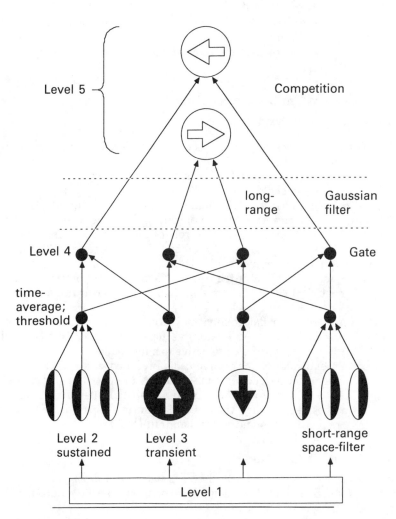

Figure 11.10   *The MOC filter. Level 1 registers the input pattern. Level 2 consists
of sustained response cells with oriented receptive fields that are sensitive to direction-
of-contrast. Level 3 consists of transient response cells with unoriented receptive
fields that are sensitive to direction-of-change in the total cell input. Level 4 cells
combine sustained cell and transient cell signals to become sensitive to direction-of-
motion and sensitive to direction-of-contrast. Level 5 cells combine level 4 cells to
become sensitive to direction-of-motion and insensitive to direction-of-contrast.*

Level 1: Preprocess Input Pattern

The image is preprocessed before activating the filter. For example, it is passed through a shunting on-center off-surround net to compensate for variable illumination, or to "discount the illuminant" (Grossberg and Todorović, 1988).

Level 2: Sustained Cell Short-range Filter

Four operations occur here:

1 *Space-average*: Inputs are processed by individual oriented receptive fields, or simple cells.
2 *Rectify*: The output signal from a simple cell grows with its activity above a signal threshold.
3 *Short-range spatial filter*: A spatially aligned array of simple cells with like direction-of-contrast pool their output signals to activate the next cell level. This spatial pooling plays the role of the short-range motion limit D_{max} (Braddick, 1974). The breadth of spatial pooling scales with the size of the simple cell receptive fields. Thus D_{max} is not independent of the spatial frequency content of the image (Nakayama and Silverman, 1984, 1985; Burr et al., 1986; Anderson and Burr, 1987), and is not a universal constant.

   The direction of spatial pooling may not be perpendicular to the oriented axis of the simple cell receptive field (Grossberg and Mingolla, 1990). The target cells are thus sensitive to a movement *direction* that may not be perpendicular to the simple cell's preferred orientation.
4 *Time-average*: The target cell time-averages the directionally sensitive inputs that it receives from the short-range spatial filter. This operation has properties akin to the "visual inertia" during apparent motion that was reported by Anstis and Ramachandran (1987).

Level 3: Transient Cell Filter

In parallel with the sustained cell filter, a transient cell filter reacts to input increments (on-cells) and decrements (off-cells) with positive outputs. This filter uses four operations too:

1 *Space-average*: This is accomplished by a receptive field that sums inputs over its entire range.
2 *Time-average*: This sum is time-averaged to generate a gradual growth and decay of total activation.
3 *Transient detector*: The on-cells are activated when the time-average increases. The off-cells are activated when the time-average decreases. This may be accomplished using a combination of feedforward inhibitory interneurons (Grossberg, 1970) and a gated dipole opponent organization of on-cells and off-cells (Grossberg, 1976).

Level 4: Sustained-transient Gating Yields Direction-of-motion Sensitivity and Direction-of-contrast Sensitivity

Maximal activation of a level 2 sustained cell filter is caused by image contrasts moving in either of two directions that differ by 180°. Multiplicative gating of each level 2 sustained cell output with a level 3 transient on-cell or off-cell removes this ambiguity. For example, consider a sustained cell output from vertically oriented light-dark simple cell receptive fields that are joined together in the horizontal direction by the short-range spatial filter. Such a sustained cell output is maximized by a light-dark image contrast moving to the right or to the left. Multiplying this level 2 output with a level 3 transient on-cell output generates a level 4 cell that responds maximally to motion to the right. Multiplying it with a level 3 off-cell output generates a level 4 cell that responds maximally to motion to the left. Multiplying a sustained cell with a transient cell is the main operation of the Marr and Ullman (1981) motion detector. Despite this point of similarity, Grossberg and Rudd (1989) described six basic differences between the MOC filter and the Marr-Ullman model. For example, none of the operations such as short-range spatial filtering, time-averaging, and rectification occurs in the Marr-Ullman model. In addition, the rationale of the MOC filter – to design a filter that is sensitive to direction-of-motion and insensitive to direction-of-contrast – is not part of the Marr-Ullman model. This difference is fundamental. The Marr-Ullman model is a product of the "independent modules" perspective. The MOC filter's insensitivity to direction-of-contrast can only be formulated within the framework of BCS/FCS complementarity: one cannot understand why a boundary filter's output needs to be insensitive to direction-of-contrast unless there exists a complementary "seeing" system that is sensitive to direction-of-contrast.

The cell outputs from level 4 are sensitive to direction-of-contrast. Level 5 consists of cells that pool outputs from level 4 cells which are sensitive to the same direction-of-motion but to opposite directions-of-contrast.

Level 5: Long-range Spatial Filter and Competition

Outputs from level 4 cells sensitive to the same direction-of-motion but opposite directions-of-contrast activate individual level 5 cells via a long-range spatial filter that is Gaussianly distributed across space. In particular, this long-range filter groups together level 4 cell outputs from level 3 short-range filters with the same directional preference but different simple cell orientations. Thus the long-range filter provides the extra degree of freedom that enables level 5 cells to function as "direction" cells, rather than "orientation" cells.

The long-range spatial filter broadcasts each level 4 signal over a wide spatial range in level 5. Competitive, or lateral inhibitory, interactions within level 5 contrast-enhance this input pattern to generate spatially sharp level 5 responses. A winner-takes-all competitive network (Grossberg, 1973, 1982) can transform even a very broad input pattern into a focal activation at the position that receives the maximal input. A contrast-enhancing competitive interaction has also been modeled at the complex cell level of the SOC filter (Grossberg, 1987b; Grossberg and Marshall, 1989). The level 5 cells of the MOC filter are, in other respects too, computationally homologous to the SOC filter complex cells. The winner-takes-all assumption is a limiting case of how competition can restore positional localization. More generally, we suggest that this competitive process partially contrast-enhances its input pattern to generate a motion signal whose breadth across space increases with the breadth of its inducing pattern.

Continuous Motion Paths from Spatially Stationary Flashes: An Emergent Property

MOC filter properties suggest an answer to long-standing questions in the vision literature concerning why individual flashes do not produce a percept of long-range motion, yet long-range interaction between spatially discrete pairs of flashes can produce a spatially sharp percept of continuous motion. Such apparent motion phenomena are a particularly useful probe of motion mechanisms because they describe controllable experimental situations in which nothing moves, yet a compelling percept of motion is generated. They also provide a simple example of a perceptual *emergent property*; namely, a property that is generated by system interactions operating in real-time, and thus that cannot be explained as a consequence of independently computed quantities, or a list of algorithmic statements.

For example, two brief flashes of light, separated in both time and space, create an illusion of movement from the location of the first flash to that of the second when the spatiotemporal parameters of the display are within the correct range (figure 11.11a). Variants of apparent motion include *phi motion*, or the *phi phenomenon*, whereby a "figureless" or "objectless" motion signal propagates from one flash to the other, analogous to the rapid motion of an object so quickly that its form cannot be clearly identified; *beta motion*, whereby a well-defined form seems to move smoothly and continuously from one flash to the other; and *gamma motion*, the apparent expansion at onset and contraction at offset of a single flash of light (Bartley, 1941; Kolers, 1972).

Outstanding theoretical issues concerning apparent motion include the resolution of a trade-off that exists between the long-range spatial interaction that is needed to generate the motion percept, and localization of the perceived motion signal that smoothly interpolates the inducing flashes. If a long-range interaction between the flashes must exist in order to generate the motion percept, then why is it not perceived when only a single light is flashed? Why are not outward waves of motion-carrying signals induced by a single flash? What kind of long-range influence is generated by each flash, yet only triggers a perceived motion signal when at least two flashes are

TWO FLASH DISPLAY

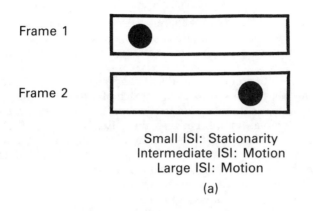

Frame 1

Frame 2

Small ISI: Stationarity
Intermediate ISI: Motion
Large ISI: Motion

(a)

TERNUS DISPLAY

Frame 1

Frame 2

Small ISI: Stationarity
Intermediate ISI: Element Motion
Large ISI: Group Motion

(b)

Figure 11.11 *Two types of apparent motion displays in which the two frames outline the same region in space into which the dots are flashed at successive times: In (a) a single dot is flashed, followed by an interstimulus interval (ISI), followed by a second dot. At small ISIs, the two dots appear to flicker in place. At longer ISIs, motion from the position of the first dot to that of the second is perceived. b, In the Ternus display, three dots are presented in each frame such that two of the dots in each frame occupy the same positions. At short ISIs, all the dots appear to be stationary. At longer ISIs the dots at the shared positions appear to be stationary, while apparent motion occurs from the left dot in frame 1 to the right dot in frame 2. At still longer ISIs, the three dots appear to move from frame 1 to frame 2 as a group.*

activated? What kind of long-range influence from individual flashes can generate a smooth motion signal between flashes placed at variable distances from one another? How does the motion signal speed up to smoothly interpolate flashes that occur at larger distances but the same time lag (Kolers, 1972)? How does the motion signal speed up to smoothly interpolate flashes when they occur at the same distance but shorter time lag (Kolers, 1972)?

A well-known apparent motion display, originally due to Ternus (1926), illustrates the fact that not only the existence of a motion percept, but also its figural identity, may depend on subtle aspects of the display, such as the interstimulus interval, or ISI, between the offset of the first flash and the onset of the second flash (figure 11.11b). In the Ternus display, a cyclic alternation of two stimulus frames gives rise to competing visual movement percepts. In frame 1, three black elements are arranged in a horizontal row on a white background. (The contrast may be reversed without consequence to the discussion which follows.) In frame 2, the elements are shifted to the right in such a way that the positions of the two leftwardmost elements in frame 2 are identical to those of the two rightwardmost elements in frame 1. Depending on the stimulus conditions, the observer will see either of two bistable motion percepts. Either the elements will appear to move to the right as a group between frames 1 and 2 and then back again during the second half of a cycle of the display or, alternatively, the leftwardmost element in frame 1 will appear to move to the location of the rightwardmost element in frame 2, jumping across two intermediate elements which appear to remain stationary. We will refer to the first percept as "group" motion; and the second percept as "element" motion. At short ISIs there is a tendency to observe element motion. At longer ISIs, there is a tendency to observe group motion.

Formal analogs of these phenomena occur at level 5 of the MOC filter in response to sequences of flashes presented to level 1. Intuitively, a signal for motion will arise when a spatially continuous flow of activation crosses the network through time. Each activation represents the peak, or maximal activity, of a broad spatial pattern of activation across the network. The broad activation pattern (figure 11.12b) is generated by the long-range spatial filter in response to a spatially localized flash to level 1 (figure 11.12a). The sharply localized response function, denoted by $x_i^{(R)}$ in figure 11.12c, is due to the contrast-enhancing action of the competitive network within level 5. A stationary localized $x_i^{(R)}$ response will be generated in response to a single flashing input every time it occurs.

Apparent motion can emerge when two input flashes occur with the following spatial and temporal separations. Let the positions of the flashes be $i = 1$ and $i = N$. Let the activity $r_1(t)$ caused by the first flash start to decay as the activity $r_N(t)$ caused by the second flash starts to grow. Suppose, moreover, that the flashes are close enough that the spatial patterns $r_1 G_{1i}$ and $r_N G_{Ni}$ overlap that are caused by broadcasting r_1 through the long-range filter G_{1i} and r_N through G_{Ni} to all level 5 positions i. Then the total input:

SPATIAL RESPONSE TO A
SINGLE FLASH

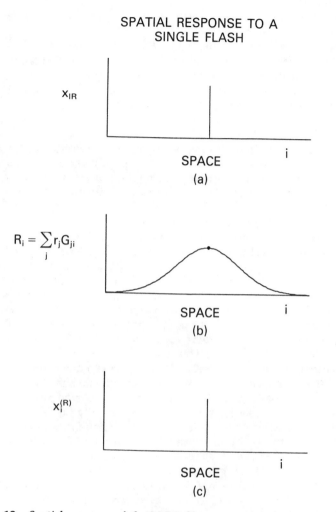

x_{IR}

SPACE   i
(a)

$R_i = \sum_j r_j G_{ji}$

SPACE   i
(b)

$x_i^{(R)}$

SPACE   i
(c)

Figure 11.12   *Spatial response of the MOC filter to a point input. a, Sustained activity of a level 2 cell; b, total input pattern to level 5; c, contrast-enhanced response at level 5.*

$$R_i = r_1 G_{1i} + r_N G_{Ni}$$

to the *i*th cell in level 5 can change in such a way that the maximum value of the spatial pattern $R_i(t)$ through time, namely $x_i^{(R)}(t)$, first occurs at $i = 1$, then $i = 2$, then $i = 3$, and so on until $i = N$. A percept of continuous motion from the position of the first flash to that of the second will result. In other words, two properly positioned and timed flashes can cause a travelling wave of activation across level 5.

This basic property of the MOC filter is illustrated by the computer simulations from Grossberg and Rudd (1989) that are schematized in figures 11.13–11.15. Figure 11.13 depicts the temporal response to a single flash at position 1 of level 1. The sustained cell response at position 1 of level 2 undergoes a gradual growth and decay of activation (figure 11.13b), although the position of maximal activation in the input to level 5 does not change through time (figure 11.13c).

Figure 11.14 illustrates an important implication of the fact that the level 2 cell activations persist after their level 1 inputs shut off. If a flash at position 1 is followed, after an appropriate delay, by a flash at position N, then the sustained response to the first flash (e.g. $x_{1R}(t)$) can decay while the response to the second flash (e.g. $x_{NR}(t)$) grows.

Assume for the moment that the transient signals computed at level 3 are held constant and consider how the waxing and waning of sustained cell responses from level 2 control the motion percept. Then the total input pattern R_i to level 5 can change through time in the manner depicted in figure 11.15. Each row of figure 11.15a illustrates the total input to level 5 caused, at a prescribed time t, by $x_{1R}(t)$ alone, by $x_{NR}(t)$ alone, and by both flashes together. Successive rows plot these functions at equally spaced later times. Note that as $x_{1R}(t)$ decays and $x_{NR}(t)$ grows, the maximum value of $R_i(t)$ moves continuously to the right. Figure 11.15b depicts the position $x_i^{(R)}(t)$ of the maximum value at the corresponding times.

In summary, the time-averaged and space-averaged responses to individual flashes do not change their position of maximal activation through time (figure 11.13c). In this case, "nothing moves." On the other hand, properly phased multiple flashes can generate a temporally and spatially averaged total response whose maximum moves continuously between the positions of the flashes through time (figure 11.15). In addition, by gating sustained cell responses by transient cell responses, the changeover occurs from element motion to group motion in response to the Ternus display as ISI is increased (figure 11.11b). Grossberg and Rudd (1989) have analyzed a wide variety of data about short-range and long-range motion using such properties of the MOC filter.

Why are Both Static and Motion Boundary Contour Systems Needed?

As illustrated above, the motion BCS has begun to provide explanations for a large body of psychophysical and neurobiological data about the perception of moving form. Once the MOC filter was defined, however, a new puzzle emerged. If Nature could design an MOC filter that is sensitive to direction-of-motion and insensitive to direction-of-contrast, then why did the SOC filter evolve, in which insensitivity to direction-of-contrast comes only

TEMPORAL RESPONSE TO A
SINGLE FLASH

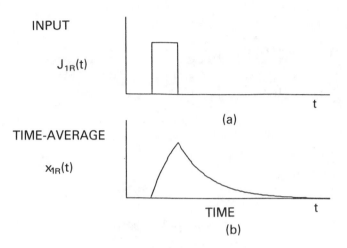

INPUT

$J_{1R}(t)$

(a)

TIME-AVERAGE

$x_{1R}(t)$

TIME   t

(b)

GROWTH OF ACTIVATION AS A
FUNCTION OF SPACE AND TIME

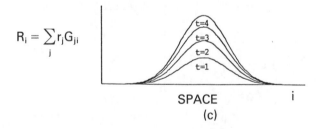

$$R_i = \sum_j r_j G_{ji}$$

t=4
t=3
t=2
t=1

SPACE   i

(c)

Figure 11.13 *Temporal response of sustained response cells to a point input. a,*
The input is presented for a brief duration at location 1. b, The activity of the
sustained response cell gradually builds up after input onset, then decays after input
offset. c, Growth of the input pattern to level 5 through time with transient cell
activity held constant. The activity pattern retains a Gaussian shape centered at the
location of the input.

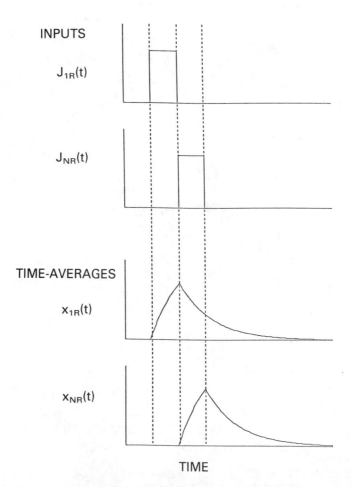

TEMPORAL RESPONSE TO
TWO SUCCESSIVE FLASHES

INPUTS

$J_{1R}(t)$

$J_{NR}(t)$

TIME-AVERAGES

$x_{1R}(t)$

$x_{NR}(t)$

TIME

Figure 11.14 *Temporal response of the sustained response cells at level 2 to two successive point inputs. One input is presented briefly at location 1, followed by a second input at location N. For an appropriately timed display, the decaying response at position 1 overlaps the rising response at position N.*

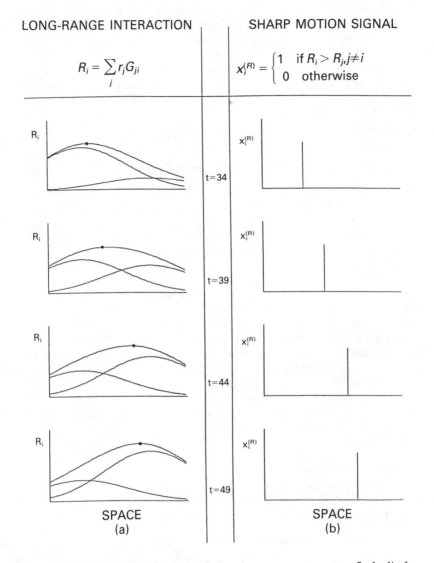

Figure 11.15 *Motion OC filter simulation in response to a two-flash display. Successive rows correspond to increasing times: a, The two lower curves in each row depict the total input to level 5 caused by each of the two flashes. The input due to the left flash decreases while the input due to the right flash increases. The total input due to both flashes is a traveling wave whose maximum value moves from the location of the first flash to that of the second flash. b, Position of the contrast-enhanced response at level 5.*

at the cost of a loss of sensitivity to direction-of-motion? This question is perplexing given the facts that animals' eyes are usually in relative motion with respect to their visual environment, and that simple cells in V1 are already sensitive to direction-of-motion.

I suggest an answer to this puzzle in which the static form and motion form systems are part of a larger design. In particular, the computation of static and motion properties are not realized by independent modules. This answer is suggested by re-analyzing the SOC filter in terms of how transient cells interact with the sustained cells depicted in figures 11.8 and 11.9.

The Symmetric Unfolding of Opponent Processes

Inspection of the CC loop in figure 11.9 provides an important clue. There, the hypercomplex cells are organized into opponent on-cells and off-cells, yet the SOC filter explicitly depicts only pathways to the hypercomplex on-cells from the simple on-cells via complex on-cells. Moreover, all of these cells are of sustained cell type. Interactions with transient cells are not described. When interactions with transient cells are added, a role for parallel SOC filter and MOC filter designs is suggested.

Let simple on-cells be defined by gating each pair of like-oriented sustained cells in figure 11.8 with a transient on-cell. Such a gated pair of on-cells is depicted in figure 11.16a, where it gives rise to a complex on-cell. Likewise, a pair of simple off-cells can be defined by gating the pair of like-oriented sustained cells in figure 11.8 with a transient off-cell. Such a gated pair of simple off-cells is depicted in figure 11.16b, where it gives rise to a complex off-cell.

Let the complex on-cell in figure 11.16a input to hypercomplex on-cells as in figure 11.9. In a similar fashion, let the complex off-cell in figure 11.16b input to hypercomplex off-cells in figure 11.9. The process of gating sustained cells by transient cells in the static BCS thus makes the overall design of this architecture more symmetric by showing how simple and complex on-cells and off-cells fit into the scheme.

Symmetry considerations also clarify why a static BCS and a motion BCS both exist. This symmetry principle controls the simultaneous satisfaction of three constraints, namely:

1 *Sustained-transient gating*: multiplicative interaction, or gating, of all combinations of sustained cell and transient cell output signals to form four sustained-transient cell types.
2 *Opponent pairs*: symmetric organization of these sustained-transient cell types into two pairs of opponent processes, such that:
3 *Independence of DOC*: output signals from the opponent processes are independent of direction-of-contrast. (DOC).

As shown above, multiplicative gating of sustained cells and transient cells generates receptive field properties of oriented on-cells and off-cells

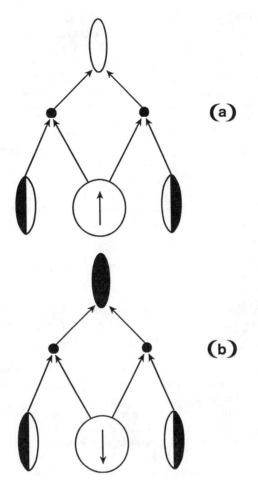

Figure 11.16 *a, A complex/orientation/on-cell. Pairs of rectified sustained cells with opposite direction-of-contrast are gated by rectified transient on-cells before the gated responses are added. b, A complex/orientation/off-cell. Pairs of rectified sustained cells with opposite direction-of-contrast are gated by rectified transient off-cells before the gated responses are added.*

within the static BCS, and direction-sensitive cells within the motion BCS. Opponent processing is a fundamental organizational principle whose role in stabilizing the self-organization of cortical circuits has been analyzed within adaptive resonance theory (Grossberg, 1980, 1982). The constraint that output signals be independent of direction-of-contrast enables both the static BCS and the motion BCS to generate emergent boundary segmentations along image contrast reversals.

Thus, the MOC filter and SOC filter realize all possible ways of symmetrically gating opponent pairs of sustained cells with transient cells to generate two opponent pairs of output signals that are insensitive to direction-of-contrast. One opponent pair of outcomes contains cell pairs that are insensitive to direction-of-motion, but sensitive to either the onset or the offset of an oriented contrast difference. These cells may be called complex/orientation/on-cells (figure 11.16a) and complex/orientation/off-cells (figure 11.16b), respectively. They belong to the SOC filter. The other opponent pair of outcomes contains the MOC filter cell pairs that are sensitive to opposite directions-of-motion. These cells may be called (for example) complex/direction/left-cells (figure 11.17a) and complex/direction/right-cells (figure 11.17b). When both sets of pairs are combined into a single symmetric diagram, the result is shown in figure 11.18, which summarizes how parallel, but interdependent, streams of static form and motion form processing are predicted to be organized in visual cortex.

90° Orientations and 180° Directions: from V1 to V2 and from V1 to MT

An important consequence of the abstract symmetries described in figures 11.16 and 11.17 is the familiar fact from daily life that opposite orientations are 90° apart, whereas opposite directions are 180° apart. In particular, the opposite orientation of "vertical" is "horizontal," and the opposite direction of "up" is "down." The symmetry implied by the former distinction is a 90° symmetry, whereas that implied by the latter distinction is 180° symmetry. How does this difference arise?

The 90° symmetry of opposite orientations is implied by the mechanisms for generating perpendicular end cuts at the hypercomplex cells of the static BCS, as sketched above and analyzed in Grossberg and Mingolla (1985b). This perpendicularity property is possible because the opponent feature of a complex/orientation/on-cell is a complex/orientation/off-cell (figure 11.16). To illustrate this property, suppose that a vertical line end excites a complex/vertical/on-cell in figure 11.18. Suppose that the end-stopped competition inhibits hypercomplex/vertical/on-cells at positions beyond the line end. Hypercomplex/horizontal/on-cells at these positions are thereby activated, and generate an end cut. As a result, a net excitatory input is generated from the horizontally oriented hypercomplex cells to the horizontally oriented bipole cells of the CC loop at that position (figure 11.9). These excitatory end cut inputs cooperate across positions to generate a horizontal emergent segmentation, that is perpendicular to the vertical line, along the entire line end.

In contrast, the opposite feature of a complex/direction cell is another complex/direction cell whose direction preference differs from it by 180° (figure 11.17). When this latter property is organized into a network topography, one finds the type of direction hypercolumns that were described in MT by Albright et al. (1984). A pictorial indication of how direction

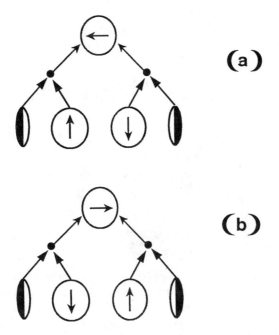

Figure 11.17 *a, A complex/direction/left-cell. Pairs of rectified sustained cells with opposite direction-of-contrast are gated by pairs of rectified transient on-cells and off-cells, before the gated responses are added. b, A complex/direction/right-cell. Same as in (a) except sustained cells are gated by the opposite transient cell.*

hypercolumns in MT may be generated from the orientation hypercolumns of V1 is shown in figure 11.19. This figure acknowledges that the pathways from V1 to MT combine signals from sustained cells and transient cells (figure 11.17) in a different way from the pathways from V1 to V2 (figure 11.16).

Opponent Rebounds: Rapid Reset Limits Smearing of Resonating Segmentations

A further example of perceptual complementarity may be understood by assuming that the opponent cell pairs shown in figures 11.16 and 11.17 are capable of *antagonistic rebound*; that is, offset of one cell in the pair after its sustained activation can trigger an antagonistic rebound that transiently activates the opponent cell in the pair (figure 11.20). A neural model of such an opponent process is called a *gated dipole* (Grossberg, 1972, 1982, 1988). Such an antagonistic rebound can rapidly reset a resonating boundary in response to rapid changes in the stimulus.

For example, consider a time interval when the horizontally oriented hypercomplex cells in figure 11.9 are cooperating with horizontally oriented

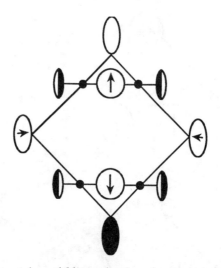

Figure 11.18   *Symmetric unfolding of pairs of opponent orientation cells and opponent direction cells whose outputs are insensitive to direction-of-contrast. The gating combinations from figures 11.16 and 11.17 are combined to emphasize their underlying symmetry.*

bipole cells to generate a horizontal boundary segmentation in the CC loop. Suppose that the input pattern is then suddenly shut off. In the absence of opponent processing, the positive feedback signals between the active hypercomplex on-cells and bipole cells could maintain the boundary segmentation for a long time after input offset, thereby causing serious smearing of the visual percept in response to rapidly changing scenes. Due to opponent processing, however, offset of the horizontal complex on-cells can trigger an antagonistic rebound that activates the horizontal complex off-cells (figure 11.20a). The horizontal hypercomplex off-cells are hereby activated, and they generate inhibitory signals to the horizontal bipole cells, as in figure 11.9. These inhibitory signals shut off the resonating segmentation. Thus antagonistic rebound by off-cells which directly inhibit bipole cells in area V2 is predicted to be one of the inhibitory processes that control the amount of smear caused by a moving image in the experiments of Hogben and Di Lollo (1985).

Relating Rapid Reset to Spatial Impenetrability

This explanation of rapid reset of a resonating segmentation uses the fact that on-cells and off-cells of a given orientation generate excitatory inputs and inhibitory inputs, respectively, to bipole cells of like orientation (figure 11.9). Grossberg and Mingolla (1985b) have shown that such a circuit design

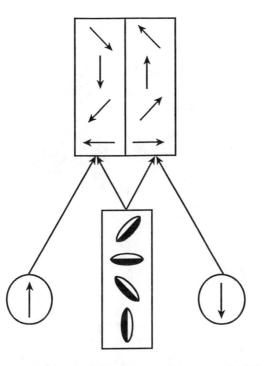

Figure 11.19   *Orientation and direction hypercolumns. A single hypercolumn of orientation cells (say in V1) can give rise to a double hypercolumn of opponent direction cells (say MT) through gating with opponent pairs of transient cells.*

also generates the property of *spatial impenetrability*, whereby emergent segmentations are prevented from penetrating figures whose boundaries are built up from non-colinear orientations. In particular, in a cartoon drawing of a person standing in a grassy field, the horizontal contours where the ground touches the sky do not generate horizontal emergent boundaries that cut the person's vertical body in half. The present discussion predicts that sudden offset of a previously sustained figure that contains many vertically oriented lines may facilitate, rather than block, the propagation of horizontal emergent boundary segmentations between the horizontally oriented lines that surround the location of the figure on both sides.

MacKay After-images, the Waterfall Effect, and Long-Range MAE

The previous sections argued that some positive after-effects may be partly due to a lingering resonance, and some negative after-effects may be partly

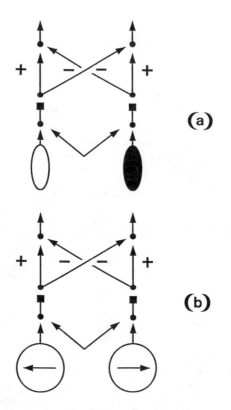

Figure 11.20   *Opponent rebounds. When opponent cells are organized into gated dipole opponent circuits, as in (a), offset of orientation on-cell can transiently activate like-oriented off-cells, as well as perpendicular on-cells (see text). Likewise, as in (b), offset of a direction cell can transiently activate cells tuned to the opposite direction.*

due to an antagonistic rebound, in a CC loop. Within the static BCS, negative after-effects tend to activate perpendicular segmentations via the same 90° symmetry of the SOC filter that generates perpendicular end cuts. Due to this symmetry, sustained inspection of a radial image can induce a circular after-effect if a blank screen is subsequently attended (MacKay, 1957). In a similar fashion, it follows from the 180° symmetry of the MOC filter that sustained inspection of a waterfall can induce an upward-moving motion after-effect (MAE) if a blank screen is subsequently attended (Sekuler, 1975).

The assumption that a level of gated dipoles occurs subsequent to level 5 of the MOC filter also provides an explanation of how a long-range MAE can occur between the locations of two flashes that previously generated apparent motion between themselves (von Grünau, 1986).

Such data properties, and the coexistence of parallel systems for the analysis of static form and moving form, may now be traced to a developmental process within the visual cortex that is predicted to realize a symmetry principle: generate all possible sustained-transient BCS output signals that are independent of direction-of-contrast and organized into opponent dipoles.

The Visual Process as a Self-organizing Quantum Sensitive System

In the preceding discussion, I have touched upon some of the design principles that seem to govern the neural architecture that subserves visual perception. These include principles of complementarity, uncertainty, symmetry, and resonance. When asked what other theory is based upon these four types of principles, most of us would answer: quantum mechanics.

The visual system is also a quantum sensitive system. Our brains are tuned to be able to see even a few light quanta. FACADE theory seems to be uncovering some of the neural designs whereby our minds achieve their competence to function perceptually in the quantized world of light.

Acknowledgments

This research was supported in part by the Air Force Office of Scientific Research (AFOSR F49620–86–C–0037 and AFOSR F49620–87–C–0018), the Army Research Office (ARO DAAL–03–88–K–0088), DARPA (AFOSR 90–0083), and Hughes Research Laboratories (S1–804481–D).

References

Albright, T. D. 1989: Centrifugal direction bias in the middle temporal visual area (MT) of the Macaque. *Visual Neuroscience*, 2, 177–88.

Albright, T. D., Desimone, R. and Gross, C. G. 1984: Columnar organization of directionally sensitive cells in visual area MT of the Macaque. *Journal of Neurophysiology*, 51, 16–31.

Aleksander, I. 1983: Emergent intelligent properties of progressively structured pattern recognition nets. *Pattern Recognition Letters*, 1, 375–84.

Alkhateeb, W., Morland, A. B., Ruddock, K. H. and Savage, C. J. 1990a: Spatial, colour and contrast response characteristics of mechanisms which mediate discrimination of pattern orientation and magnification. *Spatial Vision*, 5, 129–41.

Alkhateeb, W., Morris, R. J. and Ruddock, K. H. 1990b: Effects of stimulus complexity on simple spatial discriminations. *Spatial Vision*, 5, 143–57.

Aloimonos, J. and Liuqing Huang 1990: Motion boundary illusions and their regularization. *Proceedings of the Royal Society of London*, B242, 75–81.

Andersen, G. J. 1989: Perception of three-dimensional structure from optic flow without locally smooth velocity. *Journal of Experimental Psychology: Human Perception and Performance*, 15, 363–71.

Anderson, C. H. and Van Essen, D. C. 1987: Shifter circuits: a computational strategy for dynamic aspects of visual processing. *Proceedings of the National Academy of Sciences*, 84, 6297–301.

Anderson, J. R. and Bower, G. H. 1973: *Human Associative Memory*. New York: V. H. Winston and Sons.

Anderson, S. J. and Burr, D. C. 1987: Receptive field size of human motion detection units. *Vision Research*, 27, 621–35.

Andrews, D. P. 1967: The perception of contour orientation in the central fovea: II. Spatial integration. *Vision Research*, 7, 999–1013.

Andrews, D. P., Butcher, A. K. and Buckley, B. R. 1973: Acuities for spatial arrangement in line figures: human and ideal line observers compared. *Vision Research*, 13, 599–620.

Andrews, D. P., Webb, J. and Miller, D. 1974: Acuity for length comparison in continuous and broken lines. *Vision Research*, 14, 757–66.

Anstis, S., Howard, I. P. and Rogers B. 1978: A Craik–O'Brien–Cornsweet illusion for visual depth. *Vision Research*, 18, 213–17.

Anstis, S. and Ramachandran, V. S. 1987: Visual inertia in apparent motion. *Vision Research*, 27, 755–64.

Appelle, S. 1972: Perception and discrimination as a function of stimulus orientation. *Psychological Bulletin*, 78, 266–78.

Arend, L. E. 1973: Spatial differential and integral operations in human vision: implications of stabilized retinal image fading. *Psychological Review*, 80, 374–95.

Arend, L. E. and Goldstein, R. E. 1987: Lightness models, gradient illusions and curl. *Perception and Psychophysics*, 42, 65–80.

Arnoult, M. D. 1954: Shape discrimination as a function of the angular orientation of the stimuli. *Journal of Experimental Psychology*, 47, 323–8.

Asch, S. E. and Witkin, H. A. 1948: Studies in space orientation: I. Perception of the upright with displaced visual fields. *Journal of Experimental Psychology*, 38, 325–7.

Attneave, F. 1954: Informational aspects of visual perception. *Psychological Review*, 61, 183–93.

Attneave, F. 1968: Triangles as ambiguous figures. *American Journal of Psychology*, 81, 447–53.

Attneave, F. 1972: Representation of physical space. In A. W. Melton and E. Martin (eds), *Coding Processes in Human Memory*. Washington, DC: V. H. Winston and Sons.

Badcock, D. R. and Westheimer, G. 1985a: Spatial location and hyperacuity: the centre/surround localization contribution function has two substrates. *Vision Research*, 25, 1259–67.

Badcock, D. R. and Westheimer, G. 1985b: Spatial location and hyperacuity: flank position within the centre and surround zones. *Spatial Vision*, 1, 3–11.

Baddeley, A. 1986: *Working Memory*. New York: Oxford University Press.

Bagnara, S., Simion, F. and Umiltà, C. 1984: Reference patterns and the process of normalization. *Perception and Psychophysics*, 35, 186–92.

Barbur, J. L. and Ruddock, K. H. 1980: Spatial characteristics of movement detection mechanisms in human vision: 1. Achromatic vision. *Biological Cybernetics*, 37, 77–92.

Barbur, J. L., Ruddock, K. H. and Waterfield, V. A. 1980: Human visual responses in the absence of the geniculo-calcarine projection. *Brain*, 103, 905–28.

Bard, J. 1977: A unity underlying the different zebra striping patterns. *Journal of Zoology, London*, 183, 527–39.

Barlow, H. B., Blakemore, C. B. and Pettigrew, J. D. 1967: The neurophysiological mechanism of binocular depth discrimination. *Journal of Physiology* 193, 327–42.

Baron, R. J. 1981: Mechanisms of human facial recognition. *International Journal of Man-Machine Studies*, 15, 137–78.

Barrow, H. and Tenenbaum, J. M. 1978: Recovering intrinsic scene characteristics from images. In A. Hanson and E. Riseman (eds), *Computer Vision Systems*, pp. 3–26. New York: Academic Press.

Barrow, H. G. and Tenenbaum, J. M. 1981: Interpreting line drawings as three dimensional surfaces. *Artificial Intelligence*, 17, 75–116.

Bartlett, J. C., Hurrey, S. and Thorley, W. 1984: Typicality and familiarity of faces. *Memory and Cognition*, 12, 219–28.

Bartley, S. H. 1941: *Vision: a Study of its Basis*. New York: D. Van Nostrand.

Bell, H. H. and Lappin, J. S. 1979: The detection of rotation in random-dot patterns. *Perception and Psychophysics*, 26, 415–17.

Bergen, J. R. and Adelson, E. H. 1988: Early vision and texture perception. *Nature*, 333, 363–4.

Bergen, J. R. and Julesz, B. 1983: Parallel versus serial processing in rapid pattern discrimination. *Nature*, 303, 696–8.

Besl, P. J. and Jain, R. C. 1986: Invariant surface characteristics for 3D object recognition in range images. *Computer Vision, Graphics, and Image Processing*, 33, 33–80.

Beverley, K. I. and Regan, D. 1982: Adaptation to incomplete flow patterns: no evidence for "filling in" the perception of flow patterns. *Perception*, 11, 275–8.

Biederman, I. 1985: Human image understanding: recent research and a theory. *Computer Vision, Graphics, and Image Processing*, 32, 29–73.

Biederman, I. 1987: Recognition-by-components: a theory of human image understanding. *Psychological Review*, 94, 115–47.

Biederman, I. and Ju, G. 1988: Surface vs. edge-based determinants of visual recognition. *Cognitive Psychology*, 20, 38–64.

Binford, T. O. 1981: Inferring surfaces from images. *Artificial intelligence*, 17, 205–45.

Blake, A. and Zisserman, A. 1987: *Visual Reconstruction*. Cambridge, Mass.: MIT Press.

Blakemore, C. and Campbell, F. W. 1969: On the existence of neurones in the human visual system selectivity sensitive to the orientation and size of retinal images. *Journal of Physiology (London)* 203, 237–60.

Blakemore, C., Carpenter, R. H. S. and Georgeson, M. A. 1970: Lateral inhibition between orientation detectors in the human visual system. *Nature*, 228, 37–9.

Blakemore, C. B., Fiorentini, A. and Maffei, L. 1972: A second neural mechanism of binocular depth discrimination. *Journal of Physiology*, 226, 725–40.

Bolz, J. and Gilbert, C. D. 1986: Generation of end-inhibition in the visual cortex via interlaminar connections. *Nature*, 320, 362–5.

Boring, E. G. 1950: A *History of Experimental Psychology*, 2nd edn. New York: Appelton–Century–Crofts.

Boucart, M. and Humphreys, G. W. 1992: The computation of perceptual structure from collinearity and closure: normality and pathology. *Neuropsychologia*, in press.

Braddick, O. J. 1973: The masking of apparent motion in random-dot patterns. *Vision Research*, 13, 355–69.

Braddick, O. J. 1974: A short range process in apparent motion. *Vision Research*, 14, 519–27.

Bradshaw, J. L. and Wallace, G. 1971: Models for the processing and identification of faces. *Perception and Psychophysics*, 9, 443–8.

Brady, J. M. and Asada, H. 1983: Smoothed local symmetries. *International Journal of Robotics Research*, 3, 36–61.

Brady, J. M., Ponce, J., Yuille, A. and Asada, H. 1985: Describing surfaces. In H. Hanafusa and H. Inoue (eds), *Proceedings of the Second International Symposium of Robotics Research*, pp. 5–16. Cambridge, Mass: MIT Press.

Brady, M. 1983: Criteria for representation of shape. In J. Beck, B. Hope and A. Rosenfeld (eds), *Human and Machine Vision*. New York: Academic Press.

Braine, L. G. 1965: Disorientation of forms: an examination of Rock's theory. *Psychonomic Science*, 3, 541–2.

Braine, L. G., Relyea, L. and Davidman, L. 1981: On how adults identify the orientation of a shape. *Perception and Psychophysics*, 29, 138–44.

Braunstein, M. L. 1968: Motion and texture as sources of slant information. *Journal of Experimental Psychology*, 78, 247–53.

Braunstein, M. L. and Andersen, G. J. 1981: Velocity gradients and relative depth perception. *Perception and Psychophysics*, 29, 145–55.

Braunstein, M. L. and Andersen, G. J. 1984: Shape and depth perception for parallel projections of three-dimensional motion. *Journal of Experimental Psychology: Human Perception and Performance*, 10, 749–60.

Braunstein, M. L. and Tittle, J. S. 1988: The observer-relative velocity field as the basis for effective motion parallax. *Journal of Experimental Psychology: Human Perception and Performance*, 14, 582–90.

Bromley, J. M., Humphreys, G. W., Javadnia, A., Riddoch, M. J. and Ruddock, K. H. 1986: Pattern discrimination in a human subject suffering visual agnosia. *Journal of Physiology (London)*, 377, 67P.

Brookes, A. and Stevens, K. A. 1989a: Binocular depth from surfaces vs. volumes. *Journal of Experimental Psychology: Human Perception and Performance*, 15(3), 479–84.

Brookes, A. and Stevens, K. A. 1989b: The analogy between stereo depth and brightness contrast. *Perception*, 18(5), 601–14.

Brown, E., Deffenbacher, K. and Sturgill, W. 1977: Memory for faces and the circumstances of encounter. *Journal of Applied Psychology*, 62, 311–18.

Bruce, C., Desimone, R. and Gross, C. G. 1981: Visual properties of neurons in a polysensory area in superior temporal sulcus of the Macaque. *Journal of Neurophysiology*, 46, 369–84.

Bruce, V. 1979: Searching for politicians: an information-processing approach to face recognition. *Quarterly Journal of Experimental Psychology*, 31, 373–95.

Bruce, V. 1982: Changing faces: visual and non-visual coding processes in face recognition. *British Journal of Psychology*, 73, 105–16.

Bruce, V. 1983: Recognizing faces. *Philosophical Transactions of the Royal Society of London*, B302, 423–36.

Bruce, V. 1986a: Influences of familiarity on the processing of faces. *Perception*, 15, 387–97.

Bruce, V. 1986b: Recognising familiar faces. In H. D. Ellis, M. A. Jeeves, F. Newcombe and A. Young (eds), *Aspects of Face Processing*. Dordrecht: Martinus Nijhoff.

Bruce, V. 1988: *Recognising Faces*. London: Lawrence Erlbaum.

Bruce, V. 1989: The structure of faces. In A. W. Young and H. D. Ellis (eds), *Handbook of Research on Face Processing*. Amsterdam: North Holland.

Bruce, V. and Burton, M. 1989: Computer recognition of faces. In A. W. Young and H. D. Ellis (eds), *Handbook of Research on Face Processing*. Amsterdam: North Holland.

Bruce, V., Burton, M. and Doyle, T. in press: Faces as surfaces. In V. Bruce and M. Burton (eds), *Processing Images of Faces*. Norwood, NJ: Ablex.

Bruce, V., Burton, M., Doyle, T. and Dench, N. 1989: Further experiments on the perception of growth in three dimensions. *Perception and Psychophysics*, 46, 528–36.

Bruce, V., Doyle, T., Dench, N. and Burton, M. 1991: Remembering facial configurations. *Cognition*, 38, 109–44.

Bruce, V. and Valentine, T. 1985: Identity priming in the recognition of familiar faces. *British Journal of Psychology*, 76, 373–83.

Bruce, V. and Valentine, T. 1986: Semantic priming of familiar faces. *Quarterly Journal of Psychology*, 38A, 125–50.

Bruce, V. and Valentine, T. 1988: When a nod's as good as a wink: the role of dynamic information in face recognition. In M. Gruneberg, P. Morris and R. Sykes (eds), *Practical Aspects of Memory: Current Research and Issues*, vol. 1. Chichester: Wiley.

Bruce, V. and Young, A. 1986: Understanding face recognition. *British Journal of Psychology*, 77, 305–27.

Bruno, N. and Cutting, J. E. 1988: Minimodularity and the perception of layout. *Journal of Experimental Psychology: General*, 117(2), 161–70.

Bruyer, R., Laterre, C., Seron, X., Feyereisen, P., Strypstein, E., Pierrard, E. and Rectem, D. 1983: A case of prosopagnosia with some preserved covert remembrance of familiar faces. *Brain and Cognition*, 2, 257–84.

Bucher, N. M. and Palmer, S. E. 1985: Effects of motion on the perceived pointing of ambiguous triangles. *Perception and Psychophysics*, 38, 227–36.

Bülthoff, H. H. and Mallot, H. A. 1988: Integration of depth modules: stereo and shading. *Journal of the Optical Society of America*, A5 1749–58.

Burkhalter, A. and Van Essen, D. C. 1986: Processing of color, form and disparity information in visual areas VP and V2 of ventral extrastriate cortex in the Macaque monkey. *Journal of Neuroscience*, 6, 2327–51.

Burr, D. C., Ross, J. and Morrone, M. C. 1986: Smooth and sampled motion. *Vision Research*, 26, 643–52.

Burton, A. M., Bruce, V. and Johnston, R. A. 1990: Understanding face recognition with an interactive activation model. *British Journal of Psychology* 81, 361–80.

Caelli, T. M. and Julesz, B. 1978: On perceptual analyzers underlying visual texture discrimination, part 1. *Biological Cybernetics*, 28, 67–75.

Campbell, F. W. and Robson, J. G. 1968: Application of Fourier analysis to the visibility of gratings. *Journal of Physiology*, 197, 551–6.

Campbell, R., Landis, T. and Regard, M. 1986: Face recognition and lipreading: a neurological dissociation. *Brain*, 109, 509–21.

Canny, J. F. 1986: Edge detection. *Transactions of the IEEE PAMI-8*, 6, 679–98.

Caramazza, A. and McCloskey, M. 1988: The case for single case studies. *Cognitive Neuropsychology*, 5, 517–28.

Carpenter, G. A. and Grossberg, S. 1987a: A massively parallel architecture for a self-organizing neural pattern recognition machine. *Computer Vision, Graphics, and Image Processing*, 37, 54–115.

Carpenter, G. A. and Grossberg, S. 1987b: ART 2: stable self-organization of pattern recognition codes for analog input patterns. *Applied Optics*, 26, 4919–30.

Carpenter, G. A. and Grossberg, S. 1988: The ART of adaptive pattern recognition by a self-organizing neural network. *Computer*, 21, 77–88.

Cavanagh, P. 1977: Locus of rotation effects in recognition. *Bulletin of the Psychonomic Society*, 10, 101–4.

Cavanagh, P. and Favreau, O. E. 1980: Motion aftereffect: a global mechanism for the perception of rotation. *Perception*, 9, 175–82.

Cave, K. R. and Kosslyn, S. M. 1989: Varieties of size-specific visual selection. *Journal of Experimental Psychology: General*, 118, 148–64.

Clocksin, W. H. 1980: Perception of surface slant and edge labels from optical flow: a computational approach. *Perception*, 9, 253–69.

Cohen, M. A. and Grossberg, S. 1984: Neural dynamics of brightness perception: features, boundaries, diffusion, and resonance. *Perception and Psychophysics*, 36, 428–56.

Cohen, M. A. and Grossberg, S. 1986: Neural dynamics of speech and language coding: developmental programs, perceptual grouping, and competition for short term memory. *Human Neurobiology*, 5, 1–22.

Cohen, M. A. and Grossberg, S. 1987: Masking fields: a massively parallel neural architecture for learning, recognizing, and predicting multiple grouping of patterned data. *Applied Optics*, 26, 1866–91.

Cohen, M. A., Grossberg, S. and Stork, D. G. 1988: Speech perception and production by a self-organizing neural network. In Y. C. Lee (ed.), *Evolution, Learning, Cognition, and Advanced Architectures*. Hong Kong: World Scientific Publishers.

Cooper, L. A. and Shepard, R. N. 1973: Chronometric studies of the rotation of mental images. In W. G. Chase (ed.), *Visual Information Processing*. New York: Academic Press, 75–176.

Corballis, M. C. 1988: Recognition of disoriented shapes. *Psychological Review*, 95, 115–23.

Corballis, M. C. and Cullen, S. 1986: Decisions about the axes of disoriented shapes. *Memory and Cognition*, 14, 27–38.

Corballis, M. C. and McLaren, R. 1984: Minding One's Ps and Qs: mental rotation and mirror-image discrimination. *Journal of Experimental Psychology: Human Perception and Performance*, 10, 318–27.

Corballis, M. C. and Nagourney, B. A. 1978: Latency to categorize disoriented alphanumeric characters as letters or digits. *Canadian Journal of Psychology*, 32, 186–8.

Corballis, M. C., Zbrodoff, N. J., Shetzer, L. I. and Butler, P. B. 1978: Decisions about identity and orientation of rotated letters and digits. *Memory and Cognition*, 6, 98–107.

Cornsweet, T. N. 1970: *Visual perception*, New York: Academic Press.

Craven, B. J. and Watt, R. J. 1989: The use of image statistics in the estimation of lateral extent. *Spatial Vision*, 4, 223–39.

Craw, I. G., Ellis, H. and Lishman, J. R. 1987: Automatic extraction of face features. *Pattern Recognition Letters*, 5, 183–7.

Cumming, B. G., Johnston, E. B. and Parker, A. J. 1991: Vertical disparities and 3-D shape perception. *Nature*, 349, 411–13.

Cutting, J. E. 1986: *Perception with an Eye for Motion*. Cambridge Mass. MIT Press.

Cynader, M. and Regan, D. 1978: Neurones in cat parastriate cortex sensitive to the direction of motion in three-dimensional space. *Journal of Physiology*, 274, 549–69.

Dannenbring, G. L. and Briand, K. 1982: Semantic priming and the word repetition effect in a lexical decision task. *Canadian Journal of Psychology*, 36, 435–44.

Danta, G., Hilton, R. C. and O'Boyle, D. J. 1978: Hemisphere function and binocular depth perception. *Brain*, 101, 569–89.

Dean, A. F. and Tolhurst, D. 1983: On the distinctiveness of simple and complex cells in the visual cortex of the cat. *Journal of Physiology*, 344, 305–25.

Dearborn, G. V. N. 1899: Recognition under objective reversal. *Psychological Review*, 6, 395–406.

De Bruyn, B. and Orban, G. A. 1990a: The role of direction information in the perception of geometric optic flow components. *Perception and Psychophysics*, 47, 433–8.

De Bruyn, B. and Orban, G. A. 1990b: The importance of velocity gradients in the perception of three-dimensional rigidity. *Perception*, 19, 21–7.

Dell, G. S. 1986: A spreading-activation theory of retrieval in sentence production. *Psychological Review*, 93, 283–321.

De Renzi, E. 1986: Current issues in prosopagnosia. In H. D. Ellis, M.A. Jeeves, F. Newcombe and A. W. Young (eds). *Aspects of Face Processing*. Dordrecht: Martinus Nijhoff.

Desimone, R., Schein, S. J., Moran, J. and Ungerleider, L. G. 1985: Contour, color, and shape analysis beyond the striate cortex. *Vision Research*, 25, 441–52.

Desimone, R. and Ungerleider, L. G. 1989: Neural mechanisms of visual processing in monkeys. In F. Boller and J. Grafman (eds). *Handbook of Neuropsychology*, vol. 2. Amsterdam: Elsevier Science.

De Valois, R. L., Albrecht, D. G. and Thorell, L. G. 1982: Spatial frequency selectivity of cells in Macaque visual cortex. *Vision Research*, 22, 545–59.

De Valois, R. L. and De Valois, K. K. 1980: Spatial vision. *American Review of Psychology*, 31, 309–41.

Devlin, Lord Patrick 1976: Report to the Secretary of State for the Home Department of the Departmental Committee on Evidence of Identification in Criminal Cases. London: HMSO.

Dobbins, A., Zucker, S. and Cynader, M. 1987: Endstopping in the visual cortex as a substrate for calculating curvature. *Nature*, 329, 438–41.

Dobbins, A., Zucker, S. and Cynader, M. 1989: Endstopping and curvature. *Vision Research*, 29, 1371–88.

Dosher, B. A., Sperling, G. and Wurst, S. A. 1986: Tradeoffs between stereopsis and proximity luminance covariance as determinants of perceived 3D structure. *Vision Research*, 26, 973–90.

Duncan, G. and Humphreys, G. W. 1989: Visual search and stimulus similarity. *Psychological Review*, 96, 433–58.

Duncker, K. 1929: Uber induzierte Bewegung. *Psychologische Forschung*, 12, 180–256. (Condensed in W. Ellis (ed. and trans.), *Source Book of Gestalt Psychology*. New York: Humanities Press, 1950.)

Eckhorn, R., Bauer, R., Jordan, W., Brosch, M., Kruse, W., Munk, M. and Reitboeck, H. J. 1988: Coherent oscillations: a mechanism of feature linking in the visual cortex? *Biological Cybernetics*, 60, 121–30.

Efron, R. 1968: What is perception? *Boston Studies in the Philosophy of Science*, 4, 137–73.

Eley, M. G. 1982: Identifying rotated letter-like symbols. *Memory and Cognition*, 10, 25–32.

Ellis, A. W., Young, A. W., Flude, B. M. and Hay, D. C. 1987: Repetition priming of face recognition. *Quarterly Journal of Experimental Psychology*, 39A, 193–210.

Ellis, H. D. 1986: Processes underlying face recognition. In R. Bruyer (ed.), *The Neuropsychology of Face Perception and Facial Expression*. Hillsdale, NJ: Lawrence Erlbaum.

Engel, F. L. 1971: Visual conspicuity, directed attention and retinal focus. *Vision Research*, 11, 563–76.

Engel, F. L. 1974: Visual conspicuity and selective background interference in eccentric vision. *Vision Research*, 14, 459–71.

Enlow, D. H. 1982: *Handbook of Facial Growth*. Philadelphia: W. B. Saunders.

Enroth-Cugell, C. and Robson, J. G. 1966: The contrast sensitivity of retinal cells of the cat. *Journal of Physiology*, 187, 517–52.

Enroth-Cugell, C. and Robson, J. G. 1984: Functional characteristics and diversity of cat retinal ganglion cells. *Investigative Ophthalmology and Visual Science*, 25, 250–67.

Eriksen, C. W. and St James, J. D. 1986: Visual attention within and around the field of focal attention: a zoom lens model. *Perception and Psychophysics*, 40, 225–40.

Evans, L. 1970: Automobile-speed estimation using movie-film simulation. *Ergonomics*, 13, 231–7.

Farah, M. J. 1988: Is visual imagery really visual? Overlooked evidence from neuropsychology. *Psychological Review*, 95, 307–17.

Farah, M. J. and Hammond, K. M. 1988: Mental rotation and orientation-invariant object recognition: dissociable processes. *Cognition*, 29, 29–46.

Farber, J. M. and McConkie, A. B. 1979: Optical motions as information for unsigned depth. *Journal of Experimental Psychology: Human Perception and Performance*, 5, 494–500.

Faux, I. D. and Pratt, M. J. 1979: *Computational Geometry for Design and Manufacture*. Chichester, UK: Ellis Horwood Ltd.

Ferster, D. 1981: A comparison of binocular depth mechanisms in areas 17 and 18 of the cat visual cortex. *Journal of Physiology*, 331, 623–55.

Finke, R. A. and Kosslyn, S. M. 1980: Mental imagery acuity in the peripheral visual field. *Journal of Experimental Psychology: Human Perception and Performance*, 6, 126–39.

Finke, R. A., Pinker, S. and Farah, M. 1989: Reinterpreting visual patterns in mental imagery. *Cognitive Science*, 13, 51–78.

Finke, R. A. and Shepard, R. N. 1986: Visual functions of mental imagery. In K. R. Boff, L. Kaufman and J. P. Thomas (eds), *Handbook of Perception and Human Performance*. New York: Wiley–Interscience.

Foley, J. D., van Dam, A., Feiner, S. and Hughes, J. F. 1990: *Computer Graphics: Principles and Practice*, 2nd edn. Reading, Mass.: Addison-Wesley.

Foley, J. M. 1980: Binocular distance perception. *Psychological Review*, 87, 411–34.

Forsyth, D. and Zisserman, A. 1989: Mutual illumination. Proceedings of the IEEE Conference on Computer Vision and Pattern Recognition (CVPR89), pp. 466–75. San Diego: IEEE Press.

Forsyth, D. and Zisserman, A. 1990: Shape from shading in the light of mutual illumination. *Image and Vision Computing*, 8, 42–9.

Foster, D. H. 1980: A spatial perturbation technique for the investigation of discrete internal representations of visual patterns. *Biological Cybernetics*, 38, 159–69.

Foster, D. H. 1983: Visual discrimination, categorical identification, and categorical rating in brief displays of curved lines: implications for discrete encoding processes. *Journal of Experimental Psychology: Human Perception and Performance*, 9, 785–806.

Foster, D. H. 1984: Local and global computational factors in visual recognition. In P. C. Dodwell and T. Caelli (eds), *Figural Synthesis*. Hillsdale, NJ: Lawrence Erlbaum.

Foster, D. H. and Ward, P. A. 1991: Asymmetries in oriented-line detection indicate two orthogonal filters in early vision. *Proceedings of the Royal Society of London*, B243, 75–81.

Freeman, R. D. and Ohzawa, I. 1990: On the neurophysiological organization of binocular vision. *Vision Research*, 30, 1661–76.

Ghent, L. 1960: Recognition by children of realistic figures presented in various orientations. *Canadian Journal of Psychology*, 14, 249–56.

Gibson, E. J. 1969: *Principles of Perceptual Learning and Development*. New York: Appleton–Century–Crofts.

Gibson, J. J. 1950: *The Perception of the Visual World*. Boston: Houghton-Mifflin.

Gibson, J. J. 1979: *The Ecological Approach to Visual Perception*. Boston: Houghton-Mifflin.

Gibson, J. J. and Robinson, D. 1935: Orientation in visual perception: the recognition of familiar plane forms in differing orientations. *Psychological Monographs*, 46, 39–47.

Gilinsky, A. S. 1968: Orientation-specific effects of patterns of adapting light on visual acuity. *Journal of the Optical Society of America*, 58, 13–18.

Gillam, B. 1968: Perception of slant when perspective and stereopsis conflict: experiments with aniseikonic lenses. *Journal of Experimental Psychology*, 78(2), 299–305.

Gillam, B., Chambers, D. and Russo, T. 1988: Postfusional latencies in stereoscopic perception and the primitives of stereopsis. *Journal of Experimental Psychology*, Human Perception and Performance, 14, 163–75.

Gillam, B., Flagg, T. and Findlay, D. 1984: Evidence for disparity change as the primary stimulus for stereoscopic processing. *Perception and Psychophysics*, 36, 559–64.

Ginsburg, A. 1971: Psychological correlates of a model of the human visual system. Unpublished master's thesis. Air Force Institute of Technology.

Ginsburg, A. 1986: Spatial filtering and visual form perception. In K. R. Boff, L. Kaufman and J. P. Thomas (eds), *Handbook of Perception and Human Performance, Vol. II: Cognitive Processes and Performance*. New York: John Wiley and Sons.

Godwin-Austen, R. B. 1965: A case of visual disorientation. *Journal of Neurology, Neurosurgery and Psychiatry*, 28, 453–8.

Goldstein, A. G. and Chance, J. E. 1971: Visual recognition memory for complex configurations. *Perception and Psychophysics*, 9, 237–41.

Gomori, A. J. and Hawryluk, G. A. 1984: Visual agnosia without alexia. *Neurology*, 34, 947–50.

Gould, S. J. and Lewontin, R. 1979: The spandrels of San Marco and the panglossian paradigm: a critique of the adaptationist programme. *Proceedings of the Royal Society, Series B*, 205, 581–98.

Graham, N. and Beck, J. 1988: Unpublished manuscript.

Graham, N., Beck, J. and Sutter, A. 1989: Two nonlinearities in texture segregation. *Investigative Ophthalmology and Visual Science*, 30(3) (Suppl.) 161.

Gray, C. M., König, P., Engel, A. K. and Singer, W. 1989: Oscillatory responses in cat visual cortex exhibit inter-columnar synchronization which reflects global stimulus properties. *Nature*, 338, 334–7.

Gregory, R. L. 1970: *The Intelligent Eye*. London: Weidenfeld and Nicolson.

Gregory, R. L. 1980: Perceptions as hypotheses. *Philosophical Transactions of the Royal Society of London*, B290, 181–97.

Grimson, W. E. L. 1982: A computational theory of visual surface interpolation. *Philosophical Transactions of the Royal Society (London)*, B298, 395–427.

Grossberg, S. 1970: Neural pattern discrimination. *Journal of Theoretical Biology*, 27, 291–337.

Grossberg, S. 1972: A neural theory of punishment and avoidance, II. Quantitative theory. *Mathematical Biosciences*, 15, 253–85.

Grossberg, S. 1973: Contour enhancement, short-term memory, and constancies in reverberating neural networks. *Studies in Applied Mathematics*, 52, 217–57.

Grossberg, S. 1976: Adaptive pattern classification and universal recoding, II: Feedback, expectation, olfaction, and illusions. *Biological Cybernetics*, 23, 187–202.

Grossberg, S. 1978: A theory of human memory: self-organization and performance of sensory-motor codes, maps, and plans. In R. Rosen and F. Snell (eds), *Progress in Theoretical Biology*, vol. 5. New York: Academic Press, 233–374.

Grossberg, S. 1980: How does a brain build a cognitive code? *Psychological Review*, 87, 1–51.

Grossberg, S. 1982: *Studies of Mind and Brain: Neural Principles of Learning, Perception, Development, Cognition, and Motor Control*. Boston: Reidel Press.

Grossberg, S. 1984: Outline of a theory of brightness, color, and form perception. In E. Degreef and J. van Buggenhaut (eds), *Trends in Mathematical Psychology*. Amsterdam: North Holland.

Grossberg, S. 1986: The adaptive self-organization of serial order in behavior: speech, language, and motor control. In E. C. Schwab and H. C. Nusbaum (eds), *Pattern Recognition by Humans and Machines, Vol. 1: Speech Perception*. New York: Academic Press, 187–294.

Grossberg, S. 1987a: Cortical dynamics of three-dimensional form, color, and brightness perception, I: Monocular theory. *Perception and Psychophysics*, 41, 87–116.

Grossberg, S. 1987b: Cortical dynamics of three-dimensional form, color, and brightness perception, II: Binocular theory. *Perception and Psychophysics*, 41, 117–58.

Grossberg, S. (ed.) 1987c: *The Adaptive Brain, Vol. II: Vision, Speeh, Language, and Motor Control*. Amsterdam: North Holland.

Grossberg, S. (ed.) 1988: *Neural Networks and Natural Intelligence*. Cambridge, Mass.: MIT Press.

Grossberg, S. and Marshall, J. 1989: Stereo boundary fusion by cortical complex cells: a system of maps, filters, and feedback networks for multiplexing distributed data. *Neural Networks*, 2, 29–51.

Grossberg, S. and Mingolla, E. 1985a: Neural dynamics of form perception: boundary completion, illusory figures, and neon color spreading. *Psychological Review*, 92, 173–211.

Grossberg, S. and Mingolla, E. 1985b: Neural dynamics of perceptual grouping: textures, boundaries, and emergent segmentations. *Perception and Psychophysics*, 38, 141–71.

Grossberg, S. and Mingolla, E. 1987: Neural dynamics of surface perception: boundary webs, illuminants, and shape-from-shading. *Computer Vision, Graphics, and Image Processing*, 37, 116–65.

Grossberg, S. and Mingolla, E. 1990: Neural dynamics of motion segmentation: direction fields, apertures, and resonant grouping. In M. Caudill (ed.), *Proceedings of the International Joint Conference on Neural Networks, I.* Hillsdale, NJ: Erlbaum, 11–14.

Grossberg, S., Mingolla, E. and Todorović, D. 1989: A neural network architecture for preattentive vision. *IEEE Transactions on Biomedical Engineering*, 36, 65–84.

Grossberg, S. and Rudd, M. E. 1989: A neural architecture for visual motion perception: group and element apparent motion. *Neural Networks*, 2, 421–50.

Grossberg, S. and Stone, G. O. 1986: Neural dynamics of word recognition and recall: attentional priming, learning, and resonance. *Psychological Review*, 93, 46–74.

Grossberg, S. and Todorović, D. 1988: Neural dynamics of 1-D and 2-D brightness perception: a unified model of classical and recent phenomena. *Perception and Psychophysics*, 43, 241–77.

Grünau, M. W. von 1986: A motion aftereffect for long-range stroboscopic apparent motion. *Perception and Psychophysics*, 40, 31–8.

Haig, N. D. 1986: Investigating face recognition with an image processing computer. In H. D. Ellis, M. A. Jeeves, F. Newcombe and A. Young (eds), *Aspects of Face Processing*. Dordrecht: Martinus Nijhoff.

Hammond, P. and MacKay, D. M. 1977: Differential responsiveness of simple and complex cells in cat striate cortex to visual texture. *Experimental Brain Research*, 30, 275–96.

Hawken, M. J. and Parker, A. J. 1987: Spatial properties of neurones in the monkey striate cortex. *Proceedings of the Royal Society of London*, B231, 251–88.

Hawken, M. J. and Parker, A. J. 1990: Detection and discrimination mechanisms in the striate cortex of Old World monkeys. In C. Blakemore (ed.), *Vision: Coding and Efficiency*. Cambridge: Cambridge University Press.

Hawken, M. J., Parker, A. J. and Lund, J. S. 1988: Laminar organization and contrast sensitivity of direction-selective cells in the striate cortex of the Old-World monkey. *Journal of Neuroscience*, 8, 3541–8.

Hay, D. C. and Young, A. W. 1982. The human face. In A. W. Ellis (ed.), *Normality and Pathology in Cognitive Functions*. London: Academic Press.

Heggelund, P. 1981: Receptive field organization of simple cells in cat striate cortex. *Experimental Brain Research*, 42, 89–98.

Helmholtz, H. von (1910) *Treatise on Physiological Optics*, vol. III, translated from the 3rd edn (1910) of *Handbuch der Physiologischen Optik* by J. P. C. Southall (1925). Republished (1962) by Dover Publications Inc., New York.

Hershenson, M. 1984: Phantom spiral aftereffect: evidence for global mechanisms in perception. *Bulletin of the Psychonomic Society*, 22, 535–7.

Hershenson, M. 1987: Visual system responds to rotational and size-change components of complex proximal motion patterns. *Perception and Psychophysics*, 42, 60–4.

Heydt, R. von der, Peterhans, E. and Baumgartner, G. 1984: Illusory contours and cortical neuron responses. *Science*, 224, 1260–2.

Heywood, C. A., Wilson, B. and Cowey, A. 1987: A case study of cortical colour "blindness" with relatively intact achromatopic discrimination. *Journal of Neurology, Neurosurgery and Psychiatry*, 50, 22–9.

Hilbert, D. and Cohn-Vossen, S. (1932) *Anschauliche Geometrie*. Berlin: Springer-Verlag. Translated as *Geometry and the Imagination*. New York: Chelsea Publishing Co.

Hildreth, E. C., Grzywacz, N. M., Adeslon, E. H. and Inada, V. K. 1990: The perceptual buildup of three-dimensional structure from motion. *Perception and Psychophysics*, 48, 19–36.

Hildreth, E. C. and Koch, C. 1987: The analysis of visual motion. *Annual Review of Neuroscience*, 10, 477–533.

Hinton, G. E. 1981: A parallel computation that assigns canonical object-based frames of reference. In *Proceedings of the Seventh International Joint Conference on Artificial Intelligence*, 2. Los Altos: Kaufman, 683–5.

Hinton, G. E. and Parsons, L. M. 1981: Frames of reference and mental imagery. In A. Baddeley and J. Long (eds), *Attention and Performance*: IX. Hillsdale, NJ: Erlbaum, 261–77.

Hinton, G. E. and Shallice, T. 1991: Lesioning an attractor network: investigations of acquired dyslexia. *Psychological Review*, 98, 74–95.

Hochberg, J. and Gellman, L. 1977: The effect of landmark features on mental rotation times. *Memory and Cognition*, 5, 23–6.

Hoffman, K. -P. 1973: Conduction velocity in pathways from retina to superior colliculus in the cat: a correlation with receptive field properties. *Journal of Neurophysiology*, 36, 409–24.

Hoffman, D. D. and Richards, W. A. (1984) Parts of recognition. *Cognition*, 18, 65–96.

Hogben, J. H. and Di Lollo, V. 1985: Suppression of visual persistence in apparent motion. *Perception and Psychophysics*, 38, 450–60.

Holding, D. H. 1985: *The Psychology of Chess Skill*. Hillsdale, NJ.: Erlbaum.

Holliday, I. E. and Ruddock, K. H. 1983: Two spatio-temporal filters in human vision: I, Temporal and spatial frequency response characteristics. *Biological Cybernetics* 47, 173–90.

Holst, E. von. 1957: Aktive Leistung der menschlichen Gesichtswahrnehmung. *Studium Generale*, 10, 321–43.

Hopfield, J. J. 1982: Neural networks and physical systems with emergent collective computational properties. *Proceedings of the National Academy of Sciences, USA*, 79, 2554–8.

Hopfield, J. J. 1984: Neurons with graded response have collective computational properties like those of two-state neurons. *Proceedings of the National Academy of Sciences, USA*, 81, 3088–92.

Horn, B. K. P. 1986: *Robot Vision*. Cambridge, Mass.: MIT Press.

Horn, B. K. P. (ed.) 1989: *Shape from Shading*. Cambridge, Mass.: MIT Press.

Hubel, D. H. 1988: *Eye, Brain and Vision*. New York: W. H. Freeman.

Hubel, D. H. and Wiesel, T. N. 1962: Receptive fields, binocular interaction and functional architecture in the cat's visual cortex. *Journal of Physiology (London)*, 160, 106–54.

Hubel, D. H. and Wiesel, T. N. 1965: Receptive fields and functional architecture in two non-striate visual areas (18 and 19) of the cat. *Journal of Neurophysiology*, 28, 229–89.

Hubel, D. H. and Wiesel, T. N. 1968: Receptive fields and functional architecture of monkey striate cortex. *Journal of Physiology*, 195, 215–43.

Hubel, D. H. and Wiesel, T. N. 1977: Functional architecture of Macaque monkey visual cortex. *Proceedings of the Royal Society of London*, B198, 1–59.

Humphrey, G. K. and Jolicoeur, P. 1988: Visual object identification: some effects of foreshortening and monocular depth cues. In Z. W. Pylyshyn (ed.), *Computational Processes in Human Vision: An Interdisciplinary Perspective*. Norwood, NJ: Ablex, 429–42.

Humphreys, G. W. 1983: Reference frames and shape perception. *Cognitive Psychology*, 15, 309–41.

Humphreys, G. W. 1984: Shape constancy: the effects of changing shape orientation and the effects of changing the position of focal features. *Perception and Psychophysics*, 36, 50–64.

Humphreys, G. W., Freeman, T. and Müller, H. M. 1992a: Lesioning a connectionist model of visual search: selective effects on distractor grouping. *Canadian Journal of Psychology*, in press.

Humphreys, G. W. and Müller, H. M. 1992: SEarch via Recursive Rejection (SERR): A connectionist model of visual search. *Cognitive Psychology* in press.

Humphreys, G. W. and Quinlan, P. T. 1987: Normal and pathological processes in visual object constancy. In G. W. Humphreys and M. J. Riddoch (eds), *Visual Object Processing: A Cognitive Neuropsychological Approach*. London: Erlbaum.

Humphreys, G. W., Quinlan, P. T. and Riddoch, M. J. 1989: Grouping processes in visual search: Effects with single- and combined-feature targets. *Journal of Experimental Psychology: General*, 118, 258–79.

Humphreys, G. W. and Riddoch, M. J. 1984: Routes to object constancy: implications from neurological impairments of object constancy. *Quarterly Journal of Experimental Psychology*, 36A, 385–415.

Humphreys, G. W. and Riddoch, M. J. 1985: Authors' correction to "Routes to Object Constancy". *Quarterly Journal of Experimental Psychology*, 37A, 493–5.

Humphreys, G. W. and Riddoch, M. J. 1987a: *To See but not to See: A Case Study of Visual Agnosia*. London: Erlbaum.

Humphreys, G. W. and Riddoch, M. J. 1987b: The fractionation of visual agnosia. In G. W. Humphreys and M. J. Riddoch (eds), *Visual Object Processing: A Cognitive Neuropsychological Approach*. London: Erlbaum.

Humphreys, G. W., Riddoch, M. J., Donnelly, N., Freeman, T., Boucart, M. and Müller, H. 1992b: Intermediate visual processing and visual agnosia.

In M. J. Farah and G. Ratcliff (eds), *The Neuropsychology of High-level Vision: Collected Tutorial Essays*. Hillsdale, NJ: Erlbaum.

Humphreys, G. W., Riddoch, M. J., Quinlan, P. T., Price, C. J. and Donnelly, N. 1992c: Parallel pattern processing in visual agnosia. *Canadian Journal of Psychology*, in press.

Huttenlocher, J. 1968: Constructing spatial images: a strategy in reasoning. *Psychological Review*, 75, 550–60.

Huttenlocher, J., Higgins, E. T., Milligan, L. and Kaufman, B. 1970: The mystery of the "negative equative" construction. *Journal of Verbal Learning and Verbal Behavior*, 9, 334–41.

Huttenlocher, D. P. and Ullman, S. 1987: Object recognition using alignment. *Proceedings of the First International Conference on Computer Vision*, IEEE Computer Society Press, 102–11.

Ike, E. E., Ruddock, K. H. and Skinner, P. 1987: Visual discrimination of simple geometrical patterns: 1. Measurements for multiple element stimuli. *Spatial Vision*, 2, 13–29.

Ikeda, M. and Takeuchi, T. 1975: Influence of foveal load on the functional visual field. *Perception and Psychophysics*, 18, 255–60.

Janez, L. 1983: Stimulus control of the visual reference frame: Quantitative theory. *Informes de Psychologia*, 133–147.

Javadnia, A. and Ruddock, K. H. 1988a: The limits of parallel processing in the visual discrimination of orientation and magnification. *Spatial Vision*, 3, 97–114.

Javadnia, A. and Ruddock, K. H. 1988b: Simultaneous processing of spatial and chromatic components of patterned stimuli by the human visual system. *Spatial Vision*, 3, 115–27.

Johansson, G. 1973: Monocular movement parallax and near-space perception. *Perception* 2, 135–46.

Johnson-Laird, P. N. 1983: *Mental Models*. Cambridge, Mass.: Harvard University Press.

Johnston, E. B. 1988: Systematic distortions of shape from stereo. *Investigative Ophthalmology and Visual Science*, 29(3) (Suppl.) 399.

Johnston, E. B. 1989: Human perception of three-dimensional shape. Unpublished DPhil. thesis, University of Oxford.

Johnston, E. B. 1991: Systematic distortions of shape from stereo. *Vision Research*, 31, 1351–60.

Johnston, I. R., White, G. R. and Cumming, R. W. 1973: The role of optical expansion patterns in locomotor control. *American Journal of Psychology*, 86, 311–24.

Johnston, R. A. and Bruce, V. 1990: Lost properties? Retrieval differences between name codes and semantic codes for familiar people. *Psychological Research*, 52, 62–7.

Jolicoeur, P. 1985: The time to name disoriented natural objects. *Memory and Cognition*, 13, 289–303.

Jolicoeur, P. 1988: Mental rotation and the identification of disoriented objects. *Canadian Journal of Psychology*, 42, 461–78.

Jolicoeur, P. 1990: Orientation congruency effects on the identification of disoriented shapes. *Journal of Experimental Psychology: Human Perception and Performance*, 16, 351–64.

Jolicoeur, P. and Kosslyn, S. M. 1983: Coordinate systems in the long-term memory representation of three-dimensional shapes. *Cognitive Psychology*, 15, 301–45.

Jolicoeur, P. and Landau, M. J. 1984: Effects of orientation on the identification of simple visual patterns. *Canadian Journal of Psychology*, 38, 80–93.

Jolicoeur, P. and Milliken, B. 1989: Identification of disoriented objects: effects of context of prior presentation. *Journal of Experimental Psychology: Learning, Memory, and Cognition*, 15, 200–10.

Jolicoeur, P. and Rak, D. 1985: Memory for visual shape: evidence for viewer-centered representations. Paper presented at the Forty-sixth Annual Convention of the Canadian Psychological Association, Halifax, Nova Scotia.

Jolicoeur, P., Snow, D. and Murray, J. 1987: The time to identify disoriented letters: effects of practice and font. *Canadian Journal of Psychology*, 41, 303–16.

Julesz, B. 1971: *Foundations of Cyclopean Perception*. Chicago: University of Chicago Press.

Julesz, B. 1980: Spatial nonlinearities in the instantaneous perception of textures with identical power spectra. *Philosophical Transactions of the Royal Society of London*, B290, 83–94.

Julesz, B. 1981: Textons, the elements of texture perception, and their interactions. *Nature*, 290, 91–7.

Julesz, B. and Hesse, R. I. 1970: Inability to perceive the direction of rotation movement of line segments. *Nature*, 225, 243–4.

Karpov, B. A., Meerson, Y. A. and Tonkonogii, I. M. 1979: On some peculiarities of the visuomotor system in visual agnosia. *Neuropsychologia*, 17, 281–94.

Kato, H., Bishop, P. O. and Orban, G. A. 1978: Hypercomplex and simple/complex cell classifications in cat striate cortex. *Journal of Neurophysiology*, 41, 1071–95.

Kellman, P. J. 1984: Perception of three-dimensional form by human infants. *Perception and Psychophysics*, 36, 353–8.

Kirby, K. N. and Kosslyn, S. M. 1990: Capacity limits on visual images of "Bricks." Unpublished manuscript.

Koenderink, J. J. 1984: What does the occluding contour tell us about solid shape? *Perception*, 13, 321–30.

Koenderink, J. J. 1985: Space, form, and optical deformations. In D. T. Engle, M. Jeanerod and D. N. Lee (eds), *Brain Mechanisms and Spatial Vision*. Dordrecht: Martinus Nijhoff.

Koenderink, J. J. 1986: Optic flow. *Vision Research*, 26, 161–80.

Koenderink, J. J. and van Doorn, A. J. 1975: Invariant properties of the motion parallax field due to the movement of rigid bodies relative to the observer. *Optica Acta*, 22, 773–91.

Koenderink, J. J. and van Doorn, A. J. 1976a: Geometry of binocular vision and a model for stereopsis. *Biological Cybernetics*, 21, 29–35.

Koenderink, J. J. and van Doorn, A. J. 1976b: Local structure of movement parallax of the plane. *Journal of the Optical Society of America*, 66, 717–23.

Koenderink, J. J. and van Doorn, A. J. 1980: Photometric invariants related to solid shape. *Optica Acta*, 27, 981–96.

Koenderink, J. J. and van Doorn, A. J. 1981: Exterospecific component of the motion parallax field. *Journal of the Optical Society of America*, 71, 953–7.

Koenderink, J. J. and van Doorn, A. J. 1982: The shape of smooth objects and the way contours end. *Perception*, 11, 129–37.

Koenderink, J. J. and van Doorn, A. J. 1987: Representation of local geometry in the visual system. *Biological Cybernetics*, 55, 367–75.

Koenderink, J. J. and Richards, W. 1988: Two-dimensional curvature operators. *Journal of the Optical Society of America*, A5, 1136–41.

Kohler, W. 1920: *Die physischen Gestalten in Ruhe und im stationaren Zustand.* Braunschweig.

Kohler, W. and Held, R. 1949: The cortical correlate of pattern vision. *Science*, 110, 414–19.

Kohonen, T., Oja, E. and Lehtio, P. 1981: Storage and processing of information in distributed associative memory systems. In G. Hinton and J. A. Anderson (eds), *Parallel Models of Associative Memory.* Hillsdale, NJ: Erlbaum.

Kolers, P. A. 1972: *Aspects of Motion Perception.* Oxford: Pergamon Press.

Kolers, P. A. and Perkins, D. N. 1969a: Orientation of letters and errors in their recognition. *Perception and Psychophysics*, 5, 265–9.

Kolers, P. A. and Perkins, D. N. 1969b: Orientation of letters and their speed of recognition. *Perception and Psychophysics*, 5, 275–80.

Komatsu, H. and Wurtz, R. H. 1988a: Relation of cortical areas MT and MST to pursuit eye movements. I. Localization and visual properties of neurons. *Journal of Neurophysiology*, 60, 580–603.

Komatsu, H. and Wurtz, R. H. 1988b: Relation of cortical areas MT and MST to pursuit eye movements. III. Interaction with full field visual stimulation. *Journal of Neurophysiology*, 60, 621–44.

Kopfermann, H. 1930: Psychologische Untersuchungen uber die Wirkung zweidimensionaler korperlicher Gebilde. *Psychologische Forschung*, 13, 293–364.

Koriat, A. and Norman, J. 1985: Reading rotated words. *Journal of Experimental Psychology: Human Perception and Performance*, 11, 490–508.

Koriat, A. and Norman, J. 1989: Why is word recognition impaired by disorientation while the identification of single letters is not? *Journal of Experimental Psychology: Human Perception and Performance*, 15, 153–63.

Kosslyn, S. M. 1976: Can imagery be distinguished from other forms of internal representation? Evidence from studies of information retrieval time. *Memory and Cognition*, 4, 291–7.

Kosslyn, S. M. 1978: Measuring the visual angle of the mind's eye. *Cognitive Psychology*, 10, 356–89.

Kosslyn, S. M. 1980: *Image and Mind*. Cambridge, Mass.: Harvard University Press.

Kosslyn, S. M. 1981: The medium and the message in mental imagery: a theory. *Psychological Review*, 88, 46–66.

Kosslyn, S. M. 1984: Mental representations. In J. R. Anderson and S. M. Kosslyn (eds), *Tutorials in Learning and Memory: Essays in Honor of Gordon Bower*. New York: W. H. Freeman.

Kosslyn, S. M. 1987: Seeing and imagining in the cerebral hemispheres: a computational approach. *Psychological Review*, 94, 148–75.

Kosslyn, S. M., Brunn, J. L., Cave, K. R. and Wallach, R. W. 1984: Individual differences in mental imagery ability: a computational analysis. *Cognition*, 18, 195–243.

Kosslyn, S. M., Holyoak, K. J. and Huffman, C. S. 1976: A processing approach to the dual coding hypothesis. *Journal of Experimental Psychology: Human Learning and Memory*, 2, 223–33.

Kosslyn, S. M. and Jolicoeur, P. 1981: A theory-based approach to the study of individual differences in mental imagery. In R. E. Snow, P. A. Federico and W. E. Montague (eds), *Aptitude Learning and Instruction: Cognitive Processes Analysis of Aptitude*, Vol. I. Hillsdale, NJ.: Erlbaum .

Kosslyn, S. M. and Pomerantz, J. R. 1977: Imagery, propositions and the form of internal representations. *Cognitive Psychology*, 9, 52–76.

Kuffler, S. W. 1953: Discharge patterns and functional organisation of mammalian retina. *Journal of Neurophysiology*, 16, 37–68.

Kurucz, J. and Feldmar, G. 1979: Prosopo-affective agnosia as a symptom of cerebral organic disease. *Journal of the American Geriatrics Society*, 27, 225–30.

Kurucz, J., Feldmar, G. and Werner, W. 1979: Prosopo-affective agnosia associated with chronic organic brain syndrome. *Journal of the American Geriatrics Society*, 27, 91–5.

Land, E. H. 1977: The retinex theory of color vision. *Scientific American*, 237, 108–28.

Lappin, J. S. and Bell, H. H. 1976: The detection of coherence in moving random-dot patterns. *Vision Research*, 16, 161–8.

Larrabee, G. J., Levin, H. S., Huff, F. J., Kay, M. C. and Guinto, F. C. Jr. 1985: Visual agnosia contrasted with visual-verbal disconnection. *Neuropsychologia*, 23, 1–12.

Larsen, A. and Bundesen, C. 1978: Size scaling in visual pattern recognition. *Journal of Experimental Psychology: Human Perception and Performance*, 4, 1–20.

Lashley, K. S., Chow, K. L. and Semmes, J. 1951: An examination of the electrical field theory of cerebral integration. *Psychological Review*, 58, 123–36.

Laughery, K. R., Alexander, J. F. and Lane, A. B. 1971: Recognition of human faces: effects of target exposure time, target position, pose position, and type of photograph. *Journal of Applied Psychology*, 55, 477–83.

Laughery, K. R., Rhodes, B. and Batten, G. 1981: Computer-guided recognition and retrieval of faces. In G. Davies, H. Ellis and J. Shepherd (eds), *Perceiving and Remembering Faces*. London: Academic Press.

Lee, D. N., Lishman, J. R. and Thomson, J. A. 1982: Regulation of gait in long jumping. *Journal of Experimental Psychology: Human Perception and Performance*, 8, 448–59.

Lee, D. N. and Reddish, P. E. 1981: Plummeting gannets: a paradigm of ecological optics. *Nature*, 293, 293–4.

Lehky, S. R. and Sejnowski, T. 1990: Neural network model of visual cortex for determining surface curvature from images of shaded surfaces. *Proceedings of the Royal Society of London*, B240, 251–78.

Lehky, S. R. and Sejnowski, T. 1988: Network model of shape from shading: neural function arises from both receptive and projective fields. *Nature*, 333, 452–4.

Levine, D. N. 1978: Prosopagnosia and visual object agnosia: a behavioural study. *Brain and Language*, 5, 341–65.

Levine, M. W. and Shefner, J. M. 1981: *Fundamentals of Sensation and Perception*. Reading, Mass.: Addison-Wesley.

Light, L. L., Kayra-Stuart, F. and Hollander, S. 1979: Recognition memory for typical and unusual faces. *Journal of Experimental Psychology: Human Learning and Memory*, 5, 212–28.

Lindsay, P. H. and Norman, D. A. 1972: *Human Information Processing*. New York: Academic Press.

Lisberger, S., Morris, E. J. and Tychsen, L. 1987: Visual motion processing and sensory-motor integration for pursuit eye movements. *Annual Review of Neuroscience*, 10, 97–129.

Llewellyn, K. R. 1971: Visual guidance of locomotion. *Journal of Experimental Psychology*, 91, 245–61.

Longuet-Higgins, H. C. and Prazdny, K. 1980: The interpretation of a moving retinal image. *Proceedings of the Royal Society of London*, B208, 385–97.

Lowe, D. G. 1987a: Three-dimensional object recognition from single two-dimensional images. *Artificial Intelligence*, 31, 355–95.

Lowe, D. G. 1987b: The viewpoint consistency constraint. *International Journal of Computer Vision*, 1, 57–72.

McCarthy, R. A. and Warrington, E. K. 1986: Visual associative agnosia: a clinico-anatomical study of a single case. *Journal of Neurology, Neurosurgery and Psychiatry*, 49, 1233–40.

McClelland, J. L. and Rumelhart, D. E. 1981: An interactive activation model of context effects in letter perception, part I: an account of basic findings. *Psychological Review*, 88, 375–407.

McClelland, J. L. and Rumelhart, D. E. 1985: Distributed memory and the representation of general and specific information. *Journal of Experimental Psychology: General*, 114, 159–88.

McClelland, J. L. and Rumelhart, D. E. 1986: *Parallel Distributed Processing: Explorations in the Microstructure of Cognition, Vol. 2: Psychological and Biological Models*. Cambridge, Mass.: MIT Press/Bradford Books.

Mach, E. 1886/1959: *The Analysis of Sensations.* (Translated from the German edition, 1886) New York: Dover.

Mackay, D. M. 1957: Moving visual images produced by regular stationary patterns. *Nature,* 180, 849–50.

McLeod, R. W. and Ross, H. E. 1983: Optic flow and cognitive factors in time-to-collision. *Perception,* 12, 417–23.

McMullen, P. A. and Jolicoeur, P. 1989: Processing the identity and orientation of object line drawings. Paper presented at the 30th Annual Meeting of The Psychonomic Society, Atlanta, Georgia.

McMullen, P. A. and Jolicoeur, P. 1990: The spatial frame of reference in object naming and discrimination of left-right reflections. *Memory and Cognition,* 18, 99–115.

Maki, R. H. 1986: Naming and locating the tops of rotated pictures. *Canadian Journal of Psychology,* 40, 368–87.

Mark, L. S. and Todd, J. T. 1983: The perception of growth in three dimensions. *Perception and Psychophysics,* 33, 193–6.

Marr, D. 1976: Early processing of visual information. *Philosophical Transactions of the Royal Society of London,* B275, 484–519.

Marr, D. 1978: Representing visual information. *Lectures on Mathematics in the Live Sciences,* 10, 101–80. Reprinted in A. R. Hanson and E. M. Riseman (eds) *Computer Vision Systems.* New York: Academic Press, 1979.

Marr, D. 1980: Visual information processing: the structure and creation of visual representations. *Philosophical Transactions of the Royal Society of London* B290, 199–218.

Marr, D. 1982: *Vision.* San Francisco: W.H. Freeman.

Marr, D. and Hildreth, E. C. 1980: Theory of edge detection. *Proceedings of the Royal Society of London,* B207, 187–217.

Marr, D. and Nishihara, H. K. 1978: Representation and recognition of the spatial organisation of three-dimensional shapes. *Proceedings of the Royal Society of London,* B204, 301–28.

Marr, D. and Ullman, S. 1981: Directional selectivity and its use in early visual processing. *Proceedings of the Royal Society of London,* B211, 151–80.

Maske, R., Yamani, S. and Bishop, P. O. 1987: End-stopped cells and binocular depth discrimination in the striate cortex of the cat. *Proceedings of the Royal Society of London,* B229, 257–76.

Maunsell, J. H. R. and van Essen, D. C. 1983: Response properties of single units in middle temporal visual area of the Macaque. *Journal of Neurophysiology,* 49, 1127–47.

Mayhew, J. E. W. 1982: The interpretation of stereo-disparity information: the computation of surface orientation and depth. *Perception,* 11, 387–403.

Mayhew, J. E. W. and Longuet-Higgins, H. C. 1982: A computational model of binocular depth perception. *Nature,* 297, 376–9.

Memon, A. and Bruce, V. 1985: Context effects in episodic studies of verbal and facial memory: a review. *Current Psychological Research and Reviews,* 4, 349–69.

Mewhort, D. J. K., Campbell, A. J., Marchetti, F. M. and Campbell, J. I. D.

1981: Identification, localization, and "iconic memory": an evaluation of the bar-probe task. *Memory and Cognition*, 9, 50–67.

Milner, P. M. 1974: A model for visual shape recognition. *Psychological Review*, 81, 521–35.

Mishkin, M. 1982: A memory system in the monkey. *Philosophical Transactions of the Royal Society of London*, B298, 85–95.

Mishkin, M. and Appenzeller, T. 1987: The anatomy of memory. *Scientific American*, 256, 80–9.

Mitchison, G. J. and Westheimer, G. 1984: The perception of depth in simple figures. *Vision Research*, 24(9), 1063–73.

Miyashita, Y. 1988: Neuronal correlate of visual associative long-term memory in the primate temporal cortex. *Nature*, 335, 817–20.

Morgan, M. J. and Watt, R. J. 1989: The Weber relation for position is not an artefact of eccentricity. *Vision Research*, 29, 1457–62.

Morrone, M. C. and Burr, D. J. 1988: Feature detection in human vision: a phase-dependent energy model. *Proceedings of the Royal Society of London*, B235, 221–45.

Morton, J. 1969: Interaction of information in word recognition. *Psychological Review*, 76, 165–78.

Morton, J. 1979: Facilitation in word recognition: experiments causing change in the logogen model. In P. A. Kolers, M. Wrolstad and H. Bouma (eds), *Processing of Visible Language*. New York: Plenum.

Movshon, J. A., Adelson, E. H., Gizzi, M. and Newsome, W. T. 1985: The analysis of moving visual patterns. In C. Chagas, R. Gattas and C. G. Gross (eds), *Pattern Recognition Mechanisms*. Rome: Vatican Press.

Movshon, J. A., Thompson, I. D. and Tolhurst, D. J. 1978a: Spatial summation in the receptive field of simple cells in the cat striate cortex. *Journal of Physiology*, 283, 79–99.

Movshon, J. A., Thompson, I. D. and Tolhurst, D. J. 1978b: Receptive field organization of complex cells in the cat's striate cortex. *Journal of Physiology*, 283, 79–99.

Mozer, M. C. and Behrmann, M. 1990: On the interaction of selective attention and lexical knowledge: a connectionist account of neglect dyslexia. *Journal of Cognitive Neuroscience*, 2, 96–123.

Murray, J., Jolicoeur, P., McMullen, P. A. and Ingleton, M. A. 1990: Templates, features, and the identification of disoriented natural objects. Unpublished manuscript.

Nakayama, K. and Silverman, G. H. 1984: Temporal and spatial characteristics of the upper displacement limit for motion in random dots. *Vision Research*, 24, 293–9.

Nakayama, K. and Silverman, G. H. 1985: Detection and discrimination of sinusoidal grating displacements. *Journal of the Optical Society of America*, 2, 267–73.

Nakayama, K., Silverman, G., MacLeod, D. I. A. and Mulligan, J. 1984: Sensitivity to shearing and compressive motion in random dots. *Perception*, 13, 229–43.

Nakayama, T. and Tyler, C. W. 1981: Psychophysical isolation of movement sensitivity by removal of familiar pattern cues. *Vision Research*, 21, 427–33.

Navon D. 1977: Forest before trees: the precedence of global features in visual perception. *Cognitive Psychology*, 9, 353–83.

Navon, D. 1978: Perception of misoriented words and letter strings. *Canadian Journal of Psychology*, 32, 129–40.

Neisser, U. 1967: *Cognitive Psychology*. New York: Appleton–Century–Crofts.

Nelson, J. I., Kato, H. and Bishop, P. O. 1977: Discrimination of orientation and position disparities by binocularly activated neurons in cat striate cortex. *Journal of Neurophysiology*, 40, 260–83.

Newsome, W. T., Gizzi, M. S. and Movshon, J. A. 1983: Spatial and temporal properties of neurons in Macaque MT. *Investigative Ophthalmology and Visual Science*, 24, 106.

Newsome, W., Wurtz, R. H. and Komatsu, H. 1988: Relation of cortical areas MT and MST to pursuit eye movements. II. Differentiation of retinal from extraretinal inputs. *Journal of Neurophysiology*, 60, 621–44.

Nickerson, R. S. 1965: Short term memory for meaningful configurations: a demonstration of capacity. *Canadian Journal of Psychology*, 19, 155–60.

Orban, G. A., Kato, H. and Bishop, P. O. 1979a: End-zone region in receptive fields of hypercomplex and other striate neurons in the cat. *Journal of Neurophysiology*, 42, 819–32.

Orban, G. A., Kato, H. and Bishop, P. O. 1979b: Dimensions and properties of end-zone inhibitory areas in receptive fields of hypercomplex cells in cat striate cortex. *Journal of Neurophysiology*, 42, 833–50.

Ormrod, J. E. 1979: Cognitive Processes in the solution of three-term series problems. *American Journal of Psychology*, 92, 235–55.

Paivio, A. 1971: *Imagery and Verbal Processes*. New York: Holt, Rinehart and Winston.

Paivio, A. 1986: *Mental Representations*. New York: Oxford University Press.

Palmer, S. E. 1975: Visual Perception and world knowledge. In D. A. Norman and D. E. Rumelhart (eds), *Explorations in Cognition*. San Francisco: Freeman.

Palmer, S. E. 1980: What makes triangles point: local and global effects in configurations of ambiguous triangles. *Cognitive Psychology*, 12, 285–305.

Palmer, S. E. 1983: The psychology of perceptual organization: a transformational approach. In J. Beck, B. Hope and A. Rosenfeld (eds), *Human and Machine Vision*. New York: Academic Press.

Palmer, S. E. 1985: The role of symmetry in shape perception. *Acta Psychologica*, 59, 67–90.

Palmer, S. E. 1989: Reference frames in the perception of shape and orientation. In B. Shepp and S. Ballesteros (eds), *Object Perception: Structure and Process*. Hillsdale, NJ: Erlbaum.

Palmer, S. E. and Bucher, N. M. 1981: Configural effects in perceived pointing of ambiguous triangles. *Journal of Experimental Psychology: Human Perception and Performance*, 7, 88–114.

Palmer, S. E. and Bucher, N. M. 1982: Textural effects in perceived pointing of ambiguous triangles. *Journal of Experimental Psychology: Human Perception and Performance*, 8, 693–708.

Palmer, S. E., Rosch, E. and Chase, P. 1981: Canonical perspective and the perception of objects. In J. Long and A. Baddeley (eds), *Attention and Performance IX*. Hillsdale, NJ: Erlbaum.

Palmer, S. E., Simone, E. J. and Kube, P. 1988: Reference frame effects on shape perception in two versus three dimensions. *Perception*, 17, 147–63.

Pantle, A. and Sekuler, R. W. 1968: Size-detecting mechanisms in human vision. *Science* (NY), 162, 1146–8.

Parker, A. J. and Hawken, M. J. 1985: Capabilities of monkey cortical cells in spatial resolution tasks. *Journal of the Optical Society of America*, A2, 1101–14.

Parker, A. J., Johnston, E. B., Mansfield, J. S. and Yang, Y. 1991: Stereo, surfaces and shape. In M. S. Landy and J. A. Movshon (eds), *Computational Models of Visual Processing*, pp. 359–81. Cambridge, Mass.: MIT Press.

Patterson, K. 1978: Person recognition: more than a pretty face. In M. M. Gruneberg, P. E. Morris and R. N. Sykes (eds), *Practical Aspects of Memory*. London: Academic Press.

Patterson, K. and Baddeley, A. D. 1977: When face recognition fails. *Journal of Experimental Psychology: Human Learning and Memory*, 3, 406–17.

Patterson, K. E., Seidenberg, M. S. and McClelland, J. L. 1989: In R. G. M. Morris (ed.), *Parallel Distributed Processing: Implications for Psychology and Neuroscience*. Oxford: University of Oxford Press.

Pearson, D. E. 1986: Transmitting deaf sign language over the telecommunications network. *British Journal of Audiology*, 20, 299–305.

Pearson, D. E., Hanna, E. and Martinez, K. 1990: Computer generated cartoons. In H. Barlow and C. Blakemore (eds), *Images and Understanding*. Cambridge: Cambridge University Press.

Pearson, D. E. and Robinson, J. A. 1985: Visual communication at very low data rates. *Proceedings of the IEEE*, 73, 795–812.

Pentland, A. P. 1986: Local shading analysis. In A. P. Pentland (ed.), *From Pixels to Predicates*. New Jersey: Ablex.

Pentland, A. 1989: A possible neural mechanism for computing shape from shading. *Neural Computation*, 1, 208–17.

Perenin, M. T. and Jeannerod, M. 1975: Residual vision in cortically blind hemifields. *Neuropsychology*, 13, 1–7.

Perenin, M. T. and Jeannerod, M. 1978: Visual function within the hemianopic field following early cerebral hemidecortication in man 1: Spatial localisation. *Neuropsychology*, 16, 1–13.

Perrett, D. I., Mistlin, A. J., Potter, D. D., Smith, P. A. J., Head, A. S., Chitty, A. S., Broenniman, R., Milner, A. D. and Jeeves, M. A. 1986: Functional organisation of visual neurones processing face identity. In H. D. Ellis, M. A. Jeeves, F. Newcombe and A. Young (eds), *Aspects of Face Processing*. Dordrecht: Martinus Nijhoff.

Perrett, D. I., Smith, P. A. J., Potter, D. D., Mistlin, A. J., Head, A. S., Milner, A. D. and Jeeves, M. A. 1985: Visual cells in the temporal cortex sensitive to face view and gaze direction. *Proceedings of the Royal Society of London*, B223, 293–317.

Peterhans, E. and von der Heydt, R. 1989: Mechanisms of contour perception in monkey visual cortex. II: Contours bridging gaps. *The Journal of Neuroscience*, 9, 1749–63.

Peterhans, E. and von der Heydt, R. 1991: Subjective contours – bridging the gap between psychophysics and physiology. *Trends in Neuroscience*, 14, 112–19.

Pittenger, J. B. and Shaw, R. E. 1975: Ageing faces as viscal-elastic events: implications for a theory of non-rigid shape perception. *Journal of Experimental Psychology: Human Perception and Performance*, 1, 374–82.

Poggio, G. F. and Fischer, B. 1977: Binocular interaction and depth sensitivity in striate and prestriate cortex of behaving monkeys. *Journal of Neurophysiology*, 40, 1392–1405.

Poggio, G. F., Motter, B. C., Squatrito, S. and Trotter, Y. 1985: Responses of neurons in visual cortex (V1 and V2) of the alert Macaque to dynamic random-dot stereograms. *Vision Research*, 25, 397–406.

Prazdny, K. 1983a: On the information in optic flows. *Computer Vision, Graphics, and Image Processing*, 22, 239–59.

Prazdny, K. 1983b: Stereoscopic matching, eye position, and absolute depth. *Perception*, 12, 151–60.

Prazdny, K. 1985: On the nature of inducing forms generating perception of illusory contours. *Perception and Psychophysics*, 37, 237–42.

Price, C. J. and Humphreys, G. W. 1989: The effects of surface detail on object categorization and naming. *Quarterly Journal of Experimental Psychology*, 41A, 797–828.

Priest, H. F. and Cutting, J. E. 1985: Visual flow and direction of locomotion. *Science*, 227, 1063–4.

Pylyshyn, Z. W. 1973: What the mind's eye tells the mind's brain: a critique of mental imagery. *Psychological Bulletin*, 80, 1–24.

Pylyshyn, Z. W. 1979: The rate of "mental rotation" of images: a test of a holistic analogue hypothesis. *Memory and Cognition*, 7, 19–28.

Pylyshyn, Z. W. 1981: The imagery debate: analogue media versus tacit knowledge. *Psychological Review*, 87, 16–45.

Quine, W. V. 1960: *Word and Object*. New York: Wiley.

Ratcliff, R. and McKoon, G. 1988: A retrieval theory of priming in memory. *Psychological Review*, 95, 385–408.

Read, J. D., Vokey, J. R. and Hammersley, R. in press: Changing photos of faces: effects of exposure duration and photo similarity on recognition and the accuracy-confidence relationship. *Journal of Experimental Psychology: Learning, Memory and Cognition*.

Redies, C. and Spillmann, L. 1981: The neon color effect in the Ehrenstein illusion. *Perception*, 10, 667–81.

Regan, D. 1985: Visual flow and direction of locomotion. *Science*, 227, 1064–5.

Regan, D. and Beverley, K. I. 1978a: Looming detectors in the human visual pathway. *Vision Research*, 18, 415–21.

Regan, D. and Beverley, K. I. 1978b: Illusory motion in depth: aftereffect of adaptation to changing size. *Vision Research*, 18, 209–12.

Regan, D. and Beverley, K. I. 1979: Visually guided locomotion: psychophysical evidence for a neural mechanism sensitive to flow patterns. *Science*, 205, 311–13.

Regan, D. and Beverley, K. I. 1985: Visual responses to vorticity and the neural analysis of optic flow. *Journal of the Optical Society of America*, A2, 280–3.

Regan, D. and Cynader, M. 1979: Neurons in area 18 of cat visual cortex selectively sensitive to changing size: nonlinear interactions between responses to two edges. *Vision Research*, 19, 699–711.

Rentschler, I., Hilz, R., Sütterlin, C. and Noguchi, K. 1981: Illusions of filled lateral and angular extent. *Experimental Brain Research*, 44, 154–8.

Rewald, J. 1973: *The History of Impressionism*, 4th edn. New York: The Museum of Modern Art.

Rhodes, G. 1985: Lateralised processes in face recognition. *British Journal of Psychology*, 76, 249–71.

Rhodes, G., Brennan, S. and Carey, S. 1987: Recognition and ratings of caricatures: implications for mental representations of faces. *Cognitive Psychology*, 19, 473–97.

Richardson, A. 1969: *Mental Imagery*. New York: Springer.

Richmond, B. and Optican, L. M. 1990: Temporal encoding of two-dimensional patterns by single units in primate primary visual cortex. II. Information transmission. *Journal of Neurophysiology*, 64, 370–80.

Riddoch, M. J. and Humphreys, G. W. 1986: Neurological impairments of object constancy: the effects of orientation and size disparities. *Cognitive Neuropsychology*, 3, 207–24.

Riddoch, M. J. and Humphreys, G. W. 1987a: A case of integrative visual agnosia. *Brain*, 110, 1431–62.

Riddoch, M. J. and Humphreys, G. W. 1987b: Visual object processing in optic aphasia: a case of semantic access agnosia. *Cognitive Neuropsychology*, 4, 131–85.

Rieger, J. H. and Lawton, D. T. 1985: Processing differential image motion. *Journal of the Optical Society of America*, A2, 354–60.

Ritter, M. 1979: Perception of depth: processing of simple positional disparity as a function of viewing distance. *Perception and Psychophysics*, 25(3), 209–14.

Roberts, A. and Bruce, V. 1988: Feature saliency in judging the sex and familiarity of faces. *Perception*, 17, 485–91.

Robinson, J. O. 1972: *The Psychology of Visual Illusion*. New York: Hutchinson.

Robson, J. 1980: Neural images: the physiological basis of spatial vision. In C. S. Harnis (ed.), *Visual Coding and Adaptability*, pp. 177–214. New Jersey: Lawrence Erlbaum.

Rock, I. 1956: The orientation of forms on the retina and in the environment. *The American Journal of Psychology*, 69, 513–28.

Rock, I. 1973: *Orientation and Form*. New York: Academic Press.

Rock, I. 1974: The perception of disoriented figures. *Scientific American*, 230, 78–85.

Rock, I. 1990: The concept of reference frame in psychology. In I. Rock (ed.), *The Legacy of Solomon Asch: Essays in Cognition and Social Psychology.* Hillsdale, NJ: Erlbaum.

Rock, I. and Heimer, W. 1957: The effects of retinal and phenomenal Orientation of the perception of form. *The American Journal of Psychology*, 70, 493–511.

Rodieck, R. W. 1965: Quantitative analysis of cat retinal ganglion cell response to visual stimuli. *Vision Research*, 5, 583–601.

Rogers, B. 1986: The perception of surface curvature from motion and parallax cues. *Investigative Ophthalmology and Visual Science* ARVO Abstracts Supplement, 27, 181.

Rogers, B. 1991: Why the eye doesn't shape up. *Nature*, 349, 365–6.

Rogers, B. and Cagenello, R. 1989: Disparity curvature and the perception of three-dimensional surfaces. *Nature*, 339, 135–7.

Rogers, B. and Graham, M. 1979: Motion parallax as an independent cue for depth perception. *Perception*, 8, 125–34.

Rogers, B. and Graham, M. 1983: Anisotropies in the perception of three-dimensional surfaces. *Science*, 221, 1409–11.

Rolls, E. T. 1984: Neurons in the cortex of the temporal lobe and in the amygdala of the monkey with responses selective for faces. *Human Neurobiology*, 3, 209–22.

Rolls, E. T. 1988: Visual information processing in the primate temporal lobe. In M. Imbert (ed.), *Models of Visual Perception: from Natural to Artificial.* Oxford: Oxford University Press.

Rolls, E. T. in press: The processing of face information in the primate temporal lobe. In V. Bruce and M. Burton (eds), *Processing Images of Faces*. Norwood, NJ: Ablex.

Ruddock, K. H. 1991: Spatial vision after cortical lesions. In D. M. Regan (ed.), *Vision and Visual Dysfunction, Vol. 10, Spatial Vision*. London: Macmillan, 261–89.

Rumelhart, D. E. and McClelland, J. L. 1982: An interactive activation model of context effects in letter perception: part 2. The contextual enhancement effect and some tests and extensions of the model. *Psychological Review*, 89, 60–94.

Rumelhart, D. E. and McClelland, J. L. 1986: *Parallel Distributed Processing: Explorations in the Microstructure of Cognition*, vol. 1. Cambridge, Mass.: MIT Press.

Saito, H., Yukie, M., Tanaka, K., Hikosaka, K., Fukada, Y. and Iwai, E. 1986: Integration of direction signals of image motion in the superior temporal sulcus of the Macaque monkey. *Journal of Neuroscience*, 6, 145–57.

Sakai, T., Nagao, M. and Kanade, T. 1972: Computer analysis and classification of photographs of human faces. *Proceedings of the first USA–Japan Computer Conference*, pp. 55–62.

Sakata, H., Shibutani, H., Kawano, K. and Harrington, T. L. 1985: Neural mechanisms of space vision in the parietal association cortex of the monkey. *Vision Research*, 25, 453–63.

Scapinello, F. F. and Yarmey, A. D. 1970: The role of familiarity and orientation in immediate and delayed recognition of pictorial stimuli. *Psychonomic Science*, 21, 329–31.

Schiff, W. 1965: Perception of impending collision: a study of visually directed avoidance behavior. *Psychological Monographs: General and Applied*, 79(11), 1–25.

Schiff, W. and Detwiler, M. L. 1979: Information used in judging impending collision. *Perception*, 8, 647–58.

Schwartz, E. L., Desimone, R., Albright, T. and Gross, C. 1983: Shape recognition and inferior temporal neurons. *Proceedings of the National Academy of Sciences*, 80, 5776–8.

Sekuler, R. 1975: Visual motion perception. In E. C. Carterette and M. P. Friedman (eds), *Handbook of Perception, Vol. V: Seeing*. New York: Academic Press.

Sergent, J. 1984a: Configural processing of faces in the left and right cerebral hemispheres. *Journal of Experimental Psychology: Human Perception and Performance*, 10, 554–72.

Sergent, J. 1984b: An investigation into component and configural processes underlying face recognition. *British Journal of Psychology*, 75, 221–42.

Sergent, J. 1986: Microgenesis of face perception. In H. D. Ellis, M. A. Jeeves, F. Newcombe and A. Young (eds), *Aspects of Face Processing*. Dordrecht: Martinus Nijhoff.

Sergent, J. 1989: Structural processing of faces. In A. W. Young and H. D. Ellis (eds), *Handbook of Research on Face Processing*. Amsterdam: North-Holland.

Seymour, P. H. K. 1979: *Human Visual Cognition*. London: Collier Macmillan.

Shallice, T. 1988: *From Neuropsychology to Mental Structure*. Cambridge: Cambridge University Press.

Shapiro, P. N. and Penrod, S. 1986: Meta-analysis of facial identification studies. *Psychological Bulletin*, 100, 139–56.

Shapley, R. and Enroth-Cugell, C. 1984: Visual adaptation and retinal gain controls. In N. Osborne and G. Chader (eds), *Progress in Retinal Research*, 3, 263–346. Oxford: Pergamon Press.

Shaver, P., Pierson, L. and Lang, S. 1975: Converging evidence for the functional significance of imagery in problem solving. *Cognition*, 3, 359–75.

Shepard, R. N. 1967: Recognition memory for words, sentences and pictures. *Journal of Verbal Learning and Verbal Behaviour*, 6, 156–63.

Shepard, R. N. 1981: Psychophysical complementarity. In M. Kubovy and J. R. Pomerantz (eds), *Perceptual Organization*. Hillsdale, NJ: Erlbaum.

Shepard, R. N. and Cooper, L. A. 1982: *Mental Images and their Transformations*. Cambridge, Mass.: MIT Press.

Shepherd, J. W. 1981: Social factors in face recognition. In G. Davies, H. Ellis and J. Shepherd (eds), *Perceiving and Remembering Faces*. London: Academic Press.

Shepherd, J. W. 1986: An interactive computer system for retrieving faces. In H. D. Ellis, M. A. Jeeves, F. Newcombe and A. Young (eds), *Aspects of face Processing*. Dordrecht: Martinus Nijhoff.

Shepherd, J. W., Davies, G. M. and Ellis, H. D. 1981: Studies of cue saliency. In G. Davies, H. Ellis and J. Shepherd (eds), *Perceiving and Remembering Faces*. London: Academic Press.

Shepherd, J. W., Ellis, H. D. and Davies, G. M. 1982: *Identification Evidence: a Psychological Evaluation*. Aberdeen: University of Aberdeen Press.

Shinar, D. and Owen, D. H. 1973: Effects of form rotation on the speed of classification: the development of shape constancy. *Perception and Psychophysics*, 14, 149–54.

Shulman, G. L. and Wilson, J. 1987: Spatial frequency and selective attention to local and global information. *Perception*, 16, 89–101.

Simion, F., Bagnara, S., Roncato, S. and Umiltà, C. 1982: Transformation processes upon the visual code. *Perception and Psychophysics*, 31, 13–25.

Slater, A. and Morrison, V. 1985: Shape constancy and slant perception at birth. *Perception*, 14, 337–44.

Snodgrass, J. G. and Vanderwart, M. 1980: A standardized set of 260 pictures: norms for name agreement, image agreement, familiarity, and visual complexity. *Journal of Experimental Psychology: Human Learning and Memory*, 6, 174–215.

Sperry, R. W. and Milner, N. 1955: Pattern perception following the insertion of mica plates into visual cortex. *Journal of Comparative and Physiological Psychology*, 48, 463–9.

Spitzer, H. and Hochstein, S. 1985: A complex-cell receptive field model. *Journal of Neurophysiology*, 53, 1266–86.

Standing, L., Conezio, J. and Haber, R. N. 1970: Perception and memory for pictures: single-trial learning of 2560 visual stimuli. *Psychonomic Science*, 19, 73–4.

Sternberg, S. 1966: High-speed scanning in human memory. *Science*, 153, 652–4.

Stevens, K. A. 1981a: The visual interpretation of surface contours. *Artificial intelligence*, 217, Special Issue on Computer Vision, 47–74.

Stevens, K. A. 1981b: The information content of texture gradients. *Biological Cybernetics*, 42, 95–105.

Stevens, K. A. 1983a: Slant-tilt: the visual encoding of surface orientation. *Biological Cybernetics*, 46, 183–95.

Stevens, K. A. 1983b: Surface tilt (the direction of surface slant): a neglected psychophysical variable. *Perception and Psychophysics*, 33, 241–50.

Stevens, K. A. and Brookes, A. 1987: Probing depth in monocular images. *Biological Cybernetics*, 56, 355–66.

Stevens, K. A. and Brookes, A. 1988: Integrating stereopsis with monocular interpretations of planar surfaces. *Vision Research*, 28, 371–86.

Stevens, K. A., Lees, M. and Brookes, A in press: Effects of conflicting information on integration of stereopsis with monocular interpretations.

Stoerig, P. and Cowey, A. 1989: Wavelength sensitivity in "blindsight". *Nature*, 342, 916–18.

Stoffregen, T. A., Schmuckler, M. A. and Gibson, E. J. 1987: Use of central and peripheral optical flow in stance and locomotion in young walkers. *Perception*, 16, 113–19.

Stone, J. 1972: Morphology and physiology of the geniculocortical synapse in the cat: the question of parallel input to the striate cortex. *Investigative Ophthalmology*, 11, 338–44.

Stone, J. and Dreher, B. 1973: Projection of X- and Y-cells of the cat's lateral geniculate nucleus to areas 17 and 18 of visual cortex. *Journal of Neurophysiology*, 36, 551–67.

Stonham, J. 1986: Practical face recognition and Verification with WISARD. In H. D. Ellis, M. A. Jeeves, F. Newcombe and A. Young (eds), *Aspects of Face Processing*. Dordrecht: Martinus Nijhoff.

Sutherland, N. S. 1968: Outline of a theory of visual pattern recognition in animal and man. *Proceedings of the Royal Society of London*, B171, 297–317.

Takano, Y. 1989: Perception of rotated forms: a theory of information types. *Cognitive Psychology*, 21, 1–59.

Tanaka, H., Fukada, Y. and Saito, H. 1989: Underlying mechanisms of expansion/contraction and rotation cells in the dorsal part of the medial superior temporal area of the Macaque monkey. *Journal of Neurophysiology*, 62, 642–56.

Tanaka, K., Hikosaka, K., Saito, H., Yukie, M., Fukada, Y. and Iwai, E. 1986: Analysis of local and wide-field movements in the superior temporal visual areas of the Macaque monkey. *Journal of Neuroscience*, 6, 133–44.

Tanaka, M., Lee, B. B. and Creutzfeldt, O. D. 1983: Spectral tuning and contour representation in area 17 of the awake monkey. In. J. D. Mollon and L. T. Sharpe (eds), *Colour Vision*. New York: Academic Press.

Tanaka, H. and Saito, H. 1989: Analysis of motion of the visual field by direction, expansion/contraction, and rotation cells clustered in the dorsal part of the medial superior temporal area of the Macaque monkey. *Journal of Neurophysiology*, 62, 626–41.

Tarr, M. J. and Pinker, S. 1989: Mental rotation and orientation-dependence in shape recognition. *Cognitive Psychology*, 21, 233–82.

Ternus, J. 1926: Experimentelle Untersuchungen über phänomenale Identität. *Psychologische Forschung*, 7, 81–136. Abstracted and translated in W. D. Ellis (ed.), *A Sourcebook of Gestalt Psychology*. New York: Humanities Press, 1950.

Thomas, J. P. and Shimamura, K. K. 1975: Inhibitory interaction between visual pathways tuned to different orientations. *Vision Research*, 15, 1373–80.

Thompson, P. 1980: Margaret Thatcher: a new illusion. *Perception*, 9, 483–4.

Thorell, L. G., De Valois, R. L. and Albrecht, D. G. 1984: Spatial mapping of monkey V1 cells with pure color and luminance stimuli. *Vision Research*, 24, 751–69.

Todd, J. T. and Mingolla, E. 1983: Perception of surface curvature and direction of illumination from patterns of shading. *Journal of Experimental Psychology: Human Perception and Performance*, 9, 583–95.

Todd, J. T. and Reichel, F. D. 1989: Ordinal structure in the visual perception and cognition of smoothly curved surfaces. *Psychological Review*, 96(4), 643–57.

Tolhurst, D. J. 1973: Separate channels for the analysis of the shape and the movement of a moving visual stimulus. *Journal of Physiology*, 231, 385–402.

Torrey, C. 1985: Visual flow and direction of locomotion. *Science*, 227, 1064.

Treisman, A. 1983: The role of attention in object perception. In O. J. Braddick and A. C. Sleigh (eds), *Physical and Biological Processing of Images*. Berlin: Springer, 316–25.

Treisman, A. 1988: Features and objects. The Fourteenth Bartlett Memorial Lecture. *Quarterly Journal of Experimental Psychology*, 40A, 201–37.

Treisman, A. and Gormican, S. 1988: Feature analysis in early vision: evidence from search asymmetries. *Psychological Review*, 95, 15–48.

Treisman, A. and Schmidt, H. 1982: Illusory conjunctions in the perception of objects. *Cognitive Psychology*, 14, 107–41.

Treisman, A. and Souther, J. 1985: Search asymmetry: a diagnostic for preattentive processing of separable features. *Journal of Experimental Psychology: General*, 114, 285–310.

Treue, S., Husain, M. and Andersen, R. A. 1991: Human perception of structure from motion. *Vision Research*, 31, 59–75.

Ullman, S. 1984: Visual Routines. *Cognition*, 18, 97–159.

Ungerleider, L. G. and Mishkin, M. 1982: Two cortical visual systems. In D. Ingle, M. A. Goodale and R. J. W. Mansfield (eds), *Analysis of Visual Behavior*. Cambridge, Mass.: MIT Press.

Valentine, T. and Bruce, V. 1986a: Recognizing familiar faces: the role of distinctiveness and familiarity. *Canadian Journal of Psychology*, 40, 300–5.

Valentine, T. and Bruce, V. 1986b: The effects of distinctiveness in recognising and classifying faces. *Perception*, 15, 525–36.

Van Essen, D. 1985: Functional organization of primate visual cortex. In A. Peters and E. G. Jones (eds), *Cerebral Cortex*, vol. 3. New York: Plenum Press.

Van Essen, D. C. and Maunsell, J. 1983: Hierarchical organization and functional streams in the visual cortex. *Trends in Neuroscience*, 6, 370–5.

Voorhees, H. and Poggio, T. 1988: Computing texture boundaries. *Nature*, 336, 364–7.

Wallach, H. 1976: *On Perception*. New York: Quadrangle/The New York Times Book Company.

Waltz, D. 1975: Understanding line drawings of scenes with shadows. In P. H. Winston (ed.), *The Psychology of Computer Vision*, pp. 19–91. New York: McGraw-Hill.

Wapner, W., Judd, T. and Gardner, H. 1978: Visual agnosia in an artist. *Cortex*, 14, 343–64.

Warren, W. H. and Hannon, D. J. 1988: Direction of self-motion is perceived from optical flow. *Nature*, 336, 162–3.

Warren, W. H., Morris, M. W. and Kalish, M. 1988: Perception of translational heading from optical flow. *Journal of Experimental Psychology: Human Perception and Performance*, 14, 646–60.

Warrington, E. K. 1982: Neuropsychological studies of objects recognition. *Philosophical Transactions of the Royal Society of London*, B298, 15–33.

Warrington, E. K. and James, M. 1986: Visual object recognition in patients with right-hemisphere lesion: axes or features? *Perception*, 15, 355–66.

Warrington, E. K. and Taylor, A. M. 1973: The contribution of the right parietal lobe to object recognition. *Cortex*, 9, 152–64.

Watt, A. 1989: *Fundamentals of Three-dimensional Computer Graphics*. Wokingham: Addison-Wesley.

Watt, R. J. 1984: Towards a general theory of the visual acuities for shape and spatial arrangement. *Vision Research*, 24, 1377–86.

Watt, R. J. 1985: Structured representation in low-level vision. *Nature*, 313, 266–7.

Watt, R. J. 1987a: Scanning from coarse to fine spatial scales in the human visual system after the onset of a stimulus. *Journal of the Optical Society of America*, A4 2006–2021.

Watt, R. J. 1987b: Scale-space analysis in the human primal sketch. Proceedings of the Alvey Vision Club Conference, 1987.

Watt, R. J. 1988: *Visual Processing: Computational, Psychophysical and Cognitive Research*. Hove, Sussex: Lawrence Erlbaum.

Watt, R. and Andrews, D. P. 1982: Contour curvature analysis: hyperacuities in the discrimination of detailed shape. *Vision Research*, 22, 449–60.

Watt, R. J. and Campbell, F. W. 1985: Vernier acuity: interactions between length effects and gaps when orientation cues are eliminated. *Spatial Vision*, 1, 31–8.

Watt, R. J. and Morgan, M. J. 1985: A theory of the primitive spatial code in human vision. *Vision Research*, 25, 1661–74.

Watt, R. J., Ward, R. M. and Casco, C. 1987: The dectection of deviation from straightness in lines. *Vision Research*, 27, 1659–78.

Waxman, A. M. and Wohn, K. 1988: Image flow theory: a framework for 3-D inference from time-varying imagery. In C. Brown (ed.), *Advances in Computer Vision*, vol. 1. Hillsdale, NJ: Erlbaum.

Weber, R. J. and Harnish, R. 1974: Visual imagery for words: the Hebb test. *Journal of Experimental Psychology*, 102, 409–14.

Weiskrantz, L. 1986: *Blindsight: A Case Study and its Implications*. Oxford: Oxford University Press.

Weiskrantz, L., Warrington, E. K., Sanders, M. D. and Marshall, J. 1974: Visual capacity in the hemianopic field following a restricted occipital ablation. *Brain*, 97, 709–28.

Westheimer, G. 1981: Visual hyperacuity. *Progress in Sensory Physiology*, 1, 1–30. Berlin: Springer-Verlag.

Westheimer, G. and McKee, S. P. 1977: Spatial configurations for visual hyperacuity. *Vision Research*, 17, 941–7.

Weyl, H. 1952: *Symmetry*. Princeton, NJ: Princeton University Press.

Wheatstone, C. 1838: Contributions to the physiology of vision. I: On some remarkable, and hitherto unobserved, phenomena of binocular vision. *Philosophical Transactions of the Royal Society of London*, 128, 371–94.

Wheatstone, C. 1852: Contributions to the physiology of vision. II: On some remarkable, and hitherto unobserved, phenomena of binocular vision (continued). *Philosophical Transactions of the Royal Society of London*, 142, 1–14.

White, M. J. 1980: Naming and categorization of tilted alphanumeric characters do not require mental rotation. *Bulletin of the Psychonomic Society*, 15, 153–6.

Williams, G. H. 1989: Psychophysical measurement of shear detectors in human vision. Unpublished PhD thesis: University of Birmingham.

Wilson, H. R. and Bergen, J. R. 1979: A four mechanism model for threshold spatial vision. *Vision Research*, 19, 19–32.

Wingfield, A. 1968: Effects of frequency on identification and naming of objects. *American Journal of Psychology*, 81, 226–34.

Wiser, M. A. 1980: The role of Intrinsic axes in the mental representation of shapes. Unpublished doctoral dissertation, Massachusetts Institute of Technology.

Wiser, M. 1981: The role of intrinsic axes in shape recognition. Paper presented at the Third Annual Conference of Cognitive Science Society, Berkeley, California.

Wright, W. D. 1946: *Researches on Normal and Defective Colour Vision*. London: Kimpton.

Wright, W. D. 1964: *The Measurement of Colour*, 3rd edn. London: Hilger and Watts.

Yarbus, A. L. 1967: *Eye Movements and Vision*. New York: Plenum Press.

Yin, R. K. 1969: Looking at upside down faces. *Journal of Experimental Psychology*, 81, 141–5.

Yin, R. K. 1970: Face recognition by brain-injured patients: a dissociable ability? *Neuropsychologia*, 8, 395–402.

Young, A. W. and Bruce, V. 1991: Perceptual categories and the computation of grandmother. *European Journal of Cognitive Psychology*, 3, 5–49.

Young, A. W., Hay, D. C. and Ellis, A. W. 1985: The faces that launched a thousand slips: everyday difficulties and errors in recognizing people. *British Journal of Psychology*, 76, 495–523.

Young, A. W., Hellawell, D. and Hay, D. C. 1987: Configurational information in face perception. *Perception*, 16, 747–59.

Young, A. W., McWeeny, K. H., Ellis, A. W. and Hay, D. C. 1986a: Naming and categorisation latencies for faces and written names. *Quarterly Journal of Experimental Psychology*, 38A, 297–318.

Young, A. W., McWeeny, K. H., Hay, D. C. and Ellis, A. W. 1986b: Matching familiar and unfamiliar faces on identity and expression. *Psychological Research*, 48, 63–8.

Zeki, S. M. 1974a: Functional organization of a visual area in the posterior bank of the superior temporal sulcus of the rhesus monkey. *Journal of Physiology (London)*, 236, 549–73.

Zeki, S. M. 1974b: Cells responding to changing image size and disparity in the cortex of the rhesus monkey. *Journal of Physiology (London)*, 242, 827–41.

Zeki, S. M. 1983a: Colour coding in the cerebral cortex: the reaction of cells in monkey visual cortex to wavelengths and colours. *Neuroscience,* 9, 741–65.

Zeki, S. M. 1983b: Colour coding in the cerebral cortex: the responses of wavelength-selective and colour coded cells in monkey visual cortex to changes in wavelength composition. *Neuroscience,* 9, 767–91.

Zihl, J., Von Cramon, D. and Mai, N. 1983: Selective disturbance of movement vision after bilateral brain damage. *Brain,* 106, 313–40.

Index